ENGLISH CRITIC
Nineteenth Ce

ENGLISH CRITICAL ESSAYS

Nineteenth Century

SELECTED AND EDITED BY
EDMUND D. JONES

OXFORD UNIVERSITY PRESS
LONDON OXFORD NEW YORK
1971

Oxford University Press

LONDON OXFORD NEW YORK
GLASGOW TORONTO MELBOURNE WELLINGTON
CAPE TOWN SALISBURY IBADAN NAIROBI DAR ES SALAAM LUSAKA ADDIS ABABA
BOMBAY CALCUTTA MADRAS KARACHI LAHORE DACCA
KUALA LUMPUR SINGAPORE HONG KONG TOKYO

SBN 19 281117 7

This selection first published in THE WORLD'S CLASSICS
1916; reset 1947

First issued as an Oxford University Press paperback by
Oxford University Press, London, 1971

Printed lithographically in Great Britain
by The Camelot Press Ltd, London and Southampton

CONTENTS

Preface	vii
WILLIAM WORDSWORTH: *Poetry and Poetic Diction* (1800)	1
SAMUEL TAYLOR COLERIDGE: *Wordsworth's Theory of Diction* (1817)	33
Metrical Composition (1817)	47
WILLIAM BLAKE: *The Canterbury Pilgrims* (1809)	72
CHARLES LAMB: *On the Tragedies of Shakespeare, Considered with Reference to their Fitness for Stage Representation* (1811)	81
PERCY BYSSHE SHELLEY: *A Defence of Poetry* (1821)	102
WILLIAM HAZLITT: *My First Acquaintance with Poets* (1823)	139
JOHN KEBLE: *Sacred Poetry* (1825)	162
JOHN HENRY NEWMAN: *Poetry with reference to Aristotle's Poetics* (1829)	190
THOMAS CARLYLE: *The Hero as Poet. Dante; Shakespeare* (1840)	216
JAMES HENRY LEIGH HUNT: *An Answer to the Question, What is Poetry?* (1844)	255
MATTHEW ARNOLD: *The Choice of Subjects in Poetry* (1853)	304
JOHN RUSKIN: *Of the Pathetic Fallacy* (1856)	323
JOHN STUART MILL: *Thoughts on Poetry and its Varieties* (1833, revised 1859)	341
WALTER BAGEHOT: *Wordsworth, Tennyson, and Browning; or, Pure, Ornate, and Grotesque Art in English Poetry* (1864)	368
WALTER HORATIO PATER: *Coleridge's Writings* (1866)	421
RALPH WALDO EMERSON: *Shakespeare; or, the Poet* (1850)	458
JAMES RUSSELL LOWELL: *Wordsworth* (1876)	478

PREFACE

THE essays here brought together are meant to illustrate English literary criticism during the nineteenth century, which forms an epoch in English literature whose beginnings are more clearly defined than those of most literary epochs. The publication of the *Lyrical Ballads* in 1798, and of Wordsworth's Preface to the second edition in 1800, show the Romantic Movement grown conscious and deliberate, with results that have coloured the whole stream of English poetry and criticism ever since.

The greater part of the present collection deals with general principles rather than with criticisms of individual books or authors. The nineteenth century, having discarded the dogmas and 'rules' of Neo-classicism, had perforce to investigate afresh the Theory of Poetry, and though no systematic treatment of the subject in all its bearings appeared, some valuable contributions were made, the most notable of which came from the poets themselves.

The extracts from the *Biographia Literaria* are placed next to the Wordsworthian doctrines which they criticize; otherwise the arrangement of the English essays is chronological.

American criticism is represented—inadequately, but, it is hoped, not unworthily—by the last two essays.

In the preparation of this volume I have received much valuable help from Mr. J. C. Smith, which I now gratefully acknowledge.

1916   EDMUND D. JONES

WILLIAM WORDSWORTH
1770–1850
POETRY AND POETIC DICTION
[Preface to the Second Edition of *Lyrical Ballads*, 1800]

THE first Volume of these Poems has already been submitted to general perusal. It was published, as an experiment, which, I hoped, might be of some use to ascertain, how far, by fitting to metrical arrangement a selection of the real language of men in a state of vivid sensation, that sort of pleasure and that quantity of pleasure may be imparted, which a Poet may rationally endeavour to impart.

I had formed no very inaccurate estimate of the probable effect of those Poems: I flattered myself that they who should be pleased with them would read them with more than common pleasure: and, on the other hand, I was well aware, that by those who should dislike them, they would be read with more than common dislike. The result has differed from my expectation in this only, that a greater number have been pleased than I ventured to hope I should please.

. . . .

Several of my Friends are anxious for the success of these Poems, from a belief, that, if the views with which they were composed were indeed realized, a class of Poetry would be produced, well adapted to interest mankind permanently, and not unimportant in the quality, and in the multiplicity of its moral relations: and on this account they have advised me to prefix a systematic defence of the theory upon which the Poems were written. But I was unwilling to undertake the task, knowing that on this occasion the Reader would look coldly upon my arguments, since I might be suspected of having been principally influenced by the selfish and foolish hope of *reasoning* him into an approbation of these particular Poems: and I was still more unwilling to undertake the task, because, adequately to display the opinions, and fully to enforce the arguments, would require a space wholly disproportionate to a preface. For, to treat the subject with the clearness and coherence of which it is susceptible, it would be necessary to give a full account of the present state of the public taste in this country, and to determine how far this taste is healthy or depraved; which, again, could not be determined, without pointing out in what manner language and the human mind act and re-act on each other, and without retracing the revolutions, not of literature alone, but likewise of society itself. I have therefore altogether declined to enter regularly upon this defence; yet I am sensible, that there would be something like impropriety in abruptly obtruding upon the Public, without a few words of introduction, Poems so materially different from those upon which general approbation is at present bestowed.

It is supposed, that by the act of writing in verse an Author makes a formal engagement that he will gratify certain known habits of association; that he not only thus apprises the Reader that certain classes of ideas and expressions will be found in his book, but that others will be carefully excluded. This exponent or symbol held forth by metrical language must in different eras of literature have excited very different expectations: for example, in the age of Catullus, Terence, and Lucretius, and that of Statius or Claudian; and in our own country, in the age of Shakespeare and Beaumont and Fletcher, and that of Donne and Cowley, or Dryden, or Pope. I will not take upon me to determine the exact import of the promise which, by the act of writing in verse, an Author in the present day makes to his reader: but it will undoubtedly appear to many persons that I have not fulfilled the terms of an engagement thus voluntarily contracted. They who have been accustomed to the gaudiness and inane phraseology of many modern writers, if they persist in reading this book to its conclusion, will, no doubt, frequently have to struggle with feelings of strangeness and awkwardness: they will look round for poetry, and will be induced to inquire by what species of courtesy these attempts can be permitted to assume that title. I hope therefore the reader will not censure me for attempting to state what I have proposed to myself to perform; and also (as far as the limits of a preface will permit) to explain some of the chief reasons which have determined me in the choice of my purpose: that at least he may be spared any unpleasant feeling of disappointment, and that I myself may be protected from one of the most dishonourable accusations which can be brought against an Author; namely, that of an indolence which prevents him from endeavouring to ascertain what is his duty, or, when his duty is ascertained, prevents him from performing it.

The principal object, then, proposed in these Poems was to choose incidents and situations from common life, and to relate or describe them, throughout, as far as was possible in a selection of language really used by men, and, at the same time, to throw over them a certain colouring of imagination, whereby ordinary things should be presented to the mind in an unusual aspect; and, further, and above all, to make these incidents and situations interesting by tracing in them, truly though not ostentatiously, the primary laws of our nature: chiefly, as far as regards the manner in which we associate ideas in a state of excitement. Humble and rustic life was generally chosen, because, in that condition, the essential passions of the heart find a better soil in which they can attain their maturity, are less under restraint, and speak a plainer and more emphatic language; because in that condition of life our elementary feelings co-exist in a state of greater simplicity, and, consequently, may be more accurately contemplated, and more forcibly communicated; because the manners of rural life germinate from those elementary feelings, and, from the necessary character of rural occupations, are more easily comprehended, and are more durable; and, lastly, because in that condition the passions of men are incorporated with the beautiful and permanent forms of nature. The language, too, of these men has been adopted (purified indeed from what appear to be its real defects, from all lasting and rational causes of dislike or disgust) because such men hourly communicate with the best objects from which the best part of language is originally derived; and because, from their rank in society and the sameness and narrow circle of their intercourse, being less under the influence of social vanity, they convey their feelings and notions in simple and unelaborated expressions. Accordingly, such a language, arising out of repeated experience and regular feelings, is a more permanent, and a far more philosophical language, than that which is frequently substituted for it by Poets, who think that they are conferring honour upon themselves and their art, in proportion as they separate themselves from the sympathies of men, and indulge in arbitrary and capricious habits of expression, in order to furnish food for fickle tastes, and fickle appetites, of their own creation.[1]

I cannot, however, be insensible to the present outcry against the triviality and meanness, both of thought and language, which some of my contemporaries have occasionally introduced into their metrical compositions; and I acknowledge that this defect, where it exists, is more dishonourable to the Writer's own character than false refinement or arbitrary innovation, though I should contend at the same time, that it is far less pernicious in the sum

[1] It is worth while here to observe, that the affecting parts of Chaucer are almost always expressed in language pure and universally intelligible even to this day.

of its consequences. From such verses the Poems in these volumes will be found distinguished at least by one mark of difference, that each of them has a worthy *purpose*. Not that I always began to write with a distinct purpose formally conceived; but habits of meditation have, I trust, so prompted and regulated my feelings, that my descriptions of such objects as strongly excite those feelings, will be found to carry along with them a *purpose*. If this opinion be erroneous, I can have little right to the name of a Poet. For all good poetry is the spontaneous overflow of powerful feelings: and though this be true, Poems to which any value can be attached were never produced on any variety of subjects but by a man who, being possessed of more than usual organic sensibility, had also thought long and deeply. For our continued influxes of feeling are modified and directed by our thoughts, which are indeed the representatives of all our past feelings; and, as by contemplating the relation of these general representatives to each other, we discover what is really important to men, so, by the repetition and continuance of this act, our feelings will be connected with important subjects, till at length, if we be originally possessed of much sensibility, such habits of mind will be produced, that, by obeying blindly and mechanically the impulses of those habits, we shall describe objects, and utter sentiments, of such a nature, and in such connexion with each other, that the understanding of the Reader must necessarily be in some degree enlightened, and his affections strengthened and purified.

It has been said that each of these Poems has a purpose. Another circumstance must be mentioned which distinguishes these Poems from the popular Poetry of the day; it is this, that the feeling therein developed gives importance to the action and situation, and not the action and situation to the feeling.

A sense of false modesty shall not prevent me from asserting, that the Reader's attention is pointed to this mark of distinction, far less for the sake of these particular Poems than from the general importance of the subject. The subject is indeed important! For the human mind is capable of being excited without the application of gross and violent stimulants; and he must have a very faint perception of its beauty and dignity who does not know this, and who does not further know, that one being is elevated above another, in proportion as he possesses this capability. It has therefore appeared to me, that to endeavour to produce or enlarge this capability is one of the best services in which, at any period, a Writer can be engaged; but this service, excellent at all times, is especially so at the present day. For a multitude of causes, unknown to former times, are now acting with a combined force to blunt the discriminating powers of the mind, and, unfitting it for all voluntary exertion, to reduce it to a state of almost savage torpor. The most effective of these causes are the great national events which are daily taking place, and the increasing accumulation of men in cities, where the uniformity of their occupations produces a craving for extraordinary incident, which the rapid communication of intelligence hourly gratifies. To this tendency of life and manners the literature and theatrical exhibitions of the country have conformed themselves. The invaluable works of our elder writers, I had almost said the works of Shakespeare and Milton, are driven into neglect by frantic novels, sickly and stupid German Tragedies, and deluges of idle and extravagant stories in verse.—When I think upon this degrading thirst after outrageous stimulation, I am almost ashamed to have spoken of the feeble endeavour made in these volumes to counteract it; and, reflecting upon the magnitude of the general evil, I should be oppressed with no dishonourable melancholy, had I not a deep impression of certain inherent and indestructible qualities of the human mind, and likewise of certain powers in the great and permanent objects that act upon it, which are equally inherent and indestructible; and were there not added to this impression a belief, that the time is approaching when the evil will be systematically opposed, by men of greater powers and with far more distinguished success.

Having dwelt thus long on the subjects and aim of these Poems, I shall request the Reader's permission to apprise him of a few circumstances relating to their *style*, in order, among other reasons, that he may not censure me for not having performed what I never attempted. The Reader will find that personifications of abstract ideas rarely occur in these volumes; and are utterly rejected, as an ordinary device to elevate the style, and raise it above prose. My purpose was to imitate, and, as far as possible, to adopt the very language of men; and assuredly such personifications do not make any natural or regular part of that language. They are, indeed, a figure of speech occasionally prompted by passion, and I have made use of them as such; but have endeavoured utterly to reject them as a mechanical device of style, or as a family language which Writers in metre seem to lay claim to by prescription. I have wished to keep the Reader in the company of flesh and blood, persuaded that by so doing I shall interest him. Others who pursue a different track will interest him likewise; I do not interfere with their claim, but wish to prefer a claim of my own. There will also be found in these volumes little of what is usually called poetic diction; as much pains has been taken to avoid it as is ordinarily taken to produce it; this has been done for the reason already alleged, to bring my language near to the language of men; and further, because the pleasure which I have proposed to myself to impart, is of a kind very different from that which is supposed by many persons to be the proper object of poetry. Without being culpably particular, I do not know how to give my Reader a more exact notion of the style in which it was my wish and intention to write, than by informing him that I have at all times endeavoured to look steadily at my subject; consequently, there is I hope in these Poems little falsehood of description, and my ideas are expressed in language fitted to their respective importance. Something must have been gained by this practice, as it is friendly to one property of all good poetry, namely, good sense: but it has necessarily cut me off from a large portion of phrases and figures of speech which from father to son have long been regarded as the common inheritance of Poets. I have also thought it expedient to restrict myself still further, having abstained from the use of many expressions, in themselves proper and beautiful, but which have been foolishly repeated by bad Poets, till such feelings of disgust are connected with them as it is scarcely possible by any art of association to overpower.

If in a poem there should be found a series of lines, or even a single line, in which the language, though naturally arranged, and according to the strict laws of metre, does not differ from that of prose, there is a numerous class of critics, who, when they stumble upon these prosaisms, as they call them, imagine that they have made a notable discovery, and exult over the Poet as over a man ignorant of his own profession. Now these men would establish a canon of criticism which the Reader will conclude he must utterly reject, if he wishes to be pleased with these volumes. And it would be a most easy task to prove to him, that not only the language of a large portion of every good poem, even of the most elevated character, must necessarily, except with reference to the metre, in no respect differ from that of good prose, but likewise that some of the most interesting parts of the best poems will be found to be strictly the language of prose when prose is well written. The truth of this assertion might be demonstrated by innumerable passages from almost all the poetical writings, even of Milton himself. To illustrate the subject in a general manner, I will here adduce a short composition of Gray, who was at the head of those who, by their reasonings, have attempted to widen the space of separation betwixt Prose and Metrical composition, and was more than any other man curiously elaborate in the structure of his own poetic diction.

> In vain to me the smiling mornings shine,
> And reddening Phoebus lifts his golden fire:
> The birds in vain their amorous descant join,
> Or cheerful fields resume their green attire.
> These ears, alas! for other notes repine;
> *A different object do these eyes require;*
> *My lonely anguish melts no heart but mine;*
> *And in my breast the imperfect joys expire;*
> Yet morning smiles the busy race to cheer,
> And new-born pleasure brings to happier men;
> The fields to all their wonted tribute bear;
> To warm their little loves the birds complain.
> *I fruitless mourn to him that cannot hear,*
> *And weep the more because I weep in vain.*

It will easily be perceived, that the only part of this Sonnet which is of any value is the lines printed in Italics; it is equally obvious, that, except in the rhyme, and in the use of the single word 'fruitless' for fruitlessly, which is so far a defect, the language of these lines does in no respect differ from that of prose.

By the foregoing quotation it has been shown that the language of Prose may yet be well adapted to Poetry; and it was previously asserted, that a large portion of the language of every good poem can in no respect differ from that of good Prose. We will go further. It may be safely affirmed, that there neither is, nor can be, any *essential* difference between the language of prose and metrical composition. We are fond of tracing the resemblance between Poetry and Painting, and, accordingly, we call them Sisters: but where shall we find bonds of connexion sufficiently strict to typify the affinity betwixt metrical and prose composition? They both speak by and to the same organs; the bodies in which both of them are clothed may be said to be of the same substance, their affections are kindred, and almost identical, not necessarily differing even in degree; Poetry[1] sheds no tears 'such as Angels weep', but natural and human tears; she can boast of no celestial ichor that distinguishes her vital juices from those of prose; the same human blood circulates through the veins of them both.

If it be affirmed that rhyme and metrical arrangement of themselves constitute a distinction which overturns what has just been said on the strict affinity of metrical language with that of prose, and paves the way for other artificial distinctions which the mind voluntarily admits, I answer that the language of such Poetry as is here recommended is, as far as is possible, a selection of the language really spoken by men; that this selection, wherever it is made with true taste and feeling, will of itself form a distinction far greater than would at first be imagined, and will entirely separate the composition from the vulgarity and meanness of ordinary life; and, if metre be superadded thereto, I believe that a dissimilitude will be produced altogether sufficient for the gratification of a rational mind. What other distinction would we have? Whence is it to come? And where is it to exist? Not, surely, where the Poet speaks through the mouths of his characters: it cannot be necessary here, either for elevation of style, or any of its supposed ornaments: for, if the Poet's subject be judiciously chosen, it will naturally, and upon fit occasion, lead him to passions the language of which, if selected truly and judiciously,

---

[1] I here use the word 'Poetry' (though against my own judgement) as opposed to the word Prose, and synonymous with metrical composition. But much confusion has been introduced into criticism by this contradistinction of Poetry and Prose, instead of the more philosophical one of Poetry and Matter of Fact, or Science. The only strict antithesis to Prose is Metre; nor is this, in truth, a *strict* antithesis, because lines and passages of metre so naturally occur in writing prose, that it would be scarcely possible to avoid them, even were it desirable.

must necessarily be dignified and variegated, and alive with metaphors and figures. I forbear to speak of an incongruity which would shock the intelligent Reader, should the Poet interweave any foreign splendour of his own with that which the passion naturally suggests: it is sufficient to say that such addition is unnecessary. And, surely, it is more probable that those passages, which with propriety abound with metaphors and figures, will have their due effect, if, upon other occasions where the passions are of a milder character, the style also be subdued and temperate.

But, as the pleasure which I hope to give by the Poems now presented to the Reader must depend entirely on just notions upon this subject, and, as it is in itself of high importance to our taste and moral feelings, I cannot content myself with these detached remarks. And if, in what I am about to say, it shall appear to some that my labour is unnecessary, and that I am like a man fighting a battle without enemies, such persons may be reminded, that, whatever be the language outwardly holden by men, a practical faith in the opinions which I am wishing to establish is almost unknown. If my conclusions are admitted, and carried as far as they must be carried if admitted at all, our judgements concerning the works of the greatest Poets both ancient and modern will be far different from what they are at present, both when we praise, and when we censure: and our moral feelings influencing and influenced by these judgements will, I believe, be corrected and purified.

Taking up the subject, then, upon general grounds, let me ask, what is meant by the word Poet? What is a Poet? To whom does he address himself? And what language is to be expected from him?—He is a man speaking to men: a man, it is true, endowed with more lively sensibility, more enthusiasm and tenderness, who has a greater knowledge of human nature, and a more comprehensive soul, than are supposed to be common among mankind; a man pleased with his own passions and volitions, and who rejoices more than other men in the spirit of life that is in him; delighting to contemplate similar volitions and passions as manifested in the goings-on of the Universe, and habitually impelled to create them where he does not find them. To these qualities he has added a disposition to be affected more than other men by absent things as if they were present; an ability of conjuring up in himself passions, which are indeed far from being the same as those produced by real events, yet (especially in those parts of the general sympathy which are pleasing and delightful) do more nearly resemble the passions produced by real events, than anything which, from the motions of their own minds merely, other men are accustomed to feel in themselves:—whence, and from practice, he has acquired a greater readiness and power in expressing what he thinks and feels, and especially those thoughts and feelings which, by his own choice, or from the structure of his own mind, arise in him without immediate external excitement.

But whatever portion of this faculty we may suppose even the greatest Poet to possess, there cannot be a doubt that the language which it will suggest to him, must often, in liveliness and truth, fall short of that which is uttered by men in real life, under the actual pressure of those passions, certain shadows of which the Poet thus produces, or feels to be produced, in himself.

However exalted a notion we would wish to cherish of the character of a Poet, it is obvious, that while he describes and imitates passions, his employment is in some degree mechanical, compared with the freedom and power of real and substantial action and suffering. So that it will be the wish of the Poet to bring his feelings near to those of the persons whose feelings he describes, nay, for short spaces of time, perhaps, to let himself slip into an entire delusion, and even confound and identify his own feelings with theirs; modifying only the language which is thus suggested to him by a consideration that he describes for a particular purpose, that of giving pleasure. Here, then, he will apply the principle of selection which has been already insisted upon. He will depend upon this for removing what would otherwise be painful or disgusting in the passion; he will feel that there is no necessity to trick out or to elevate nature: and, the more industriously he applies this principle, the deeper will be his faith that no words, which *his* fancy or imagination can suggest, will be to be compared with those which are the emanations of reality and truth.

But it may be said by those who do not object to the general spirit of these remarks, that, as it is impossible for the Poet to produce upon all occasions language as exquisitely fitted for the passion as that which the real passion itself suggests, it is proper that he should consider himself as in the situation of a translator, who does not scruple to substitute excellencies of another kind for those which are unattainable by him; and endeavours occasionally to surpass his original, in order to make some amends for the general inferiority to which he feels that he must submit. But this would be to encourage idleness and unmanly despair. Further, it is the language of men who speak of what they do not understand; who talk of Poetry as of a matter of amusement and idle pleasure; who will converse with us as gravely about a *taste* for Poetry, as they express it, as if it were a thing as indifferent as a taste for rope-dancing or Frontiniac or Sherry. Aristotle, I have been told, has said, that Poetry is the most philosophic of all writing: it is so: its object is truth, not individual and local, but general, and operative; not standing upon external testimony, but carried alive into the heart by passion; truth which is its own testimony, which gives competence and confidence to the tribunal to which it appeals, and receives them from the same tribunal. Poetry is the image of man and nature. The obstacles which stand in the way of the fidelity of the Biographer and Historian, and of their consequent utility, are incalculably greater than those which are to be encountered by the Poet who comprehends the dignity of his art. The Poet writes under one restriction only, namely, the necessity of giving immediate pleasure to a human Being possessed of that information which may be expected from him, not as a lawyer, a physician, a mariner, an astronomer, or a natural philosopher, but as a Man. Except this one restriction, there is no object standing between the Poet and the image of things; between this, and the Biographer and Historian, there are a thousand.

Nor let this necessity of producing immediate pleasure be considered as a degradation of the Poet's art. It is far otherwise. It is an acknowledgement of the beauty of the universe, an acknowledgement the more sincere, because not formal, but indirect; it is a task light and easy to him who looks at the world in the spirit of love: further, it is a homage paid to the native and naked dignity of man, to the grand elementary principle of pleasure, by which he knows, and feels, and lives, and moves. We have no sympathy but what is propagated by pleasure: I would not be misunderstood; but wherever we sympathize with pain, it will be found that the sympathy is produced and carried on by subtle combinations with pleasure. We have no knowledge, that is, no general principles drawn from the contemplation of particular facts, but what has been built up by pleasure, and exists in us by pleasure alone. The Man of science, the Chemist and Mathematician, whatever difficulties and disgusts they may have had to struggle with, know and feel this. However painful may be the objects with which the Anatomist's knowledge is connected, he feels that his knowledge is pleasure; and where he has no pleasure he has no knowledge. What then does the Poet? He considers man and the objects that surround him as acting and re-acting upon each other, so as to produce an infinite complexity of pain and pleasure; he considers man in his own nature and in his ordinary life as contemplating this with a certain quantity of immediate knowledge, with certain convictions, intuitions, and deductions, which from habit acquire the quality of intuitions; he considers him as looking upon this complex scene of ideas and sensations, and finding everywhere objects that immediately excite in him sympathies which, from the necessities of his nature, are accompanied by an overbalance of enjoyment.

To this knowledge which all men carry about with them, and to these sympathies in which, without any other discipline than that of our daily life, we are fitted to take delight, the Poet principally directs his attention. He considers man and nature as essentially adapted to each other, and the mind of man as naturally the mirror of the fairest and most interesting properties of nature. And thus the Poet, prompted by this feeling of pleasure, which accompanies him through the whole course of his studies, converses with general nature, with affections akin to those, which, through labour and length of time, the Man of science has raised up in himself, by conversing with those particular parts of nature which are the objects of his studies. The knowledge both of the Poet and the Man of science is pleasure; but the knowledge of the one cleaves to us as a necessary part of our existence, our natural and unalienable inheritance; the other is a personal and individual acquisition, slow to come to us, and by no habitual and direct sympathy connecting us with our fellow-beings. The Man of science seeks truth as a remote and unknown benefactor; he cherishes and loves it in his solitude: the Poet, singing a song in which all human beings join with him, rejoices in the presence of truth as our visible friend and hourly companion. Poetry is the breath and finer spirit of all knowledge; it is the impassioned expression which is in the countenance of all Science. Emphatically may it be said of the Poet, as Shakespeare hath said of man, 'that he looks before and after.' He is the rock of defence for human nature; an upholder and preserver, carrying everywhere with him relationship and love. In spite of difference of soil and climate, of language and manners, of laws and customs: in spite of things silently gone out of mind, and things violently destroyed; the Poet binds together by passion and knowledge the vast empire of human society, as it is spread over the whole earth, and over all time. The objects of the Poet's thoughts are everywhere; though the eyes and senses of man are, it is true, his favourite guides, yet he will follow wheresoever he can find an atmosphere of sensation in which to move his wings. Poetry is the first and last of all knowledge—it is as immortal as the heart of man. If the labours of Men of science should ever create any material revolution, direct or indirect, in our condition, and in the impressions which we habitually receive, the Poet will sleep then no more than at present; he will be ready to follow the steps of the Man of science, not only in those general indirect effects, but he will be at his side, carrying sensation into the midst of the objects of the science itself. The remotest discoveries of the Chemist, the Botanist, or Mineralogist, will be as proper objects of the Poet's art as any upon which it can be employed, if the time should ever come when these things shall be familiar to us, and the relations under which they are contemplated by the followers of these respective sciences shall be manifestly and palpably material to us as enjoying and suffering beings. If the time should ever come when what is now called science, thus familiarized to men, shall be ready to put on, as it were, a form of flesh and blood, the Poet will lend his divine spirit to aid the transfiguration, and will welcome the Being thus produced, as a dear and genuine inmate of the household of man.—It is not, then, to be supposed that any one, who holds that sublime notion of Poetry which I have attempted to convey, will break in upon the sanctity and truth of his pictures by transitory and accidental ornaments, and endeavour to excite admiration of himself by arts, the necessity of which must manifestly depend upon the assumed meanness of his subject.

What has been thus far said applies to Poetry in general; but especially to those parts of composition where the Poet speaks through the mouths of his characters; and upon this point it appears to authorize the conclusion that there are few persons of good sense, who would not allow that the dramatic parts of composition are defective, in proportion as they deviate from the real language of nature, and are coloured by a diction of the Poet's own, either peculiar to him as an individual Poet or belonging simply to Poets in general; to a body of men who, from the circumstance of their compositions being in metre, it is expected will employ a particular language.

It is not, then, in the dramatic parts of composition that we look for this distinction of language; but still it may be proper and necessary where the Poet speaks to us in his own person and character. To this I answer by referring the Reader to the description before given of a Poet. Among the qualities there enumerated as principally conducing to form a Poet, is implied nothing differing in kind from other men, but only in degree. The sum of what was said is, that the Poet is chiefly distinguished from other men by a greater promptness to think and feel without immediate external excitement, and a greater power in expressing such thoughts and feelings as are produced in him in that manner. But these passions and thoughts and feelings are the general passions and thoughts and feelings of men. And with what are they connected? Undoubtedly with our moral sentiments and animal sensations, and with the causes which excite these; with the operations of the elements, and the appearances of the visible universe; with storm and sunshine, with the revolutions of the seasons, with cold and heat, with loss of friends and kindred, with injuries and resentments, gratitude and hope, with fear and sorrow. These, and the like, are the sensations and objects which the Poet describes, as they are the sensations of other men, and the objects which interest them. The Poet thinks and feels in the spirit of human passions. How, then, can his language differ in any material degree from that of all other men who feel vividly and see clearly? It might be *proved* that it is impossible. But supposing that this were not the case, the Poet might then be allowed to use a peculiar language when expressing his feelings for his own gratification, or that of men like himself. But Poets do not write for Poets alone, but for men. Unless therefore we are advocates for that admiration which subsists upon ignorance, and that pleasure which arises from hearing what we do not understand, the Poet must descend from this supposed height; and, in order to excite rational sympathy, he must express himself as other men express themselves. To this it may be added, that while he is only selecting from the real language of men, or, which amounts to the same thing, composing accurately in the spirit of such selection, he is treading upon safe ground, and we know what we are to expect from him. Our feelings are the same with respect to metre; for, as it may be proper to remind the Reader, the distinction of metre is regular and uniform, and not, like that which is produced by what is usually called POETIC DICTION, arbitrary, and subject to infinite caprices upon which no calculation whatever can be made. In the one case, the Reader is utterly at the mercy of the Poet, respecting what imagery or diction he may choose to connect with the passion; whereas, in the other, the metre obeys certain laws, to which the Poet and Reader both willingly submit because they are certain, and because no interference is made by them with the passion, but such as the concurring testimony of ages has shown to heighten and improve the pleasure which co-exists with it.

It will now be proper to answer an obvious question, namely, Why, professing these opinions, have I written in verse? To this, in addition to such answer as is included in what has been already said, I reply, in the first place, Because, however I may have restricted myself, there is still left open to me what confessedly constitutes the most valuable object of all writing, whether in prose or verse; the great and universal passions of men, the most general and interesting of their occupations, and the entire world of nature before me—to supply endless combinations of forms and imagery. Now, supposing for a moment that whatever is interesting in these objects may be as vividly described in prose, why should I be condemned for attempting to superadd to such description the charm which, by the consent of all nations, is acknowledged to exist in metrical language? To this, by such as are yet unconvinced, it may be answered that a very small part of the pleasure given by Poetry depends upon the metre, and that it is injudicious to write in metre, unless it be accompanied with the other artificial distinctions of style with which metre is usually accompanied, and that, by such deviation, more will be lost from the shock which will thereby be given to the Reader's associations than will be counterbalanced by any pleasure which he can derive from the general power of numbers. In answer to those who still contend for the necessity of accompanying metre with certain appropriate colours of style in order to the accomplishment of its appropriate end, and who also, in my opinion, greatly underrate the power of metre in itself, it might, perhaps, as far as relates to these Volumes, have been almost sufficient to observe, that poems are extant, written upon more humble subjects, and in a still more naked and simple style, which have continued to give pleasure from generation to generation. Now, if nakedness and simplicity be a defect, the fact here mentioned affords a strong presumption that poems somewhat less naked and simple are capable of affording pleasure at the present day; and, what I wished *chiefly* to attempt, at present, was to justify myself for having written under the impression of this belief.

But various causes might be pointed out why, when the style is manly, and the subject of some importance, words metrically arranged will long continue to impart such a pleasure to mankind as he who proves the extent of that pleasure will be desirous to impart. The end of Poetry is to produce excitement in co-existence with an overbalance of pleasure; but, by the supposition, excitement is an unusual and irregular state of the mind; ideas and feelings do not, in that state, succeed each other in accustomed order. If the words, however, by which this excitement is produced be in themselves powerful, or the images and feelings have an undue proportion of pain connected with them, there is some danger that the excitement may be carried beyond its proper bounds. Now the co-presence of something regular, something to which the mind has been accustomed in various moods and in a less excited state, cannot but have great efficacy in tempering and restraining the passion by an intertexture of ordinary feeling, and of feeling not strictly and necessarily connected with the passion. This is unquestionably true; and hence, though the opinion will at first appear paradoxical, from the tendency of metre to divest language, in a certain degree, of its reality, and thus to throw a sort of half-consciousness of unsubstantial existence over the whole composition, there can be little doubt but that more pathetic situations and sentiments, that is, those which have a greater proportion of pain connected with them, may be endured in metrical composition, especially in rhyme, than in prose. The metre of the old ballads is very artless; yet they contain many passages which would illustrate this opinion; and, I hope, if the following Poems be attentively perused, similar instances will be found in them. This opinion may be further illustrated by appealing to the Reader's own experience of the reluctance with which he comes to the re-perusal of the distressful parts of *Clarissa Harlowe*, or the *Gamester*; while Shakespeare's writings, in the most pathetic scenes, never act upon us, as pathetic, beyond the bounds of pleasure—an effect which, in a much greater degree than might at first be imagined, is to be ascribed to small, but continual and regular impulses of pleasurable surprise from the metrical arrangement.—On the other hand (what it must be allowed will much more frequently happen) if the Poet's words should be incommensurate with the passion, and inadequate to raise the Reader to a height of desirable excitement, then (unless the Poet's choice of his metre has been grossly injudicious), in the feelings of pleasure which the Reader has been accustomed to connect with metre in general, and in the feeling, whether cheerful or melancholy, which he has been accustomed to connect with that particular movement of metre, there will be found something which will greatly contribute to impart passion to the words, and to effect the complex end which the Poet proposes to himself.

If I had undertaken a SYSTEMATIC defence of the theory here maintained, it would have been my duty to develop the various causes upon which the pleasure received from metrical language depends. Among the chief of these causes is to be reckoned a principle which must be well known to those who have made any of the Arts the object of accurate reflection; namely, the pleasure which the mind derives from the perception of similitude in dissimilitude. This principle is the great spring of the activity of our minds, and their chief feeder. From this principle the direction of the sexual appetite, and all the passions connected with it, take their origin: it is the life of our ordinary conversation; and upon the accuracy with which similitude in dissimilitude, and dissimilitude in similitude are perceived, depend our taste and our moral feelings. It would not be a useless employment to apply this principle to the consideration of metre, and to show that metre is hence enabled to afford much pleasure, and to point out in what manner that pleasure is produced. But my limits will not permit me to enter upon this subject, and I must content myself with a general summary.

I have said that poetry is the spontaneous overflow of powerful feelings: it takes its origin from emotion recollected in tranquillity: the emotion is contemplated till, by a species of reaction, the tranquillity gradually disappears, and an emotion, kindred to that which was before the subject of contemplation, is gradually produced, and does itself actually exist in the mind. In this mood successful composition generally begins, and in a mood similar to this it is carried on; but the emotion, of whatever kind, and in whatever degree, from various causes, is qualified by various pleasures, so that in describing any passions whatsoever, which are voluntarily described, the mind will, upon the whole, be in a state of enjoyment. If Nature be thus cautious to preserve in a state of enjoyment a being so employed, the Poet ought to profit by the lesson held forth to him, and ought especially to take care, that, whatever passions he communicates to his Reader, those passions, if his Reader's mind be sound and vigorous, should always be accompanied with an overbalance of pleasure. Now the music of harmonious metrical language, the sense of difficulty overcome, and the blind association of pleasure which has been previously received from works of rhyme or metre of the same or similar construction, an indistinct perception perpetually renewed of language closely resembling that of real life, and yet, in the circumstance of metre, differing from it so widely—all these imperceptibly make up a complex feeling of delight, which is of the most important use in tempering the painful feeling always found intermingled with powerful descriptions of the deeper passions. This effect is always produced in pathetic and impassioned poetry; while, in lighter compositions, the ease and gracefulness with which the Poet manages his numbers are themselves confessedly a principal source of the gratification of the Reader. All that it is *necessary* to say, however, upon this subject, may be effected by affirming, what few persons will deny, that, of two descriptions, either of passions, manners, or characters, each of them equally well executed, the one in prose and the other in verse, the verse will be read a hundred times where the prose is read once.

Having thus explained a few of my reasons for writing in verse, and why I have chosen subjects from common life, and endeavoured to bring my language near to the real language of men, if I have been too minute in pleading my own cause, I have at the same time been treating a subject of general interest; and for this reason a few words shall be added with reference solely to these particular poems, and to some defects which will probably be found in them. I am sensible that my associations must have sometimes been particular instead of general, and that, consequently, giving to things a false importance, I may have sometimes written upon unworthy subjects; but I am less apprehensive on this account, than that my language may frequently have suffered from those arbitrary connexions of feelings and ideas with particular words and phrases, from which no man can altogether protect himself. Hence I have no doubt, that, in some instances, feelings, even of the ludicrous, may be given to my Readers by expressions which appeared to me tender and pathetic. Such faulty expressions, were I convinced they were faulty at present, and that they must necessarily continue to be so, I would willingly take all reasonable pains to correct. But it is dangerous to make these alterations on the simple authority of a few individuals, or even of certain classes of men; for where the understanding of an Author is not convinced, or his feelings altered, this cannot be done without great injury to himself: for his own feelings are his stay and support; and, if he set them aside in one instance, he may be induced to repeat this act till his mind shall lose all confidence in itself, and become utterly debilitated. To this it may be added, that the critic ought never to forget that he is himself exposed to the same errors as the Poet, and, perhaps, in a much greater degree: for there can be no presumption in saying of most readers, that it is not probable they will be so well acquainted with the various stages of meaning through which words have passed, or with the fickleness or stability of the relations of particular ideas to each other; and, above all, since they are so much less interested in the subject, they may decide lightly and carelessly.

Long as the Reader has been detained, I hope he will permit me to caution him against a mode of false criticism which has been applied to Poetry, in which the language closely resembles that of life and nature. Such verses have been triumphed over in parodies, of which Dr. Johnson's stanza is a fair specimen:—

>   I put my hat upon my head
>   And walked into the Strand,
>   And there I met another man
>   Whose hat was in his hand.

Immediately under these lines let us place one of the most justly-admired stanzas of the 'Babes in the Wood.'

>   These pretty Babes with hand in hand
>   Went wandering up and down;
>   But never more they saw the Man
>   Approaching from the Town.

In both these stanzas the words, and the order of the words, in no respect differ from the most unimpassioned conversation. There are words in both, for example, 'the Strand', and 'the Town', connected with none but the most familiar ideas; yet the one stanza we admit as admirable, and the other as a fair example of the superlatively contemptible. Whence arises this difference? Not from the metre, not from the language, not from the order of the words; but the *matter* expressed in Dr. Johnson's stanza is contemptible. The proper method of treating trivial and simple verses, to which Dr. Johnson's stanza would be a fair parallelism, is not to say, this is a bad kind of poetry, or, this is not poetry; but, this wants sense; it is neither interesting in itself, nor can *lead* to anything interesting; the images neither originate in that sane state of feeling which arises out of thought, nor can excite thought or feeling in the Reader. This is the only sensible manner of dealing with such verses. Why trouble yourself about the species till you have previously decided upon the genus? Why take pains to prove that an ape is not a Newton, when it is self-evident that he is not a man?

One request I must make of my reader, which is, that in judging these Poems he would decide by his own feelings genuinely, and not by reflection upon what will probably be the judgement of others. How common is it to hear a person say, I myself do not object to this style of composition, or this or that expression, but, to such and such classes of people it will appear mean or ludicrous! This mode of criticism, so destructive of all sound unadulterated judgement, is almost universal: let the Reader then abide, independently, by his own feelings, and, if he finds himself affected, let him not suffer such conjectures to interfere with his pleasure.

If an Author, by any single composition, has impressed us with respect for his talents, it is useful to consider this as affording a presumption, that on other occasions where we have been displeased, he, nevertheless, may not have written ill or absurdly; and further, to give him so much credit for this one composition as may induce us to review what has displeased us, with more care than we should otherwise have bestowed upon it. This is not only an act of justice, but, in our decisions upon poetry especially, may conduce, in a high degree, to the improvement of our own taste; for an *accurate* taste in poetry, and in all the other arts, as Sir Joshua Reynolds has observed, is an *acquired* talent, which can only be produced by thought and a long-continued intercourse with the best models of composition. This is mentioned, not with so ridiculous a purpose as to prevent the most inexperienced Reader from judging for himself, (I have already said that I wish him to judge for himself;) but merely to temper the rashness of decision, and to suggest, that, if Poetry be a subject on which much time has not been bestowed, the judgement may be erroneous; and that, in many cases, it necessarily will be so.

Nothing would, I know, have so effectually contributed to further the end which I have in view, as to have shown of what kind the pleasure is, and how that pleasure is produced, which is confessedly produced by metrical composition essentially different from that which I have here endeavoured to recommend: for the Reader will say that he has been pleased by such composition; and what more can be done for him? The power of any art is limited; and he will suspect, that, if it be proposed to furnish him with new friends, that can be only upon condition of his abandoning his old friends. Besides, as I have said, the Reader is himself conscious of the pleasure which he has received from such composition, composition to which he has peculiarly attached the endearing name of Poetry; and all men feel an habitual gratitude, and something of an honourable bigotry, for the objects which have long continued to please them:

we not only wish to be pleased, but to be pleased in that particular way in which we have been accustomed to be pleased. There is in these feelings enough to resist a host of arguments; and I should be the less able to combat them successfully, as I am willing to allow, that, in order entirely to enjoy the Poetry which I am recommending, it would be necessary to give up much of what is ordinarily enjoyed. But, would my limits have permitted me to point out how this pleasure is produced, many obstacles might have been removed, and the Reader assisted in perceiving that the powers of language are not so limited as he may suppose; and that it is possible for poetry to give other enjoyments, of a purer, more lasting, and more exquisite nature. This part of the subject has not been altogether neglected, but it has not been so much my present aim to prove, that the interest excited by some other kinds of poetry is less vivid, and less worthy of the nobler powers of the mind, as to offer reasons for presuming, that if my purpose were fulfilled, a species of poetry would be produced, which is genuine poetry; in its nature well adapted to interest mankind permanently, and likewise important in the multiplicity and quality of its moral relations.

From what has been said, and from a perusal of the Poems, the Reader will be able clearly to perceive the object which I had in view: he will determine how far it has been attained; and, what is a much more important question, whether it be worth attaining: and upon the decision of these two questions will rest my claim to the approbation of the Public.

APPENDIX

ON POETIC DICTION

Perhaps, as I have no right to expect that attentive perusal, without which, confined, as I have been, to the narrow limits of a preface, my meaning cannot be thoroughly understood, I am anxious to give an exact notion of the sense in which the phrase poetic diction has been used; and for this purpose, a few words shall here be added, concerning the origin and characteristics of the phraseology, which I have condemned under that name.

The earliest poets of all nations generally wrote from passion excited by real events; they wrote naturally, and as men: feeling powerfully as they did, their language was daring, and figurative. In succeeding times, Poets, and Men ambitious of the fame of Poets, perceiving the influence of such language, and desirous of producing the same effect without being animated by the same passion, set themselves to a mechanical adoption of these figures of speech, and made use of them, sometimes with propriety, but much more frequently applied them to feelings and thoughts with which they had no natural connexion whatsoever. A language was thus insensibly produced, differing materially from the real language of men in *any situation*. The Reader or Hearer of this distorted language found himself in a perturbed and unusual state of mind: when affected by the genuine language of passion he had been in a perturbed and unusual state of mind also: in both cases he was willing that his common judgement and understanding should be laid asleep, and he had no instinctive and infallible perception of the true to make him reject the false; the one served as a passport for the other. The emotion was in both cases delightful, and no wonder if he confounded the one with the other, and believed them both to be produced by the same, or similar causes. Besides, the Poet spake to him in the character of a man to be looked up to, a man of genius and authority. Thus, and from a variety of other causes, this distorted language was received with admiration; and Poets, it is probable, who had before contented themselves for the most part with misapplying only expressions which at first had been dictated by real passion, carried the abuse still further, and introduced phrases composed apparently in the spirit of the original figurative language of passion, yet altogether of their own invention, and characterized by various degrees of wanton deviation from good sense and nature.

It is indeed true, that the language of the earliest Poets was felt to differ materially from ordinary language, because it was the language of extraordinary occasions; but it was really spoken by men, language which the Poet himself had uttered when he had been affected by the events which he described, or which he had heard uttered by those around him. To this language it is probable that metre of some sort or other was early superadded. This separated the genuine language of Poetry still further from common life, so that whoever read or heard the poems of these earliest Poets felt himself moved in a way in which he had not been accustomed to be moved in real life, and by causes manifestly different from those which acted upon him in real life. This was the great temptation to all the corruptions which have followed: under the protection of this feeling succeeding Poets constructed a phraseology which had one thing, it is true, in common with the genuine language of poetry, namely, that it was not heard in ordinary conversation; that it was unusual. But the first Poets, as I have said, spake a language which, though unusual, was still the language of men. This circumstance, however, was disregarded by their successors; they found that they could please by easier means: they became proud of modes of expression which they themselves had invented, and which were uttered only by themselves. In process of time metre became a symbol or promise of this unusual language, and whoever took upon him to write in metre, according as he possessed more or less of true poetic genius, introduced less or more of this adulterated phraseology into his compositions, and the true and the false were inseparably interwoven until, the taste of men becoming gradually perverted, this language was received as a natural language: and at length, by the influence of books upon men, did to a certain degree really become so. Abuses of this kind were imported from one nation to another, and with the progress of refinement this diction became daily more and more corrupt, thrusting out of sight the plain humanities of nature by a motley masquerade of tricks, quaintnesses, hieroglyphics, and enigmas.

It would not be uninteresting to point out the causes of the pleasure given by this extravagant and absurd diction. It depends upon a great variety of causes, but upon none, perhaps, more than its influence in impressing a notion of the peculiarity and exaltation of the Poet's character, and in flattering the Reader's self-love by bringing him nearer to a sympathy with that character; an effect which is accomplished by unsettling ordinary habits of thinking, and thus assisting the Reader to approach to that perturbed and dizzy state of mind in which if he does not find himself, he imagines that he is *balked* of a peculiar enjoyment which poetry can and ought to bestow.

The sonnet quoted from Gray, in the Preface, except the lines printed in Italics, consists of little else but this diction, though not of the worst kind; and indeed, if one may be permitted to say so, it is far too common in the best writers both ancient and modern. Perhaps in no way, by positive example, could more easily be given a notion of what I mean by the phrase *poetic diction* than by referring to a comparison between the metrical paraphrase which we have of passages in the Old and New Testament, and those passages as they exist in our common Translation. See Pope's 'Messiah' throughout; Prior's 'Did sweeter sounds adorn my flowing tongue,' &c. &c. 'Though I speak with the tongues of men and of angels,' &c. &c. 1 Corinthians, chap. xiii. By way of immediate example take the following of Dr. Johnson:—

Turn on the prudent Ant thy heedless eyes,
Observe her labours, Sluggard, and be wise;
No stern command, no monitory voice,
Prescribes her duties, or directs her choice;
Yet, timely provident, she hastes away
To snatch the blessings of a plenteous day;
When fruitful Summer loads the teeming plain,
She crops the harvest, and she stores the grain.
How long shall sloth usurp thy useless hours,
Unnerve thy vigour, and enchain thy powers?
While artful shades thy downy couch enclose,
And soft solicitation courts repose,
Amidst the drowsy charms of dull delight,
Year chases year with unremitted flight,
Till Want now following, fraudulent and slow,
Shall spring to seize thee, like an ambush'd foe.

From this hubbub of words pass to the original. 'Go to the Ant, thou Sluggard, consider her ways, and be wise: which having no guide, overseer, or ruler, provideth her meat in the summer, and gathereth her food in the harvest. How long wilt thou sleep, O Sluggard? when wilt thou arise out of thy sleep? Yet a little sleep, a little slumber, a little folding of the hands to sleep. So shall thy poverty come as one that travelleth, and thy want as an armed man.' Proverbs, chap. vi.

One more quotation, and I have done. It is from Cowper's *Verses supposed to be written by Alexander Selkirk*:

Religion! what treasure untold
Resides in that heavenly word!
More precious than silver and gold,
Or all that this earth can afford.
But the sound of the church-going bell
These valleys and rocks never heard,
Ne'er sighed at the sound of a knell,
Or smiled when a sabbath appeared.

Ye winds, that have made me your sport,
Convey to this desolate shore
Some cordial endearing report
Of a land I must visit no more.

> My Friends, do they now and then send
> A wish or a thought after me?
> O tell me I yet have a friend,
> Though a friend I am never to see.

This passage is quoted as an instance of three different styles of composition. The first four lines are poorly expressed; some Critics would call the language prosaic; the fact is, it would be bad prose, so bad, that it is scarcely worse in metre. The epithet 'church-going' applied to a bell, and that by so chaste a writer as Cowper, is an instance of the strange abuses which Poets have introduced into their language, till they and their Readers take them as matters of course, if they do not single them out expressly as objects of admiration. The two lines 'Ne'er sighed at the sound', &c., are, in my opinion, an instance of the language of passion wrested from its proper use, and, from the mere circumstance of the composition being in metre, applied upon an occasion that does not justify such violent expressions; and I should condemn the passage, though perhaps few Readers will agree with me, as vicious poetic diction. The last stanza is throughout admirably expressed: it would be equally good whether in prose or verse, except that the Reader has an exquisite pleasure in seeing such natural language so naturally connected with metre. The beauty of this stanza tempts me to conclude with a principle which ought never to be lost sight of, and which has been my chief guide in all I have said,—namely, that in works of *imagination and sentiment*, for of these only have I been treating, in proportion as ideas and feelings are valuable, whether the composition be in prose or in verse, they require and exact one and the same language. Metre is but adventitious to composition, and the phraseology for which that passport is necessary, even where it may be graceful at all, will be little valued by the judicious.

SAMUEL TAYLOR COLERIDGE
1772–1834
WORDSWORTH'S THEORY OF DICTION
[*Biographia Literaria*, chap. xvii, 1817]

AS far as Mr. Wordsworth in his preface contended, and most ably contended, for a reformation in our poetic diction, as far as he has evinced the truth of passion, and the *dramatic* propriety of those figures and metaphors in the original poets, which, stripped of their justifying reasons, and converted into mere artifices of connexion or ornament, constitute the characteristic falsity in the poetic style of the moderns; and as far as he has, with equal acuteness and clearness, pointed out the process by which this change was effected, and the resemblances between that state into which the reader's mind is thrown by the pleasureable confusion of thought from an unaccustomed train of words and images; and that state which is induced by the natural language of impassioned feeling; he undertook a useful task, and deserves all praise, both for the attempt and for the execution. The provocations to this remonstrance in behalf of truth and nature were still of perpetual recurrence before and after the publication of this preface. I cannot likewise but add, that the comparison of such poems of merit, as have been given to the public within the last ten or twelve years, with the majority of those produced previously to the appearance of that preface, leave no doubt on my mind, that Mr. Wordsworth is fully justified in believing his efforts to have been by no means ineffectual. Not only in the verses of those who have professed their admiration of his genius, but even of those who have distinguished themselves by hostility to his theory, and depreciation of his writings, are the impressions of his principles plainly visible. It is possible, that with these principles others may have been blended, which are not equally evident; and some which are unsteady and subvertible from the narrowness or imperfection of their basis. But it is more than possible, that these errors of defect or exaggeration, by kindling and feeding the controversy, may have conduced not only to the wider propagation of the accompanying truths, but that, by their frequent presentation to the mind in an excited state, they may have won for them a more permanent and practical result. A man will borrow a part from his opponent the more easily, if he feels himself justified in continuing to reject a part. While there remain important points in which he can still feel himself in the right, in which he still finds firm footing for continued resistance, he will gradually adopt those opinions, which were the least remote from his own convictions, as not less congruous with his own theory than with that which he reprobates. In like manner with a kind of instinctive prudence, he will abandon by little and little his weakest posts, till at length he seems to forget that they had ever belonged to him, or affects to consider them at most as accidental and 'petty annexments', the removal of which leaves the citadel unhurt and unendangered.

My own differences from certain supposed parts of Mr. Wordsworth's theory ground themselves on the assumption, that his words had been rightly interpreted, as purporting that the proper diction for poetry in general consists altogether in a language taken, with due exceptions, from the mouths of men in real life, a language which actually constitutes the natural conversation of men under the influence of natural feelings. My objection is, first, that in any sense this rule is applicable only to certain classes of poetry; secondly, that even to these classes it is not applicable, except in such a sense, as hath never by any one (as far as I know or have read) been denied

WORDSWORTH'S THEORY OF DICTION

or doubted; and lastly, that as far as, and in that degree in which it is practicable, yet as a rule it is useless, if not injurious, and therefore either need not, or ought not to be practised. The poet informs his reader that he had generally chosen low and rustic life; but not *as* low and rustic, or in order to repeat that pleasure of doubtful moral effect, which persons of elevated rank and of superior refinement oftentimes derive from a happy imitation of the rude unpolished manners and discourse of their inferiors. For the pleasure so derived may be traced to three exciting causes. The first is the naturalness, in fact, of the things represented. The second is the apparent naturalness of the representation, as raised and qualified by an imperceptible infusion of the author's own knowledge and talent, which infusion does, indeed, constitute it an imitation as distinguished from a mere copy. The third cause may be found in the reader's conscious feeling of his superiority awakened by the contrast presented to him; even as for the same purpose the kings and great barons of yore retained sometimes actual clowns and fools, but more frequently shrewd and witty fellows in that character. These, however, were not Mr. Wordsworth's objects. He chose low and rustic life, 'because in that condition the essential passions of the heart find a better soil, in which they can attain their maturity, are less under restraint, and speak a plainer and more emphatic language; because in that condition of life our elementary feelings co-exist in a state of greater simplicity, and consequently may be more accurately contemplated, and more forcibly communicated; because the manners of rural life germinate from those elementary feelings; and from the necessary character of rural occupations are more easily comprehended, and are more durable; and lastly, because in that condition the passions of men are incorporated with the beautiful and permanent forms of nature.'

Now it is clear to me, that in the most interesting of the poems, in which the author is more or less dramatic, as the *Brothers*, *Michael*, *Ruth*, the *Mad Mother*, &c., the persons introduced are by no means taken from low or rustic life in the common acceptation of those words; and it is not less clear, that the sentiments and language, as far as they can be conceived to have been really transferred from the minds and conversation of such persons, are attributable to causes and circumstances not necessarily connected with 'their occupations and abode'. The thoughts, feelings, language, and manners of the shepherd-farmers in the vales of Cumberland and Westmoreland, as far as they are actually adopted in those poems, may be accounted for from causes, which will and do produce the same results in every state of life, whether in town or country. As the two principal I rank that INDEPENDENCE, which raises a man above servitude, or daily toil for the profit of others, yet not above the necessity of industry and a frugal simplicity of domestic life; and the accompanying unambitious, but solid and religious, EDUCATION, which has rendered few books familiar, but the Bible, and the liturgy or hymnbook. To the latter cause, indeed, which is so far accidental, that it is the blessing of particular countries and a particular age, not the product of particular places or employments, the poet owes the show of probability, that his personages might really feel, think, and talk with any tolerable resemblance to his representation. It is an excellent remark of Dr. Henry More's that 'a man of confined education, but of good parts, by constant reading of the Bible will naturally form a more winning and commanding rhetoric than those that are learned: the intermixture of tongues and of artificial phrases debasing their style'.

It is, moreover, to be considered that to the formation of healthy feelings, and a reflecting mind, negations involve impediments not less formidable than sophistication and vicious intermixture. I am convinced, that for the human soul to prosper in rustic life a certain vantage-ground is pre-requisite. It is not every man that is likely to be improved by a country life or by country labours. Education, or original sensibility, or both, must pre-exist, if the changes, forms, and incidents of nature are to prove a sufficient stimulant. And where these are not sufficient, the mind contracts and hardens by want of stimulants: and the man becomes selfish, sensual, gross, and hard-hearted. Let the management of the POOR LAWS in Liverpool, Manchester, or Bristol be compared with the ordinary dispensation of the poor rates in agricultural villages, where the farmers are the overseers and guardians of the poor. If my own experience have not been particularly unfortunate, as well as that of the many respectable country clergymen with whom I have conversed on the subject, the result would engender more than scepticism concerning the desirable influences of low and rustic life in and for itself. Whatever may be concluded on the other side, from the stronger local attachments and enterprising spirit of the Swiss, and other mountaineers, applies to a particular mode of pastoral life, under forms of property that permit and beget manners truly republican, not to rustic life in general, or to the absence of artificial cultivation. On the contrary the mountaineers, whose manners have been so often eulogized, are in general better educated and greater readers than men of equal rank elsewhere. But where this is not the case, as among the peasantry of North Wales, the ancient mountains, with all their terrors and all their glories, are pictures to the blind, and music to the deaf.

I should not have entered so much into detail upon this passage, but here seems to be the point, to which all the lines of difference converge as to their source and centre;—I mean, as far as, and in whatever respect, my poetic creed does differ from the doctrines promulgated in this preface. I adopt with full faith the principle of Aristotle, that poetry, as poetry, is essentially ideal, that it avoids and excludes all accident; that its apparent individualities of rank, character, or occupation must be representative of a class; and that the persons of poetry must be clothed with generic attributes, with the common attributes of the class: not with such as one gifted individual might possibly possess, but such as from his situation it is most probable beforehand that he would possess. If my premises are right and my deductions legitimate, it follows that there can be no poetic medium between the swains of Theocritus and those of an imaginary golden age.

The characters of the vicar and the shepherd-mariner in the poem of *The Brothers*, that of the shepherd of Green-head Ghyll in the *Michael*, have all the verisimilitude and representative quality, that the purposes of poetry can require. They are persons of a known and abiding class, and their manners and sentiments the natural product of circumstances common to the class. Take Michael for instance:

> An old man stout of heart, and strong of limb:
> His bodily frame had been from youth to age
> Of an unusual strength: his mind was keen,
> Intense, and frugal, apt for all affairs,
> And in his shepherd's calling he was prompt
> And watchful more than ordinary men.
> Hence he had learned the meaning of all winds,
> Of blasts of every tone; and oftentimes
> When others heeded not, he heard the South
> Make subterraneous music, like the noise
> Of bagpipers on distant Highland hills.
> The shepherd, at such warning, of his flock
> Bethought him, and he to himself would say,
> The winds are now devising work for me!
> And truly at all times the storm, that drives
> The traveller to a shelter, summon'd him
> Up to the mountains. He had been alone
> Amid the heart of many thousand mists,

That came to him and left him on the heights.
So liv'd he, until his eightieth year was pass'd.
And grossly that man errs, who should suppose
That the green valleys, and the streams and rocks,
Were things indifferent to the shepherd's thoughts.
Fields, where with chearful spirits he had breath'd
The common air; the hills, which he so oft
Had climb'd with vigorous steps; which had impress'd
So many incidents upon his mind
Of hardship, skill or courage, joy or fear;
Which, like a book, preserved the memory
Of the dumb animals, whom he had sav'd,
Had fed or shelter'd, linking to such acts,
So grateful in themselves, the certainty
Of honourable gain; these fields, these hills
Which were his living being, even more
Than his own blood—what could they less? had laid
Strong hold on his affections, were to him
A pleasureable feeling of blind love,
The pleasure which there is in life itself.

On the other hand, in the poems which are pitched at a lower note, as the *Harry Gill*, *Idiot Boy*, the feelings are those of human nature in general; though the poet has judiciously laid the scene in the country, in order to place himself in the vicinity of interesting images, without the necessity of ascribing a sentimental perception of their beauty to the persons of his drama. In *The Idiot Boy*, indeed, the mother's character is not so much a real and native product of a 'situation where the essential passions of the heart find a better soil, in which they can attain their maturity, and speak a plainer and more emphatic language', as it is an impersonation of an instinct abandoned by judgement. Hence the two following charges seem to me not wholly groundless: at least, they are the only plausible objections, which I have heard to that fine poem. The one is, that the author has not, in the poem itself, taken sufficient care to preclude from the reader's fancy the disgusting images of ordinary morbid idiocy, which yet it was by no means his intention to represent. He has even by the 'burr, burr, burr', uncounteracted by any preceding description of the boy's beauty, assisted in recalling them. The other is, that the idiocy of the boy is so evenly balanced by the folly of the mother, as to present to the general reader rather a laughable burlesque on the blindness of anile dotage, than an analytic display of maternal affection in its ordinary workings.

In *The Thorn*, the poet himself acknowledges in a note the necessity of an introductory poem, in which he should have portrayed the character of the person from whom the words of the poem are supposed to proceed: a superstitious man moderately imaginative, of slow faculties and deep feelings, 'a captain of a small trading vessel, for example, who, being past the middle age of life, had retired upon an annuity, or small independent income, to some village or country town of which he was not a native, or in which he had not been accustomed to live. Such men having nothing to do become credulous and talkative from indolence'. But in a poem, still more in a lyric poem—and the Nurse in Shakespeare's *Romeo and Juliet* alone prevents me from extending the remark even to dramatic poetry, if indeed even the Nurse itself can be deemed altogether a case in point—it is not possible to imitate truly a dull and garrulous discourser, without repeating the effects of dullness and garrulity. However this may be, I dare assert, that the parts—(and these form the far larger portion of the whole)—which might as well or still better have proceeded from the poet's own imagination, and have been spoken in his own character, are those which have given, and which will continue to give, universal delight; and that the passages exclusively appropriate to the supposed narrator, such as the last couplet of the third stanza;[1] the seven last lines of the tenth;[2] and

---

[1] I've measured it from side to side;
'Tis three feet long, and two feet wide.

[2] Nay, rack your brain—'tis all in vain,
I'll tell you every thing I know;

WORDSWORTH'S THEORY OF DICTION

the five following stanzas, with the exception of the four admirable lines at the commencement of the fourteenth, are felt by many unprejudiced and unsophisticated hearts, as sudden and unpleasant sinkings from the height to which the poet had previously

> But to the Thorn, and to the Pond
> Which is a little step beyond,
> I wish that you would go:
> Perhaps, when you are at the place,
> You something of her tale may trace.
>
> I'll give you the best help I can:
> Before you up the mountain go,
> Up to the dreary mountain-top,
> I'll tell you all I know.
> 'Tis now some two-and-twenty years
> Since she (her name is Martha Ray)
> Gave, with a maiden's true good will,
> Her company to Stephen Hill;
> And she was blithe and gay,
> And she was happy, happy still
> Whene'er she thought of Stephen Hill.
>
> And they had fix'd the wedding-day,
> The morning that must wed them both;
> But Stephen to another maid
> Had sworn another oath;
> And, with this other maid, to church
> Unthinking Stephen went—
> Poor Martha! on that woeful day
> A pang of pitiless dismay
> Into her soul was sent;
> A fire was kindled in her breast,
> Which might not burn itself to rest.
>
> They say, full six months after this,
> While yet the summer leaves were green,
> She to the mountain-top would go,
> And there was often seen.
> 'Tis said a child was in her womb,
> As now to any eye was plain;
> She was with child, and she was mad;
> Yet often she was sober sad
> From her exceeding pain.

lifted them, and to which he again re-elevates both himself and his reader.

If then I am compelled to doubt the theory, by which the choice of characters was to be directed, not only *à priori*, from grounds of reason, but both from the few instances in which the poet himself need be supposed to have been governed by it, and from the comparative inferiority of those instances; still more must I hesitate in my assent to the sentence which immediately follows the former citation; and which I can neither admit as particular fact, nor as general rule. 'The language, too, of these men is adopted (purified indeed from what appear to be its real defects, from all lasting and rational causes of dislike or disgust) because such men hourly communicate with the best objects from which the best part of

> Oh me! ten thousand times I'd rather
> That he had died, that cruel father!
>
> *   *   *   *   *   *   *
> *   *   *   *   *   *   *
> *   *   *   *   *   *   *
> *   *   *   *   *   *   *
>
> Last Christmas when we talked of this,
> Old farmer Simpson did maintain,
> That in her womb the infant wrought
> About its mother's heart, and brought
> Her senses back again:
> And, when at last her time drew near,
> Her looks were calm, her senses clear.
>
> No more I know, I wish I did,
> And I would tell it all to you:
> For what became of this poor child
> There's none that ever knew:
> And if a child was born or no,
> There's no one that could ever tell;
> And if 'twas born alive or dead,
> There's no one knows, as I have said:
> But some remember well,
> That Martha Ray about this time
> Would up the mountain often climb.

language is originally derived; and because, from their rank in society and the sameness and narrow circle of their intercourse, being less under the action of social vanity, they convey their feelings and notions in simple and unelaborated expressions.' To this I reply; that a rustic's language, purified from all provincialism and grossness, and so far reconstructed as to be made consistent with the rules of grammar— (which are in essence no other than the laws of universal logic, applied to psychological materials)— will not differ from the language of any other man of common sense, however learned or refined he may be, except as far as the notions, which the rustic has to convey, are fewer and more indiscriminate. This will become still clearer, if we add the consideration— (equally important though less obvious)—that the rustic, from the more imperfect development of his faculties, and from the lower state of their cultivation, aims almost solely to convey insulated facts, either those of his scanty experience or his traditional belief; while the educated man chiefly seeks to discover and express those connexions of things, or those relative bearings of fact to fact, from which some more or less general law is deducible. For facts are valuable to a wise man, chiefly as they lead to the discovery of the indwelling law, which is the true being of things, the sole solution of their modes of existence, and in the knowledge of which consists our dignity and our power.

As little can I agree with the assertion, that from the objects with which the rustic hourly communicates the best part of language is formed. For first, if to communicate with an object implies such an acquaintance with it, as renders it capable of being discriminately reflected on; the distinct knowledge of an uneducated rustic would furnish a very scanty vocabulary. The few things and modes of action requisite for his bodily conveniences would alone be individualized; while all the rest of nature would be expressed by a small number of confused general terms. Secondly, I deny that the words and combinations of words derived from the objects, with which the rustic is familiar, whether with distinct or confused knowledge, can be justly said to form the best part of language. It is more than probable, that many classes of the brute creation possess discriminating sounds, by which they can convey to each other notices of such objects as concern their food, shelter, or safety. Yet we hesitate to call the aggregate of such sounds a language, otherwise than metaphorically. The best part of human language, properly so called, is derived from reflection on the acts of the mind itself. It is formed by a voluntary appropriation of fixed symbols to internal acts, to processes and results of imagination, the greater part of which have no place in the consciousness of uneducated man; though in civilized society, by imitation and passive remembrance of what they hear from their religious instructors and other superiors, the most uneducated share in the harvest which they neither sowed nor reaped. If the history of the phrases in hourly currency among our peasants were traced, a person not previously aware of the fact would be surprised at finding so large a number, which three or four centuries ago were the exclusive property of the universities and the schools; and, at the commencement of the Reformation, had been transferred from the school to the pulpit, and thus gradually passed into common life. The extreme difficulty, and often the impossibility, of finding words for the simplest moral and intellectual processes of the languages of uncivilized tribes has proved perhaps the weightiest obstacle to the progress of our most zealous and adroit missionaries. Yet these tribes are surrounded by the same nature as our peasants are; but in still more impressive forms; and they are, moreover, obliged to particularize many more of them. When, therefore, Mr. Wordsworth adds, 'accordingly, such a language'—(meaning, as before, the language of rustic life purified from provincialism)—'arising out of repeated experience and regular feelings, is a more permanent, and a far more philosophical language, than that which is frequently substituted for it by poets, who think that they are conferring honour upon themselves and their art in proportion as they indulge in arbitrary and capricious habits of expression;' it may be answered, that the language, which he has in view, can be attributed to rustics with no greater right, than the style of Hooker or Bacon to Tom Brown or Sir Roger L'Estrange. Doubtless, if what is peculiar to each were omitted in each, the result must needs be the same. Further, that the poet, who uses an illogical diction, or a style fitted to excite only the low and changeable pleasure of wonder by means of groundless novelty, substitutes a language of folly and vanity, not for that of the rustic, but for that of good sense and natural feeling.

Here let me be permitted to remind the reader, that the positions, which I controvert, are contained in the sentences—'*a selection of the* REAL *language of men*';—'*the language of these men*' (i.e. men in low and rustic life) '*I propose to myself to imitate, and, as far as is possible, to adopt the very language of men.*' '*Between the language of prose and that of metrical composition, there neither is, nor can be, any essential difference.*' It is against these exclusively that my opposition is directed.

I object, in the very first instance, to an equivocation in the use of the word 'real'. Every man's language varies, according to the extent of his knowledge, the activity of his faculties, and the depth or quickness of his feelings. Every man's language has, first, its individualities; secondly, the common properties of the class to which he belongs; and thirdly, words and phrases of universal use. The language of Hooker, Bacon, Bishop Taylor, and Burke differs from the common language of the learned class only by the superior number and novelty of the thoughts and relations which they had to convey. The language of

Algernon Sidney differs not at all from that, which every well-educated gentleman would wish to write, and (with due allowance for the undeliberateness, and less connected train, of thinking natural and proper to conversation) such as he would wish to talk. Neither one nor the other differ half so much from the general language of cultivated society, as the language of Mr. Wordsworth's homeliest composition differs from that of a common peasant. For 'real' therefore, we must substitute ordinary, or *lingua communis*. And this, we have proved, is no more to be found in the phraseology of low and rustic life than in that of any other class. Omit the peculiarities of each and the result of course must be common to all. And assuredly the omissions and changes to be made in the language of rustics, before it could be transferred to any species of poem, except the drama or other professed imitation, are at least as numerous and weighty, as would be required in adapting to the same purpose the ordinary language of tradesmen and manufacturers. Not to mention, that the language so highly extolled by Mr. Wordsworth varies in every county, nay in every village, according to the accidental character of the clergyman, the existence or non-existence of schools; or even, perhaps, as the exciseman, publican, and barber happen to be, or not to be, zealous politicians, and readers of the weekly newspaper *pro bono publico*. Anterior to cultivation the *lingua communis* of every country, as Dante has well observed, exists everywhere in parts, and nowhere as a whole.

Neither is the case rendered at all more tenable by the addition of the words, *in a state of excitement.* For the nature of a man's words, where he is strongly affected by joy, grief, or anger, must necessarily depend on the number and quality of the general truths, conceptions and images, and of the words expressing them, with which his mind had been previously stored. For the property of passion is not to

WORDSWORTH'S THEORY OF DICTION

create; but to set in increased activity. At least, whatever new connexions of thoughts or images, or (which is equally, if not more than equally, the appropriate effect of strong excitement) whatever generalizations of truth or experience the heat of passion may produce; yet the terms of their convevance must have pre-existed in his former conversations, and are only collected and crowded together by the unusual stimulation. It is indeed very possible to adopt in a poem the unmeaning repetitions, habitual phrases, and other blank counters, which an unfurnished or confused understanding interposes at short intervals, in order to keep hold of his subject, which is still slipping from him, and to give him time for recollection; or, in mere aid of vacancy, as in the scanty companies of a country stage the same player pops backwards and forwards, in order to prevent the appearance of empty spaces, in the procession of *Macbeth*, or *Henry VIII*. But what assistance to the poet, or ornament to the poem, these can supply, I am at a loss to conjecture. Nothing assuredly can differ either in origin or in mode more widely from the apparent tautologies of intense and turbulent feeling, in which the passion is greater and of longer endurance than to be exhausted or satisfied by a single representation of the image or incident exciting it. Such repetitions I admit to be a beauty of the highest kind; as illustrated by Mr. Wordsworth himself from the song of Deborah. *At her feet he bowed, he fell, he lay down: at her feet he bowed, he fell: where he bowed, there he fell down dead.*

METRICAL COMPOSITION
[*Biographia Literaria*, chap. xviii, 1817]

I CONCLUDE, therefore, that the attempt is impracticable; and that, were it not impracticable, it would still be useless. For the very power of making the selection implies the previous possession of the language selected. Or where can the poet have lived? And by what rules could he direct his choice, which would not have enabled him to select and arrange his words by the light of his own judgement? We do not adopt the language of a class by the mere adoption of such words exclusively, as that class would use, or at least understand; but likewise by following the order, in which the words of such men are wont to succeed each other. Now this order, in the intercourse of uneducated men, is distinguished from the diction of their superiors in knowledge and power, by the greater disjunction and separation in the component parts of that, whatever it be, which they wish to communicate. There is a want of that prospectiveness of mind, that surview, which enables a man to foresee the whole of what he is to convey, appertaining to any one point; and by this means so to subordinate and arrange the different parts according to their relative importance, as to convey it at once, and as an organized whole.

Now I will take the first stanza, on which I have chanced to open, in the *Lyrical Ballads*. It is one the most simple and the least peculiar in its language.

> In distant countries have I been,
> And yet I have not often seen
> A healthy man, a man full grown,
> Weep in the public roads, alone.
> But such a one, on English ground,
> And in the broad highway, I met;
> Along the broad highway he came,
> His cheeks with tears were wet:
> Sturdy he seem'd, though he was sad;
> And in his arms a lamb he had.

The words here are doubtless such as are current in all ranks of life; and of course not less so in the hamlet and cottage than in the shop, manufactory, college, or palace. But is this the order, in which the rustic would have placed the words? I am grievously deceived, if the following less compact mode of com-

METRICAL COMPOSITION

mencing the same tale be not a far more faithful copy. 'I have been in a many parts, far and near, and I don't know that I ever saw before a man crying by himself in the public road; a grown man I mean, that was neither sick nor hurt,' &c., &c. But when I turn to the following stanza in *The Thorn*:

> At all times of the day and night
> This wretched woman thither goes,
> And she is known to every star,
> And every wind that blows:
> And there, beside the thorn, she sits,
> When the blue day-light's in the skies;
> And when the whirlwind's on the hill,
> Or frosty air is keen and still;
> And to herself she cries,
> Oh misery! Oh misery!
> Oh woe is me! Oh misery!

and compare this with the language of ordinary men; or with that which I can conceive at all likely to proceed, in real life, from such a narrator, as is supposed in the note to the poem; compare it either in the succession of the images or of the sentences; I am reminded of the sublime prayer and hymn of praise, which MILTON, in opposition to an established liturgy, presents as a fair specimen of common extemporary devotion, and such as we might expect to hear from every self-inspired minister of a conventicle! And I reflect with delight, how little a mere theory, though of his own workmanship, interferes with the processes of genuine imagination in a man of true poetic genius, who possesses, as Mr. Wordsworth, if ever man did, most assuredly does possess,

> The Vision and the Faculty Divine.

One point then alone remains, but that the most important; its examination having been, indeed, my chief inducement for the preceding inquisition. '*There neither is nor can be any essential difference between the language of prose and metrical composition.*' Such is Mr. Wordsworth's assertion. Now prose itself, at least in all argumentative and consecutive works, differs, and ought to differ, from the language of conversation; even as reading ought to differ from talking. Unless therefore the difference denied be that of the mere words, as materials common to all styles of writing, and not of the style itself in the universally admitted sense of the term, it might be naturally presumed that there must exist a still greater between the ordonnance of poetic composition and that of prose, than is expected to distinguish prose from ordinary conversation.

There are not, indeed, examples wanting in the history of literature, of apparent paradoxes that have summoned the public wonder as new and startling truths, but which, on examination, have shrunk into tame and harmless truisms; as the eyes of a cat, seen in the dark, have been mistaken for flames of fire. But Mr. Wordsworth is among the last men, to whom a delusion of this kind would be attributed by any one who had enjoyed the slightest opportunity of understanding his mind and character. Where an objection has been anticipated by such an author as natural, his answer to it must needs be interpreted in some sense which either is, or has been, or is capable of being controverted. My object then must be to discover some other meaning for the term '*essential difference*' in this place, exclusive of the indistinction and community of the words themselves. For whether there ought to exist a class of words in the English, in any degree resembling the poetic dialect of the Greek and Italian, is a question of very subordinate importance. The number of such words would be small indeed, in our language; and even in the Italian and Greek, they consist not so much of different words, as of slight differences in the forms of declining and conjugating the same words; forms, doubtless, which having been, at some period more or less remote, the common grammatic flexions of some tribe or province, had been accidentally appropriated to poetry by the general admiration of certain master intellects, the first established lights of inspiration, to whom that dialect happened to be native.

Essence, in its primary signification, means the principle of individuation, the inmost principle of the possibility of any thing, as that particular thing. It is equivalent to the idea of a thing, whenever we use the word, idea, with philosophic precision. Existence, on the other hand, is distinguished from essence, by the superinduction of reality. Thus we speak of the essence, and essential properties of a circle; but we do not therefore assert, that any thing, which really exists, is mathematically circular. Thus too, without any tautology we contend for the existence of the Supreme Being; that is, for a reality correspondent to the idea. There is, next, a secondary use of the word essence, in which it signifies the point or ground of contra-distinction between two modifications of the same substance or subject. Thus we should be allowed to say, that the style of architecture of Westminster Abbey is essentially different from that of St. Paul's, even though both had been built with blocks cut into the same form, and from the same quarry. Only in this latter sense of the term must it have been denied by Mr. Wordsworth (for in this sense alone is it affirmed by the general opinion) that the language of poetry (i.e. the formal construction, or architecture, of the words and phrases) is essentially different from that of prose. Now the burthen of the proof lies with the oppugner, not with the supporters of the common belief. Mr. Wordsworth, in consequence, assigns as the proof of his position, 'that not only the language of a large portion of every good poem, even of the most elevated character, must necessarily, except with reference to the metre, in no respect differ from that of good prose, but likewise that some of the most interesting parts of the best poems will be found to be strictly the language of prose, when prose is well written. The truth of this assertion might be demonstrated by innumerable passages from almost all the poetical writings even of Milton himself.' He then quotes Gray's sonnet:—

In vain to me the smiling mornings shine,
And reddening Phoebus lifts his golden fire;
The birds in vain their amorous descant join,
Or cheerful fields resume their green attire.
These ears, alas! for other notes repine;
A different object do these eyes require;
My lonely anguish melts no heart but mine;
And in my breast the imperfect joys expire.
Yet morning smiles the busy race to cheer,
And newborn pleasure brings to happier men;
The fields to all their wonted tribute bear,
To warm their little loves the birds complain.
I fruitless mourn to him that cannot hear,
And weep the more because I weep in vain,

and adds the following remark:—'It will easily be perceived, that the only part of this Sonnet, which is of any value, is the lines printed in italics. It is equally obvious, that, except in the rhyme, and in the use of the single word "fruitless" for "fruitlessly", which is so far a defect, the language of these lines does in no respect differ from that of prose.'

An idealist defending his system by the fact, that when asleep we often believe ourselves awake, was well answered by his plain neighbour, 'Ah, but when awake do we ever believe ourselves asleep?'—Things identical must be convertible. The preceding passage seems to rest on a similar sophism. For the question is not, whether there may not occur in prose an order of words, which would be equally proper in a poem; nor whether there are not beautiful lines and sentences of frequent occurrence in good poems, which would be equally becoming as well as beautiful in good prose; for neither the one nor the other has ever been either denied or doubted by any one. The true question must be, whether there are not modes

METRICAL COMPOSITION

of expression, a construction, and an order of sentences, which are in their fit and natural place in a serious prose composition, but would be disproportionate and heterogeneous in metrical poetry; and, vice versa, whether in the language of a serious poem there may not be an arrangement both of words and sentences, and a use and selection of (what are called) *figures of speech*, both as to their kind, their frequency, and their occasions, which on a subject of equal weight would be vicious and alien in correct and manly prose. I contend, that in both cases this unfitness of each for the place of the other frequently will and ought to exist.

And first from the origin of metre. This I would trace to the balance in the mind effected by that spontaneous effort which strives to hold in check the workings of passion. It might be easily explained likewise in what manner this salutary antagonism is assisted by the very state, which it counteracts; and how this balance of antagonists became organized into metre (in the usual acceptation of that term) by a supervening act of the will and judgement, consciously and for the foreseen purpose of pleasure. Assuming these principles, as the data of our argument, we deduce from them two legitimate conditions, which the critic is entitled to expect in every metrical work. First, that, as the elements of metre owe their existence to a state of increased excitement, so the metre itself should be accompanied by the natural language of excitement. Secondly, that as these elements are formed into metre artificially, by a voluntary act, with the design and for the purpose of blending delight with emotion, so the traces of present volition should throughout the metrical language be proportionately discernible. Now these two conditions must be reconciled and co-present. There must be not only a partnership, but a union; an interpenetration of passion and of will, of spontaneous impulse and of voluntary purpose. Again, this union can be manifested only in a frequency of forms and figures of speech (originally the offspring of passion, but now the adopted children of power), greater than would be desired or endured, where the emotion is not voluntarily encouraged and kept up for the sake of that pleasure, which such emotion, so tempered and mastered by the will, is found capable of communicating. It not only dictates, but of itself tends to produce, a more frequent employment of picturesque and vivifying language, than would be natural in any other case, in which there did not exist, as there does in the present, a previous and well understood, though tacit, *compact* between the poet and his reader, that the latter is entitled to expect, and the former bound to supply, this species and degree of pleasurable excitement. We may in some measure apply to this union the answer of POLIXENES, in the *Winter's Tale*, to PERDITA's neglect of the streaked gilly-flowers, because she had heard it said:

There is an art which, in their piedness, shares
With great creating nature.
      Pol. Say there be;
Yet nature is made better by no mean,
But nature makes that mean; so, ev'n that art,
Which, you say, adds to nature, is an art,
That nature makes. You see, sweet maid, we marry
A gentler scion to the wildest stock;
And make conceive a bark of ruder kind
By bud of nobler race. This is an art,
Which does mend nature—change it rather; but
The art itself is nature.

Secondly, I argue from the EFFECTS of metre. As far as metre acts in and for itself, it tends to increase the vivacity and susceptibility both of the general feelings and of the attention. This effect it produces by the continued excitement of surprise, and by the quick reciprocations of curiosity still gratified and still re-excited, which are too slight indeed to be at any one moment objects of distinct consciousness, yet become considerable in their aggregate influence.

METRICAL COMPOSITION

As a medicated atmosphere, or as wine during animated conversation, they act powerfully, though themselves unnoticed. Where, therefore, correspondent food and appropriate matter are not provided for the attention and feelings thus roused, there must needs be a disappointment felt; like that of leaping in the dark from the last step of a staircase, when we had prepared our muscles for a leap of three or four.

The discussion on the powers of metre in the preface is highly ingenious and touches at all points on truth. But I cannot find any statement of its powers considered abstractly and separately. On the contrary Mr. Wordsworth seems always to estimate metre by the powers which it exerts during (and, as I think, in consequence of) its combination with other elements of poetry. Thus the previous difficulty is left unanswered, what the elements are with which it must be combined, in order to produce its own effects to any pleasureable purpose. Double and tri-syllable rhymes, indeed, form a lower species of wit, and, attended to exclusively for their own sake, may become a source of momentary amusement; as in poor Smart's distich to the Welsh Squire who had promised him a hare:

> Tell me, thou son of great Cadwallader!
> Hast sent the hare? or hast thou swallowed her?

But for any poetic purposes, metre resembles (if the aptness of the simile may excuse its meanness) yeast, worthless or disagreeable by itself, but giving vivacity and spirit to the liquor with which it is proportionately combined.

The reference to *The Children in the Wood* by no means satisfies my judgement. We all willingly throw ourselves back for awhile into the feelings of our childhood. This ballad, therefore, we read under such recollections of our own childish feelings, as would equally endear to us poems, which Mr. Wordsworth himself would regard as faulty in the opposite extreme of gaudy and technical ornament. Before the invention of printing, and in a still greater degree, before the introduction of writing, metre, especially alliterative metre (whether alliterative at the beginning of the words, as in *Piers Plowman*, or at the end, as in rhymes), possessed an independent value as assisting the recollection, and consequently the preservation, of *any* series of truths or incidents. But I am not convinced by the collation of facts, that *The Children in the Wood* owes either its preservation, or its popularity, to its metrical form. Mr. Marshal's repository affords a number of tales in prose inferior in pathos and general merit, some of as old a date, and many as widely popular. *Tom Hickathrift*, *Jack the Giant-killer*, *Goody Two-shoes*, and *Little Red Riding-hood* are formidable rivals. And that they have continued in prose, cannot be fairly explained by the assumption, that the comparative meanness of their thoughts and images precluded even the humblest forms of metre. The scene of *Goody Two-shoes* in the church is perfectly susceptible of metrical narration; and, among the Θαύματα θαυμαστότατα even of the present age, I do not recollect a more astonishing image than that of the '*whole rookery, that flew out of the giant's beard*', scared by the tremendous voice, with which this monster answered the challenge of the heroic *Tom Hickathrift*!

If from these we turn to compositions universally, and independently of all early associations, beloved and admired, would *The Maria*, *The Monk*, or *The Poor Man's Ass* of Sterne, be read with more delight, or have a better chance of immortality, had they without any change in the diction been composed in rhyme, than in their present state? If I am not grossly mistaken, the general reply would be in the negative. Nay, I will confess, that, in Mr. Wordsworth's own volumes, the *Anecdote for Fathers*, *Simon Lee*, *Alice Fell*, *The Beggars*, and *The Sailor's Mother*, notwithstanding the beauties which are to be found in each of them where the poet interposes the music of his own thoughts, would have been more delightful to me in prose, told and managed, as by Mr. Wordsworth they would have been, in a moral essay, or pedestrian tour.

Metre in itself is simply a stimulant of the attention, and therefore excites the question: Why is the attention to be thus stimulated? Now the question cannot be answered by the pleasure of the metre itself: for this we have shown to be conditional, and dependent on the appropriateness of the thoughts and expressions, to which the metrical form is superadded. Neither can I conceive any other answer that can be rationally given, short of this: I write in metre, because I am about to use a language different from that of prose. Besides, where the language is not such, how interesting soever the reflections are, that are capable of being drawn by a philosophic mind from the thoughts or incidents of the poem, the metre itself must often become feeble. Take the last three stanzas of *The Sailor's Mother*, for instance. If I could for a moment abstract from the effect produced on the author's feelings, as a man, by the incident at the time of its real occurrence, I would dare appeal to his own judgement, whether in the metre itself he found a sufficient reason for their being written metrically?

> And, thus continuing, she said,
> I had a son, who many a day
> Sailed on the seas; but he is dead;
> In Denmark he was cast away;
> And I have travelled far as Hull, to see
> What clothes he might have left, or other property.
>
> The bird and cage they both were his:
> 'Twas my son's bird; and neat and trim
> He kept it: many voyages
> This singing-bird hath gone with him;
> When last he sailed he left the bird behind;
> As it might be, perhaps, from bodings of his mind.

> He to a fellow-lodger's care
> Had left it, to be watched and fed,
> Till he came back again; and there
> I found it when my son was dead;
> And now, God help me for my little wit!
> I trail it with me, Sir! he took so much delight in it.

If disproportioning the emphasis we read these stanzas so as to make the rhymes perceptible, even tri-syllable rhymes could scarcely produce an equal sense of oddity and strangeness, as we feel here in finding rhymes at all in sentences so exclusively colloquial. I would further ask whether, but for that visionary state, into which the figure of the woman and the susceptibility of his own genius had placed the poet's imagination (a state, which spreads its influence and colouring over all, that co-exists with the exciting cause, and in which

> The simplest, and the most familiar things
> Gain a strange power of spreading awe around them),

I would ask the poet whether he would not have felt an abrupt downfall in these verses from the preceding stanza?

> The ancient spirit is not dead;
> Old times, thought I, are breathing there;
> Proud was I that my country bred
> Such strength, a dignity so fair:
> She begged an alms, like one in poor estate;
> I looked at her again, nor did my pride abate.

It must not be omitted, and is besides worthy of notice, that those stanzas furnish the only fair instance that I have been able to discover in all Mr. Wordsworth's writings, of an actual adoption, or true imitation, of the real and very language of low and rustic life, freed from provincialisms.

Thirdly, I deduce the position from all the causes elsewhere assigned, which render metre the proper form of poetry, and poetry imperfect and defective without metre. Metre, therefore, having been connected with poetry most often and by a peculiar fitness, whatever else is combined with metre must, though it be not itself essentially poetic, have nevertheless some property in common with poetry, as an intermedium of affinity, a sort (if I may dare borrow a well-known phrase from technical chemistry) of *mordaunt* between it and the super-added metre. Now poetry, Mr. Wordsworth truly affirms, does always imply PASSION: which word must be here understood in its most general sense, as an excited state of the feelings and faculties. And as every passion has its proper pulse, so will it likewise have its characteristic modes of expression. But where there exists that degree of genius and talent which entitles a writer to aim at the honours of a poet, the very act of poetic composition itself is, and is allowed to imply and to produce, an unusual state of excitement, which of course justifies and demands a correspondent difference of language, as truly, though not perhaps in as marked a degree, as the excitement of love, fear, rage, or jealousy. The vividness of the descriptions or declamations in DONNE or DRYDEN is as much and as often derived from the force and fervour of the describer, as from the reflections, forms or incidents, which constitute their subject and materials. The wheels take fire from the mere rapidity of their motion. To what extent, and under what modifications, this may be admitted to act, I shall attempt to define in an after remark on Mr. Wordsworth's reply to this objection, or rather on his objection to this reply, as already anticipated in his preface.

Fourthly, and as intimately connected with this, if not the same argument in a more general form, I adduce the high spiritual instinct of the human being impelling us to seek unity by harmonious adjustment, and thus establishing the principle, that all the parts of an organized whole must be assimilated to the more important and essential parts. This and the preceding arguments may be strengthened by the reflection, that the composition of a poem is among the imitative arts; and that imitation, as opposed to copying, consists either in the interfusion of the same throughout the radically different, or of the different throughout a base radically the same.

Lastly, I appeal to the practice of the best poets, of all countries and in all ages, as authorizing the opinion, (deduced from all the foregoing,) that in every import of the word essential, which would not here involve a mere truism, there may be, is, and ought to be an essential difference between the language of prose and of metrical composition.

In Mr. Wordsworth's criticism of Gray's Sonnet, the readers' sympathy with his praise or blame of the different parts is taken for granted rather perhaps too easily. He has not, at least, attempted to win or compel it by argumentative analysis. In my conception at least, the lines rejected as of no value do, with the exception of the two first, differ as much and as little from the language of common life, as those which he has printed in italics as possessing genuine excellence. Of the five lines thus honourably distinguished, two of them differ from prose, even more widely than the lines which either precede or follow, in the position of the words.

> *A different object do these eyes require;*
> *My lonely anguish melts no heart but mine;*
> *And in my breast the imperfect joys expire.*

But were it otherwise, what would this prove, but a truth, of which no man ever doubted? Videlicet, that there are sentences, which would be equally in their place both in verse and prose. Assuredly it does not prove the point, which alone requires proof; namely, that there are not passages, which would suit the one and not suit the other. The first line of this sonnet is distinguished from the ordinary language of men by the epithet to *'morning'*. (For we will set aside, at present, the consideration, that the particular word '*smiling*' is hackneyed and (as it involves a sort of personification) not quite congruous with the common and material attribute of *shining*.) And, doubtless, this adjunction of epithets for the purpose of additional description, where no particular attention is demanded for the quality of the thing, would be noticed as giving a poetic cast to a man's conversation. Should the sportsman exclaim, '*Come boys! the rosy morning calls you up*', he will be supposed to have some song in his head. But no one suspects this, when he says, 'A wet morning shall not confine us to our beds.' This then is either a defect in poetry, or it is not. Whoever should decide in the affirmative, I would request him to re-peruse any one poem, of any confessedly great poet from Homer to Milton, or from Aeschylus to Shakespeare; and to strike out (in thought I mean) every instance of this kind. If the number of these fancied erasures did not startle him, or if he continued to deem the work improved by their total omission, he must advance reasons of no ordinary strength and evidence, reasons grounded in the essence of human nature. Otherwise, I should not hesitate to consider him as a man not so much proof against all authority, as dead to it.

The second line,

And reddening Phoebus lifts his golden fire;—

has indeed almost as many faults as words. But then it is a bad line, not because the language is distinct from that of prose, but because it conveys incongruous images, because it confounds the cause and the effect, the real thing with the personified representative of the thing; in short, because it differs from the language of good sense! That the 'Phoebus' is hackneyed, and a school-boy image, is an accidental fault, dependent on the age in which the author wrote, and not deduced from the nature of the thing. That it is part of an exploded mythology, is an objection more deeply grounded. Yet when the torch of ancient learning was rekindled, so cheering were its beams, that our eldest poets, cut off by Christianity from all accredited machinery, and deprived of all acknowledged guardians and symbols of the great objects of nature, were naturally induced to adopt, as a poetic language, those fabulous personages, those forms of the supernatural in nature, which had given them such dear delight in the poems of their great masters. Nay, even at this day what scholar of genial taste will not so far sympathize with them, as to read with pleasure in Petrarch, Chaucer, or Spenser, what he would perhaps condemn as puerile in a modern poet?

I remember no poet, whose writings would safelier stand the test of Mr. Wordsworth's theory, than Spenser. Yet will Mr. Wordsworth say, that the style of the following stanza is either undistinguished from prose, and the language of ordinary life? Or that it is vicious, and that the stanzas are blots in the *Faerie Queene*?

> By this the northern wagoner had set
> His sevenfold teme behind the steadfast starre,
> That was in ocean waves yet never wet,
> But firme is fixt, and sendeth light from farre
> To all that in the wild deep wandering are:
> And chearful chanticleer with his note shrill
> Had warned once that Phoebus' fiery carre
> In haste was climbing up the easterne hill,
> Full envious that night so long his roome did fill.
>
> Book I, Can. 2, St. 2.
>
> At last the golden orientall gate
> Of greatest heaven gan to open fayre,
> And Phœbus fresh, as brydegrome to his mate,
> Came dauncing forth, shaking his deawie hayre,
> And hurl'd his glist'ring beams through gloomy ayre:
> Which when the wakeful elfe perceived, streightway
> He started up, and did him selfe prepayre
> In sun-bright armes and battailous array;
> For with that pagan proud he combat will that day.
>
> Book I, Can. 5, St. 2.

METRICAL COMPOSITION

On the contrary to how many passages, both in hymn books and in blank verse poems, could I (were it not invidious) direct the reader's attention, the style of which is most unpoetic, because, and only because, it is the style of prose? He will not suppose me capable of having in my mind such verses, as

> I put my hat upon my head
> And walk'd into the Strand;
> And there I met another man,
> Whose hat was in his hand.

To such specimens it would indeed be a fair and full reply, that these lines are not bad, because they are unpoetic; but because they are empty of all sense and feeling; and that it were an idle attempt to prove that an ape is not a Newton, when it is evident that he is not a man. But the sense shall be good and weighty, the language correct and dignified, the subject interesting and treated with feeling; and yet the style shall, notwithstanding all these merits, be justly blamable as prosaic, and solely because the words and the order of the words would find their appropriate place in prose, but are not suitable to metrical composition. The *Civil Wars* of Daniel is an instructive, and even interesting work; but take the following stanzas (and from the hundred instances which abound I might probably have selected others far more striking):

> And to the end we may with better ease
> Discern the true discourse, vouchsafe to show
> What were the times foregoing near to these,
> That these we may with better profit know.
> Tell how the world fell into this disease;
> And how so great distemperature did grow;
> So shall we see with what degrees it came;
> How things at full do soon wax out of frame.
>
> Ten kings had from the Norman conqu'ror reign'd
> With intermixt and variable fate,
> When England to her greatest height attain'd
> Of power, dominion, glory, wealth, and state;

> After it had with much ado sustain'd
> The violence of princes, with debate
> For titles and the often mutinies
> Of nobles for their ancient liberties.
>
> For first, the Norman, conqu'ring all by might,
> By might was forc'd to keep what he had got;
> Mixing our customs and the form of right
> With foreign constitutions he had brought;
> Mast'ring the mighty, humbling the poorer wight,
> By all severest means that could be wrought;
> And, making the succession doubtful, rent
> His new-got state, and left it turbulent.
> Book I, St. vii, viii, and ix.

Will it be contended on the one side, that these lines are mean and senseless? Or on the other, that they are not prosaic, and for that reason unpoetic? This poet's well-merited epithet is that of the '*well-languaged Daniel*'; but likewise, and by the consent of his contemporaries no less than of all succeeding critics, the 'prosaic Daniel.' Yet those, who thus designate this wise and amiable writer, from the frequent incorrespondency of his diction to his metre in the majority of his compositions, not only deem them valuable and interesting on other accounts, but willingly admit that there are to be found throughout his poems, and especially in his *Epistles* and in his *Hymen's Triumph*, many and exquisite specimens of that style which, as the neutral ground of prose and verse, is common to both. A fine and almost faultless extract, eminent, as for other beauties, so for its perfection in these species of diction, may be seen in Lamb's *Dramatic Specimens*, &c., a work of various interest from the nature of the selections themselves, (all from the plays of Shakespeare's contemporaries), and deriving a high additional value from the notes, which are full of just and original criticism, expressed with all the freshness of originality.

Among the possible effects of practical adherence to a theory that aims to identify the style of prose

METRICAL COMPOSITION

and verse,—(if it does not indeed claim for the latter a yet nearer resemblance to the average style of men in the viva voce intercourse of real life)—we might anticipate the following as not the least likely to occur. It will happen, as I have indeed before observed, that the metre itself, the sole acknowledged difference, will occasionally become metre to the eye only. The existence of prosaisms, and that they detract from the merit of a poem, must at length be conceded, when a number of successive lines can be rendered, even to the most delicate ear, unrecognizable as verse, or as having even been intended for verse, by simply transcribing them as prose; when if the poem be in blank verse, this can be effected without any alteration, or at most by merely restoring one or two words to their proper places, from which they have been transplanted[1] for no assignable cause

---

[1] As the ingenious gentleman under the influence of the Tragic Muse contrived to dislocate, 'I wish you a good morning, Sir! Thank you, Sir, and I wish you the same,' into two blank-verse heroics:—

To you a good morning, good Sir! I wish.
You, Sir! I thank: to you the same wish I.

In those parts of Mr. Wordsworth's works which I have thoroughly studied, I find fewer instances in which this would be practicable than I have met in many poems, where an approximation of prose has been sedulously and on system guarded against. Indeed excepting the stanzas already quoted from *The Sailor's Mother*, I can recollect but one instance: viz. a short passage of four or five lines in *The Brothers*, that model of English pastoral, which I never yet read with unclouded eye.—'James, pointing to its summit, over which they had all purposed to return together, informed them that he would wait for them there. They parted, and his comrades passed that way some two hours after, but they did not find him at the appointed place, *a circumstance of which they took no heed*: but one of them, going by chance into the house, which at this time was James's house, learnt *there*, that nobody had seen him all that day.' The only change which has been made is in

or reason but that of the author's convenience; but if it be in rhyme, by the mere exchange of the final word of each line for some other of the same meaning, equally appropriate, dignified and euphonic.

The answer or objection in the preface to the anticipated remark 'that metre paves the way to other distinctions', is contained in the following words. 'The distinction of rhyme and metre is voluntary and uniform, and not, like that produced by (what is called) poetic diction, arbitrary, and subject to infinite caprices, upon which no calculation whatever can be made. In the one case the reader is utterly at the mercy of the poet respecting what imagery or diction he may choose to connect with the passion.' But is this a poet, of whom a poet is speaking? No surely! rather of a fool or madman: or at best of a vain or ignorant phantast! And might not brains so wild and so deficient make just the same havoc with rhymes and metres, as they are supposed to effect with modes and figures of speech? How is the reader at the mercy of such men? If he continue to read their nonsense, is it not his own fault? The ultimate end of criticism is much more to establish the principles of writing, than to furnish rules how to pass judgement on what has been written by others; if indeed it were possible that the two could be separated. But if it be asked, by what principles the

the position of the little word *there* in two instances, the position in the original being clearly such as is not adopted in ordinary conversation. The other words printed in *italics* were so marked because, though good and genuine English, they are not the phraseology of common conversation either in the word put in apposition, or in the connexion by the genitive pronoun. Men in general would have said, 'but that was a circumstance they paid no attention to, or took no notice of;' and the language is, on the theory of the preface, justified only by the narrator's being the *Vicar*. Yet if any ear *could* suspect, that these sentences were ever printed as metre, on those very words alone could the suspicion have been grounded.

poet is to regulate his own style, if he do not adhere closely to the sort and order of words which he hears in the market, wake, high-road, or plough-field? I reply; by principles, the ignorance or neglect of which would convict him of being no poet, but a silly or presumptuous usurper of the name! By the principles of grammar, logic, psychology! In one word, by such a knowledge of the facts, material and spiritual, that most appertain to his art, as, if it have been governed and applied by good sense, and rendered instinctive by habit, becomes the representative and reward of our past conscious reasonings, insights, and conclusions, and acquires the name of TASTE. By what rule that does not leave the reader at the poet's mercy, and the poet at his own, is the latter to distinguish between the language suitable to suppressed, and the language, which is characteristic of indulged, anger? Or between that of rage and that of jealousy? Is it obtained by wandering about in search of angry or jealous people in uncultivated society, in order to copy their words? Or not far rather by the power of imagination proceeding upon the all in each of human nature? By meditation, rather than by observation? And by the latter in consequence only of the former? As eyes, for which the former has pre-determined their field of vision, and to which, as to its organ, it communicates a microscopic power? There is not, I firmly believe, a man now living, who has, from his own inward experience, a clearer intuition than Mr. Wordsworth himself, that the last mentioned are the true sources of genial discrimination. Through the same process and by the same creative agency will the poet distinguish the degree and kind of the excitement produced by the very act of poetic composition. As intuitively will he know, what differences of style it at once inspires and justifies; what intermixture of conscious volition is natural to that state; and in what instances such figures and colours of speech degenerate into mere creatures of an arbitrary purpose, cold technical artifices of ornament or connexion. For, even as truth is its own light and evidence, discovering at once itself and falsehood, so is it the prerogative of poetic genius to distinguish by parental instinct its proper offspring from the changelings, which the gnomes of vanity or the fairies of fashion may have laid in its cradle or called by its names. Could a rule be given from without, poetry would cease to be poetry, and sink into a mechanical art. It would be μόρφωσις, not ποίησις. The rules of the IMAGINATION are themselves the very powers of growth and production. The words to which they are reducible, present only the outlines and external appearance of the fruit. A deceptive counterfeit of the superficial form and colours may be elaborated; but the marble peach feels cold and heavy, and children only put it to their mouths. We find no difficulty in admitting as excellent, and the legitimate language of poetic fervour self-impassioned, Donne's apostrophe to the Sun in the second stanza of his *Progress of the Soul*.

> Thee, eye of heaven! this great soul envies not;
> By thy male force is all, we have, begot.
> In the first East thou now beginn'st to shine,
> Suck'st early balm and island spices there,
> And wilt anon in thy loose-rein'd career
> At Tagus, Po, Seine, Thames, and Danow dine,
> And see at night this western world of mine:
> Yet hast thou not more nations seen than she,
> Who before thee one day began to be,
> And, thy frail light being quench'd, shall long,
>   long outlive thee!

Or the next stanza but one:

> Great destiny, the commissary of God,
> That hast mark'd out a path and period
> For ev'ry thing! Who, where we offspring took,
> Our way and ends see'st at one instant: thou
> Knot of all causes! Thou, whose changeless brow
> Ne'er smiles nor frowns! O! vouchsafe thou to look,
> And show my story in thy eternal book, &c.

METRICAL COMPOSITION

As little difficulty do we find in excluding from the honours of unaffected warmth and elevation the madness prepense of pseudo-poesy, or the startling hysteric of weakness over-exerting itself, which bursts on the unprepared reader in sundry odes and apostrophes to abstract terms. Such are the Odes to Jealousy, to Hope, to Oblivion, and the like, in Dodsley's collection and the magazines of that day, which seldom fail to remind me of an Oxford copy of verses on the two Suttons, commencing with

INOCULATION, heavenly maid! descend!

It is not to be denied that men of undoubted talents, and even poets of true, though not of first-rate, genius, have from a mistaken theory deluded both themselves and others in the opposite extreme. I once read to a company of sensible and well-educated women the introductory period of Cowley's preface to his *Pindaric Odes, written in imitation of the style and manner of the odes of Pindar*. 'If (says Cowley) a man should undertake to translate Pindar, word for word, it would be thought that one madman had translated another: as may appear, when he, that understands not the original, reads the verbal traduction of him into Latin prose, than which nothing seems more raving.' I then proceeded with his own free version of the second Olympic, composed for the charitable purpose of rationalizing the Theban Eagle.

Queen of all harmonious things,
Dancing words and speaking strings,
What God, what hero, wilt thou sing?
What happy man to equal glories bring?
Begin, begin thy noble choice,
And let the hills around reflect the image of thy voice.
Pisa does to Jove belong,
Jove and Pisa claim thy song.
The fair first-fruits of war, th' Olympic games,
Alcides offer'd up to Jove;
Alcides too thy strings may move!
But, oh! what man to join with these can worthy prove?

> Join Theron boldly to their sacred names;
> Theron the next honour claims;
> Theron to no man gives place,
> Is first in Pisa's and in Virtue's race;
> Theron there, and he alone,
> Ev'n his own swift forefathers has outgone.

One of the company exclaimed, with the full assent of the rest, that if the original were madder than this, it must be incurably mad. I then translated the ode from the Greek, and as nearly as possible, word for word; and the impression was, that in the general movement of the periods, in the form of the connexions and transitions, and in the sober majesty of lofty sense, it appeared to them to approach more nearly, than any other poetry they had heard, to the style of our Bible in the prophetic books. The first strophe will suffice as a specimen:

> Ye harp-controuling hymns! (or) ye hymns the sovereigns of harps!
> What God? what Hero?
> What Man shall we celebrate?
> Truly Pisa indeed is of Jove,
> But the Olympiad (or the Olympic games) did Hercules establish,
> The first-fruits of the spoils of war.
> But Theron for the four-horsed car,
> That bore victory to him,
> It behoves us now to voice aloud:
> The Just, the Hospitable,
> The Bulwark of Agrigentum.
> Of renowned fathers
> The Flower, even him
> Who preserves his native city erect and safe.

But are such rhetorical caprices condemnable only for their deviation from the language of real life? and are they by no other means to be precluded, but by the rejection of all distinctions between prose and verse, save that of metre? Surely good sense, and a moderate insight into the constitution of the human mind, would be amply sufficient to prove, that such language and such combinations are the native produce neither of the fancy nor of the imagination; that their operation consists in the excitement of surprise by the juxtaposition and apparent reconciliation of widely different or incompatible things. As when, for instance, the hills are made to reflect the image of a voice. Surely, no unusual taste is requisite to see clearly, that this compulsory juxtaposition is not produced by the presentation of impressive or delightful forms to the inward vision, nor by any sympathy with the modifying powers with which the genius of the poet had united and inspirited all the objects of his thought; that it is therefore a species of wit, a pure work of the will, and implies a leisure and self-possession both of thought and of feeling, incompatible with the steady fervour of a mind possessed and filled with the grandeur of its subject. To sum up the whole in one sentence. When a poem, or a part of a poem, shall be adduced, which is evidently vicious in the figures and contexture of its style, yet for the condemnation of which no reason can be assigned, except that it differs from the style in which men actually converse, then, and not till then, can I hold this theory to be either plausible, or practicable, or capable of furnishing either rule, guidance, or precaution, that might not, more easily and more safely, as well as more naturally, have been deduced in the author's own mind from considerations of grammar, logic, and the truth and nature of things, confirmed by the authority of works, whose fame is not of ONE country nor of ONE age.

WILLIAM BLAKE
1757–1827
THE CANTERBURY PILGRIMS (1809)
SIR GEFFREY CHAUCER AND THE NINE-AND-TWENTY PILGRIMS ON THEIR JOURNEY TO CANTERBURY[1]

THE time chosen is early morning, before sunrise, when the jolly company are just quitting the Tabarde Inn. The Knight and Squire with the Squire's Yeoman lead the Procession; next follow the youthful Abbess, her Nun, and three Priests; her greyhounds attend her:

> Of small hounds had she that she fed
> With roast flesh, milk, and wastel bread.

Next follow the Friar and Monk; then the Tapiser, the Pardoner, and the Sompnour and Manciple. After these 'Our Host', who occupies the centre of the cavalcade, directs them to the Knight as the person who would be likely to commence their task of each telling a tale in their order. After the Host follow the Shipman, the Haberdasher, the Dyer, the Franklin, the Physician, the Ploughman, the Lawyer, the Poor Parson, the Merchant, the Wife of Bath, the Miller, the Cook, the Oxford Scholar, Chaucer himself; and the Reeve comes as Chaucer has described:

> And ever he rode hinderest of the rout.

These last are issuing from the gateway of the Inn; the Cook and the Wife of Bath are both taking their morning's draught of comfort. Spectators stand at the gateway of the Inn, and are composed of an old Man, a Woman, and Children.

The Landscape is an eastward view of the country, from the Tabarde Inn in Southwark, as it may be supposed to have appeared in Chaucer's time, inter-

[1] From *A Descriptive Catalogue of Pictures*.

spersed with cottages and villages. The first beams of the Sun are seen above the horizon; some buildings and spires indicate the situation of the Great City. The Inn is a Gothic building, which Thynne in his Glossary says was the lodging of the Abbot of Hyde, by Winchester. On the Inn is inscribed its title, and a proper advantage is taken of this circumstance to describe the subject of the Picture. The words written over the gateway of the Inn are as follow: 'The Tabarde Inn, by Henry Baillie, the lodgynge-house for Pilgrims who journey to Saint Thomas's Shrine at Canterbury.'

The characters of Chaucer's Pilgrims are the characters which compose all ages and nations. As one age falls, another rises, different to mortal sight, but to immortals only the same; for we see the same characters repeated again and again, in animals, vegetables, minerals, and in men. Nothing new occurs in identical existence; Accident ever varies, Substance can never suffer change nor decay.

Of Chaucer's characters, as described in his *Canterbury Tales*, some of the names or titles are altered by time, but the characters themselves for ever remain unaltered; and consequently they are the physiognomies or lineaments of universal human life, beyond which Nature never steps. Names alter, things never alter. I have known multitudes of those who would have been monks in the age of monkery, who in this deistical age are deists. As Newton numbered the stars, and as Linnaeus numbered the plants, so Chaucer numbered the classes of men.

The Painter has consequently varied the heads and forms of his personages into all Nature's varieties; the horses he has also varied to accord to their riders; the costume is correct according to authentic monuments.

The Knight and Squire with the Squire's Yeoman lead the Procession, as Chaucer has also placed them first in his Prologue. The Knight is a true

Hero, a good, great and wise man; his whole-length portrait on horseback, as written by Chaucer, cannot be surpassed. He has spent his life in the field, has ever been a conqueror, and is that species of character which in every age stands as the guardian of man against the oppressor. His son is like him, with the germ of perhaps greater perfection still, as he blends literature and the arts with his warlike studies. Their dress and their horses are of the first rate, without ostentation, and with all the true grandeur that unaffected simplicity when in high rank always displays. The Squire's Yeoman is also a great character, a man perfectly knowing in his profession:

> And in his hand he bare a mighty bow.

Chaucer describes here a mighty man, one who in war is the worthy attendant on noble heroes.

The Prioress follows these with her female Chaplain:

> Another Nonne also with her had she,
> That was her Chaplaine, and Priests three.

This Lady is described also as of the first rank, rich and honoured. She has certain peculiarities and little delicate affectations, not unbecoming in her, being accompanied with what is truly grand and really polite; her person and face Chaucer has described with minuteness; it is very elegant, and was the beauty of our ancestors till after Elizabeth's time, when voluptuousness and folly began to be accounted beautiful.

Her companion and her three Priests were no doubt all perfectly delineated in those parts of Chaucer's work which are now lost; we ought to suppose them suitable attendants on rank and fashion.

The Monk follows these with the Friar. The Painter has also grouped with these the Pardoner and the Sompnour and the Manciple, and has here also introduced one of the rich citizens of London—characters likely to ride in company, all being above the common rank in life, or attendants on those who were so.

For the Monk is described by Chaucer, as a man of the first rank in society, noble, rich, and expensively attended; he is a leader of the age, with certain humorous accompaniments in his character, that do not degrade, but render him an object of dignified mirth, but also with other accompaniments not so respectable.

The Friar is a character of a mixed kind:

> A friar there was, a wanton and a merry;

but in his office he is said to be a 'full solemn man'; eloquent, amorous, witty and satirical; young, handsome and rich; he is a complete rogue, with constitutional gaiety enough to make him a master of all the pleasures of the world:

> His neck was white as the flour de lis,
> Thereto strong he was as a champioun.

It is necessary here to speak of Chaucer's own character, that I may set certain mistaken critics right in their conception of the humour and fun that occur on the journey. Chaucer is himself the great poetical observer of men, who in every age is born to record and eternize its acts. This he does as a master, as a father and superior, who looks down on their little follies from the Emperor to the Miller, sometimes with severity, oftener with joke and sport.

Accordingly Chaucer has made his Monk a great tragedian, one who studied poetical art. So much so that the generous Knight is, in the compassionate dictates of his soul, compelled to cry out:

> 'Ho,' quoth the Knyght, 'good Sir, no more of this;
> That ye have said is right ynough, I wis,
> And mokell more; for little heaviness
> Is right enough for much folk, as I guesse.
> I say, for me, it is a great disease,
> Whereas men have been in wealth and ease,
> To heare of their sudden fall, alas!
> And the contrary is joy and solas.'

The Monk's definition of tragedy in the proem to his tale is worth repeating:

> Tragedie is to tell a certain story,
> As old books us maken memory,
> Of hem that stood in great prosperity,
> And be fallen out of high degree,
> Into miserie, and ended wretchedly.

Though a man of luxury, pride and pleasure, he is a master of art and learning, though affecting to despise it. Those who can think that the proud huntsman and noble housekeeper, Chaucer's Monk, is intended for a buffoon or burlesque character, know little of Chaucer.

For the Host who follows this group, and holds the centre of the cavalcade, is a first-rate character, and his jokes are no trifles; they are always, though uttered with audacity, and equally free with the Lord and the Peasant—they are always substantially and weightily expressive of knowledge and experience; Henry Baillie, the keeper of the greatest Inn of the greatest City, for such was the Tabarde Inn in Southwark near London, our Host, was also a leader of the age.

By way of illustration I instance Shakespeare's Witches in *Macbeth*. Those who dress them for the stage, consider them as wretched old women, and not, as Shakespeare intended, the Goddesses of Destiny; this shows how Chaucer has been misunderstood in his sublime work. Shakespeare's Fairies also are the rulers of the vegetable world, and so are Chaucer's; let them be so considered, and then the poet will be understood, and not else.

But I have omitted to speak of a very prominent character, the Pardoner, the Age's Knave, who always commands and domineers over the high and low vulgar. This man is sent in every age for a rod and scourge, and for a blight, for a trial of men, to divide the classes of men; he is in the most holy

THE CANTERBURY PILGRIMS 77

sanctuary, and he is suffered by Providence for wise ends, and has also his great use, and his grand leading destiny.

His companion the Sompnour is also a Devil of the first magnitude, grand, terrific, rich, and honoured in the rank of which he holds the destiny. The uses to society are perhaps equal of the Devil and of the Angel; their sublimity who can dispute?

> In daunger had he at his own gise,
> The young girls of his diocese,
> And he knew well their counsel, &c.

The principal figure in the next group is the Good Parson; an Apostle, a real Messenger of Heaven, sent in every age for its light and its warmth. This man is beloved and venerated by all, and neglected by all: he serves all, and is served by none. He is, according to Christ's definition, the greatest of his age: yet he is a Poor Parson of a town. Read Chaucer's description of the Good Parson, and bow the head and the knee to Him, Who in every age sends us such a burning and a shining light. Search, O ye rich and powerful, for these men and obey their counsel; then shall the golden age return. But alas! you will not easily distinguish him from the Friar or the Pardoner; they also are 'full solemn men', and their counsel you will continue to follow.

I have placed by his side the Sergeant-at-Lawe, who appears delighted to ride in his company, and between him and his brother the Ploughman; as I wish men of law would always ride with them, and take their counsel, especially in all difficult points. Chaucer's Lawyer is a character of great venerableness, a Judge and a real master of the jurisprudence of his age.

The Doctor of Physic is in this group; and the Franklin, the voluptuous country gentleman, contrasted with the Physician, and, on his other hand, with two Citizens of London. Chaucer's characters live age after age. Every age is a Canterbury Pilgrimage; we all pass on, each sustaining one of these characters; nor can a child be born who is not one or other of these characters of Chaucer. The Doctor of Physic is described as the first of his profession, perfect, learned, completely Master and Doctor in his art. Thus the reader will observe that Chaucer makes every one of his characters perfect in his kind; every one is an Antique Statue, the image of a class and not of an imperfect individual.

This group also would furnish substantial matter, on which volumes might be written. The Franklin is one who keeps open table, who is the genius of eating and drinking, the Bacchus; as the Doctor of Physic is the Aesculapius, the Host is the Silenus, the Squire is the Apollo, the Miller is the Hercules, &c. Chaucer's characters are a description of the eternal Principles that exist in all ages. The Franklin is voluptuousness itself, most nobly portrayed:

> It snewed in his house of meat and drink.

The Ploughman is simplicity itself, with wisdom and strength for its stamina. Chaucer has divided the ancient character of Hercules between his Miller and his Ploughman. Benevolence is the Ploughman's great characteristic; he is thin with excessive labour, and not with old age as some have supposed:

> He would thresh, and thereto dike and delve,
> For Christe's sake, for every poore wight,
> Withouten hire, if it lay in his might.

Visions of these eternal principles or characters of human life appear to poets in all ages; the Grecian gods were the ancient Cherubim of Phoenicia; but the Greeks, and since them the Moderns, have neglected to subdue the gods of Priam. These gods are visions of the eternal attributes, or divine names, which, when erected into gods, become destructive to humanity. They ought to be the servants, and not the masters of man or of society. They ought to be made to sacrifice to man, and not man compelled to sacrifice to them; for, when separated from man or humanity, who is Jesus the Saviour, the Vine of Eternity? They are thieves and rebels, they are destroyers.

The Ploughman of Chaucer is Hercules in his supreme Eternal State, divested of his Spectrous Shadow, which is the Miller, a terrible fellow, such as exists in all times and places for the trial of men, to astonish every neighbourhood with brutal strength and courage, to get rich and powerful, to curb the pride of Man.

The Reeve and the Manciple are two characters of the most consummate worldly wisdom. The Shipman, or Sailor, is a similar genius of Ulyssean art, but with the highest courage superadded.

The Citizens and their Cook are each leaders of a class. Chaucer has been somehow made to number four citizens, which would make his whole company, himself included, thirty-one. But he says there was but nine-and-twenty in his company:

> Full nine and twenty in a company.

The Webbe, or Weaver, and the Tapiser, or Tapestry Weaver, appear to me to be the same person; but this is only an opinion, for 'full nine and twenty' may signify one more or less. But I daresay that Chaucer wrote 'A Webbe Dyer', that is a Cloth Dyer:

> A Webbe Dyer and a Tapiser.

The Merchant cannot be one of the Three Citizens, as his dress is different, and his character is more marked, whereas Chaucer says of his rich citizens:

> All were yclothed in o liverie.

The characters of Women Chaucer has divided into two classes, the Lady Prioress and the Wife of Bath. Are not these leaders of the ages of men? The Lady Prioress in some ages predominates; and in some the Wife of Bath, in whose character Chaucer has been equally minute and exact; because she is also a scourge and a blight. I shall say no more of her, nor expose what Chaucer has left hidden; let the young reader study what he has said of her: it is useful as a scarecrow. There are of such characters born too many for the peace of the world.

I come at length to the Clerk of Oxenford. This character varies from that of Chaucer, as the contemplative philosopher varies from the poetical genius. There are always these two classes of learned sages, the poetical and the philosophical. The Painter has put them side by side, as if the youthful clerk had put himself under the tuition of the mature poet. Let the Philosopher always be the servant and scholar of Inspiration, and all will be happy.

CHARLES LAMB
1775–1834
ON THE TRAGEDIES OF SHAKESPEARE
CONSIDERED WITH REFERENCE TO THEIR FITNESS FOR STAGE REPRESENTATION (1811)

TAKING a turn the other day in the Abbey, I was struck with the affected attitude of a figure, which I do not remember to have seen before, and which upon examination proved to be a whole-length of the celebrated Mr. Garrick. Though I would not go so far with some good Catholics abroad as to shut players altogether out of consecrated ground, yet I own I was not a little scandalized at the introduction of theatrical airs and gestures into a place set apart to remind us of the saddest realities. Going nearer, I found inscribed under this harlequin figure the following lines:

> To paint fair Nature, by divine command,
> Her magic pencil in his glowing hand,
> A Shakespeare rose: then, to expand his fame
> Wide o'er this breathing world, a Garrick came.
> Though sunk in death the forms the Poet drew,
> The Actor's genius bade them breathe anew;
> Though, like the bard himself, in night they lay,
> Immortal Garrick call'd them back to day:
> And till Eternity with power sublime
> Shall mark the mortal hour of hoary Time,
> Shakespeare and Garrick like twin-stars shall shine,
> And earth irradiate with a beam divine.

It would be an insult to my readers' understandings to attempt anything like a criticism on this farrago of false thoughts and nonsense. But the reflection it led me into was a kind of wonder, how, from the days of the actor here celebrated to our own, it should have been the fashion to compliment every performer in his turn, that has had the luck to please the town in any of the great characters of Shakespeare, with the notion of possessing a *mind congenial with the poet's*: how people should come thus unaccountably to confound the power of originating poetical images and conceptions with the faculty of being able to read or recite the same when put into words;[1] or what connexion that absolute mastery over the heart and soul of man, which a great dramatic poet possesses, has with those low tricks upon the eye and ear, which a player by observing a few general effects, which some common passion, as grief, anger, &c. usually has upon the gestures and exterior, can so easily compass. To know the internal workings and movements of a great mind, of an Othello or a Hamlet for instance, the *when* and the *why* and the *how far* they should be moved; to what pitch a passion is becoming; to give the reins and to pull in the curb exactly at the moment when the drawing in or the slackening is most graceful; seems to demand a reach of intellect of a vastly different extent from that which is employed upon the bare imitation of the signs of these passions in the countenance or gesture, which signs are usually observed to be most lively and emphatic in the weaker sort of minds, and which signs can after all but indicate some passion, as I said before, anger, or grief, generally; but of the motives and grounds of the passion, wherein it differs from the same passion in low and vulgar natures, of these the actor can give no more idea by his face or gesture than the eye (without a

---

[1] It is observable that we fall into this confusion only in *dramatic* recitations. We never dream that the gentleman who reads Lucretius in public with great applause, is therefore a great poet and philosopher; nor do we find that Tom Davies, the bookseller, who is recorded to have recited the *Paradise Lost* better than any man in England in his day (though I cannot help thinking there must be some mistake in this tradition), was therefore, by his intimate friends, set upon a level with Milton.

metaphor) can speak, or the muscles utter intelligible sounds. But such is the instantaneous nature of the impressions which we take in at the eye and ear at a playhouse, compared with the slow apprehension oftentimes of the understanding in reading, that we are apt not only to sink the play-writer in the consideration which we pay to the actor, but even to identify in our minds in a perverse manner, the actor with the character which he represents. It is difficult for a frequent playgoer to disembarrass the idea of Hamlet from the person and voice of Mr. K. We speak of Lady Macbeth, while we are in reality thinking of Mrs. S. Nor is this confusion incidental alone to unlettered persons, who, not possessing the advantage of reading, are necessarily dependent upon the stage-player for all the pleasure which they can receive from the drama, and to whom the very idea of *what an author is* cannot be made comprehensible without some pain and perplexity of mind: the error is one from which persons otherwise not meanly lettered, find it almost impossible to extricate themselves.

Never let me be so ungrateful as to forget the very high degree of satisfaction which I received some years back from seeing for the first time a tragedy of Shakespeare performed, in which these two great performers sustained the principal parts. It seemed to embody and realize conceptions which had hitherto assumed no distinct shape. But dearly do we pay all our life after for this juvenile pleasure, this sense of distinctness. When the novelty is past, we find to our cost that instead of realizing an idea, we have only materialized and brought down a fine vision to the standard of flesh and blood. We have let go a dream, in quest of an unattainable substance.

How cruelly this operates upon the mind, to have its free conceptions thus crampt and pressed down to the measure of a strait-lacing actuality, may be judged from that delightful sensation of freshness with which we turn to those plays of Shakespeare which have escaped being performed, and to those passages in the acting plays of the same writer which have happily been left out in performance. How far the very custom of hearing anything *spouted*, withers and blows upon a fine passage, may be seen in those speeches from *Henry the Fifth*, &c. which are current in the mouths of school-boys from their being to be found in *Enfield Speakers*, and such kind of books. I confess myself utterly unable to appreciate that celebrated soliloquy in *Hamlet*, beginning 'To be or not to be', or to tell whether it be good, bad, or indifferent, it has been so handled and pawed about by declamatory boys and men, and torn so inhumanly from its living place and principle of continuity in the play, till it is become to me a perfect dead member.

It may seem a paradox, but I cannot help being of opinion that the plays of Shakespeare are less calculated for performance on a stage, than those of almost any other dramatist whatever. Their distinguished excellence is a reason that they should be so. There is so much in them, which comes not under the province of acting, with which eye, and tone, and gesture, have nothing to do.

The glory of the scenic art is to personate passion, and the turns of passion; and the more coarse and palpable the passion is, the more hold upon the eyes and ears of the spectators the performer obviously possesses. For this reason, scolding scenes, scenes where two persons talk themselves into a fit of fury, and then in a surprising manner talk themselves out of it again, have always been the most popular upon our stage. And the reason is plain, because the spectators are here most palpably appealed to, they are the proper judges in this war of words, they are the legitimate ring that should be formed round such 'intellectual prize-fighters'. Talking is the direct object of the imitation here. But in all the best dramas, and in Shakespeare above all, how obvious it

ON THE TRAGEDIES OF SHAKESPEARE

is, that the form of *speaking*, whether it be in soliloquy or dialogue, is only a medium, and often a highly artificial one, for putting the reader or spectator into possession of that knowledge of the inner structure and workings of mind in a character, which he could otherwise never have arrived at *in that form of composition* by any gift short of intuition. We do here as we do with novels written in the *epistolary form*. How many improprieties, perfect solecisms in letter-writing, do we put up with in *Clarissa* and other books, for the sake of the delight which that form upon the whole gives us.

But the practice of stage representation reduces everything to a controversy of elocution. Every character, from the boisterous blasphemings of Bajazet to the shrinking timidity of womanhood, must play the orator. The love-dialogues of Romeo and Juliet, those silver-sweet sounds of lovers' tongues by night; the more intimate and sacred sweetness of nuptial colloquy between an Othello or a Posthumus with their married wives, all those delicacies which are so delightful in the reading, as when we read of those youthful dalliances in Paradise

> As beseem'd
> Fair couple link'd in happy nuptial league
> Alone:

by the inherent fault of stage representation, how are these things sullied and turned from their very nature by being exposed to a large assembly; when such speeches as Imogen addresses to her lord, come drawling out of the mouth of a hired actress, whose courtship, though nominally addressed to the personated Posthumus, is manifestly aimed at the spectators, who are to judge of her endearments and her returns of love.

The character of Hamlet is perhaps that by which, since the days of Betterton, a succession of popular performers have had the greatest ambition to distinguish themselves. The length of the part may be one of their reasons. But for the character itself, we find it in a play, and therefore we judge it a fit subject of dramatic representation. The play itself abounds in maxims and reflections beyond any other, and therefore we consider it as a proper vehicle for conveying moral instruction. But Hamlet himself—what does he suffer meanwhile by being dragged forth as a public schoolmaster, to give lectures to the crowd! Why, nine parts in ten of what Hamlet does, are transactions between himself and his moral sense, they are the effusions of his solitary musings, which he retires to holes and corners and the most sequestered parts of the palace to pour forth; or rather, they are the silent meditations with which his bosom is bursting, reduced to *words* for the sake of the reader, who must else remain ignorant of what is passing there. These profound sorrows, these light-and-noise-abhorring ruminations, which the tongue scarce dares utter to deaf walls and chambers, how can they be represented by a gesticulating actor, who comes and mouths them out before an audience, making four hundred people his confidants at once? I say not that it is the fault of the actor so to do; he must pronounce them *ore rotundo*, he must accompany them with his eye, he must insinuate them into his auditory by some trick of eye, tone, or gesture, or he fails. *He must be thinking all the while of his appearance, because he knows that all the while the spectators are judging of it.* And this is the way to represent the shy, negligent, retiring Hamlet.

It is true that there is no other mode of conveying a vast quantity of thought and feeling to a great portion of the audience, who otherwise would never earn it for themselves by reading, and the intellectual acquisition gained this way may, for aught I know, be inestimable; but I am not arguing that Hamlet should not be acted, but how much Hamlet is made another thing by being acted. I have heard much of the wonders which Garrick performed in this part; but as I never saw him, I must have leave to doubt whether the representation of such a character came within the province of his art. Those who tell me of him, speak of his eye, of the magic of his eye, and of his commanding voice: physical properties, vastly desirable in an actor, and without which he can never insinuate meaning into an auditory,—but what have they to do with Hamlet? what have they to do with intellect? In fact, the things aimed at in theatrical representation, are to arrest the spectator's eye upon the form and the gesture, and so to gain a more favourable hearing to what is spoken: it is not what the character is, but how he looks; not what he says, but how he speaks it. I see no reason to think that if the play of *Hamlet* were written over again by some such writer as Banks or Lillo, retaining the process of the story, but totally omitting all the poetry of it, all the divine features of Shakespeare, his stupendous intellect; and only taking care to give us enough of passionate dialogue, which Banks or Lillo were never at a loss to furnish; I see not how the effect could be much different upon an audience, nor how the actor has it in his power to represent Shakespeare to us differently from his representation of Banks or Lillo. Hamlet would still be a youthful accomplished prince, and must be gracefully personated; he might be puzzled in his mind, wavering in his conduct, seemingly-cruel to Ophelia, he might see a ghost, and start at it, and address it kindly when he found it to be his father; all this in the poorest and most homely language of the servilest creeper after nature that ever consulted the palate of an audience; without troubling Shakespeare for the matter: and I see not but there would be room for all the power which an actor has, to display itself. All the passions and changes of passion might remain: for those are much less difficult to write or act than is thought, it is a trick easy to be attained, it is but rising or falling a note or two in the voice, a whisper with a significant foreboding look to announce its approach, and so contagious the counterfeit appearance of any emotion is, that let the words be what they will, the look and tone shall carry it off and make it pass for deep skill in the passions.

It is common for people to talk of Shakespeare's plays being *so natural*; that everybody can understand him. They are natural indeed, they are grounded deep in nature, so deep that the depth of them lies out of the reach of most of us. You shall hear the same persons say that George Barnwell is very natural, and Othello is very natural, that they are both very deep; and to them they are the same kind of thing. At the one they sit and shed tears, because a good sort of young man is tempted by a naughty woman to commit *a trifling peccadillo*, the murder of an uncle or so, that is all, and so comes to an untimely end, which is *so moving*; and at the other, because a blackamoor in a fit of jealousy kills his innocent white wife: and the odds are that ninety-nine out of a hundred would willingly behold the same catastrophe happen to both the heroes, and have thought the rope more due to Othello than to Barnwell. For of the texture of Othello's mind, the inward construction marvellously laid open with all its strengths and weaknesses, its heroic confidences and its human misgivings, its agonies of hate springing from the depths of love, they see no more than the spectators at a cheaper rate, who pay their pennies a-piece to look through the man's telescope in Leicester-fields, see into the inward plot and topography of the moon. Some dim thing or other they see, they see an actor personating a passion, of grief, or anger, for instance, and they recognize it as a copy of the usual external effects of such passions; for at least as being true to *that symbol of the emotion which passes current at the theatre for it*, for it is often no more than that: but of the grounds of the passion, its correspondence to a great or heroic nature, which is the only worthy object of tragedy,— that common auditors know any thing of this, or can have any such notions dinned into them by the mere strength of an actor's lungs,—that apprehensions foreign to them should be thus infused into them by storm, I can neither believe, nor understand how it can be possible.

We talk of Shakespeare's admirable observation of life, when we should feel, that not from a petty inquisition into those cheap and every-day characters which surrounded him, as they surround us, but from his own mind, which was, to borrow a phrase of Ben Jonson's, the very 'sphere of humanity', he fetched those images of virtue and of knowledge, of which every one of us recognizing a part, think we comprehend in our natures the whole; and oftentimes mistake the powers which he positively creates in us, for nothing more than indigenous faculties of our own minds which only waited the action of corresponding virtues in him to return a full and clear echo of the same.

To return to Hamlet.—Among the distinguishing features of that wonderful character, one of the most interesting (yet painful) is that soreness of mind which makes him treat the intrusions of Polonius with harshness, and that asperity which he puts on in his interviews with Ophelia. These tokens of an unhinged mind (if they be not mixed in the latter case with a profound artifice of love, to alienate Ophelia by affected discourtesies, so to prepare her mind for the breaking off of that loving intercourse, which can no longer find a place amidst business so serious as that which he has to do) are parts of his character, which to reconcile with our admiration of Hamlet, the most patient consideration of his situation is no more than necessary; they are what we *forgive afterwards*, and explain by the whole of his character, but *at the time* they are harsh and unpleasant. Yet such is the actor's necessity of giving strong blows to the audience, that I have never seen a player in this character, who did not exaggerate and strain to the utmost these ambiguous features,—these temporary deformities in the character. They make him express a vulgar scorn at Polonius which utterly degrades his gentility, and which no explanation can render palatable; they make him show contempt, and curl up the nose at Ophelia's father,—contempt in its very grossest and most hateful form; but they get applause by it: it is natural, people say; that is, the words are scornful, and the actor expresses scorn, and that they can judge of: but why so much scorn, and of that sort, they never think of asking.

So to Ophelia.—All the Hamlets that I have ever seen, rant and rave at her as if she had committed some great crime, and the audience are highly pleased, because the words of the part are satirical, and they are enforced by the strongest expression of satirical indignation of which the face and voice are capable. But then, whether Hamlet is likely to have put on such brutal appearances to a lady whom he loved so dearly, is never thought on. The truth is, that in all such deep affections as had subsisted between Hamlet and Ophelia, there is a stock of *supererogatory love*, (if I may venture to use the expression) which in any great grief of heart, especially where that which preys upon the mind cannot be communicated, confers a kind of indulgence upon the grieved party to express itself, even to its heart's dearest object, in the language of a temporary alienation; but it is not alienation, it is a distraction purely, and so it always makes itself to be felt by that object: it is not anger, but grief assuming the appearance of anger,—love awkwardly counterfeiting hate, as sweet countenances when they try to frown: but such sternness and fierce disgust as Hamlet is made to show, is no counterfeit, but the real face of absolute aversion,—of irreconcilable alienation. It may be said he puts on the madman; but then he should only so far put on this counterfeit lunacy as his own real distraction will give him leave; that is, incompletely, imperfectly; not in that confirmed practised way, like a master of his art, or, as Dame Quickly would say, 'like one of those harlotry players.'

I mean no disrespect to any actor, but the sort of pleasure which Shakespeare's plays give in the acting seems to me not at all to differ from that which the audience receive from those of other writers; and, *they being in themselves essentially so different from all others*, I must conclude that there is something in the nature of acting which levels all distinctions. And in fact, who does not speak indifferently of the *Gamester* and of *Macbeth* as fine stage performances, and praise the Mrs. Beverley in the same way as the Lady Macbeth of Mrs. S.? Belvidera, and Calista, and Isabella, and Euphrasia, are they less liked than Imogen, or than Juliet, or than Desdemona? Are they not spoken of and remembered in the same way? Is not the female performer as great (as they call it) in one as in the other? Did not Garrick shine, and was not he ambitious of shining in every drawling tragedy that his wretched day produced,—the productions of the Hills and the Murphys and the Browns,—and shall he have that honour to dwell in our minds for ever as an inseparable concomitant with Shakespeare? A kindred mind! O who can read that affecting sonnet of Shakespeare which alludes to his profession as a player:

> Oh for my sake do you with Fortune chide,
> The guilty goddess of my harmful deeds,
> That did not better for my life provide
> Than public means which public custom breeds—
> Thence comes it that my name receives a brand;
> And almost thence my nature is subdued
> To what it works in, like the dyer's hand—

Or that other confession:

> Alas! 'tis true, I have gone here and there,
> And made myself a motley to thy view,
> Gor'd mine own thoughts, sold cheap what is most dear—

Who can read these instances of jealous self-watchfulness in our sweet Shakespeare, and dream of any congeniality between him and one that, by every tradition of him, appears to have been as mere a player as ever existed; to have had his mind tainted with the lowest players' vices,—envy and jealousy, and miserable cravings after applause; one who in the exercise of his profession was jealous even of the women-performers that stood in his way; a manager full of managerial tricks and stratagems and finesse: that any resemblance should be dreamed of between him and Shakespeare,—Shakespeare who, in the plenitude and consciousness of his own powers, could with that noble modesty, which we can neither imitate nor appreciate, express himself thus of his own sense of his own defects:

> Wishing me like to one more rich in hope,
> Featur'd like him, like him with friends possest;
> Desiring *this man's art, and that man's scope.*

I am almost disposed to deny to Garrick the merit of being an admirer of Shakespeare. A true lover of his excellences he certainly was not; for would any true lover of them have admitted into his matchless scenes such ribald trash as Tate and Cibber, and the rest of them, that

> With their darkness durst affront his light,

have foisted into the acting plays of Shakespeare? I believe it impossible that he could have had a proper reverence for Shakespeare, and have condescended to go through that interpolated scene in Richard the Third, in which Richard tries to break his wife's heart by telling her he loves another woman, and says, 'if she survives this she is immortal.' Yet I doubt not he delivered this vulgar stuff with as much anxiety of emphasis as any of the genuine parts; and for acting, it is as well calculated as any. But we have seen the part of Richard lately produce great fame to an actor by his manner of playing it, and it lets us into the secret of acting, and of popular judgements of Shakespeare derived from acting. Not one of the spectators who have witnessed Mr. C.'s exertions in that part, but has come away with a proper conviction that Richard is a very wicked man, and kills little children in their beds, with something like the pleasure which the giants and ogres in children's books are represented to have taken in that practice; moreover, that he is very close and shrewd and devilish cunning, for you could see that by his eye.

But is in fact this the impression we have in reading the Richard of Shakespeare? Do we feel anything like disgust, as we do at that butcher-like representation of him that passes for him on the stage? A horror at his crimes blends with the effect which we feel, but how is it qualified, how is it carried off, by the rich intellect which he displays, his resources, his wit, his buoyant spirits, his vast knowledge and insight into characters, the poetry of his part,—not an atom of all which is made perceivable in Mr. C.'s way of acting it. Nothing but his crimes, his actions, is visible; they are prominent and staring; the murderer stands out, but where is the lofty genius, the man of vast capacity,—the profound, the witty, accomplished Richard?

The truth is, the Characters of Shakespeare are so much the objects of meditation rather than of interest or curiosity as to their actions, that while we are reading any of his great criminal characters,—Macbeth, Richard, even Iago,—we think not so much of the crimes which they commit, as of the ambition, the aspiring spirit, the intellectual activity, which prompts them to overleap those moral fences. Barnwell is a wretched murderer; there is a certain fitness between his neck and the rope; he is the legitimate heir to the gallows; nobody who thinks at all can think of any alleviating circumstances in his case to make him a fit object of mercy. Or to take an instance from the higher tragedy, what else but a mere assassin is Glenalvon! Do we think of anything but of the crime which he commits, and the rack which he deserves? That is all which we really think about him. Whereas in corresponding characters in Shakespeare so little do the actions comparatively affect us, that while the impulses, the inner mind in all its perverted greatness, solely seems real and is exclusively attended to, the crime is comparatively nothing. But when we see these things represented, the acts which they do are comparatively everything, their impulses nothing. The state of sublime emotion into which we are elevated by those images of night and horror which Macbeth is made to utter, that solemn prelude with which he entertains the time till the bell shall strike which is to call him to murder Duncan,—when we no longer read it in a book, when we have given up that vantage-ground of abstraction which reading possesses over seeing, and come to see a man in his bodily shape before our eyes actually preparing to commit a murder, if the acting be true and impressive, as I have witnessed it in Mr. K.'s performance of that part, the painful anxiety about the act, the natural longing to prevent it while it yet seems unperpetrated, the too close pressing semblance of reality, give a pain and an uneasiness which totally destroy all the delight which the words in the book convey, where the deed doing never presses upon us with the painful sense of presence: it rather seems to belong to history,—to something past and inevitable, if it has anything to do with time at all. The sublime images, the poetry alone, is that which is present to our minds in the reading.

So to see Lear acted—to see an old man tottering about the stage with a walking-stick, turned out of doors by his daughters in a rainy night, has nothing in it but what is painful and disgusting. We want to take him into shelter and relieve him. That is all the feeling which the acting of Lear ever produced in me. But the Lear of Shakespeare cannot be acted. The contemptible machinery by which they mimic the storm which he goes out in, is not more inadequate to represent the horrors of the real elements, than any actor can be to represent Lear: they might more easily propose to personate the Satan of Milton upon a stage, or one of Michael Angelo's terrible figures. The greatness of Lear is not in corporal dimension, but in intellectual: the explosions of his passion are terrible as a volcano: they are storms turning up and disclosing to the bottom that sea, his mind, with all its vast riches. It is his mind which is laid bare. This case of flesh and blood seems too insignificant to be thought on; even as he himself neglects it. On the stage we see nothing but corporal infirmities and weakness, the impotence of rage; while we read it, we see not Lear, but we are Lear,—we are in his mind, we are sustained by a grandeur which baffles the malice of daughters and storms; in the aberrations of his reason, we discover a mighty irregular power of reasoning, immethodized from the ordinary purposes of life, but exerting its powers, as the wind blows where it listeth, at will upon the corruptions and abuses of mankind. What have looks, or tones, to do with that sublime identification of his age with that of the *heavens themselves*, when in his reproaches to them for conniving at the injustice of his children, he reminds them that 'they themselves are old'. What gesture shall we appropriate to this? What has the voice or the eye to do with such things? But the play is beyond all art, as the tamperings with it show: it is too hard and stony; it must have love-scenes, and a happy ending. It is not enough that Cordelia is a daughter, she must shine as a lover too. Tate has put his hook in the nostrils of this Leviathan, for Garrick and his followers, the showmen of the scene, to draw the mighty beast about more easily. A happy ending! —as if the living martyrdom that Lear had gone through,—the flaying of his feelings alive, did not make a fair dismissal from the stage of life the only decorous thing for him. If he is to live and be happy after, if he could sustain this world's burden after, why all this pudder and preparation,—why torment us with all this unnecessary sympathy? As if the childish pleasure of getting his gilt robes and sceptre again could tempt him to act over again his misused station, —as if at his years, and with his experience, anything was left but to die.

Lear is essentially impossible to be represented on a stage. But how many dramatic personages are there in Shakespeare, which though more tractable and feasible (if I may so speak) than Lear, yet from some circumstance, some adjunct to their character, are improper to be shown to our bodily eye. Othello for instance. Nothing can be more soothing, more flattering to the nobler parts of our natures, than to read of a young Venetian lady of highest extraction, through the force of love and from a sense of merit in him whom she loved, laying aside every consideration of kindred, and country, and colour, and wedding with *a coal-black Moor*—(for such he is represented, in the imperfect state of knowledge respecting foreign countries in those days, compared with our own, or in compliance with popular notions, though the Moors are now well enough known to be by many shades less unworthy of a white woman's fancy)—it is the perfect triumph of virtue over accidents, of the imagination over the senses. She sees Othello's colour in his mind. But upon the stage, when the imagination is no longer the ruling faculty, but we are left to our poor unassisted senses, I appeal to every one that has seen Othello played, whether he did not, on the contrary, sink Othello's mind in his colour; whether he did not find something extremely revolting in the courtship and wedded caresses of Othello and Desdemona; and whether the actual sight of the thing did not overweigh all that beautiful compromise which we make in reading;—and the reason it should do so is obvious, because there is just so much reality presented to our senses as to give a perception of disagreement, with not enough of belief in the internal motives—all that which is unseen—to overpower and reconcile the first and obvious prejudices.[1] What we see upon a stage is body and bodily action; what we are conscious of in reading is almost exclusively the mind, and its movements: and this I think may sufficiently account for the very different sort of delight with which the same play so often affects us in the reading and the seeing.

It requires little reflection to perceive, that if those characters in Shakespeare which are within the precincts of nature, have yet something in them which appeals too exclusively to the imagination, to admit of their being made objects to the senses without suffering a change and a diminution,—that still stronger the objection must lie against representing another line of characters, which Shakespeare has introduced to give a wildness and a supernatural elevation to his scenes, as if to remove them still farther from that assimilation to common life in which their excellence is vulgarly supposed to consist. When we read the incantations of those terrible beings the Witches in *Macbeth*, though some of the ingredients of their hellish composition savour of the grotesque, yet is the effect upon us other than the most serious and appalling that can be imagined? Do we not feel spell-bound as Macbeth was? Can any mirth accompany a sense of their presence? We might as well laugh under a consciousness of the principle of Evil himself being truly and really present with us. But

[1] The error of supposing that because Othello's colour does not offend us in the reading, it should also not offend us in the seeing, is just such a fallacy as supposing that an Adam and Eve in a picture shall affect us just as they do in the poem. But in the poem we for a while have Paradisaical senses given us, which vanish when we see a man and his wife without clothes in the picture. The painters themselves feel this, as is apparent by the awkward shifts they have recourse to, to make them look not quite naked; by a sort of prophetic anachronism, antedating the invention of fig-leaves. So in the reading of the play, we see with Desdemona's eyes; in the seeing of it, we are forced to look with our own.

attempt to bring these beings on to a stage, and you turn them instantly into so many old women, that men and children are to laugh at. Contrary to the old saying, that 'seeing is believing', the sight actually destroys the faith; and the mirth in which we indulge at their expense, when we see these creatures upon a stage, seems to be a sort of indemnification which we make to ourselves for the terror which they put us in when reading made them an object of belief,—when we surrendered up our reason to the poet, as children to their nurses and their elders; and we laugh at our fears, as children who thought they saw something in the dark, triumph when the bringing in of a candle discovers the vanity of their fears. For this exposure of supernatural agents upon a stage is truly bringing in a candle to expose their own delusiveness. It is the solitary taper and the book that generates a faith in these terrors: a ghost by chandelier light, and in good company, deceives no spectators,—a ghost that can be measured by the eye, and his human dimensions made out at leisure. The sight of a well-lighted house, and a well-dressed audience, shall arm the most nervous child against any apprehensions: as Tom Brown says of the impenetrable skin of Achilles with his impenetrable armour over it, 'Bully Dawson would have fought the devil with such advantages.'

Much has been said, and deservedly, in reprobation of the vile mixture which Dryden has thrown into the *Tempest*: doubtless without some such vicious alloy, the impure ears of that age would never have sate out to hear so much innocence of love as is contained in the sweet courtship of Ferdinand and Miranda. But is the *Tempest* of Shakespeare at all a subject for stage representation? It is one thing to read of an enchanter, and to believe the wondrous tale while we are reading it; but to have a conjurer brought before us in his conjuring-gown, with his spirits about him, which none but himself and some hundred of favoured spectators before the curtain are supposed to see, involves such a quantity of the *hateful incredible*, that all our reverence for the author cannot hinder us from perceiving such gross attempts upon the senses to be in the highest degree childish and inefficient. Spirits and fairies cannot be represented, they cannot even be painted,—they can only be believed. But the elaborate and anxious provision of scenery, which the luxury of the age demands, in these cases works a quite contrary effect to what is intended. That which in comedy, or plays of familiar life, adds so much to the life of the imitation, in plays which appeal to the higher faculties, positively destroys the illusion which it is introduced to aid. A parlour or a drawing-room, —a library opening into a garden,—a garden with an alcove in it,—a street, or the piazza of Covent Garden, does well enough in a scene; we are content to give as much credit to it as it demands; or rather, we think little about it,—it is little more than reading at the top of a page, 'Scene, a Garden;' we do not imagine ourselves there, but we readily admit the imitation of familiar objects. But to think by the help of painted trees and caverns, which we know to be painted, to transport our minds to Prospero, and his island and his lonely cell;[1] or by the aid of a fiddle dexterously thrown in, in an interval of speaking, to make us believe that we hear those supernatural noises of which the isle was full:—the Orrery Lecturer at the Haymarket might as well hope, by his musical glasses cleverly stationed out of sight behind his apparatus, to make us believe that we do indeed hear the chrystal spheres ring out that chime, which if it were to inwrap our fancy long, Milton thinks,

Time would run back and fetch the age of gold,
And speckled vanity

[1] It will be said these things are done in pictures. But pictures and scenes are very different things. Painting is a world of itself, but in scene-painting there is the attempt to deceive; and there is the discordancy, never to be got over, between painted scenes and real people.

Would sicken soon and die,
   And leprous Sin would melt from earthly mould;
   Yea Hell itself would pass away,
   And leave its dolorous mansions to the peering day.

The Garden of Eden, with our first parents in it, is not more impossible to be shown on a stage, than the Enchanted Isle, with its no less interesting and innocent first settlers.

The subject of Scenery is closely connected with that of the Dresses, which are so anxiously attended to on our stage. I remember the last time I saw Macbeth played, the discrepancy I felt at the changes of garment which he varied—the shiftings and re-shiftings, like a Romish priest at mass. The luxury of stage-improvements, and the importunity of the public eye, require this. The coronation robe of the Scottish monarch was fairly a counterpart to that which our king wears when he goes to the Parliament-house,—just so full and cumbersome, and set out with ermine and pearls. And if things must be represented, I see not what to find fault with in this. But in reading, what robe are we conscious of? Some dim images of royalty—a crown and sceptre, may float before our eyes, but who shall describe the fashion of it? Do we see in our mind's eye what Webb or any other robe-maker could pattern? This is the inevitable consequence of imitating everything, to make all things natural. Whereas the reading of a tragedy is a fine abstraction. It presents to the fancy just so much of external appearances as to make us feel that we are among flesh and blood, while by far the greater and better part of our imagination is employed upon the thoughts and internal machinery of the character. But in acting, scenery, dress, the most contemptible things, call upon us to judge of their naturalness.

Perhaps it would be no bad similitude, to liken the pleasure which we take in seeing one of these fine plays acted, compared with that quiet delight which we find in the reading of it, to the different feelings with which a reviewer, and a man that is not a reviewer, reads a fine poem. The accursed critical habit,—the being called upon to judge and pronounce, must make it quite a different thing to the former. In seeing these plays acted, we are affected just as judges. When Hamlet compares the two pictures of Gertrude's first and second husband, who wants to see the pictures? But in the acting, a miniature must be lugged out; which we know not to be the picture, but only to show how finely a miniature may be represented. This showing of everything, levels all things: it makes tricks, bows, and curtesies, of importance. Mrs. S. never got more fame by anything than by the manner in which she dismisses the guests in the banquet-scene in *Macbeth*: it is as much remembered as any of her thrilling tones or impressive looks. But does such a trifle as this enter into the imaginations of the readers of that wild and wonderful scene? Does not the mind dismiss the feasters as rapidly as it can? Does it care about the gracefulness of the doing it? But by acting, and judging of acting, all these non-essentials are raised into an importance, injurious to the main interest of the play.

I have confined my observations to the tragic parts of Shakespeare. It would be no very difficult task to extend the inquiry to his comedies; and to show why Falstaff, Shallow, Sir Hugh Evans, and the rest, are equally incompatible with stage representation. The length to which this essay has run, will make it, I am afraid, sufficiently distasteful to the Amateurs of the Theatre, without going any deeper into the subject at present.

PERCY BYSSHE SHELLEY

1792-1822

A DEFENCE OF POETRY (1821)

ACCORDING to one mode of regarding those two classes of mental action, which are called reason and imagination, the former may be considered as mind contemplating the relations borne by one thought to another, however produced; and the latter, as mind acting upon those thoughts so as to colour them with its own light, and composing from them, as from elements, other thoughts, each containing within itself the principle of its own integrity. The one is the τὸ ποιεῖν, or the principle of synthesis, and has for its objects those forms which are common to universal nature and existence itself; the other is the τὸ λογίζειν, or principle of analysis, and its action regards the relations of things, simply as relations; considering thoughts, not in their integral unity, but as the algebraical representations which conduct to certain general results. Reason is the enumeration of quantities already known; imagination is the perception of the value of those quantities, both separately and as a whole. Reason respects the differences, and imagination the similitudes of things. Reason is to the imagination as the instrument to the agent, as the body to the spirit, as the shadow to the substance.

Poetry, in a general sense, may be defined to be 'the expression of the imagination': and poetry is connate with the origin of man. Man is an instrument over which a series of external and internal impressions are driven, like the alternations of an ever-changing wind over an Aeolian lyre, which move it by their motion to ever-changing melody. But there is a principle within the human being, and perhaps within all sentient beings, which acts otherwise than in the lyre, and produces not melody alone, but harmony, by an internal adjustment of the sounds or motions thus excited to the impressions which excite them. It is as if the lyre could accommodate its chords to the motions of that which strikes them, in a determined proportion of sound; even as the musician can accommodate his voice to the sound of the lyre. A child at play by itself will express its delight by its voice and motions; and every inflexion of tone and every gesture will bear exact relation to a corresponding antitype in the pleasurable impressions which awakened it; it will be the reflected image of that impression; and as the lyre trembles and sounds after the wind has died away,. so the child seeks, by prolonging in its voice and motions the duration of the effect, to prolong also a consciousness of the cause. In relation to the objects which delight a child, these expressions are, what poetry is to higher objects. The savage (for the savage is to ages what the child is to years) expresses the emotions produced in him by surrounding objects in a similar manner; and language and gesture, together with plastic or pictorial imitation, become the image of the combined effect of those objects, and of his apprehension of them. Man in society, with all his passions and his pleasures, next becomes the object of the passions and pleasures of man; an additional class of emotions produces an augmented treasure of expressions; and language, gesture, and the imitative arts, become at once the representation and the medium, the pencil and the picture, the chisel and the statue, the chord and the harmony. The social sympathies, or those laws from which, as from its elements, society results, begin to develop themselves from the moment that two human beings coexist; the future is contained within the present, as the plant within the seed; and equality, diversity, unity, contrast, mutual dependence, become the principles alone capable of affording the motives according to which the will of a social being is determined to action, inasmuch as he is social; and constitute pleasure in sensation, virtue in sentiment, beauty in art, truth in reasoning, and love in the intercourse of kind. Hence men, even in the infancy of society, observe a certain order in their words and actions, distinct from that of the objects and the impressions represented by them, all expression being subject to the laws of that from which it proceeds. But let us dismiss those more general considerations which might involve an inquiry into the principles of society itself, and restrict our view to the manner in which the imagination is expressed upon its forms.

In the youth of the world, men dance and sing and imitate natural objects, observing in these actions, as in all others, a certain rhythm or order. And, although all men observe a similar, they observe not the same order, in the motions of the dance, in the melody of the song, in the combinations of language, in the series of their imitations of natural objects. For there is a certain order or rhythm belonging to each of these classes of mimetic representation, from which the hearer and the spectator receive an intenser and purer pleasure than from any other: the sense of an approximation to this order has been called taste by modern writers. Every man in the infancy of art observes an order which approximates more or less closely to that from which this highest delight results: but the diversity is not sufficiently marked, as that its gradations should be sensible, except in those instances where the predominance of this faculty of approximation to the beautiful (for so we may be permitted to name the relation between this highest pleasure and its cause) is very great. Those in whom it exists in excess are poets, in the most universal sense of the word; and the pleasure resulting from the manner in which they express the influence of society or nature upon their own minds, communicates itself to others, and gathers a sort of reduplication from that community. Their language is vitally metaphorical;

that is, it marks the before unapprehended relations of things and perpetuates their apprehension, until the words which represent them become, through time, signs for portions or classes of thoughts instead of pictures of integral thoughts; and then if no new poets should arise to create afresh the associations which have been thus disorganized, language will be dead to all the nobler purposes of human intercourse. These similitudes or relations are finely said by Lord Bacon to be 'the same footsteps of nature impressed upon the various subjects of the world';[1] and he considers the faculty which perceives them as the storehouse of axioms common to all knowledge. In the infancy of society every author is necessarily a poet, because language itself is poetry; and to be a poet is to apprehend the true and the beautiful, in a word, the good which exists in the relation, subsisting, first between existence and perception, and secondly between perception and expression. Every original language near to its source is in itself the chaos of a cyclic poem: the copiousness of lexicography and the distinctions of grammar are the works of a later age, and are merely the catalogue and the form of the creations of poetry.

But poets, or those who imagine and express this indestructible order, are not only the authors of language and of music, of the dance, and architecture, and statuary, and painting; they are the institutors of laws, and the founders of civil society, and the inventors of the arts of life, and the teachers who draw into a certain propinquity with the beautiful and the true, that partial apprehension of the agencies of the invisible world which is called religion. Hence all original religions are allegorical, or susceptible of allegory, and, like Janus, have a double face of false and true. Poets, according to the circumstances of the age and nation in which they appeared, were called, in the earlier epochs of the world, legislators, or prophets: a poet essentially comprises and unites both

[1] *De Augment. Scient.*, cap. i, lib. iii.

these characters. For he not only beholds intensely the present as it is, and discovers those laws according to which present things ought to be ordered, but he beholds the future in the present, and his thoughts are the germs of the flower and the fruit of latest time. Not that I assert poets to be prophets in the gross sense of the word, or that they can foretell the form as surely as they foreknow the spirit of events: such is the pretence of superstition, which would make poetry an attribute of prophecy, rather than prophecy an attribute of poetry. A poet participates in the eternal, the infinite, and the one; as far as relates to his conceptions, time and place and number are not. The grammatical forms which express the moods of time, and the difference of persons, and the distinction of place, are convertible with respect to the highest poetry without injuring it as poetry; and the choruses of Aeschylus, and the book of *Job*, and Dante's *Paradise*, would afford, more than any other writings, examples of this fact, if the limits of this essay did not forbid citation. The creations of sculpture, painting, and music, are illustrations still more decisive.

Language, colour, form, and religious and civil habits of action, are all the instruments and materials of poetry; they may be called poetry by that figure of speech which considers the effect as a synonym of the cause. But poetry in a more restricted sense expresses those arrangements of language, and especially metrical language, which are created by that imperial faculty, whose throne is curtained within the invisible nature of man. And this springs from the nature itself of language, which is a more direct representation of the actions and passions of our internal being, and is susceptible of more various and delicate combinations, than colour, form, or motion, and is more plastic and obedient to the control of that faculty of which it is the creation. For language is arbitrarily produced by the imagination, and has relation to thoughts alone; but all other materials, instruments, and conditions of art, have relations among each other, which limit and interpose between conception and expression. The former is as a mirror which reflects, the latter as a cloud which enfeebles, the light of which both are mediums of communication. Hence the fame of sculptors, painters, and musicians, although the intrinsic powers of the great masters of these arts may yield in no degree to that of those who have employed language as the hieroglyphic of their thoughts, has never equalled that of poets in the restricted sense of the term; as two performers of equal skill will produce unequal effects from a guitar and a harp. The fame of legislators and founders of religions, so long as their institutions last, alone seems to exceed that of poets in the restricted sense; but it can scarcely be a question, whether, if we deduct the celebrity which their flattery of the gross opinions of the vulgar usually conciliates, together with that which belonged to them in their higher character of poets, any excess will remain.

We have thus circumscribed the word poetry within the limits of that art which is the most familiar and the most perfect expression of the faculty itself. It is necessary, however, to make the circle still narrower, and to determine the distinction between measured and unmeasured language; for the popular division into prose and verse is inadmissible in accurate philosophy.

Sounds as well as thoughts have relation both between each other and towards that which they represent, and a perception of the order of those relations has always been found connected with a perception of the order of the relations of thoughts. Hence the language of poets has ever affected a certain uniform and harmonious recurrence of sound, without which it were not poetry, and which is scarcely less indispensable to the communication of its influence, than the words themselves, without reference to that peculiar order. Hence the vanity of translation; it were as wise to cast a violet into a crucible that you might discover the formal principle of its colour and odour, as seek to transfuse from one language into another the creations of a poet. The plant must spring again from its seed, or it will bear no flower—and this is the burthen of the curse of Babel.

An observation of the regular mode of the recurrence of harmony in the language of poetical minds, together with its relation to music, produced metre, or a certain system of traditional forms of harmony and language. Yet it is by no means essential that a poet should accommodate his language to this traditional form, so that the harmony, which is its spirit, be observed. The practice is indeed convenient and popular, and to be preferred, especially in such composition as includes much action: but every great poet must inevitably innovate upon the example of his predecessors in the exact structure of his peculiar versification. The distinction between poets and prose writers is a vulgar error. The distinction between philosophers and poets has been anticipated. Plato was essentially a poet—the truth and splendour of his imagery, and the melody of his language, are the most intense that it is possible to conceive. He rejected the measure of the epic, dramatic, and lyrical forms, because he sought to kindle a harmony in thoughts divested of shape and action, and he forbore to invent any regular plan of rhythm which would include, under determinate forms, the varied pauses of his style. Cicero sought to imitate the cadence of his periods, but with little success. Lord Bacon was a poet.[1] His language has a sweet and majestic rhythm, which satisfies the sense, no less than the almost superhuman wisdom of his philosophy satisfies the intellect; it is a strain which distends, and then bursts the circumference of the reader's mind, and pours itself forth

[1] See the *Filum Labyrinthi*, and the Essay on Death particularly.

together with it into the universal element with which it has perpetual sympathy. All the authors of revolutions in opinion are not only necessarily poets as they are inventors, nor even as their words unveil the permanent analogy of things by images which participate in the life of truth; but as their periods are harmonious and rhythmical, and contain in themselves the elements of verse; being the echo of the eternal music. Nor are those supreme poets, who have employed traditional forms of rhythm on account of the form and action of their subjects, less capable of perceiving and teaching the truth of things, than those who have omitted that form. Shakespeare, Dante, and Milton (to confine ourselves to modern writers) are philosophers of the very loftiest power.

A poem is the very image of life expressed in its eternal truth. There is this difference between a story and a poem, that a story is a catalogue of detached facts, which have no other connexion than time, place, circumstance, cause and effect; the other is the creation of actions according to the unchangeable forms of human nature, as existing in the mind of the Creator, which is itself the image of all other minds. The one is partial, and applies only to a definite period of time, and a certain combination of events which can never again recur; the other is universal, and contains within itself the germ of a relation to whatever motives or actions have place in the possible varieties of human nature. Time, which destroys the beauty and the use of the story of particular facts, stripped of the poetry which should invest them, augments that of poetry, and for ever develops new and wonderful applications of the eternal truth which it contains. Hence epitomes have been called the moths of just history; they eat out the poetry of it. A story of particular facts is as a mirror which obscures and distorts that which should be beautiful; poetry is a mirror which makes beautiful that which is distorted.

The parts of a composition may be poetical, without the composition as a whole being a poem. A single sentence may be considered as a whole, though it may be found in the midst of a series of unassimilated portions: a single word even may be a spark of inextinguishable thought. And thus all the great historians, Herodotus, Plutarch, Livy, were poets; and although the plan of these writers, especially that of Livy, restrained them from developing this faculty in its highest degree, they made copious and ample amends for their subjection, by filling all the interstices of their subjects with living images.

Having determined what is poetry, and who are poets, let us proceed to estimate its effects upon society.

Poetry is ever accompanied with pleasure: all spirits on which it falls open themselves to receive the wisdom which is mingled with its delight. In the infancy of the world, neither poets themselves nor their auditors are fully aware of the excellence of poetry: for it acts in a divine and unapprehended manner, beyond and above consciousness; and it is reserved for future generations to contemplate and measure the mighty cause and effect in all the strength and splendour of their union. Even in modern times, no living poet ever arrived at the fullness of his fame; the jury which sits in judgement upon a poet, belonging as he does to all time, must be composed of his peers: it must be impanelled by Time from the selectest of the wise of many generations. A poet is a nightingale, who sits in darkness and sings to cheer its own solitude with sweet sounds; his auditors are as men entranced by the melody of an unseen musician, who feel that they are moved and softened, yet know not whence or why. The poems of Homer and his contemporaries were the delight of infant Greece; they were the elements of that social system which is the column upon which all succeeding civilization has reposed. Homer embodied the ideal perfection of his age in human character; nor can we doubt that those who read his verses were awakened to an ambition of becoming like to Achilles, Hector, and Ulysses: the truth and beauty of friendship, patriotism, and persevering devotion to an object, were unveiled to the depths in these immortal creations: the sentiments of the auditors must have been refined and enlarged by a sympathy with such great and lovely impersonations, until from admiring they imitated, and from imitation they identified themselves with the objects of their admiration. Nor let it be objected, that these characters are remote from moral perfection, and that they can by no means be considered as edifying patterns for general imitation. Every epoch, under names more or less specious, has deified its peculiar errors; Revenge is the naked idol of the worship of a semi-barbarous age; and Self-deceit is the veiled image of unknown evil, before which luxury and satiety lie prostrate. But a poet considers the vices of his contemporaries as a temporary dress in which his creations must be arrayed, and which cover without concealing the eternal proportions of their beauty. An epic or dramatic personage is understood to wear them around his soul, as he may the ancient armour or the modern uniform around his body; whilst it is easy to conceive a dress more graceful than either. The beauty of the internal nature cannot be so far concealed by its accidental vesture, but that the spirit of its form shall communicate itself to the very disguise, and indicate the shape it hides from the manner in which it is worn. A majestic form and graceful motions will express themselves through the most barbarous and tasteless costume. Few poets of the highest class have chosen to exhibit the beauty of their conceptions in its naked truth and splendour; and it is doubtful whether the alloy of costume, habit, &c., be not necessary to temper this planetary music for mortal ears.

The whole objection, however, of the immorality of poetry rests upon a misconception of the manner in which poetry acts to produce the moral improvement of man. Ethical science arranges the elements which poetry has created, and propounds schemes and proposes examples of civil and domestic life: nor is it for want of admirable doctrines that men hate, and despise, and censure, and deceive, and subjugate one another. But poetry acts in another and diviner manner. It awakens and enlarges the mind itself by rendering it the receptacle of a thousand unapprehended combinations of thought. Poetry lifts the veil from the hidden beauty of the world, and makes familiar objects be as if they were not familiar; it reproduces all that it represents, and the impersonations clothed in its Elysian light stand thenceforward in the minds of those who have once contemplated them, as memorials of that gentle and exalted content which extends itself over all thoughts and actions with which it coexists. The great secret of morals is love; or a going out of our own nature, and an identification of ourselves with the beautiful which exists in thought, action, or person, not our own. A man, to be greatly good, must imagine intensely and comprehensively; he must put himself in the place of another and of many others; the pains and pleasures of his species must become his own. The great instrument of moral good is the imagination; and poetry administers to the effect by acting upon the cause. Poetry enlarges the circumference of the imagination by replenishing it with thoughts of ever new delight, which have the power of attracting and assimilating to their own nature all other thoughts, and which form new intervals and interstices whose void for ever craves fresh food. Poetry strengthens the faculty which is the organ of the moral nature of man, in the same manner as exercise strengthens a limb. A poet therefore would do ill to embody his own conceptions of right and wrong, which are usually those of his place and time, in his poetical creations, which participate in neither. By this assumption of the inferior office of interpreting the effect, in which perhaps after all he might acquit himself but imperfectly, he would resign a glory in a participation in the cause. There was little danger that Homer, or any of the eternal poets, should have so far misunderstood themselves as to have abdicated this throne of their widest dominion. Those in whom the poetical faculty, though great, is less intense, as Euripides, Lucan, Tasso, Spenser, have frequently affected a moral aim, and the effect of their poetry is diminished in exact proportion to the degree in which they compel us to advert to this purpose.

Homer and the cyclic poets were followed at a certain interval by the dramatic and lyrical poets of Athens, who flourished contemporaneously with all that is most perfect in the kindred expressions of the poetical faculty; architecture, painting, music, the dance, sculpture, philosophy, and, we may add, the forms of civil life. For although the scheme of Athenian society was deformed by many imperfections which the poetry existing in chivalry and Christianity has erased from the habits and institutions of modern Europe; yet never at any other period has so much energy, beauty, and virtue, been developed; never was blind strength and stubborn form so disciplined and rendered subject to the will of man, or that will less repugnant to the dictates of the beautiful and the true, as during the century which preceded the death of Socrates. Of no other epoch in the history of our species have we records and fragments stamped so visibly with the image of the divinity in man. But it is poetry alone, in form, in action, or in language, which has rendered this epoch memorable above all others, and the storehouse of examples to everlasting time. For written poetry existed at that epoch simultaneously with the other arts, and it is an idle inquiry to demand which gave and which received the light, which all, as from a common focus, have scattered over the darkest periods of succeeding time. We know no more of cause and effect than a constant conjunction of events: poetry is ever found to co-exist with whatever other arts contribute to the happiness and perfection of man. I appeal to what has already been established to distinguish between the cause and the effect.

It was at the period here adverted to, that the drama had its birth; and however a succeeding writer may have equalled or surpassed those few great specimens of the Athenian drama which have been preserved to us, it is indisputable that the art itself never was understood or practised according to the true philosophy of it, as at Athens. For the Athenians employed language, action, music, painting, the dance, and religious institutions, to produce a common effect in the representation of the highest idealisms of passion and of power; each division in the art was made perfect in its kind by artists of the most consummate skill, and was disciplined into a beautiful proportion and unity one towards the other. On the modern stage a few only of the elements capable of expressing the image of the poet's conception are employed at once. We have tragedy without music and dancing; and music and dancing without the highest impersonations of which they are the fit accompaniment, and both without religion and solemnity. Religious institution has indeed been usually banished from the stage. Our system of divesting the actor's face of a mask, on which the many expressions appropriated to his dramatic character might be moulded into one permanent and unchanging expression, is favourable only to a partial and inharmonious effect; it is fit for nothing but a monologue, where all the attention may be directed to some great master of ideal mimicry. The modern practice of blending comedy with tragedy, though liable to great abuse in point of practice, is undoubtedly an extension of the dramatic circle; but the comedy should be as in *King Lear*, universal, ideal, and sublime. It is perhaps the intervention of this principle which determines the balance in favour of

King Lear against the *Oedipus Tyrannus* or the *Agamemnon*, or, if you will, the trilogies with which they are connected; unless the intense power of the choral poetry, especially that of the latter, should be considered as restoring the equilibrium. *King Lear*, if it can sustain this comparison, may be judged to be the most perfect specimen of the dramatic art existing in the world; in spite of the narrow conditions to which the poet was subjected by the ignorance of the philosophy of the drama which has prevailed in modern Europe. Calderon, in his religious *Autos*, has attempted to fulfil some of the high conditions of dramatic representation neglected by Shakespeare; such as the establishing a relation between the drama and religion, and the accommodating them to music and dancing; but he omits the observation of conditions still more important, and more is lost than gained by the substitution of the rigidly-defined and ever-repeated idealisms of a distorted superstition for the living impersonations of the truth of human passion.

But I digress.—The connexion of scenic exhibitions with the improvement or corruption of the manners of men, has been universally recognized: in other words, the presence or absence of poetry in its most perfect and universal form, has been found to be connected with good and evil in conduct or habit. The corruption which has been imputed to the drama as an effect, begins, when the poetry employed in its constitution ends: I appeal to the history of manners whether the periods of the growth of the one and the decline of the other have not corresponded with an exactness equal to any example of moral cause and effect.

The drama at Athens, or wheresoever else it may have approached to its perfection, ever co-existed with the moral and intellectual greatness of the age. The tragedies of the Athenian poets are as mirrors in which the spectator beholds himself, under a thin disguise of circumstance, stript of all but that ideal perfection and energy which every one feels to be the internal type of all that he loves, admires, and would become. The imagination is enlarged by a sympathy with pains and passions so mighty, that they distend in their conception the capacity of that by which they are conceived; the good affections are strengthened by pity, indignation, terror, and sorrow; and an exalted calm is prolonged from the satiety of this high exercise of them into the tumult of familiar life: even crime is disarmed of half its horror and all its contagion by being represented as the fatal consequence of the unfathomable agencies of nature; error is thus divested of its wilfulness; men can no longer cherish it as the creation of their choice. In a drama of the highest order there is little food for censure or hatred; it teaches rather self-knowledge and self-respect. Neither the eye nor the mind can see itself, unless reflected upon that which it resembles. The drama, so long as it continues to express poetry, is as a prismatic and many-sided mirror, which collects the brightest rays of human nature and divides and reproduces them from the simplicity of these elementary forms, and touches them with majesty and beauty, and multiplies all that it reflects, and endows it with the power of propagating its like wherever it may fall.

But in periods of the decay of social life, the drama sympathizes with that decay. Tragedy becomes a cold imitation of the form of the great masterpieces of antiquity, divested of all harmonious accompaniment of the kindred arts; and often the very form misunderstood, or a weak attempt to teach certain doctrines, which the writer considers as moral truths; and which are usually no more than specious flatteries of some gross vice or weakness, with which the author, in common with his auditors, are infected. Hence what has been called the classical and domestic drama. Addison's *Cato* is a specimen of the one; and would it were not superfluous to cite examples of the other! To such purposes poetry cannot be made subservient.

Poetry is a sword of lightning, ever unsheathed, which consumes the scabbard that would contain it. And thus we observe that all dramatic writings of this nature are unimaginative in a singular degree; they affect sentiment and passion, which, divested of imagination, are other names for caprice and appetite. The period in our own history of the grossest degradation of the drama is the reign of Charles II, when all forms in which poetry had been accustomed to be expressed became hymns to the triumph of kingly power over liberty and virtue. Milton stood alone illuminating an age unworthy of him. At such periods the calculating principle pervades all the forms of dramatic exhibition, and poetry ceases to be expressed upon them. Comedy loses its ideal universality: wit succeeds to humour; we laugh from self-complacency and triumph, instead of pleasure; malignity, sarcasm, and contempt, succeed to sympathetic merriment; we hardly laugh, but we smile. Obscenity, which is ever blasphemy against the divine beauty in life, becomes, from the very veil which it assumes, more active if less disgusting: it is a monster for which the corruption of society for ever brings forth new food, which it devours in secret.

The drama being that form under which a greater number of modes of expression of poetry are susceptible of being combined than any other, the connexion of poetry and social good is more observable in the drama than in whatever other form. And it is indisputable that the highest perfection of human society has ever corresponded with the highest dramatic excellence; and that the corruption or the extinction of the drama in a nation where it has once flourished, is a mark of a corruption of manners, and an extinction of the energies which sustain the soul of social life. But, as Machiavelli says of political institutions, that life may be preserved and renewed, if men should arise capable of bringing back the drama to its principles. And this is true with respect to poetry in its most extended sense: all language, institution and form, require not only to be produced but to be sustained: the office and character of a poet participates in the divine nature as regards providence, no less than as regards creation.

Civil war, the spoils of Asia, and the fatal predominance first of the Macedonian, and then of the Roman arms, were so many symbols of the extinction or suspension of the creative faculty in Greece. The bucolic writers, who found patronage under the lettered tyrants of Sicily and Egypt, were the latest representatives of its most glorious reign. Their poetry is intensely melodious; like the odour of the tuberose, it overcomes and sickens the spirit with excess of sweetness; whilst the poetry of the preceding age was as a meadow-gale of June, which mingles the fragrance of all the flowers of the field, and adds a quickening and harmonizing spirit of its own, which endows the sense with a power of sustaining its extreme delight. The bucolic and erotic delicacy in written poetry is correlative with that softness in statuary, music, and the kindred arts, and even in manners and institutions, which distinguished the epoch to which I now refer. Nor is it the poetical faculty itself, or any misapplication of it, to which this want of harmony is to be imputed. An equal sensibility to the influence of the senses and the affections is to be found in the writings of Homer and Sophocles: the former, especially, has clothed sensual and pathetic images with irresistible attractions. Their superiority over these succeeding writers consists in the presence of those thoughts which belong to the inner faculties of our nature, not in the absence of those which are connected with the external: their incomparable perfection consists in a harmony of the union of all. It is not what the erotic poets have, but what they have not, in which their imperfection consists. It is not inasmuch as they were poets, but inasmuch as they were not poets, that they can be considered with any plausibility as connected with the corruption of their age. Had that corruption availed so as to extinguish in them the sensibility to pleasure, passion, and natural scenery, which is imputed to them as an imperfection, the last triumph of evil would have been achieved. For the end of social corruption is to destroy all sensibility to pleasure; and, therefore, it is corruption. It begins at the imagination and the intellect as at the core, and distributes itself thence as a paralysing venom, through the affections into the very appetites, until all become a torpid mass in which hardly sense survives. At the approach of such a period, poetry ever addresses itself to those faculties which are the last to be destroyed, and its voice is heard, like the footsteps of Astraea, departing from the world. Poetry ever communicates all the pleasure which men are capable of receiving: it is ever still the light of life; the source of whatever of beautiful or generous or true can have place in an evil time. It will readily be confessed that those among the luxurious citizens of Syracuse and Alexandria, who were delighted with the poems of Theocritus, were less cold, cruel, and sensual than the remnant of their tribe. But corruption must utterly have destroyed the fabric of human society before poetry can ever cease. The sacred links of that chain have never been entirely disjoined, which descending through the minds of many men is attached to those great minds, whence as from a magnet the invisible effluence is sent forth, which at once connects, animates, and sustains the life of all. It is the faculty which contains within itself the seeds at once of its own and of social renovation. And let us not circumscribe the effects of the bucolic and erotic poetry within the limits of the sensibility of those to whom it was addressed. They may have perceived the beauty of those immortal compositions, simply as fragments and isolated portions: those who are more finely organized, or born in a happier age, may recognize them as episodes to that great poem, which all poets, like the co-operating thoughts of one great mind, have built up since the beginning of the world.

The same revolutions within a narrower sphere had place in ancient Rome; but the actions and forms of its social life never seem to have been perfectly saturated with the poetical element. The Romans appear to have considered the Greeks as the selectest treasuries of the selectest forms of manners and of nature, and to have abstained from creating in measured language, sculpture, music, or architecture, anything which might bear a particular relation to their own condition, whilst it should bear a general one to the universal constitution of the world. But we judge from partial evidence, and we judge perhaps partially. Ennius, Varro, Pacuvius, and Accius, all great poets, have been lost. Lucretius is in the highest, and Virgil in a very high sense, a creator. The chosen delicacy of expressions of the latter, are as a mist of light which conceal from us the intense and exceeding truth of his conceptions of nature. Livy is instinct with poetry. Yet Horace, Catullus, Ovid, and generally the other great writers of the Virgilian age, saw man and nature in the mirror of Greece. The institutions also, and the religion of Rome were less poetical than those of Greece, as the shadow is less vivid than the substance. Hence poetry in Rome seemed to follow, rather than accompany, the perfection of political and domestic society. The true poetry of Rome lived in its institutions; for whatever of beautiful, true, and majestic, they contained, could have sprung only from the faculty which creates the order in which they consist. The life of Camillus, the death of Regulus; the expectation of the senators, in their godlike state, of the victorious Gauls: the refusal of the republic to make peace with Hannibal, after the battle of Cannae, were not the consequences of a refined calculation of the probable personal advantage to result from such a rhythm and order in the shows of life, to those who were at once the poets and the actors of these immortal dramas. The imagination beholding the beauty of this order, created it out of itself according to its own idea; the consequence was empire, and the reward everliving fame. These things are not the less poetry *quia carent vate sacro*. They are the episodes of that cyclic poem written by Time upon the memories of men. The Past, like an inspired rhapsodist, fills the theatre of everlasting generations with their harmony.

At length the ancient system of religion and manners had fulfilled the circle of its revolutions. And the world would have fallen into utter anarchy and darkness, but that there were found poets among the authors of the Christian and chivalric systems of manners and religion, who created forms of opinion and action never before conceived; which, copied into the imaginations of men, become as generals to the bewildered armies of their thoughts. It is foreign to the present purpose to touch upon the evil produced by these systems: except that we protest, on the ground of the principles already established, that no portion of it can be attributed to the poetry they contain.

It is probable that the poetry of Moses, Job, David, Solomon, and Isaiah, had produced a great effect upon the mind of Jesus and his disciples. The scattered fragments preserved to us by the biographers of this extraordinary person, are all instinct with the most vivid poetry. But his doctrines seem to have been quickly distorted. At a certain period after the prevalence of a system of opinions founded upon those promulgated by him, the three forms into which Plato had distributed the faculties of mind underwent a sort of apotheosis, and became the object of the worship of the civilized world. Here it is to be confessed that 'Light seems to thicken', and

> The crow makes wing to the rooky wood,
> Good things of day begin to droop and drowse,
> And night's black agents to their preys do rouse.

But mark how beautiful an order has sprung from the dust and blood of this fierce chaos! how the world, as from a resurrection, balancing itself on the golden wings of knowledge and of hope, has reassumed its yet unwearied flight into the heaven of time. Listen to the music, unheard by outward ears, which is as a ceaseless and invisible wind, nourishing its everlasting course with strength and swiftness.

The poetry in the doctrines of Jesus Christ, and the mythology and institutions of the Celtic conquerors of the Roman empire, outlived the darkness and the convulsions connected with their growth and victory, and blended themselves in a new fabric of manners and opinion. It is an error to impute the ignorance of the dark ages to the Christian doctrines or the predominance of the Celtic nations. Whatever of evil their agencies may have contained sprang from the extinction of the poetical principle, connected with the progress of despotism and superstition. Men, from causes too intricate to be here discussed, had become insensible and selfish: their own will had become feeble, and yet they were its slaves, and thence the slaves of the will of others; lust, fear, avarice, cruelty, and fraud, characterized a race amongst whom no one was to be found capable of *creating* in form, language, or institution. The moral anomalies of such a state of society are not justly to be charged upon any class of events immediately connected with them, and those events are most entitled to our approbation which could dissolve it most expeditiously. It is unfortunate for those who cannot distinguish words from thoughts, that many of these anomalies have been incorporated into our popular religion.

It was not until the eleventh century that the effects of the poetry of the Christian and chivalric systems began to manifest themselves. The principle of equality had been discovered and applied by Plato in his *Republic*, as the theoretical rule of the mode in which the materials of pleasure and of power, produced by the common skill and labour of human beings, ought to be distributed among them. The limitations of this rule were asserted by him to be determined only by the sensibility of each, or the utility to result to all. Plato, following the doctrines of Timaeus and Pythagoras, taught also a moral and intellectual system of doctrine, comprehending at once the past, the present, and the future condition of man. Jesus Christ divulged the sacred and eternal truths contained in these views to mankind, and Christianity, in its abstract purity, became the exoteric expression of the esoteric doctrines of the poetry and wisdom of antiquity. The incorporation of the Celtic nations with the exhausted population of the south, impressed upon it the figure of the poetry existing in their mythology and institutions. The result was a sum of the action and reaction of all the causes included in it; for it may be assumed as a maxim that no nation or religion can supersede any other without incorporating into itself a portion of that which it supersedes. The abolition of personal and domestic slavery, and the emancipation of women from a great part of the degrading restraints of antiquity, were among the consequences of these events.

The abolition of personal slavery is the basis of the highest political hope that it can enter into the mind of man to conceive. The freedom of women produced the poetry of sexual love. Love became a religion, the idols of whose worship were ever present. It was as if the statues of Apollo and the Muses had been endowed with life and motion, and had walked forth among their worshippers; so that earth became peopled by the inhabitants of a diviner world. The familiar appearance and proceedings of life became wonderful and heavenly, and a paradise was created as out of the wrecks of Eden. And as this creation itself is poetry, so its creators were poets; and language was the instrument of their art: 'Galeotto fù il libro, e chi lo scrisse.' The Provençal Trouveurs, or inventors, preceded Petrarch, whose verses are as spells, which unseal the inmost enchanted fountains of the delight which is in the grief of love. It is impossible to feel them without becoming a portion of that beauty which we contemplate: it were superfluous to explain how the gentleness and the elevation of mind connected with these sacred emotions can render men more amiable, more generous and wise, and lift them out of the dull vapours of the little world of self. Dante understood the secret things of love even more than Petrarch. His *Vita Nuova* is an inexhaustible fountain of purity of sentiment and language: it is the idealized history of that period, and those intervals of his life which were dedicated to love. His apotheosis of Beatrice in Paradise, and the gradations of his own love and her loveliness, by which as by steps he feigns himself to have ascended to the throne of the Supreme Cause, is the most glorious imagination of modern poetry. The acutest critics have justly reversed the judgement of the vulgar, and the order of the great acts of the 'Divine Drama', in the measure of the admiration which they accord to the Hell, Purgatory, and Paradise. The latter is a perpetual hymn of everlasting love. Love, which found a worthy poet in Plato alone of all the ancients, has been celebrated by a chorus of the greatest writers of the renovated world; and the music has penetrated the caverns of society, and its echoes still drown the dissonance of arms and superstition. At successive intervals, Ariosto, Tasso, Shakespeare, Spenser, Calderon, Rousseau, and the great writers of our own age, have celebrated the dominion of love, planting as it were trophies in the human mind of that sublimest victory over sensuality and force. The true relation borne to each other by the sexes into which human kind is distributed, has become less misunderstood; and if the error which confounded diversity with inequality of the powers of the two sexes has been partially recognized in the opinions and institutions of modern Europe, we owe this great benefit to the worship of which chivalry was the law, and poets the prophets.

The poetry of Dante may be considered as the bridge thrown over the stream of time, which unites the modern and ancient world. The distorted notions of invisible things which Dante and his rival Milton have idealized, are merely the mask and the mantle in which these great poets walk through eternity enveloped and disguised. It is a difficult question to determine how far they were conscious of the distinction which must have subsisted in their minds between their own creeds and that of the people. Dante at least appears to wish to mark the full extent of it by placing Riphaeus, whom Virgil calls *iustissimus unus*, in Paradise, and observing a most heretical caprice in his distribution of rewards and punishments. And Milton's poem contains within itself a philosophical refutation of that system, of which, by a strange and natural antithesis, it has been a chief popular support. Nothing can exceed the energy and magnificence of the character of Satan as expressed in *Paradise Lost*. It is a mistake to suppose that he could ever have been intended for the popular personification of evil. Implacable hate, patient cunning, and a sleepless refinement of device to inflict the extremest anguish on an enemy, these things are evil; and, although venial in a slave, are not to be forgiven in a tyrant; although redeemed by much that ennobles his defeat in one subdued, are marked by all that dishonours his conquest in the victor. Milton's Devil as a moral being is as far superior to his God, as one who perseveres in some purpose which he has conceived to be excellent in spite of adversity and torture, is to one who in the cold security of undoubted triumph inflicts the most horrible revenge upon his enemy, not from any mistaken notion of inducing him to repent of a perseverance in enmity, but with the alleged design of exasperating him to deserve new torments. Milton has so far violated the popular creed (if this shall be judged to be a violation) as to have alleged no superiority of moral virtue to his God over his Devil.

And this bold neglect of a direct moral purpose is the most decisive proof of the supremacy of Milton's genius. He mingled as it were the elements of human nature as colours upon a single pallet, and arranged them in the composition of his great picture according to the laws of epic truth; that is, according to the laws of that principle by which a series of actions of the external universe and of intelligent and ethical beings is calculated to excite the sympathy of succeeding generations of mankind. The *Divina Commedia* and *Paradise Lost* have conferred upon modern mythology a systematic form; and when change and time shall have added one more superstition to the mass of those which have arisen and decayed upon the earth, commentators will be learnedly employed in elucidating the religion of ancestral Europe, only not utterly forgotten because it will have been stamped with the eternity of genius.

Homer was the first and Dante the second epic poet: that is, the second poet, the series of whose creations bore a defined and intelligible relation to the knowledge and sentiment and religion of the age in which he lived, and of the ages which followed it: developing itself in correspondence with their development. For Lucretius had limed the wings of his swift spirit in the dregs of the sensible world; and Virgil, with a modesty that ill became his genius, had affected the fame of an imitator, even whilst he created anew all that he copied; and none among the flock of mockbirds, though their notes were sweet, Apollonius Rhodius, Quintus Calaber, Nonnus, Lucan, Statius, or Claudian, have sought even to fulfil a single condition of epic truth. Milton was the third epic poet. For if the title of epic in its highest sense be refused to the *Aeneid*, still less can it be conceded to the *Orlando Furioso*, the *Gerusalemme Liberata*, the *Lusiad*, or the *Faerie Queene*.

Dante and Milton were both deeply penetrated with the ancient religion of the civilized world; and its spirit exists in their poetry probably in the same proportion as its forms survived in the unreformed worship of modern Europe. The one preceded and the other followed the Reformation at almost equal intervals. Dante was the first religious reformer, and Luther surpassed him rather in the rudeness and acrimony, than in the boldness of his censures of papal usurpation. Dante was the first awakener of entranced Europe; he created a language, in itself music and persuasion, out of a chaos of inharmonious barbarisms. He was the congregator of those great spirits who presided over the resurrection of learning; the Lucifer of that starry flock which in the thirteenth century shone forth from republican Italy, as from a heaven, into the darkness of the benighted world. His very words are instinct with spirit; each is as a spark, a burning atom of inextinguishable thought; and many yet lie covered in the ashes of their birth, and pregnant with a lightning which has yet found no conductor. All high poetry is infinite; it is as the first acorn, which contained all oaks potentially. Veil after veil may be undrawn, and the inmost naked beauty of the meaning never exposed. A great poem is a fountain for ever overflowing with the waters of wisdom and delight; and after one person and one age has exhausted all its divine effluence which their peculiar relations enable them to share, another and yet another succeeds, and new relations are ever developed, the source of an unforeseen and an unconceived delight.

The age immediately succeeding to that of Dante, Petrarch, and Boccaccio, was characterized by a revival of painting, sculpture, and architecture. Chaucer caught the sacred inspiration, and the superstructure of English literature is based upon the materials of Italian invention.

But let us not be betrayed from a defence into a critical history of poetry and its influence on society. Be it enough to have pointed out the effects of poets, in the large and true sense of the word, upon their own and all succeeding times.

But poets have been challenged to resign the civic crown to reasoners and mechanists, on another plea. It is admitted that the exercise of the imagination is most delightful, but it is alleged that that of reason is more useful. Let us examine as the grounds of this distinction, what is here meant by utility. Pleasure or good, in a general sense, is that which the consciousness of a sensitive and intelligent being seeks, and in which, when found, it acquiesces. There are two kinds of pleasure, one durable, universal and permanent; the other transitory and particular. Utility may either express the means of producing the former or the latter. In the former sense, whatever strengthens and purifies the affections, enlarges the imagination, and adds spirit to sense, is useful. But a narrower meaning may be assigned to the word utility, confining it to express that which banishes the importunity of the wants of our animal nature, the surrounding men with security of life, the dispersing the grosser delusions of superstition, and the conciliating such a degree of mutual forbearance among men as may consist with the motives of personal advantage.

Undoubtedly the promoters of utility, in this limited sense, have their appointed office in society. They follow the footsteps of poets, and copy the sketches of their creations into the book of common life. They make space and give time. Their exertions are of the highest value, so long as they confine their administration of the concerns of the inferior powers of our nature within the limits due to the superior ones. But whilst the sceptic destroys gross superstitions, let him spare to deface, as some of the French writers have defaced, the eternal truths charactered upon the imaginations of men. Whilst the mechanist abridges, and the political economist combines labour, let them beware that their speculations, for want of correspondence with those first principles which belong to the imagination,

A DEFENCE OF POETRY

do not tend, as they have in modern England, to exasperate at once the extremes of luxury and want. They have exemplified the saying, 'To him that hath, more shall be given; and from him that hath not, the little that he hath shall be taken away.' The rich have become richer, and the poor have become poorer; and the vessel of the state is driven between the Scylla and Charybdis of anarchy and despotism. Such are the effects which must ever flow from an unmitigated exercise of the calculating faculty.

It is difficult to define pleasure in its highest sense; the definition involving a number of apparent paradoxes. For, from an inexplicable defect of harmony in the constitution of human nature, the pain of the inferior is frequently connected with the pleasures of the superior portions of our being. Sorrow, terror, anguish, despair itself, are often the chosen expressions of an approximation to the highest good. Our sympathy in tragic fiction depends on this principle; tragedy delights by affording a shadow of the pleasure which exists in pain. This is the source also of the melancholy which is inseparable from the sweetest melody. The pleasure that is in sorrow is sweeter than the pleasure of pleasure itself. And hence the saying, 'It is better to go to the house of mourning, than to the house of mirth.' Not that this highest species of pleasure is necessarily linked with pain. The delight of love and friendship, the ecstasy of the admiration of nature, the joy of the perception and still more of the creation of poetry, is often wholly unalloyed.

The production and assurance of pleasure in this highest sense is true utility. Those who produce and preserve this pleasure are poets or poetical philosophers.

The exertions of Locke, Hume, Gibbon, Voltaire, Rousseau,[1] and their disciples, in favour of oppressed

---

[1] Although Rousseau has been thus classed, he was essentially a poet. The others, even Voltaire, were mere reasoners.

and deluded humanity, are entitled to the gratitude of mankind. Yet it is easy to calculate the degree of moral and intellectual improvement which the world would have exhibited, had they never lived. A little more nonsense would have been talked for a century or two; and perhaps a few more men, women, and children, burnt as heretics. We might not at this moment have been congratulating each other on the abolition of the Inquisition in Spain. But it exceeds all imagination to conceive what would have been the moral condition of the world if neither Dante, Petrarch, Boccaccio, Chaucer, Shakespeare, Calderon, Lord Bacon, nor Milton, had ever existed; if Raphael and Michael Angelo had never been born; if the Hebrew poetry had never been translated; if a revival of the study of Greek literature had never taken place; if no monuments of ancient sculpture had been handed down to us; and if the poetry of the religion of the ancient world had been extinguished together with its belief. The human mind could never, except by the intervention of these excitements, have been awakened to the invention of the grosser sciences, and that application of analytical reasoning to the aberrations of society, which it is now attempted to exalt over the direct expression of the inventive and creative faculty itself.

We have more moral, political and historical wisdom, than we know how to reduce into practice; we have more scientific and economical knowledge than can be accommodated to the just distribution of the produce which it multiplies. The poetry in these systems of thought, is concealed by the accumulation of facts and calculating processes. There is no want of knowledge respecting what is wisest and best in morals, government, and political economy, or at least, what is wiser and better than what men now practise and endure. But we let '*I dare not* wait upon *I would*, like the poor cat in the adage.' We want the creative faculty to imagine that which we know; we want the generous impulse to act that which we imagine; we want the poetry of life: our calculations have outrun conception; we have eaten more than we can digest. The cultivation of those sciences which have enlarged the limits of the empire of man over the external world, has, for want of the poetical faculty, proportionally circumscribed those of the internal world; and man, having enslaved the elements, remains himself a slave. To what but a cultivation of the mechanical arts in a degree disproportioned to the presence of the creative faculty, which is the basis of all knowledge, is to be attributed the abuse of all invention for abridging and combining labour, to the exasperation of the inequality of mankind? From what other cause has it arisen that the discoveries which should have lightened, have added a weight to the curse imposed on Adam? Poetry, and the principle of Self, of which money is the visible incarnation, are the God and Mammon of the world.

The functions of the poetical faculty are twofold; by one it creates new materials of knowledge and power and pleasure; by the other it engenders in the mind a desire to reproduce and arrange them according to a certain rhythm and order which may be called the beautiful and the good. The cultivation of poetry is never more to be desired than at periods when, from an excess of the selfish and calculating principle, the accumulation of the materials of external life exceed the quantity of the power of assimilating them to the internal laws of human nature. The body has then become too unwieldy for that which animates it.

Poetry is indeed something divine. It is at once the centre and circumference of knowledge; it is that which comprehends all science, and that to which all science must be referred. It is at the same time the root and blossom of all other systems of thought; it is that from which all spring, and that which adorns all; and that which, if blighted, denies the fruit and the seed, and withholds from the barren world the nourishment and the succession of the scions of the tree of life. It is the perfect and consummate surface and bloom of all things: it is as the odour and the colour of the rose to the texture of the elements which compose it, as the form and splendour of unfaded beauty to the secrets of anatomy and corruption. What were virtue, love, patriotism, friendship—what were the scenery of this beautiful universe which we inhabit; what were our consolations on this side of the grave—and what were our aspirations beyond it, if poetry did not ascend to bring light and fire from those eternal regions where the owl-winged faculty of calculation dare not ever soar? Poetry is not like reasoning, a power to be exerted according to the determination of the will. A man cannot say, 'I will compose poetry.' The greatest poet even cannot say it; for the mind in creation is as a fading coal, which some invisible influence, like an inconstant wind, awakens to transitory brightness; this power arises from within, like the colour of a flower which fades and changes as it is developed, and the conscious portions of our natures are unprophetic either of its approach or its departure. Could this influence be durable in its original purity and force, it is impossible to predict the greatness of the results; but when composition begins, inspiration is already on the decline, and the most glorious poetry that has ever been communicated to the world is probably a feeble shadow of the original conceptions of the poet. I appeal to the greatest poets of the present day, whether it is not an error to assert that the finest passages of poetry are produced by labour and study. The toil and the delay recommended by critics can be justly interpreted to mean no more than a careful observation of the inspired moments, and an artificial connexion of the spaces between their suggestions by the intertexture of conventional expressions; a necessity only imposed by the limitedness of the poetical faculty itself; for

Milton conceived the *Paradise Lost* as a whole before he executed it in portions. We have his own authority also for the muse having 'dictated' to him the 'unpremeditated song'. And let this be an answer to those who would allege the fifty-six various readings of the first line of the *Orlando Furioso*. Compositions so produced are to poetry what mosaic is to painting. This instinct and intuition of the poetical faculty is still more observable in the plastic and pictorial arts; a great statue or picture grows under the power of the artist as a child in the mother's womb; and the very mind which directs the hands in formation is incapable of accounting to itself for the origin, the gradations, or the media of the process.

Poetry is the record of the best and happiest moments of the happiest and best minds. We are aware of evanescent visitations of thought and feeling sometimes associated with place or person, sometimes regarding our own mind alone, and always arising unforeseen and departing unbidden, but elevating and delightful beyond all expression: so that even in the desire and regret they leave, there cannot but be pleasure, participating as it does in the nature of its object. It is as it were the interpenetration of a diviner nature through our own; but its footsteps are like those of a wind over the sea, which the coming calm erases, and whose traces remain only, as on the wrinkled sand which paves it. These and corresponding conditions of being are experienced principally by those of the most delicate sensibility and the most enlarged imagination; and the state of mind produced by them is at war with every base desire. The enthusiasm of virtue, love, patriotism, and friendship, is essentially linked with such emotions; and whilst they last, self appears as what it is, an atom to a universe. Poets are not only subject to these experiences as spirits of the most refined organization, but they can colour all that they combine with the evanescent hues of this ethereal world; a word, a trait in the representation of a scene or a passion, will touch the enchanted chord, and reanimate, in those who have ever experienced these emotions, the sleeping, the cold, the buried image of the past. Poetry thus makes immortal all that is best and most beautiful in the world; it arrests the vanishing apparitions which haunt the interlunations of life, and veiling them, or in language or in form, sends them forth among mankind, bearing sweet news of kindred joy to those with whom their sisters abide—abide, because there is no portal of expression from the caverns of the spirit which they inhabit into the universe of things. Poetry redeems from decay the visitations of the divinity in man.

Poetry turns all things to loveliness; it exalts the beauty of that which is most beautiful, and it adds beauty to that which is most deformed; it marries exultation and horror, grief and pleasure, eternity and change; it subdues to union under its light yoke all irreconcilable things. It transmutes all that it touches, and every form moving within the radiance of its presence is changed by wondrous sympathy to an incarnation of the spirit which it breathes: its secret alchemy turns to potable gold the poisonous waters which flow from death through life; it strips the veil of familiarity from the world, and lays bare the naked and sleeping beauty, which is the spirit of its forms.

All things exist as they are perceived; at least in relation to the percipient. 'The mind is its own place, and of itself can make a heaven of hell, a hell of heaven.' But poetry defeats the curse which binds us to be subjected to the accident of surrounding impressions. And whether it spreads its own figured curtain, or withdraws life's dark veil from before the scene of things, it equally creates for us a being within our being. It makes us the inhabitants of a world to which the familiar world is a chaos. It reproduces the common universe of which we are portions and percipients, and it purges from our inward sight the film of familiarity which obscures from us the wonder of our being. It compels us to feel that which we perceive, and to imagine that which we know. It creates anew the universe, after it has been annihilated in our minds by the recurrence of impressions blunted by reiteration. It justifies the bold and true words of Tasso: *Non merita nome di creatore, se non Iddio ed il Poeta.*

A poet, as he is the author to others of the highest wisdom, pleasure, virtue and glory, so he ought personally to be the happiest, the best, the wisest, and the most illustrious of men. As to his glory, let time be challenged to declare whether the fame of any other institutor of human life be comparable to that of a poet. That he is the wisest, the happiest, and the best, inasmuch as he is a poet, is equally incontrovertible: the greatest poets have been men of the most spotless virtue, of the most consummate prudence, and, if we would look into the interior of their lives, the most fortunate of men: and the exceptions, as they regard those who possessed the poetic faculty in a high yet inferior degree, will be found on consideration to confine rather than destroy the rule. Let us for a moment stoop to the arbitration of popular breath, and usurping and uniting in our own persons the incompatible characters of accuser, witness, judge, and executioner, let us decide without trial, testimony, or form, that certain motives of those who are 'there sitting where we dare not soar', are reprehensible. Let us assume that Homer was a drunkard, that Virgil was a flatterer, that Horace was a coward, that Tasso was a madman, that Lord Bacon was a peculator, that Raphael was a libertine, that Spenser was a poet laureate. It is inconsistent with this division of our subject to cite living poets, but posterity has done ample justice to the great names now referred to. Their errors have been weighed and found to have been dust in the balance; if their sins 'were as scarlet, they are now white as snow': they have been washed in the blood of the mediator and redeemer, Time. Observe in what a ludicrous chaos the imputations of real or fictitious crime have been confused in the contemporary calumnies against poetry and poets; consider how little is, as it appears —or appears, as it is; look to your own motives, and judge not, lest ye be judged.

Poetry, as has been said, differs in this respect from logic, that it is not subject to the control of the active powers of the mind, and that its birth and recurrence have no necessary connexion with the consciousness or will. It is presumptuous to determine that these are the necessary conditions of all mental causation, when mental effects are experienced unsusceptible of being referred to them. The frequent recurrence of the poetical power, it is obvious to suppose, may produce in the mind a habit of order and harmony correlative with its own nature and with its effects upon other minds. But in the intervals of inspiration, and they may be frequent without being durable, a poet becomes a man, and is abandoned to the sudden reflux of the influences under which others habitually live. But as he is more delicately organized than other men, and sensible to pain and pleasure, both his own and that of others, in a degree unknown to them, he will avoid the one and pursue the other with an ardour proportioned to this difference. And he renders himself obnoxious to calumny, when he neglects to observe the circumstances under which these objects of universal pursuit and flight have disguised themselves in one another's garments.

But there is nothing necessarily evil in this error, and thus cruelty, envy, revenge, avarice, and the passions purely evil, have never formed any portion of the popular imputations on the lives of poets.

I have thought it most favourable to the cause of truth to set down these remarks according to the order in which they were suggested to my mind, by a consideration of the subject itself, instead of observing the formality of a polemical reply; but if the view which they contain be just, they will be found to involve a refutation of the arguers against poetry, so far at least as regards the first division of the subject. I can readily conjecture what should have moved the gall of some learned and intelligent writers who quarrel with certain versifiers; I confess myself, like them, unwilling to be stunned by the Theseids of the hoarse Codri of the day. Bavius and Maevius undoubtedly are, as they ever were, insufferable persons. But it belongs to a philosophical critic to distinguish rather than confound.

The first part of these remarks has related to poetry in its elements and principles; and it has been shown, as well as the narrow limits assigned them would permit, that what is called poetry, in a restricted sense, has a common source with all other forms of order and of beauty, according to which the materials of human life are susceptible of being arranged, and which is poetry in a universal sense.

The second part[1] will have for its object an application of these principles to the present state of the cultivation of poetry, and a defence of the attempt to idealize the modern forms of manners and opinions, and compel them into a subordination to the imaginative and creative faculty. For the literature of England, an energetic development of which has ever preceded or accompanied a great and free development of the national will, has arisen as it were from a new birth. In spite of the low-thoughted envy which would undervalue contemporary merit, our own will be a memorable age in intellectual achievements, and we live among such philosophers and poets as surpass beyond comparison any who have appeared since the last national struggle for civil and religious liberty. The most unfailing herald, companion, and follower of the awakening of a great people to work a beneficial change in opinion or institution, is poetry. At such periods there is an accumulation of the power of communicating and receiving intense and impassioned conceptions respecting man and nature. The

[1] This was never written.

persons in whom this power resides may often, as far as regards many portions of their nature, have little apparent correspondence with that spirit of good of which they are the ministers. But even whilst they deny and abjure, they are yet compelled to serve, the power which is seated on the throne of their own soul. It is impossible to read the compositions of the most celebrated writers of the present day without being startled with the electric life which burns within their words. They measure the circumference and sound the depths of human nature with a comprehensive and all-penetrating spirit, and they are themselves perhaps the most sincerely astonished at its manifestations; for it is less their spirit than the spirit of the age. Poets are the hierophants of an unapprehended inspiration; the mirrors of the gigantic shadows which futurity casts upon the present; the words which express what they understand not; the trumpets which sing to battle, and feel not what they inspire; the influence which is moved not, but moves. Poets are the unacknowledged legislators of the world.

WILLIAM HAZLITT
1778–1830
MY FIRST ACQUAINTANCE WITH POETS
[From *The Liberal*, No. III, April 1823]

MY father was a Dissenting Minister at Wem in Shropshire; and in the year 1798 (the figures that compose the date are to me like the 'dreaded name of Demogorgon') Mr. Coleridge came to Shrewsbury, to succeed Mr. Rowe in the spiritual charge of a Unitarian congregation there. He did not come till late on the Saturday afternoon before he was to preach; and Mr. Rowe, who himself went down to the coach in a state of anxiety and expectation to look for the arrival of his successor, could find no one at all answering the description but a round-faced man in a short black coat (like a shooting-jacket) which hardly seemed to have been made for him, but who seemed to be talking at a great rate to his fellow-passengers. Mr. Rowe had scarce returned to give an account of his disappointment, when the round-faced man in black entered, and dissipated all doubts on the subject, by beginning to talk. He did not cease while he stayed; nor has he since, that I know of. He held the good town of Shrewsbury in delightful suspense for three weeks that he remained there, 'fluttering the *proud Salopians* like an eagle in a dove-cote'; and the Welsh mountains that skirt the horizon with their tempestuous confusion, agree to have heard no such mystic sounds since the days of

> High-born Hoel's harp or soft Llewelyn's lay!

As we passed along between Wem and Shrewsbury, and I eyed their blue tops seen through the wintry branches, or the red rustling leaves of the sturdy oak-trees by the road-side, a sound was in my ears as of a

Siren's song; I was stunned, startled with it, as from deep sleep; but I had no notion then that I should ever be able to express my admiration to others in motley imagery or quaint allusion, till the light of his genius shone into my soul, like the sun's rays glittering in the puddles of the road. I was at that time dumb, inarticulate, helpless, like a worm by the wayside, crushed, bleeding, lifeless; but now, bursting from the deadly bands that 'bound them,

> With Styx nine times round them,'

my ideas float on winged words, and as they expand their plumes, catch the golden light of other years. My soul has indeed remained in its original bondage, dark, obscure, with longings infinite and unsatisfied; my heart, shut up in the prison-house of this rude clay, has never found, nor will it ever find, a heart to speak to; but that my understanding also did not remain dumb and brutish, or at length found a language to express itself, I owe to Coleridge. But this is not to my purpose.

My father lived ten miles from Shrewsbury, and was in the habit of exchanging visits with Mr. Rowe, and with Mr. Jenkins of Whitchurch (nine miles farther on) according to the custom of Dissenting Ministers in each other's neighbourhood. A line of communication is thus established, by which the flame of civil and religious liberty is kept alive, and nourishes its smouldering fire unquenchable, like the fires in the *Agamemnon* of Aeschylus, placed at different stations, that waited for ten long years to announce with their blazing pyramids the destruction of Troy. Coleridge had agreed to come over to see my father, according to the courtesy of the country, as Mr. Rowe's probable successor; but in the meantime I had gone to hear him preach the Sunday after his arrival. A poet and a philosopher getting up into a Unitarian pulpit to preach the Gospel, was a romance in these degenerate days, a sort of revival of the primitive spirit of Christianity, which was not to be resisted.

It was in January, 1798, that I rose one morning before daylight, to walk ten miles in the mud, to hear this celebrated person preach. Never, the longest day I have to live, shall I have such another walk as this cold, raw, comfortless one, in the winter of the year 1798. *Il y a des impressions que ni le temps ni les circonstances peuvent effacer. Dussé-je vivre des siècles entiers, le doux temps de ma jeunesse ne peut renaître pour moi, ni s'effacer jamais dans ma mémoire.* When I got there, the organ was playing the 100th psalm, and, when it was done, Mr. Coleridge rose and gave out his text, 'And he went up into the mountain to pray, HIMSELF, ALONE.' As he gave out this text, his voice 'rose like a steam of rich distilled perfumes,' and when he came to the two last words, which he pronounced loud, deep, and distinct, it seemed to me, who was then young, as if the sounds had echoed from the bottom of the human heart, and as if that prayer might have floated in solemn silence through the universe. The idea of St. John came into mind, 'of one crying in the wilderness, who had his loins girt about, and whose food was locusts and wild honey.' The preacher then launched into his subject, like an eagle dallying with the wind. The sermon was upon peace and war; upon church and state—not their alliance, but their separation—on the spirit of the world and the spirit of Christianity, not as the same, but as opposed to one another. He talked of those who had 'inscribed the cross of Christ on banners dripping with human gore.' He made a poetical and pastoral excursion,—and to show the fatal effects of war, drew a striking contrast between the simple shepherd boy, driving his team afield, or sitting under the hawthorn, piping to his flock, 'as though he should never be old,' and the same poor country-lad, crimped, kidnapped, brought into town, made drunk at an alehouse, turned into a wretched drummer-boy, with his hair sticking on end with powder and pomatum, a long cue at his back, and tricked out in the loathsome finery of the profession of blood.

Such were the notes our once-lov'd poet sung.

And for myself, I could not have been more delighted if I had heard the music of the spheres. Poetry and Philosophy had met together, Truth and Genius had embraced, under the eye and with the sanction of Religion. This was even beyond my hopes. I returned home well satisfied. The sun that was still labouring pale and wan through the sky, obscured by thick mists, seemed an emblem of the *good cause*; and the cold dank drops of dew that hung half-melted on the beard of the thistle, had something genial and refreshing in them; for there was a spirit of hope and youth in all nature, that turned everything into good. The face of nature had not then the brand of JUS DIVINUM on it:

Like to that sanguine flower inscrib'd with woe.

On the Tuesday following, the half-inspired speaker came. I was called down into the room where he was, and went half-hoping, half-afraid. He received me very graciously, and I listened for a long time without uttering a word. I did not suffer in his opinion by my silence. 'For those two hours,' he afterwards was pleased to say, 'he was conversing with W. H.'s forehead!' His appearance was different from what I had anticipated from seeing him before. At a distance, and in the dim light of the chapel, there was to me a strange wildness in his aspect, a dusky obscurity, and I thought him pitted with the smallpox. His complexion was at that time clear, and even bright—

As are the children of yon azure sheen.

His forehead was broad and high, light as if built of ivory, with large projecting eyebrows, and his eyes rolling beneath them like a sea with darkened lustre.

'A certain tender bloom his face o'erspread,' a purple tinge as we see it in the pale thoughtful complexions of the Spanish portrait-painters, Murillo and Velasquez. His mouth was gross, voluptuous, open, eloquent; his chin good-humoured and round; but his nose, the rudder of the face, the index of the will, was small, feeble, nothing—like what he has done. It might seem that the genius of his face as from a height surveyed and projected him (with sufficient capacity and huge aspiration) into the world unknown of thought and imagination, with nothing to support or guide his veering purpose, as if Columbus had launched his adventurous course for the New World in a scallop, without oars or compass. So at least I comment on it after the event. Coleridge in his person was rather above the common size, inclining to the corpulent, or like Lord Hamlet, 'somewhat fat and pursy.' His hair (now, alas! grey) was then black and glossy as the raven's, and fell in smooth masses over his forehead. This long pendulous hair is peculiar to enthusiasts, to those whose minds tend heavenward; and is traditionally inseparable (though of a different colour) from the pictures of Christ. It ought to belong, as a character to all who preach *Christ crucified*, and Coleridge was at that time one of those!

It was curious to observe the contrast between him and my father, who was a veteran in the cause, and then declining into the vale of years. He had been a poor Irish lad, carefully brought up by his parents, and sent to the University of Glasgow (where he studied under Adam Smith) to prepare him for his future destination. It was his mother's proudest wish to see her son a Dissenting Minister. So if we look back to past generations (as far as eye can reach) we see the same hopes, fears, wishes, followed by the same disappointments, throbbing in the human heart; and so we may see them (if we look forward) rising up for ever, and disappearing, like vapourish bubbles, in the human breast! After being tossed about from congregation to congregation in the heats of the Unitarian controversy, and squabbles about the American war, he had been relegated to an obscure village, where he was to spend the last thirty years of his life, far from the only converse that he loved, the talk about disputed texts of Scripture and the cause of civil and religious liberty. Here he passed his days, repining but resigned, in the study of the Bible, and the perusal of the Commentators—huge folios, not easily got through, one of which would outlast a winter! Why did he pore on these from morn to night (with the exception of a walk in the fields or a turn in the garden to gather broccoli-plants or kidney-beans of his own rearing, with no small degree of pride and pleasure)?—Here were 'no figures nor no fantasies,'—neither poetry nor philosophy—nothing to dazzle, nothing to excite modern curiosity; but to his lack-lustre eyes there appeared, within the pages of the ponderous, unwieldy, neglected tomes, the sacred name of JEHOVAH in Hebrew capitals: pressed down by the weight of the style, worn to the last fading thinness of the understanding, there were glimpses, glimmering notions of the patriarchal wanderings, with palm-trees hovering in the horizon, and processions of camels at the distance of three thousand years; there was Moses with the Burning Bush, the number of the Twelve Tribes, types, shadows, glosses on the law and the prophets; there were discussions (dull enough) on the age of Methuselah, a mighty speculation! there were outlines, rude guesses at the shape of Noah's Ark and at the riches of Solomon's Temple; questions as to the date of the creation, predictions of the end of all things; the great lapses of time, the strange mutations of the globe were unfolded with the voluminous leaf, as it turned over; and though the soul might slumber with an hieroglyphic veil of inscrutable mysteries drawn over it, yet it was in a slumber ill-exchanged for all the sharpened realities of sense, wit, fancy, or reason. My father's life was

MY FIRST ACQUAINTANCE WITH POETS

comparatively a dream; but it was a dream of infinity and eternity, of death, the resurrection, and a judgement to come!

No two individuals were ever more unlike than were the host and his guest. A poet was to my father a sort of nondescript: yet whatever added grace to the Unitarian cause was to him welcome. He could hardly have been more surprised or pleased, if our visitor had worn wings. Indeed, his thoughts had wings; and as the silken sounds rustled round our little wainscoted parlour, my father threw back his spectacles over his forehead, his white hairs mixing with its sanguine hue; and a smile of delight beamed across his rugged cordial face, to think that Truth had found a new ally in Fancy![1] Besides, Coleridge seemed to take considerable notice of me, and that of itself was enough. He talked very familiarly, but agreeably, and glanced over a variety of subjects. At dinner-time he grew more animated, and dilated in a very edifying manner on Mary Wollstonecraft and Mackintosh. The last, he said, he considered (on my father's speaking of his *Vindiciae Gallicae* as a capital performance) as a clever scholastic man—a master of the topics,—or as the ready warehouseman of letters, who knew exactly where to lay his hand on what he wanted, though the goods were not his own. He thought him no match for Burke, either in style or matter. Burke was a metaphysician, Mackintosh a mere logician. Burke was an orator (almost a poet) who reasoned in figures, because he had an eye for nature: Mackintosh, on the other hand, was a rhetorician, who had only an eye to commonplaces. On this I ventured to say that I had always entertained a great

---

[1] My father was one of those who mistook his talent after all. He used to be very much dissatisfied that I preferred his Letters to his Sermons. The last were forced and dry; the first came naturally from him. For ease, half-plays on words, and a supine, monkish, indolent pleasantry, I have never seen them equalled.

opinion of Burke, and that (as far as I could find) the speaking of him with contempt might be made the test of a vulgar democratical mind. This was the first observation I ever made to Coleridge, and he said it was a very just and striking one. I remember the leg of Welsh mutton and the turnips on the table that day had the finest flavour imaginable. Coleridge added that Mackintosh and Tom Wedgwood (of whom, however, he spoke highly) had expressed a very indifferent opinion of his friend Mr. Wordsworth, on which he remarked to them—'He strides on so far before you, that he dwindles in the distance!' Godwin had once boasted to him of having carried on an argument with Mackintosh for three hours with dubious success; Coleridge told him—'If there had been a man of genius in the room he would have settled the question in five minutes.' He asked me if I had ever seen Mary Wollstonecraft, and I said, I had once for a few moments, and that she seemed to me to turn off Godwin's objections to something she advanced with quite a playful, easy air. He replied, that 'this was only one instance of the ascendancy which people of imagination exercised over those of mere intellect.' He did not rate Godwin very high[1] (this was caprice or prejudice, real or affected) but he had a great idea of Mrs. Wollstonecraft's powers of conversation, none at all of her talent for book-making. We talked a little about Holcroft. He had been asked if he was not much struck *with* him, and he said, he thought himself in more danger of being struck *by* him. I complained that he would not let me get on at all, for he required a definition of every the commonest word, exclaiming, 'What do you mean by a *sensation*, Sir? What do you mean by an *idea*?' This, Coleridge said,

[1] He complained in particular of the presumption of his attempting to establish the future immortality of man, 'without' (as he said) 'knowing what Death was or what Life was'—and the tone in which he pronounced these two words seemed to convey a complete image of both.

was barricadoing the road to truth:—it was setting up a turnpike-gate at every step we took. I forget a great number of things, many more than I remember; but the day passed off pleasantly, and the next morning Mr. Coleridge was to return to Shrewsbury. When I came down to breakfast, I found that he had just received a letter from his friend, T. Wedgwood, making him an offer of 150*l.* a year if he chose to waive his present pursuit, and devote himself entirely to the study of poetry and philosophy. Coleridge seemed to make up his mind to close with this proposal in the act of tying on one of his shoes. It threw an additional damp on his departure. It took the wayward enthusiast quite from us to cast him into Deva's winding vales, or by the shores of old romance. Instead of living at ten miles' distance, of being the pastor of a Dissenting congregation at Shrewsbury, he was henceforth to inhabit the Hill of Parnassus, to be a Shepherd on the Delectable Mountains. Alas! I knew not the way thither, and felt very little gratitude for Mr. Wedgwood's bounty. I was presently relieved from this dilemma; for Mr. Coleridge, asking for a pen and ink, and going to a table to write something on a bit of card, advanced towards me with undulating step, and giving me the precious document, said that that was his address, *Mr. Coleridge, Nether-Stowey, Somersetshire*; and that he should be glad to see me there in a few weeks' time, and, if I chose, would come half-way to meet me. I was not less surprised than the shepherd-boy (this simile is to be found in *Cassandra*) when he sees a thunderbolt fall close at his feet. I stammered out my acknowledgements and acceptance of this offer (I thought Mr. Wedgwood's annuity a trifle to it) as well as I could; and this mighty business being settled, the poet-preacher took leave, and I accompanied him six miles on the road. It was a fine morning in the middle of winter, and he talked the whole way. The scholar in Chaucer is described as going
——Sounding on his way.

So Coleridge went on his. In digressing, in dilating, in passing from subject to subject, he appeared to me to float in air, to slide on ice. He told me in confidence (going along) that he should have preached two sermons before he accepted the situation at Shrewsbury, one on Infant Baptism, the other on the Lord's Supper, showing that he could not administer either, which would have effectually disqualified him for the object in view. I observed that he continually crossed me on the way by shifting from one side of the footpath to the other. This struck me as an odd movement; but I did not at that time connect it with any instability of purpose or involuntary change of principle, as I have done since. He seemed unable to keep on in a straight line. He spoke slightingly of Hume (whose Essay on Miracles he said was stolen from an objection started in one of South's Sermons—*Credat Judaeus Apella!*). I was not very much pleased at this account of Hume, for I had just been reading, with infinite relish, that completest of all metaphysical *choke-pears*, his *Treatise on Human Nature*, to which the *Essays*, in point of scholastic subtlety and close reasoning, are mere elegant trifling, light summer-reading. Coleridge even denied the excellence of Hume's general style, which I think betrayed a want of taste or candour. He however made me amends by the manner in which he spoke of Berkeley. He dwelt particularly on his *Essay on Vision* as a masterpiece of analytical reasoning. So it undoubtedly is. He was exceedingly angry with Dr. Johnson for striking the stone with his foot, in allusion to this author's Theory of Matter and Spirit, and saying, 'Thus I confute him, Sir.' Coleridge drew a parallel (I don't know how he brought about the connexion) between Bishop Berkeley and Tom Paine. He said the one was an instance of a subtle, the other of an acute mind, than which no two things could be more distinct. The one was a shop-boy's quality, the other the characteristic of a philosopher. He considered Bishop Butler as a true philosopher, a profound and conscientious thinker, a genuine reader of nature and his own mind. He did not speak of his *Analogy*, but of his *Sermons at the Rolls' Chapel*, of which I had never heard. Coleridge somehow always contrived to prefer the *unknown* to the *known*. In this instance he was right. The *Analogy* is a tissue of sophistry, of wire-drawn, theological special-pleading; the *Sermons* (with the Preface to them) are in a fine vein of deep, matured reflection, a candid appeal to our observation of human nature, without pedantry and without bias. I told Coleridge I had written a few remarks, and was sometimes foolish enough to believe that I had made a discovery on the same subject (the *Natural Disinterestedness of the Human Mind*)—and I tried to explain my view of it to Coleridge, who listened with great willingness, but I did not succeed in making myself understood. I sat down to the task shortly afterwards for the twentieth time, got new pens and paper, determined to make clear work of it, wrote a few meagre sentences in the skeleton style of a mathematical demonstration, stopped half-way down the second page; and, after trying in vain to pump up any words, images, notions, apprehensions, facts, or observations, from that gulf of abstraction in which I had plunged myself for four or five years preceding, gave up the attempt as labour in vain, and shed tears of helpless despondency on the blank unfinished paper. I can write fast enough now. Am I better than I was then? Oh no! One truth discovered, one pang of regret at not being able to express it, is better than all the fluency and flippancy in the world. Would that I could go back to what I then was! Why can we not revive past times as we can revisit old places? If I had the quaint Muse of Sir Philip Sidney to assist me, I would write a *Sonnet to the Road between Wem and Shrewsbury*, and immortalize every step of it by some fond enigmatical conceit. I would swear that the very milestones had ears, and that Harmer-hill stooped with all its pines, to listen to a poet, as he passed! I remember but one other topic of discourse in this walk. He mentioned Paley, praised the naturalness and clearness of his style, but condemned his sentiments, thought him a mere time-serving casuist, and said that 'the fact of his work on Moral and Political Philosophy being made a text-book in our Universities was a disgrace to the national character.' We parted at the six-mile stone; and I returned homeward pensive but much pleased. I had met with unexpected notice from a person whom I believed to have been prejudiced against me. 'Kind and affable to me had been his condescension, and should be honoured ever with suitable regard.' He was the first poet I had known, and he certainly answered to that inspired name. I had heard a great deal of his powers of conversation, and was not disappointed. In fact, I never met with any thing at all like them, either before or since. I could easily credit the accounts which were circulated of his holding forth to a large party of ladies and gentlemen, an evening or two before, on the Berkeleian Theory, when he made the whole material universe look like a transparency of fine words; and another story (which I believe he has somewhere told himself) of his being asked to a party at Birmingham, of his smoking tobacco and going to sleep after dinner on a sofa, where the company found him to their no small surprise, which was increased to wonder when he started up of a sudden, and rubbing his eyes, looked about him, and launched into a three hours' description of the third heaven, of which he had had a dream, very different from Mr. Southey's Vision of Judgement, and also from that other Vision of Judgement, which Mr. Murray, the Secretary of the Bridge Street Junto, has taken into his especial keeping.

On my way back, I had a sound in my ears, it was the voice of Fancy: I had a light before me, it was the face of Poetry. The one still lingers there, the other has not quitted my side! Coleridge in truth met me half-way on the ground of philosophy, or I should not have been won over to his imaginative creed. I had an uneasy, pleasurable sensation all the time, till I was to visit him. During those months the chill breath of winter gave me a welcoming; the vernal air was balm and inspiration to me. The golden sunsets, the silver star of evening, lighted me on my way to new hopes and prospects. *I was to visit Coleridge in the Spring.* This circumstance was never absent from my thoughts, and mingled with all my feelings. I wrote to him at the time proposed, and received an answer postponing my intended visit for a week or two, but very cordially urging me to complete my promise then. This delay did not damp, but rather increase my ardour. In the meantime I went to Llangollen Vale, by way of initiating myself in the mysteries of natural scenery; and I must say I was enchanted with it. I had been reading Coleridge's description of England, in his fine *Ode on the Departing Year,* and I applied it, *con amore,* to the objects before me. That valley was to me (in a manner) the cradle of a new existence: in the river that winds through it, my spirit was baptized in the waters of Helicon!

I returned home, and soon after set out on my journey with unworn heart and untried feet. My way lay through Worcester and Gloucester, and by Upton, where I thought of Tom Jones and the adventure of the muff. I remember getting completely wet through one day, and stopping at an inn (I think it was at Tewkesbury) where I sat up all night to read *Paul and Virginia.* Sweet were the showers in early youth that drenched my body, and sweet the drops of pity that fell upon the books I read! I recollect a remark of Coleridge's upon this very book, that nothing could show the gross indelicacy of French manners and the entire corruption of their imagination more strongly than the behaviour of the heroine in the last fatal scene, who turns away from a person on board the sinking vessel, that offers to save her life, because he has thrown off his clothes to assist him in swimming. Was this a time to think of such a circumstance? I once hinted to Wordsworth, as we were sailing in his boat on Grasmere lake, that I thought he had borrowed the idea of his *Poems on the Naming of Places* from the local inscriptions of the same kind in *Paul and Virginia*. He did not own the obligation, and stated some distinction without a difference, in defence of his claim to originality. And the slightest variation would be sufficient for this purpose in his mind; for whatever *he* added or omitted would inevitably be worth all that any one else had done, and contain the marrow of the sentiment.—I was still two days before the time fixed for my arrival, for I had taken care to set out early enough. I stopped these two days at Bridgewater, and when I was tired of sauntering on the banks of its muddy river, returned to the inn, and read *Camilla*. So have I loitered my life away, reading books, looking at pictures, going to plays, hearing, thinking, writing on what pleased me best. I have wanted only one thing to make me happy; but wanting that, have wanted everything!

I arrived, and was well received. The country about Nether Stowey is beautiful, green and hilly, and near the sea-shore. I saw it but the other day, after an interval of twenty years, from a hill near Taunton. How was the map of my life spread out before me, as the map of the country lay at my feet! In the afternoon, Coleridge took me over to All-Foxden, a romantic old family mansion of the St. Aubins, where Wordsworth lived. It was then in the possession of a friend of the poet's, who gave him the free use of it. Somehow that period (the time just after the French Revolution) was not a time when *nothing was given for nothing*. The mind opened, and a softness might be perceived coming over the heart of individuals, beneath 'the scales that fence' our self-interest. Wordsworth himself was from home, but his sister kept house, and set before us a frugal repast; and we had free access to her brother's poems, the *Lyrical Ballads*, which were still in manuscript, or in the form of *Sibylline Leaves*. I dipped into a few of these with great satisfaction, and with the faith of a novice. I slept that night in an old room with blue hangings, and covered with the round-faced family-portraits of the age of George I and II, and from the wooded declivity of the adjoining park that overlooked my window, at the dawn of day, could

———hear the loud stag speak.

In the outset of life (and particularly at this time I felt it so) our imagination has a body to it. We are in a state between sleeping and waking, and have indistinct but glorious glimpses of strange shapes, and there is always something to come better than what we see. As in our dreams the fullness of the blood gives warmth and reality to the coinage of the brain, so in youth our ideas are clothed, and fed, and pampered with our good spirits; we breathe thick with thoughtless happiness, the weight of future years presses on the strong pulses of the heart, and we repose with undisturbed faith in truth and good. As we advance, we exhaust our fund of enjoyment and of hope. We are no longer wrapped in *lamb's-wool*, lulled in Elysium. As we taste the pleasures of life, their spirit evaporates, the sense palls; and nothing is left but the phantoms, the lifeless shadows of what *has been*!

That morning, as soon as breakfast was over, we strolled out into the park, and seating ourselves on the trunk of an old ash-tree that stretched along the ground, Coleridge read aloud with a sonorous and musical voice, the ballad of *Betty Foy*. I was not critically or sceptically inclined. I saw touches of truth and nature, and took the rest for granted. But in the *Thorn*, the *Mad Mother*, and the *Complaint of a Poor Indian Woman*, I felt that deeper power and pathos which have been since acknowledged,

In spite of pride, in erring reason's spite,

as the characteristics of this author; and the sense of a new style and a new spirit in poetry came over me. It had to me something of the effect that arises from the turning up of the fresh soil, or of the first welcome breath of Spring,

> While yet the trembling year is unconfirmed.

Coleridge and myself walked back to Stowey that evening, and his voice sounded high

> Of Providence, foreknowledge, will, and fate,
> Fix'd fate, free-will, foreknowledge absolute,

as we passed through echoing grove, by fairy stream or waterfall, gleaming in the summer moonlight! He lamented that Wordsworth was not prone enough to believe in the traditional superstitions of the place, and that there was a something corporeal, a *matter-of-fact-ness*, a clinging to the palpable, or often to the petty, in his poetry, in consequence. His genius was not a spirit that descended to him through the air; it sprung out of the ground like a flower, or unfolded itself from a green spray, on which the goldfinch sang. He said, however (if I remember right), that this objection must be confined to his descriptive pieces, that his philosophic poetry had a grand and comprehensive spirit in it, so that his soul seemed to inhabit the universe like a palace, and to discover truth by intuition, rather than by deduction. The next day Wordsworth arrived from Bristol at Coleridge's cottage. I think I see him now. He answered in some degree to his friend's description of him, but was more gaunt and Don Quixote-like. He was quaintly dressed (according to the *costume* of that unconstrained period) in a brown fustian jacket and striped pantaloons. There was something of a roll, a lounge in his gait, not unlike his own Peter Bell. There was a severe, worn pressure of thought about his temples, a fire in his eye (as if he saw something in objects more than the outward appearance), an intense high narrow forehead, a Roman nose, cheeks furrowed by strong purpose and feeling, and a convulsive inclination to laughter about the mouth, a good deal at variance with the solemn, stately expression of the rest of his face. Chantrey's bust wants the marking traits; but he was teased into making it regular and heavy: Haydon's head of him, introduced into the *Entrance of Christ into Jerusalem*, is the most like his drooping weight of thought and expression. He sat down and talked very naturally and freely, with a mixture of clear gushing accents in his voice, a deep gutteral intonation, and a strong tincture of the northern *burr*, like the crust on wine. He instantly began to make havoc of the half of a Cheshire cheese on the table, and said triumphantly that 'his marriage with experience had not been so productive as Mr. Southey's in teaching him a knowledge of the good things of this life.' He had been to see the *Castle Spectre* by Monk Lewis, while at Bristol, and described it very well. He said 'it fitted the taste of the audience like a glove.' This *ad captandum* merit was, however, by no means a recommendation of it, according to the severe principles of the new school, which reject rather than court popular effect. Wordsworth, looking out of the low, latticed window, said, 'How beautifully the sun sets on that yellow bank!' I thought within myself, 'With what eyes these poets see nature!' and ever after, when I saw the sunset stream upon the objects facing it, conceived I had made a discovery, or thanked Mr. Wordsworth for having made one for me! We went over to All-Foxden again the day following, and Wordsworth read us the story of Peter Bell in the open air; and the comment made upon it by his face and voice was very different from that of some later critics! Whatever might be thought of the poem, 'his face was as a book where men might read strange matters,' and he announced the fate of his hero in prophetic tones. There is a *chaunt* in the recitation both of Coleridge and Wordsworth, which acts as a spell upon the hearer, and disarms the judgement. Perhaps they have deceived themselves by making habitual use of this ambiguous accompaniment. Coleridge's manner is more full, animated, and varied; Wordsworth's more equable, sustained, and internal. The one might be termed more *dramatic*, the other more *lyrical*. Coleridge has told me that he himself liked to compose in walking over uneven ground, or breaking through the straggling branches of a copse wood; whereas Wordsworth always wrote (if he could) walking up and down a straight gravel-walk, or in some spot where the continuity of his verse met with no collateral interruption. Returning that same evening, I got into a metaphysical argument with Wordsworth, while Coleridge was explaining the different notes of the nightingale to his sister, in which we neither of us succeeded in making ourselves perfectly clear and intelligible. Thus I passed three weeks at Nether Stowey and in the neighbourhood, generally devoting the afternoons to a delightful chat in an arbour made of bark by the poet's friend Tom Poole, sitting under two fine elm-trees, and listening to the bees humming round us, while we quaffed our *flip*. It was agreed, among other things, that we should make a jaunt down the Bristol Channel, as far as Lynton. We set off together on foot, Coleridge, John Chester, and I. This Chester was a native of Nether Stowey, one of those who were attracted to Coleridge's discourse as flies are to honey, or bees in swarming-time to the sound of a brass pan. He 'followed in the chace, like a dog who hunts, not like one that made up the cry.' He had on a brown cloth coat, boots, and corduroy breeches, was low in stature, bow-legged, had a drag in his walk like a drover, which he assisted by a hazel switch, and kept on a sort of trot by the side of Coleridge, like a running footman by a state coach, that he might not lose a syllable or sound, that fell from Coleridge's lips. He told me his private opinion, that Coleridge was a wonderful man. He scarcely opened his lips, much less offered an opinion the whole way:

yet of the three, had I to choose during that journey, I would be John Chester. He afterwards followed Coleridge into Germany, where the Kantean philosophers were puzzled how to bring him under any of their categories. When he sat down at table with his idol, John's felicity was complete; Sir Walter Scott's, or Mr. Blackwood's, when they sat down at the same table with the King, was not more so. We passed Dunster on our right, a small town between the brow of a hill and the sea. I remember eyeing it wistfully as it lay below us: contrasted with the woody scene around, it looked as clear, as pure, as *embrowned* and ideal as any landscape I have seen since, of Gaspar Poussin's or Domenichino's. We had a long day's march—(our feet kept time to the echoes of Coleridge's tongue)—through Minehead and by the Blue Anchor, and on to Lynton, which we did not reach till near midnight, and where we had some difficulty in making a lodgement. We, however, knocked the people of the house up at last, and we were repaid for our apprehensions and fatigue by some excellent rashers of fried bacon and eggs. The view in coming along had been splendid. We walked for miles and miles on dark brown heaths overlooking the channel, with the Welsh hills beyond, and at times descended into little sheltered valleys close by the sea-side, with a smuggler's face scowling by us, and then had to ascend conical hills with a path winding up through a coppice to a barren top, like a monk's shaven crown, from one of which I pointed out to Coleridge's notice the bare masts of a vessel on the very edge of the horizon, and within the red-orbed disk of the setting sun, like his own spectre-ship in the *Ancient Mariner*. At Lynton the character of the sea-coast becomes more marked and rugged. There is a place called the 'Valley of Rocks' (I suspect this was only the poetical name for it) bedded among precipices overhanging the sea, with rocky caverns beneath, into which the waves dash, and where the sea-gull for ever wheels its screaming flight. On the tops of these are huge stones thrown transverse, as if an earthquake had tossed them there, and behind these is a fretwork of perpendicular rocks, something like the 'Giant's Causeway'. A thunder-storm came on while we were at the inn, and Coleridge was running out bareheaded to enjoy the commotion of the elements in the 'Valley of Rocks', but as if in spite, the clouds only muttered a few angry sounds, and let fall a few refreshing drops. Coleridge told me that he and Wordsworth were to have made this place the scene of a prose-tale, which was to have been in the manner of, but far superior to, the *Death of Abel*, but they had relinquished the design. In the morning of the second day, we breakfasted luxuriously in an old-fashioned parlour on tea, toast, eggs, and honey, in the very sight of the beehives from which it had been taken, and a garden full of thyme and wild flowers that had produced it. On this occasion Coleridge spoke of Virgil's *Georgics*, but not well. I do not think he had much feeling for the classical or elegant. It was in this room that we found a little worn-out copy of the *Seasons*, lying in a window-seat, on which Coleridge exclaimed, '*That* is true fame!' He said Thomson was a great poet, rather than a good one; his style was as meretricious as his thoughts were natural. He spoke of Cowper as the best modern poet. He said the *Lyrical Ballads* were an experiment about to be tried by him and Wordsworth, to see how far the public taste would endure poetry written in a more natural and simple style than had hitherto been attempted; totally discarding the artifices of poetical diction, and making use only of such words as had probably been common in the most ordinary language since the days of Henry II. Some comparison was introduced between Shakespeare and Milton. He said 'he hardly knew which to prefer. Shakespeare appeared to him a mere stripling in the art; he was as tall and as strong, with infinitely more activity than Milton, but he never appeared to have come to man's estate; or if he had, he would not have been a man, but a monster.' He spoke with contempt of Gray, and with intolerance of Pope. He did not like the versification of the latter. He observed that 'the ears of these couplet-writers might be charged with having short memories, that could not retain the harmony of whole passages.' He thought little of Junius as a writer; he had a dislike of Dr. Johnson; and a much higher opinion of Burke as an orator and politician, than of Fox or Pitt. He however thought him very inferior in richness of style and imagery to some of our elder prose-writers, particularly Jeremy Taylor. He liked Richardson, but not Fielding; nor could I get him to enter into the merits of *Caleb Williams*.[1] In short, he was profound and discriminating with respect to those authors whom he liked, and where he gave his judgement fair play; capricious, perverse, and prejudiced in his antipathies and distastes. We loitered on the 'ribbed sea-sands', in such talk as this, a whole morning, and I recollect met with a curious sea-weed, of which John Chester told us the country name! A fisherman gave Coleridge an account of a boy that had been drowned the day before, and that they had tried to save him at the risk of their own lives. He said 'he did not know how it was that they ventured, but, Sir, we have a *nature* towards one another.' This expression, Coleridge remarked to me, was a fine illustration of that theory of disinterestedness which I (in common with Butler) had adopted. I broached to him an argument of mine to prove

---

[1] He had no idea of pictures, of Claude or Raphael, and at this time I had as little as he. He sometimes gives a striking account at present of the Cartoons at Pisa by Buffamalco and others; of one in particular, where Death is seen in the air brandishing his scythe, and the great and mighty of the earth shudder at his approach, while the beggars and the wretched kneel to him as their deliverer. He would, of course, understand so broad and fine a moral as this at any time.

that *likeness* was not mere association of ideas. I said that the mark in the sand put one in mind of a man's foot, not because it was part of a former impression of a man's foot (for it was quite new) but because it was like the shape of a man's foot. He assented to the justness of this distinction (which I have explained at length elsewhere, for the benefit of the curious) and John Chester listened; not from any interest in the subject, but because he was astonished that I should be able to suggest anything to Coleridge that he did not already know. We returned on the third morning, and Coleridge remarked the silent cottage-smoke curling up the valleys where, a few evenings before, we had seen the lights gleaming through the dark.

In a day or two after we arrived at Stowey, we set out, I on my return home, and he for Germany. It was a Sunday morning, and he was to preach that day for Dr. Toulmin of Taunton. I asked him if he had prepared anything for the occasion? He said he had not even thought of the text, but should as soon as we parted. I did not go to hear him,—this was a fault,—but we met in the evening at Bridgewater. The next day we had a long day's walk to Bristol, and sat down, I recollect, by a well-side on the road, to cool ourselves and satisfy our thirst, when Coleridge repeated to me some descriptive lines of his tragedy of *Remorse*; which I must say became his mouth and that occasion better than they, some years after, did Mr. Elliston's and the Drury Lane boards,—

> Oh memory! shield me from the world's poor strife,
> And give those scenes thine everlasting life.

I saw no more of him for a year or two, during which period he had been wandering in the Hartz Forest in Germany; and his return was cometary, meteorous, unlike his setting out. It was not till some time after that I knew his friends Lamb and Southey. The last always appears to me (as I first saw him) with a commonplace book under his arm, and the first

MY FIRST ACQUAINTANCE WITH POETS

with a *bon-mot* in his mouth. It was at Godwin's that I met him with Holcroft and Coleridge, where they were disputing fiercely which was the best—*Man as he was, or man as he is to be*. 'Give me', says Lamb, 'man as he is *not* to be.' This saying was the beginning of a friendship between us, which I believe still continues.—Enough of this for the present.

> But there is matter for another rhyme,
> And I to this may add a second tale.

JOHN KEBLE
1792–1866

SACRED POETRY (1825)

The Star in the East; with other Poems. By
Josiah Conder. London. 1824

THERE are many circumstances about this little volume, which tend powerfully to disarm criticism. In the first place, it is, for the most part, of a *sacred* character: taken up with those subjects which least of all admit, with propriety, either in the author or critic, the exercise of intellectual subtlety. For the *practical* tendency, indeed, of such compositions, both are most deeply responsible; the author who publishes, and the critic who undertakes to recommend or to censure them. But if they appear to be written with any degree of sincerity and earnestness, we naturally shrink from treating them merely as literary efforts. To interrupt the current of a reader's sympathy in such a case, by critical objections, is not merely to deprive him of a little harmless pleasure, it is to disturb him almost in a devotional exercise. The most considerate reviewer, therefore, of a volume of sacred poetry, will think it a subject on which it is easier to say too much than too little.

In the present instance, this consideration is enforced by the unpretending tone of the volume, which bears internal evidence, for the most part, of not having been written to meet the eye of the world. It is in vain to say that this claim on the critic's favour is nullified by publication. The author may give it up, and yet the work may retain it. We may still feel that we have no right to judge severely of what was not, at first, intended to come before our judgement at all. This of course applies only to those compositions, which indicate, by something within themselves, this freedom from the pretension of authorship. And such are most of those to which we are now bespeaking our readers' attention.

Most of them, we say, because the first poem in the volume, *The Star in the East*, is of a more ambitious and less pleasing character. Although in blank verse, it is, in fact, a lyrical effusion; an ode on the rapid progress and final triumph of the Gospel. It looks like the composition of a young man: harsh and turgid in parts, but interspersed with some rather beautiful touches. The opening lines are a fair specimen.

> O to have heard th' unearthly symphonies,
> Which o'er the starlight peace of Syrian skies
> Came floating like a dream, that blessed night
> When angel songs were heard by sinful men,
> Hymning Messiah's advent! O to have watch'd
> The night with those poor shepherds, whom, when first
> The glory of the Lord shed sudden day—
> Day without dawn, starting from midnight, day
> Brighter than morning—on those lonely hills
> Strange fear surpris'd—fear lost in wondering joy,
> When from th' angelic multitude swell'd forth
> The many-voicèd consonance of praise:—
> Glory in th' highest to God, and upon earth
> Peace, towards men good will. But once before,
> In such glad strains of joyous fellowship,
> The silent earth was greeted by the heavens,
> When at its first foundation they looked down
> From their bright orbs, those heavenly ministries,
> Hailing the new-born world with bursts of joy.

Notwithstanding beauties scattered here and there, there is an effort and constrained stateliness in the poem, very different from the rapidity and simplicity of many of the shorter lyrics, which follow under the titles of Sacred and Domestic Poems. Such, for instance, as the Poor Man's Hymn

> As much have I of worldly good
>   As e'er my master had:
> I diet on as dainty food,
>   And am as richly clad,

Tho' plain my garb, though scant my board,
As Mary's Son and Nature's Lord.

The manger was his infant bed,
  His home, the mountain-cave,
He had not where to lay his head,
  He borrow'd even his grave.
Earth yielded him no resting spot,—
Her Maker, but she knew him not.

As much the world's good will I bear,
  Its favours and applause,
As He, whose blessed name I bear,—
  Hated without a cause,
Despis'd, rejected, mock'd by pride,
Betray'd, forsaken, crucified.

Why should I court my Master's foe?
  Why should I fear its frown?
Why should I seek for rest below,
  Or sigh for brief renown?—
A pilgrim to a better land,
An heir of joys at GOD's right hand?

Or the following sweet lines on Home, which occur among the Domestic poems:

That is not home, where day by day
I wear the busy hours away.
That is not home, where lonely night
Prepares me for the toils of light—
'Tis hope, and joy, and memory, give
A home in which the heart can live—
These walls no lingering hopes endear,
No fond remembrance chains me here,
Cheerless I heave the lonely sigh—
Eliza, canst thou tell me why?
'Tis where thou art is home to me,
And home without thee cannot be.

There are who strangely love to roam,
And find in wildest haunts their home;
And some in halls of lordly state,
Who yet are homeless, desolate.
The sailor's home is on the main,
The warrior's, on the tented plain,

The maiden's, in her bower of rest,
The infant's, on his mother's breast—
But where thou art is home to me,
And home without thee cannot be.

There is no home in halls of pride,
They are too high, and cold, and wide.
No home is by the wanderer found:
'Tis not in place: it hath no bound.
It is a circling atmosphere
Investing all the heart holds dear;—
A law of strange attractive force,
That holds the feelings in their course;

It is a presence undefin'd,
O'er-shadowing the conscious mind;
Where love and duty sweetly blend
To consecrate the name of friend;—
Where'er thou art is home to me,
And home without thee cannot be.

My love, forgive the anxious sigh—
I hear the moments rushing by,
And think that life is fleeting fast,
That youth with us will soon be past.
Oh! when will time, consenting, give
The home in which my heart can live?
There shall the past and future meet,
And o'er our couch, in union sweet,
Extend their cherub wings, and shower
Bright influence on the present hour,
Oh! when shall Israel's mystic guide,
The pillar'd cloud, our steps decide,
Then, resting, spread its guardian shade,
To bless the home which love hath made?
Daily, my love, shall thence arise
Our hearts' united sacrifice;
And home indeed a home will be,
Thus consecrate and shar'd with thee.

We will add one more specimen of the same kind, which forms a natural and pleasing appendix to the preceding lines.

Louise! you wept, that morn of gladness
  Which made your Brother blest;

And tears of half-reproachful sadness
    Fell on the Bridegroom's vest:
Yet, pearly tears were those, to gem
    A Sister's bridal diadem.

No words could half so well have spoken,
    What thus was deeply shown
By Nature's simplest, dearest token,
    How much was then my own;
Endearing her for whom they fell,
And Thee, for having loved so well.

But now no more—nor let a Brother,
    Louise, regretful see,
That still 'tis sorrow to another,
    That he should happy be.
Those were, I trust, the only tears
That day shall cost through coming years.

Smile with us. Happy and light-hearted,
    We three the time will while.
And, when sometimes a season parted,
    Still think of us, and smile.
But come to us in gloomy weather;
We'll weep, when we must weep, together.

Now, what is the reason of the great difference between these extracts and that from the *Star in the East*?—a difference which the earlier date of the latter, so far from accounting for, only makes the more extraordinary. In some instances, the interval of time is very short, but at all events more effort and turgidness might have been expected in the earlier poems, more simplicity and care and a more subdued tone in the later. We suspect a reason, which both poets and poetical readers are too apt to leave out of sight. There is a want of *truth* in the *Star in the East*—not that the author is otherwise than quite in earnest—but his earnestness seems rather an artificial glow, to which he has been worked up by reading and conversation of a particular cast, than the overflowing warmth of his own natural feelings, kindled by circumstances in which he was himself placed. In a word, when he writes of the success of the Bible

Society, and the supposed amelioration of the world in consequence, he writes from report and fancy only; but when he speaks of a happy home, of kindly affections, of the comforts which piety can administer in disappointment and sorrow; either we are greatly mistaken, or he speaks from real and present experience. The poetical result is what the reader has seen:

>   ——mens onus reponit, et peregrino
> Labore fessi venimus Larem ad nostrum——

We turn gladly from our fairy voyage round the world to refresh ourselves with a picture, which we feel to be drawn from the life, of a happy and innocent fireside. Nor is it, in the slightest degree, derogatory to an author's talent to say that he has failed, comparatively, on that subject of which he must have known comparatively little.

Let us here pause a moment to explain what is meant when we speak of such prospects as are above alluded to, being shadowy and unreal in respect of what is matter of experience. It is not that we doubt the tenor of the Scripture, regarding the final conversion of the whole world, or that we close our eyes to the wonderful arrangements, if the expression may be used, which Divine Providence seems everywhere making, with a view to that great consummation. One circumstance, in particular, arrests our attention, as pervading the whole of modern history, but gradually standing out in a stronger light as the view draws nearer our own times: we mean the rapid increase of colonization *from Christian nations only*. So that the larger half of the globe, and what in the nature of things will soon become the more populous, is already, in profession, Christian. The event, therefore, is unquestionable: but experience, we fear, will hardly warrant the exulting anticipations, which our author, in common with many of whose sincerity there is no reason to doubt, has raised upon it. It is but too conceivable that the whole world may become nominally

Christian, yet the face of things may be very little changed for the better. And any view of the progress of the gospel, whether in verse or in prose, which leaves out this possibility, is so far wanting in truth, and in that depth of thought which is as necessary to the higher kinds of poetical beauty as to philosophy or theology itself.

This, however, is too solemn and comprehensive a subject to be lightly or hastily spoken of. It is enough to have glanced at it, as accounting, in some measure, for the general failure of modern poets in their attempts to describe the predicted triumph of the gospel in the latter days.

To return to the sacred and domestic poems, thus advantageously distinguished from that which gives name to the volume. Affection, whether heavenly or earthly, is the simplest idea that can be; and in the graceful and harmonious expression of it lies the principal beauty of these poems. In the descriptive parts, and in the development of abstract sentiment, there is more of effort, and occasionally something very like affectation: approaching, in one instance (the *Nightingale*,) far nearer than we could wish, to the most vicious of all styles, the style of Mr. Leigh Hunt and his miserable followers.

Now, these are just the sort of merit and the sort of defect, which one might naturally expect to find united; the very simplicity of attachment, which qualifies the mind for sacred or domestic poetry, making its movements awkward and constrained, when scenes are to be described, or thoughts unravelled of more complication and less immediate interest. This is the rather to be observed, as many other sacred poets have become less generally pleasing and useful, than they otherwise would have been, from this very circumstance. The simple and touching devoutness of many of Bishop Ken's lyrical effusions has been unregarded, because of the ungraceful contrivances, and heavy movement of his narrative.

The same may be said, in our own times, of some parts of Montgomery's writings. His bursts of sacred poetry, compared with his *Greenland*, remind us of a person singing enchantingly by ear, but becoming languid and powerless the moment he sits down to a note-book.

Such writers, it is obvious, do not sufficiently trust to the command which the simple expression of their feelings would obtain over their readers. They think it must be relieved with something of more variety and imagery, to which they work themselves up with laborious, and therefore necessarily unsuccessful, efforts. The model for correcting their error is to be found in the inspired volume. We can, in general, be but incompetent judges of this, because we have been used to it from our boyhood. But let us suppose a person, whose ideas of poetry were entirely gathered from modern compositions, taking up the Psalms for the first time. Among many other remarkable differences, he would surely be impressed with the sacred writer's total carelessness about originality, and what is technically called *effect*. He would say, 'This is something better than merely attractive poetry; it is absolute and divine truth.' The same remark ought to be suggested by all sacred hymns; and it is, indeed, greatly to be lamented, that such writers as we have just mentioned should have ever lost sight of it—should have had so little confidence in the power of simplicity, and have condescended so largely to the laborious refinements of the profane Muse.

To put the same truth in a light somewhat different; it is required, we apprehend, in all poets, but particularly in sacred poets, that they should seem to write with a view of unburthening their minds, and not for the sake of writing; for love of the subject, not of the employment. The distinction is very striking in descriptive poetry. Compare the landscapes of Cowper with those of Burns. There is, if we mistake not, the same sort of difference between them, as in the conversation of two persons on scenery, the one originally an enthusiast in his love of the works of nature, the other driven, by disappointment or weariness, to solace himself with them as he might. It is a contrast which every one must have observed, when such topics come under discussion in society; and those who think it worth while, may find abundant illustration of it in the writings of this unfortunate but illustrious pair. The one all overflowing with the love of nature, and indicating, at every turn, that whatever his lot in life, he could not have been happy without her. The other visibly and wisely soothing himself, but not without effort, by attending to rural objects, in default of some more congenial happiness, of which he had almost come to despair. The latter, in consequence, laboriously sketching every object that came in his way: the other, in one or two rapid lines, which operate, as it were, like a magician's spell, presenting to the fancy just that picture, which was wanted to put the reader's mind in unison with the writer's. We would quote, as an instance, the description of Evening in the Fourth Book of the *Task*:

> Come Ev'ning, once again, season of peace;
> Return, sweet Ev'ning, and continue long!
> Methinks I see thee in the streaking west
> With matron-step slow-moving, while the night
> Treads on thy sweeping train; one hand employ'd
> In letting fall the curtain of repose
> On bird and beast, the other charg'd for man
> With sweet oblivion of the cares of day:
> Not sumptuously adorn'd, nor needing aid,
> Like homely-featur'd night, of clust'ring gems;
> A star or two, just twinkling on thy brow,
> Suffices thee; save that the moon is thine
> No less than her's, not worn indeed on high
> With ostentatious pageantry, but set
> With modest grandeur in thy purple zone,
> Resplendent less, but of an ampler round.
> Come then, and thou shalt find thy vot'ry calm,
> Or make me so. Composure is thy gift.

SACRED POETRY

And we would set over against it that purely pastoral chant:

> Now rosy May comes in wi' flowers
> To deck her gay, green spreading bowers;
> And now comes in my happy hours,
>   To wander wi' my Davie.
>   Meet me on the warlock knowe,
>   Dainty Davie, dainty Davie.
>   There I'll spend the day wi' you.
>   My ain dear dainty Davie.
>
> The crystal waters round us fa',
> The merry birds are lovers a',
> The scented breezes round us blaw,
>   A wandering wi' my Davie.
>   Meet me, &c.
> When purple morning starts the hare
> To steal upon her early fare,
> Then thro' the dews I will repair,
>   To meet my faithful Davie.
>   Meet me, &c.
> When day, expiring in the west,
> The curtain draws o' nature's rest,
> I flee to his arms I lo'e best,
>   And that's my ain dear Davie.
>   Meet me, &c.

There is surely no need to explain how this instinctive attachment to his subject is especially requisite in the sacred poet. If even the description of material objects is found to languish without it, much more will it be looked for when the best and highest of all affections is to be expressed and communicated to others. The nobler and worthier the object, the greater our disappointment to find it approached with anything like languor or constraint.

We must just mention one more quality, which may seem, upon consideration, essential to perfection in this kind: viz. that the feelings the writer expresses should appear to be specimens of his general tone of thought, not sudden bursts and mere flashes of goodness. Wordsworth's beautiful description of the

Stock-dove might not unaptly be applied to him. He should sing

>   'of love with silence blending,
>   Slow to begin, yet never ending,
>   Of serious faith and inward glee'.

Some may, perhaps, object to this, as a dull and languid strain of sentiment. But before we yield to their censures we would inquire of them what style they consider, themselves, as most appropriate to similar subjects in a kindred art. If grave, simple, sustained melodies—if tones of deep but subdued emotion are what our minds naturally suggest to us upon the mention of sacred *music*—why should there not be something analogous, a kind of plain chant, in sacred *poetry* also? fervent, yet sober; awful, but engaging; neither wild and passionate, nor light and airy; but such as we may with submission presume to be the most acceptable offering in its kind, as being indeed the truest expression of the best state of the affections. To many, perhaps to most, men, a tone of more violent emotion may sound at first more attractive. But before we *indulge* such a preference, we should do well to consider, whether it is quite agreeable to that spirit, which alone can make us worthy readers of sacred poetry. "Ένθεον ἡ ποιήσις", it is true; there must be rapture and inspiration, but these will naturally differ in their character as the powers do from whom they proceed. The worshippers of Baal may be rude and frantic in their cries and gestures; but the true Prophet, speaking to or of the true GOD, is all dignity and calmness.

If then, in addition to the ordinary difficulties of poetry, all these things are essential to the success of the Christian lyrist—if what he sets before us must be true in substance, and in manner marked by a noble simplicity and confidence in that truth, by a sincere attachment to it, and entire familiarity with it—then we need not wonder that so few should have become eminent in this branch of their art, nor need we have recourse to the disheartening and unsatisfactory solutions which are sometimes given of that circumstance.

'Contemplative piety,' says Dr. Johnson, 'or the intercourse between God and the human soul, cannot be poetical. Man, admitted to implore the mercy of his Creator, and plead the merits of his Redeemer, is already in a higher state than poetry can confer.'[1]

The sentiment is not uncommon among serious, but somewhat fearful, believers; and though we believe it erroneous, we desire to treat it not only with tenderness, but with reverence. They start at the very mention of sacred poetry, as though poetry were in its essence a profane amusement. It is, unquestionably, by far the safer extreme to be too much afraid of venturing with the imagination upon sacred ground. Yet, if it be an error, and a practical error, it may be worth while cautiously to examine the grounds of it. In the generality, perhaps, it is not so much a deliberate opinion, as a prejudice against the use of the art, arising out of its abuse. But the great writer just referred to has endeavoured to establish it by direct reasoning. He argues the point, first, from the nature of poetry, and afterwards from that of devotion.

The essence of poetry is invention; such invention as, by producing something unexpected, surprises and delights. The topics of devotion are few.

It is to be hoped that many men's experience will refute the latter part of this statement. How can the topics of devotion be few, when we are taught to make every part of life, every scene in nature, an occasion—in other words, a topic—of devotion? It might as well be said that connubial love is an unfit subject for poetry, as being incapable of novelty, because, after all, it is only ringing the changes upon

[1] *Life of Waller.*

one simple affection, which every one understands. The novelty there consists, not in the original topic, but in continually bringing ordinary things, by happy strokes of natural ingenuity, into new associations with the ruling passion.

> There's not a bonny flower that springs
> By fountain, shaw, or green;
> There's not a bonnie bird that sings
> But minds me of my Jean.

Why need we fear to extend this most beautiful and natural sentiment to 'the intercourse between the human soul and its Maker', possessing, as we do, the very highest warrant for the analogy which subsists between conjugal and divine love?

Novelty, therefore, sufficient for all the purposes of poetry, we may have on sacred subjects. Let us pass to the next objection.

Poetry pleases by exhibiting an idea more grateful to the mind than things themselves afford. This effect proceeds from the display of those parts of nature which attract, and the concealment of those which repel, the imagination; but religion must be shown as it is, suppression and addition equally corrupt it; and, such as it is, it is known already.

A fallacy may be apprehended in both parts of this statement. There are, surely, real landscapes which delight the mind as sincerely and intensely as the most perfect description could; and there are family groups which give a more exquisite sensation of domestic happiness than anything in Milton, or even Shakespeare. It is partly by association with these, the treasures of the memory, and not altogether by mere excitement of the imagination, that Poetry does her work. By the same rule sacred pictures and sacred songs cannot fail to gratify the mind which is at all exercised in devotion; recalling, as they will, whatever of highest perfection in that way she can remember in herself, or has learned of others.

Then again, it is not the religious doctrine itself,

so much as the effect of it upon the human mind and heart, which the sacred poet has to describe. What is said of suppression and addition may be true enough with regard to the former, but is evidently incorrect when applied to the latter: it being an acknowledged difficulty in all devotional writings, and not in devotional verse only, to keep clear of the extreme of languor on the one hand, and debasing rapture on the other. This requires a delicacy in the perception and enunciation of truth, of which the most earnest believer may be altogether destitute. And since, probably, no man's condition, in regard to eternal things, is exactly like that of any other man, and yet it is the business of the sacred poet to sympathize with all, his store of subjects is clearly inexhaustible, and his powers of discrimination—in other words, of suppression and addition—are kept in continual exercise.

Nor is he, by any means, so straitly limited in the other and more difficult branch of his art, the exhibition of religious doctrine itself, as is supposed in the following statement:

> Whatever is great, desirable, or tremendous, is comprised in the name of the Supreme Being. Omnipotence cannot be exalted; infinity cannot be amplified; perfection cannot be improved.

True: all perfection is implied in the name of GOD; and so all the beauties and luxuries of spring are comprised in that one word. But is it not the very office of poetry to develop and display the particulars of such complex ideas? in such a way, for example, as the idea of GOD's omnipresence is developed in the 139th Psalm? and thus detaining the mind for a while, to force or help her to think steadily on truths which she would hurry unprofitably over, how strictly soever they may be implied in the language which she uses. It is really surprising that this great and acute critic did not perceive that the objection applies as strongly against any kind of composition of which the Divine Nature is the subject, as against devotional poems.

We forbear to press the consideration that, even if the objection were allowed in respect of natural religion, it would not hold against the devotional composition of a Christian; the object of whose worship has condescended also to become the object of description, affection, and sympathy, in the literal sense of these words. But this is, perhaps, too solemn and awful an argument for this place; and therefore we pass on to the concluding statement of the passage under consideration, in which the writer turns his view downwards, and argues against sacred poetry from the nature of man, as he had before from the nature of GOD.

The employments of pious meditation are faith, thanksgiving, repentance and supplication. Faith, invariably uniform, cannot be invested by fancy with decorations. Thanksgiving, the most joyful of all holy effusions, yet addressed to a Being without passions, is confined to a few modes, and is to be felt rather than expressed.

What we have said of the variation of the devout affections, as they exist in various persons, is sufficient, we apprehend, to answer this. But the rest of the paragraph requires some additional reflection:

Repentance, trembling in the presence of the Judge, is not at leisure for cadences and epithets.

This is rather invidiously put, and looks as if the author had not entire confidence in the truth of what he was saying. Indeed, it may very well be questioned; since many of the more refined passions, it is certain, naturally express themselves in poetical language. But repentance is not merely a passion, nor is its only office to tremble in the presence of the Judge. So far from it, that one great business of sacred poetry, as of sacred music, is to quiet and sober the feelings of the penitent—to make his compunction as much of 'a reasonable service' as possible.

To proceed:

Supplication of man to man may diffuse itself through many topics of persuasion: but supplication to God can only cry for mercy.

Certainly, this would be true, if the abstract nature of the Deity were alone considered. But if we turn to the sacred volume, which corrects so many of our erring anticipations, we there find that, whether in condescension to our infirmities, or for other wise purposes, we are furnished with inspired precedents for addressing ourselves to God in all the various tones, and by all the various topics, which we should use to a good and wise man standing in the highest and nearest relation to us. This is so palpably the case throughout the scriptures, that it is quite surprising how a person of so much serious thought as Dr. Johnson could have failed to recollect it when arguing on the subject of prayer. In fact, there is a simple test, by which, perhaps, the whole of his reasoning on Sacred Poetry might be fairly and decisively tried. Let the reader, as he goes over it, bear in mind the Psalms of David, and consider whether every one of his statements and arguments is not there practically refuted.

It is not, then, because sacred subjects are peculiarly unapt for poetry, that so few sacred poets are popular. We have already glanced at some of the causes to which we attribute it—we ought to add another, which strikes us as important. Let us consider how the case stands with regard to books of devotion in *prose*.

We may own it reluctantly, but must it not be owned? that if two new publications meet the eye at once, of which no more is known than that the one is what is familiarly called *a good book*, the other a work of mere literature, nine readers out of ten will take up the second rather than the first? If this be allowed, whatever accounts for it will contribute to account also for the comparative failure of devotional poetry. For this sort of coldness and languor in the reader must act upon the author in more ways than one. The large class who write for money or applause will of course be carried, by the tide of popularity, towards some other subject. Men of more sincere minds, either from true or false delicacy, will have little heart to expose their retired thoughts to the risk of mockery or neglect; and, if they do venture, will be checked every moment, like an eager but bashful musician before a strange audience, not knowing how far the reader's feelings will harmonize with their own. This leaves the field open, in a great measure, to harder or more enthusiastic spirits; who offending continually, in their several ways, against delicacy, the one by wildness, the other by coarseness, aggravate the evil which they wished to cure; till the sacred subject itself comes at last to bear the blame due to the indifference of the reader and the indiscretion of the writer.

Such, we apprehend, would be a probable account of the condition of sacred poetry, in a country where religion was coldly acknowledged, and literature earnestly pursued. How far the description may apply to England and English literature, in their various changes since the Reformation—how far it may hold true of our own times—is an inquiry which would lead us too far at present; but it is surely worth considering. It goes deeper than any question of mere literary curiosity. It is a sort of test of the genuineness of those pretensions, which many of us are, perhaps, too forward to advance, to a higher state of morality and piety, as well as knowledge and refinement, than has been known elsewhere or in other times.

Those who, in spite of such difficulties, desire in earnest to do good by the poetical talent, which they may happen to possess, have only, as it should seem, the following alternative. Either they must veil, as it were, the sacredness of the subject—not necessarily by allegory, for it may be done in a thousand other ways—and so deceive the world of taste into devotional reading—

> Succhi amari intanto ei beve,
> E dall' inganno sua vita riceve—

or else, directly avowing that their subject as well as purpose is devotion, they must be content with a smaller number of readers; a disadvantage, however, compensated by the fairer chance of doing good to each.

It may be worth while to endeavour to trace this distinction, as exemplified in the most renowned of the sacred poets of England; and to glean from such a survey the best instruction we can, in the happy art of turning the most fascinating part of literature to the highest purposes of religion.

We must premise that we limit the title of 'sacred poet' by excluding those who only devoted a small portion of their time and talent now and then, to sacred subjects. In all ages of our literary history it seems to have been considered almost as an essential part of a poet's duty to give up some pages to scriptural story, or to the praise of his Maker, how remote so ever from anything like religion the general strain of his writings might be. Witness the Lamentation of Mary Magdalene in the works of Chaucer, and the beautiful legend of Hew of Lincoln, which he has inserted in his Canterbury Tales; witness also the hymns of Ben Jonson. But these fragments alone will not entitle their authors to be enrolled among sacred poets. They indicate the taste of their age, rather than their own; a fact which may be thought to stand rather in painful contrast with the literary history of later days.

There is another class likewise, of whom little need be said in this place; we mean those who composed, strictly and only, for the sake of unburthening their own minds, without any thought of publication. But as Chaucer's sacred effusions indicate chiefly the character of the times, so poems such as those we now allude to, mark only the turn of mind of the individual writers; and our present business is rather with that sort of poetry which combines both sorts of instruction; that, namely, which bears internal evidence of having been written by sincere men, with an intention of doing good, and with consideration of the taste of the age in which they lived.

Recurring then to the distinction above laid down, between the direct and indirect modes of sacred poetry; at the head of the two classes, as the reader may perhaps have anticipated, we set the glorious names of Spenser and of Milton. The claim of Spenser to be considered as a sacred poet does by no means rest upon his hymns alone: although even those would be enough alone to embalm and consecrate the whole volume which contains them; as a splinter of the true cross is supposed by Catholic sailors to ensure the safety of the vessel. But whoever will attentively consider the *Faerie Queene* itself, will find that it is, almost throughout, such as might have been expected from the author of those truly sacred hymns. It is a continual, deliberate endeavour to enlist the restless intellect and chivalrous feeling of an inquiring and romantic age, on the side of goodness and faith, of purity and justice.

This position is to be made good, not solely or perhaps chiefly, yet with no small force, from the allegorical structure of the poem. Most of us, perhaps, are rather disposed to undervalue this contrivance; and even among the genuine admirers of Spenser, there are not a few who on purpose leave it out of their thoughts; finding, as they say, that it only embarrasses their enjoyment of the poetry. This is certainly far from reasonable: it is a relic of childish feeling, and mere love of amusement, which ill becomes any one who is old enough to appreciate the real beauties of Spenser. Yet it is so natural, so obviously to be expected, that we must suppose a scholar and philosopher (for such Spenser was, as well as a poet) to have been aware of it, and to have made up his mind to it, with all its disadvantages, for some strong reason or other. And what reason so likely as the hope of being seriously useful, both to himself and his readers?

To *himself*, because the constant recurrence to his allegory would serve as a check upon a fancy otherwise too luxuriant, and would prevent him from indulging in such liberties as the Italian poets, in other respects his worthy masters, were too apt to take. The consequence is, that even in his freest passages, and those which one would most wish unwritten, Spenser is by no means a *seductive* poet. Vice in him, however truly described, is always made contemptible or odious. The same may be said of Milton and Shakespeare; but Milton was of a cast of mind originally austere and rigorous. He looked on vice as a judge; Shakespeare, as a satirist. Spenser was far more indulgent than either, and acted therefore the more wisely in setting himself a rule, which should make it essential to the plan of his poem to be always recommending some virtue; and remind him, like a voice from heaven, that the place on which he was standing was holy ground.

Then as to the benefit which the *readers* of the *Faerie Queene* may derive from its allegorical form; a good deal surely is to be gained from the mere habit of looking at things with a view to something beyond their qualities merely sensible; to their sacred and moral meaning, and to the high associations they were intended to create in us. Neither the works nor the word of God, neither poetry nor theology, can be duly comprehended without constant mental exercise of this kind. The comparison of the Old Testament with the New is nothing else from beginning to end. And without something of this sort, poetry, and all the other arts, would indeed be relaxing to the tone of the mind. The allegory obviates this ill effect, by serving as a frequent remembrancer of this higher application.

Not that it is necessary to bend and strain everything into conformity with it; a little leaven, of the genuine kind, will go a good way towards leavening the whole lump. And so it is in the *Faerie Queene*; for one stanza of direct allegory there are perhaps fifty of poetical embellishment; and it is in these last, after all, that the chief moral excellency of the poem lies; as we are now about to show.

But to be understood rightly, we would premise, that there is a disposition,—the very reverse of that which leads to parody and caricature,—which is common indeed to all generous minds, but is perhaps unrivalled in Spenser. As parody and caricature debase what is truly noble, by connecting it with low and ludicrous associations; so a mind, such as we are now speaking of, ennobles what of itself might seem trivial; its thoughts and language, on all occasions, taking a uniform and almost involuntary direction towards the best and highest things.

This, however, is a subject which can be hardly comprehended without examples. The first which occurs to us is the passage which relates the origin of Belphœbe.

> Her birth was of the womb of morning dew,
> And her conception of the joyous prime,
> And all her whole creation did her show
> Pure and unspotted from all loathly crime
> That is ingenerate in fleshly slime.
> So was this Virgin born, so was she bred,
> So was she trained up from time to time,
> In all chaste virtue and true bounti-hed,
> Till to her due perfection she was ripenèd.

It is evident how high and sacred a subject was present to the poet's mind in composing this stanza; and any person who is well read in the Bible, with a clue like this may satisfy himself that all Spenser's writings are replete with similar tacit allusions to the language and the doctrines of sacred writ; allusions breathed, if we may so speak, rather than uttered, and much fitter to be silently considered, than to be dragged forward for quotation or minute criticism. Of course, the more numerous and natural such allusions are, the more entirely are we justified in the denomination we have ventured to bestow on their author, of a truly 'sacred' poet.

It may be felt, as some derogation from this high character, what he has himself avowed—that much of his allegory has a turn designedly given it in honour of Queen Elizabeth; a turn which will be called courtly or adulatory according to the humour of the critic. But, in the first place, such was the custom of the times; it was adopted even in sermons by men whose sincerity it would be almost sacrilege to question. Then, the merits of Queen Elizabeth in respect of the Protestant cause were of that dazzling order, which might excuse a little poetical exuberance in her praise. And, what is very deserving of consideration, it is certain that the most gentle and generous spirits are commonly found laying themselves open to this charge of excessive compliment in addressing princes and patrons. Witness the high style adopted by the venerable Hooker, in speaking of this very Queen Elizabeth: 'Whose sacred power, matched with incomparable goodness of nature, hath hitherto been God's most happy instrument, by him miraculously kept for works of so miraculous preservation and safety unto others,' &c. Another instance of the same kind may be seen in Jeremy Taylor's dedication of his *Worthy Communicant* to the Princess of Orange. Nor is it any wonder it should be so, since such men feel most ardently the blessing and benefit as well as the difficulty of whatever is right in persons of such exalted station; and are also most strongly tempted to bear their testimony against the illiberal and envious censures of the vulgar. All these things, duly weighed, may seem to leave little, if anything, in their panegyrical strains of this greatest of laureates, to be excused by the common infirmity of human nature;

little to detract from our deliberate conviction that he was seriously guided, in the exercise of his art, by a sense of duty, and zeal for what is durably important.

Spenser then was essentially a *sacred* poet; but the delicacy and insinuating gentleness of his disposition were better fitted to the veiled than the direct mode of instruction. His was a mind which would have shrunk more from the chance of debasing a sacred subject by unhandsome treatment, than of incurring ridicule by what would be called unseasonable attempts to hallow things merely secular. It was natural therefore for him to choose not a scriptural story, but a tale of chivalry and romance; and the popular literature, and, in no small measure, the pageantry and manners of his time, would join to attract his efforts that way. In this way too he was enabled, with more propriety and grace, to introduce allusions, political or courtly, to subjects with which his readers were familiar; thus agreeably diversifying his allegory, and gratifying his affection for his friends and patrons, without the coarseness of direct compliment.

In Milton, most evidently, a great difference was to be expected: both from his own character and from that of the times in which he lived. Religion was in those days the favourite topic of discussion; and it is indeed painful to reflect, how sadly it was polluted by intermixture with earthly passions: the most awful turns and most surprising miracles of the Jewish history being made to serve the base purposes of persons, of whom it is hard to say whether they were more successful in misleading others, or in deceiving themselves. It was an effort worthy of a manly and devout spirit to rescue religion from such degradation, by choosing a subject, which, being scriptural, would suit the habit of the times, yet, from its universal and eternal importance, would give least opportunity for debasing temporary application. Then it was the temper of the man always to speak out. He carried it to a faulty excess, as his prose works too amply demonstrate. The more unfashionable his moral was, the more he would have disdained to veil it: neither had he the shrinking delicacy of Spenser to keep him back, through fear of profaning things hallowed by an unworthy touch.

Thus the great epic poem of our language came to be, avowedly, a sacred poem. One hardly dares to wish any thing other than it is in such a composition; yet it may be useful to point out in what respects the moral infirmity of the times, or of the author, has affected the work; so that we are occasionally tempted to regret even Milton's choice. But as the leading error of his mind appears to have been *intellectual* pride, and as the leading fault of the generation with which he acted was unquestionably *spiritual* pride, so the main defects of his poetry may probably be attributed to the same causes.

There is a studious undervaluing of the female character, which may be most distinctly perceived by comparing the character of Eve with that of the Lady in Comus: the latter conceived, as we imagine, before the mind of the poet had become so deeply tainted with the fault here imputed to him. A remarkable instance of it is his describing Eve as unwilling, or unworthy, to discourse herself with the angel.

> Such pleasure she reserved,
> Adam relating, she sole auditress.—

The sentiment may be natural enough, since the primaeval curse upon women: but does it not argue rather too strong a sense of her original inferiority, to put it into her mind before the fall?

What again can be said for the reproachful and insulting tone, in which, more than once, the good angels are made to address the bad ones? or of the too attractive colours, in which, perhaps unconsciously, the poet has clothed the Author of Evil himself? It is a well-known complaint among many of the readers of *Paradise Lost*, that they can hardly keep themselves from sympathizing, in some sort, with Satan, as the hero of the poem. The most probable account of which surely is, that the author himself partook largely of the haughty and vindictive republican spirit which he has assigned to the character, and consequently, though perhaps unconsciously, drew the portrait with a peculiar zest.

These blemishes are in part attributable to the times in which he lived: but there is another now to be mentioned, which cannot be so accounted for: we mean a want of purity and spirituality in his conceptions of Heaven and heavenly joys. His Paradise is a vision not to be surpassed; but his attempts to soar higher are embarrassed with too much of earth still clinging as it were to his wings. Remarks of this kind are in general best understood by comparison, and we invite our readers to compare Milton with Dante, in their descriptions of Heaven. The one as simple as possible in his imagery, producing intense effect by little more than various combinations of *three* leading ideas—light, motion, and music—as if he feared to introduce anything more gross and earthly, and would rather be censured, as doubtless he often is, for coldness and poverty of invention. Whereas Milton, with very little selection or refinement, transfers to the immediate neighbourhood of God's throne the imagery of Paradise and Earth. Indeed he seems himself to have been aware of something unsatisfactory in this, and has inserted into the mouth of an angel, a kind of apology for it:

> Though what if earth
> Be but the shadow of heav'n, and things therein
> Each to other like, more than on earth is thought?

These are blemishes, and sometimes almost tempt us to wish that even Milton had taken some subject not so immediately and avowedly connected with religion. But they do not affect his claim to be considered as the very lodestar and pattern of that class of sacred poets in England. As such we have here considered him next to Spenser; not that there were wanting others of the same order before him. In fact, most of the distinguished names in the poetical annals of Elizabeth, James I, and Charles I, might be included in the list. It may be enough just to recollect Drayton and Cowley, Herbert, Crashaw and Quarles.

The mention of these latter names suggests the remark, how very desirable it is to encourage as indulgent and, if we may so term it, *catholic* a spirit as may be, in poetical criticism. From having been over-praised in their own days, they are come now to be as much undervalued; yet their quaintness of manner and constrained imagery, adopted perhaps in compliance with the taste of their age, should hardly suffice to overbalance their sterling merits. We speak especially of Crashaw and Quarles: for Herbert is a name too venerable to be more than mentioned in our present discussion.

After Milton, sacred poetry seems to have greatly declined, both in the number and merit of those who cultivated it. No other could be expected from the conflicting evils of those times: in which one party was used to brand everything sacred with the name of Puritanism, and the other to suspect every thing poetical of being contrary to morality and religion.

Yet most of the great names of that age, especially among the Romanists, as Dryden, Pope, and before them Habington, continued to dedicate some of their poetry to religion. By their faith they were remote from the controversies which agitated the established church, and their devotion might indulge itself without incurring the suspicion of a fanatical spirit. Then the solemnity of their worship is fitted to inspire splendid and gorgeous strains, such as Dryden's paraphrase of the Veni Creator; and their own fallen fortunes in England, no less naturally, would fill them with a sense of decay very favourable to the plaintive tenderness of Habington and Crashaw.

A feeling of this kind, joined to the effect of

distressing languor and sickness, may be discerned, occasionally, in the writings of Bishop Ken; though he was far indeed from being a Romanist. We shall hardly find, in all ecclesiastical history, a greener spot than the later years of this courageous and affectionate pastor; persecuted alternately by both parties, and driven from his station in his declining age; yet singing on, with unabated cheerfulness, to the last. His poems are not popular, nor probably ever will be, for reasons already touched upon; but whoever in earnest loves his three well-known hymns, and knows how to value such unaffected strains of poetical devotion, will find his account, in turning over his four volumes, half narrative and half lyric, and all avowedly on sacred subjects; the narrative often cumbrous, and the lyric verse not seldom languid and redundant: yet all breathing such an angelic spirit, interspersed with such pure and bright touches of poetry, that such a reader as we have supposed will scarcely find it in his heart to criticize them.

Between that time and ours, the form of sacred poetry which has succeeded best in attracting public attention, is the didactic: of which Davies in Queen Elizabeth's reign, Sir Richard Blackmore in King William's, Young in the middle, and Cowper in the close, of the last century, may fairly be taken as specimens, differing from each other according to the differences of their respective literary eras. Davies, with his Lucretian majesty (although he wants the moral pathos of the Roman poet), representing aptly enough the age of Elizabeth; Blackmore, with his easy paragraphs, the careless style of King Charles's days; Young, with his pointed sentences, transferring to graver subjects a good deal of the manner of Pope; and Cowper, with his agreeable but too unsparing descriptions, coming nearer to the present day, which appears, both in manners and in scenery, to delight in Dutch painting, rather than in what is more delicately classical.

SACRED POETRY

With regard to the indirect, and, perhaps, more effective, species of sacred poetry, we fear it must be acknowledged, to the shame of the last century, that there is hardly a single specimen of it (excepting, perhaps, Gray's Elegy, and possibly some of the most perfect of Collins's poems) which has obtained any celebrity. We except the writers of our own times, who do not fall within the scope of this inquiry.

To Spenser, therefore, upon the whole, the English reader must revert, as being, pre-eminently, the sacred poet of his country: as most likely, in every way, to answer the purposes of his art; especially in an age of excitation and refinement, in which the gentler and more homely beauties, both of character and of scenery, are too apt to be despised: with passion and interest enough to attract the most ardent, and grace enough to win the most polished; yet by a silent preference everywhere inculcating the love of better and more enduring things; and so most exactly fulfilling what he has himself declared to be 'the general end of all his book'—'to fashion a gentleman, or noble person, in virtuous and gentle discipline': and going the straight way to the accomplishment of his own high-minded prayer:

> That with the glory of so goodly sight,
> The hearts of men, which fondly here admire
> Fair-seeming shows, and feed on vain delight,
> Transported with celestial desire
> Of those fair forms, may lift themselves up higher,
> And learn to love, with zealous humble duty,
> Th' eternal fountain of that heavenly beauty.

JOHN HENRY NEWMAN

1801–1890

POETRY

WITH REFERENCE TO ARISTOTLE'S POETICS (1829)

The Theatre of the Greeks; or the History, Literature, and Criticism of the Grecian Drama. With an original Treatise on the Principal Tragic and Comic Metres. Second Edition. Cambridge. 1827

THIS work is well adapted for the purpose it has in view—the illustration of the Greek drama. It has been usual for the young student to engage in a perusal of this difficult branch of classical literature, with none of that previous preparation or collateral assistance which it pre-eminently requires. Not to mention his ordinary want of information as regards the history of the drama, which, though necessary to the full understanding the nature of that kind of poetry, may still seem too remotely connected with the existing Greek plays to be an actual deficiency; nor, again, his ignorance of the dramatic dialect and metres, which, without external helps, may possibly be overcome by minds of superior talent while engaged upon them; at least without some clear ideas of the usages of the ancient stage, the Greek dramas are but partially intelligible. The circumstances under which the representation was conducted, the form and general arrangements of the theatre, the respective offices and disposition of the actors, the nature and duties of the chorus, the proprieties of the scene itself, are essential subjects of information, yet they are generally neglected. The publication before us is a compilation of the most useful works or parts of works on the criticism, history, and antiquities of the drama; among which will be found extracts from Bentley's *Dissertation on the Epistles of Phalaris* and from Schlegel's work on Dramatic Literature; the more important parts of Twining's Translation of Aristotle's *Poetics*, and critical remarks, by Dawes, Porson, Elmsley, Tate, and the writers in the *Museum Criticum*.

If we were disposed to find fault with a useful work, we should describe it as over-liberal of condensed critical information. Such ample assistance is given to the student, that little is left to exercise his own personal thought and judgement. This is a fault of not a few publications of the present day, written for our universities. From a false estimate of the advantages of accurate scholarship, the reader is provided with a multitude of minute facts, which are useful to his mind, not when barely remembered, but chiefly when he has acquired them for himself. It is of comparatively trifling importance, whether the scholar knows the force of οὐ μή or ἀλλὰ γάρ; but it may considerably improve his acumen or taste, to have gone through a process of observation, comparison, and induction, more or less original and independent of grammarians and critics. It is an officious aid which renders the acquisition of a language mechanical. Commentators are of service to stimulate the mind, and suggest thought; and though, when we view the wide field of criticism, it is impossible they should do more, yet, when that field is narrowed to the limit of academical success, there is a danger of their indulging indolence, or confirming the contracted views of dullness. These remarks are not so much directed against a valuable work like the present, the very perusal of which may be made an exercise for the mind, as against an especial fault of the age. The uses of knowledge in forming the intellectual and moral character, are too commonly overlooked; and the possession itself being viewed as a peculiar good, short ways are on all subjects excogitated for avoiding the labour of learning; whereas the very length and process of the journey is in many the chief, in all an important advantage.

But, dismissing a train of thought which would soon lead us very far from the range of subjects which the *Theatre of the Greeks* introduces to our notice, we propose to offer some speculations of our own on Greek tragedy and poetry in general, founded on the doctrine of Aristotle as contained in the publication before us. A compilation of standard works, (and such in its general character is the *Greek Theatre*,) scarcely affords the occasion of lengthened criticism on itself; whereas it may be of use to the classical student to add some further illustrations of the subject which is the common basis of the works compiled.

Aristotle considers the excellence of a tragedy to depend upon its *plot*—and, since a tragedy, as such, is obviously the exhibition of an *action*, no one can deny his statement to be abstractedly true. Accordingly he directs his principal attention to the economy of the fable; determines its range of subjects, delineates its proportions, traces its progress from a complication of incidents to their just and satisfactory arrangement, investigates the means of making a train of events striking or affecting, and shows how the exhibition of character may be made subservient to the purposes of the action. His treatise is throughout interesting and valuable. It is one thing, however, to form the beau idéal of a tragedy on scientific principles; another to point out the actual beauty of a particular school of dramatic composition. The Greek tragedians are not generally felicitous in the construction of their plots. Aristotle, then, rather tells us what tragedy should be, than what Greek tragedy really was. And this doubtless was the intention of the philosopher. Since, however, the Greek drama has obtained so extended and lasting a celebrity, and yet its excellence does not fall under the strict rules of the critical art, we should inquire in what it consists.

That the charm of Greek tragedy does not ordinarily arise from scientific correctness of plot, is certain as a matter of fact. Seldom does any great interest arise from the action; which, instead of being progressive and sustained, is commonly either a mere necessary condition of the drama, or a convenience for the introduction of matter more important than itself. It is often stationary—often irregular—sometimes either wants or outlives the catastrophe. In the plays of Aeschylus it is always simple and inartificial—in four out of the seven there is hardly any plot at all;—and, though it is of more prominent importance in those of Sophocles, yet even here the *Oedipus at Colonos* is a mere series of incidents, and the *Ajax* a union of two separate tales; while in the *Philoctetes*, which is apparently busy, the circumstances of the action are but slightly connected with the *dénouement*. The carelessness of Euripides in the construction of his plots is well known. The action then will be more justly viewed as the vehicle for introducing the personages of the drama, than as the principal object of the poet's art; it is not in the plot, but in the characters, sentiments, and diction, that the actual merit and poetry of the composition is placed. To show this to the satisfaction of the reader, would require a minuter investigation of details than our present purpose admits; yet a few instances in point may suggest others to the memory. E.g. in neither the *Oedipus Coloneus* nor the *Philoctetes*, the two most beautiful plays of Sophocles, is the plot striking; but how exquisite is the delineation of the characters of Antigone and Oedipus, in the former tragedy, particularly in their interview with Polynices, and the various descriptions of the scene itself which the Chorus furnishes! In the *Philoctetes*, again, it is the contrast between the worldly wisdom of Ulysses, the inexperienced frankness of Neoptolemus, and the simplicity of the afflicted Philoctetes, which constitutes the principal charm of the drama. Or we may instance the spirit and nature displayed in the grouping of the characters in the *Prometheus* which is almost without action;—the stubborn enemy of the new dynasty of gods; Oceanus trimming, as an accomplished politician, with the change of affairs; the single-hearted and generous Nereids; and Hermes the favourite and instrument of the usurping potentate. So again, the beauties of the *Thebae* are almost independent of the plot;—it is the Chorus which imparts grace and interest to the actionless scene; and the speech of Antigone at the end, one of the most simply striking in any play, has, scientifically speaking, no place in the tragedy, which should already have been brought to its conclusion. Amid the multitude of the beauties of the irregular Euripides, it is obvious to notice the characters of Alcestis and the Clytemnestra of the *Electra*; the soliloquies of *Medea*; the picturesque situation of Ion, the minister of the Pythian temple; the opening scene of the *Orestes*; and the dialogues between Phaedra and her attendant in the *Hippolytus*, and the old man and Antigone in the *Phoenissae*;—passages which are either unconnected with the development of the plot, or of an importance superior to it. Thus the Greek drama, as a fact, was modelled on no scientific principle. It was a pure recreation of the imagination, revelling without object or meaning beyond its own exhibition. Gods, heroes, kings, and dames, enter and retire: they may have a good reason for appearing—they may have a very poor one; whatever it is, still we have no right to ask for it;—the question is impertinent. Let us listen to their harmonious and majestic language— to the voices of sorrow, joy, compassion, or religious emotion—to the animated odes of the chorus. Why interrupt so divine a display of poetical genius by inquiries degrading it to the level of every-day events, and implying incompleteness in the action till a catastrophe arrives? The very spirit of beauty breathes through every part of the composition. We may liken the Greek drama to the music of the Italian school; in which the wonder is, how so much richness of invention in detail can be accommodated to a style so simple and uniform. Each is the development of grace, fancy, pathos, and taste, in the respective media of representation and sound.

However true then it may be, that one or two of the most celebrated dramas answer to the requisitions of Aristotle's doctrine, still, for the most part, Greek Tragedy has its own distinct and peculiar praise, which must not be lessened by a criticism conducted on principles, whether correct or not, still leading to excellence of another character. This being, as we hope, shown, we shall be still bolder, and proceed to question even the sufficiency of the rules of Aristotle for the production of dramas of the highest order. These rules, it would appear, require a plot not merely natural and unaffected, as a vehicle of more poetical matter, but one laboured and complicated as the sole legitimate channel of tragic effect; and thus tend to withdraw the mind of the poet from the spontaneous exhibition of pathos or imagination, to a minute diligence in the formation of a plan. To explain our views on the subject, we will institute a short comparison between three tragedies, the *Agamemnon*, the *Oedipus*, and the *Bacchae*, one of each of the tragic poets, where, by reference to Aristotle's principles, we think it will be found that the most perfect in plot is not the most poetical.

Of these the action of the *Oedipus Tyrannus* is frequently instanced by the critic as a specimen of judgement and skill in the selection and combination of the incidents; and in this point of view it is truly a masterly composition. The clearness, precision, certainty, and vigour, with which the line of the action moves on to its termination, is admirable. The character of Oedipus too is finely drawn, and identified with the development of the action.

The *Agamemnon* of Aeschylus presents us with the slow and difficult birth of a portentous secret—an event of old written in the resolves of destiny, a crime long meditated in the bosom of the human agents. The Chorus here has an importance altogether wanting in the Chorus of the *Oedipus*. They throw a pall of ancestral honour over the bier of the hereditary monarch, which would have been unbecoming in the case of the upstart king of Thebes. Till the arrival of Agamemnon, they occupy our attention, as the prophetic organ, not commissioned indeed but employed by heaven, to proclaim the impending horrors. Succeeding to the brief intimation of the watcher who opens the play, they seem oppressed with forebodings of woe and crime which they can neither justify nor analyse. The expression of their anxiety forms the stream in which the plot flows—every thing, even news of joy, takes a colouring from the depth of their gloom. On the arrival of the king, they retire before Cassandra, a more regularly commissioned prophetess; who, speaking first in figure, then in plain terms, only ceases that we may hear the voice of the betrayed monarch himself, informing us of the striking of the fatal blow. Here then the very simplicity of the fable constitutes its especial beauty. The death of Agamemnon is intimated at first—it is accomplished at last: throughout we find but the growing in volume and intensity of one and the same note—it is a working up of one musical ground, by fugue and imitation, into the richness of combined harmony. But we look in vain for the progressive and thickening incidents of the *Oedipus*.

The action of the *Bacchae* is also simple. It is the history of the reception of the worship of Bacchus in Thebes; who, first depriving Pentheus of his reason, and thereby drawing him on to his ruin, establishes his divinity. The interest of the scene arises from the gradual process by which the derangement of the Theban king is effected, which is powerfully and originally described. It would be comic, were it unconnected with religion. As it is, it exhibits the grave irony of a god triumphing over the impotent presumption of man, the sport and terrible mischievousness of an insulted deity. It is an exemplification of the adage, *quem deus vult perdere, prius dementat.* So delicately balanced is the action along the verge of the sublime and grotesque, that it is both solemn and humorous, without violence to the propriety of the composition: the mad and merry fire of the Chorus, the imbecile mirth of old Cadmus and Tiresias, and the infatuation of Pentheus, who is ultimately induced to dress himself in female garb to gain admittance among the Bacchae, are made to harmonize with the terrible catastrophe which concludes the life of the intruder. Perhaps the victim's first discovery of the disguised deity is the finest conception in this splendid drama. His madness enables him to discern the emblematic horns on the head of Bacchus, which were hid from him when in his sound mind; yet this discovery, instead of leading him to an acknowledgement of the divinity, provides him only with matter for a stupid and perplexed astonishment.

> καὶ ταῦρος ἡμῖν πρόσθεν ἡγεῖσθαι δοκεῖς,
> καὶ σῷ κέρατε κρατὶ προσπεφυκέναι.
> ἀλλ' ἦ ποτ' ἦσθα θήρ; τεταύρωσαι γὰρ οὖν.[1]

This play is on the whole the most favourable specimen of the genius of Euripides—not breathing the sweet composure, the melodious fullness, the majesty and grace of Sophocles; nor rudely and overpoweringly tragic as Aeschylus; but brilliant, versatile, imaginative, as well as deeply pathetic.

Here then are two dramas of extreme poetical power, but deficient in skilfulness of plot. Are they on that account to be rated below the *Oedipus*, which, in spite of its many beauties, has not even a share of the richness and sublimity of either?

Aristotle, then, it must be allowed, treats dramatic composition more as an exhibition of ingenious workmanship, than as a free and unfettered effusion of

---

[1] A Bull, thou seem'st to lead us; on thy head
   Horns have grown forth: wast heretofore a beast?
   For such thy semblance now.

genius. The inferior poem may, on his principle, be the better tragedy. He may indeed have intended solely to delineate the outward framework most suitable to the reception of the spirit of poetry, not to discuss the nature of poetry itself. If so, it cannot be denied that, the poetry being given equal in the two cases, the more perfect plot will merit the greater share of praise. And it may seem to agree with this view of his meaning, that he pronounces Euripides, in spite of the irregularity of his plots, to be, after all, the most tragic of the Greek dramatists, inasmuch (i.e.) as he excels in his appeal to those passions which the outward form of the drama merely subserves. Still there is surely too much stress laid by the philosopher upon the artificial part; which, after all, leads to negative, more than to positive excellence; and should rather be the natural and (so to say) unintentional result of the poet's feeling and imagination, than be separated from them as the direct object of his care. Perhaps it is hardly fair to judge of Aristotle's sentiments by the fragment of his work which has come down to us. Yet as his natural taste led him to delight in the explication of systems, and in those large and connected views which his vigorous talent for thinking through subjects supplied, we may be allowed to suspect him of entertaining too cold and formal conceptions of the nature of poetical composition, as if its beauties were less subtle and delicate than they really are. A word has power to convey a world of information to the imagination, and to act as a spell upon the feelings: there is no need of sustained fiction—often no room for it.[1] Some confirmation of the judgement we

[1] The sudden inspiration, e.g. of the blind Oedipus, in the second play bearing his name, by which he is enabled, ἄθικτος ἡγητῆρος ['without a guide'], to lead the way to his place of death, in our judgement, produces more poetical effect than all the skilful intricacy of the plot of the *Tyrannus*. The latter excites an interest which scarcely lasts beyond the first reading—the former *decies repetita placebit*.

have ventured to pass on the greatest of analytical philosophers, is the account he gives of the source of poetical pleasure; which he almost identifies with a gratification of the reasoning faculty, placing it in the satisfaction derived from recognizing in fiction a resemblance to the realities of life—συμβαίνει θεωροῦντας μανθάνειν καὶ συλλογίζεσθαι, τί ἕκαστον.[1]

But as we have treated, rather unceremoniously, a deservedly high authority, we will try to compensate for our rudeness, by illustrating his general doctrine of the nature of poetry, which we hold to be most true and philosophical.

Poetry, according to Aristotle, is a representation of the ideal. Biography and history represent individual characters and actual facts; poetry, on the contrary, generalizing from the phenomena of nature and life, supplies us with pictures drawn not after an existing pattern, but after a creation of the mind. *Fidelity* is the primary merit of biography and history; the essence of poetry is *fiction*. *Poesis nihil aliud est* (says Bacon) *quam historiae imitatio ad placitum.* It delineates that perfection which the imagination suggests, and to which as a limit the present system of divine Providence actually tends. Moreover, by confining the attention to one series of events and scene of action, it bounds and finishes off the confused luxuriance of real nature; while, by a skilful adjustment of circumstances, it brings into sight the connexion of cause and effect, completes the dependence of the parts one on another, and harmonizes the proportions of the whole. It is then but the type and model of history or biography, if we may be allowed the comparison, bearing some resemblance to the abstract mathematical formula of physics, before it is modified by the contingencies of gravity and friction. Hence, while it recreates the imagination by the superhuman loveliness of its views, it provides a solace for the mind broken

[1] In seeing the picture one is at the same time learning, —gathering the meaning of things.

by the disappointments and sufferings of actual life; and becomes, moreover, the utterance of the inward emotions of a right moral feeling, seeking a purity and a truth which this world will not give.

It follows that the poetical mind is one full of the eternal forms of beauty and perfection; these are its material of thought, its instrument and medium of observation—these colour each object to which it directs its view. It is called imaginative or creative, from the originality and independence of its modes of thinking, compared with the common-place and matter-of-fact conceptions of ordinary minds, which are fettered down to the particular and individual. At the same time it feels a natural sympathy with everything great and splendid in the physical and moral world; and selecting such from the mass of common phenomena, incorporates them, as it were, into the substance of its own creations. From living thus in a world of its own, it speaks the language of dignity, emotion, and refinement. Figure is its necessary medium of communication with man; for in the feebleness of ordinary words to express its ideas, and in the absence of terms of abstract perfection, the adoption of metaphorical language is the only poor means allowed it for imparting to others its intense feelings. A metrical garb has, in all languages, been appropriated to poetry—it is but the outward development of the music and harmony within. The verse, far from being a restraint on the true poet, is the suitable index of his sense, and is adopted by his free and deliberate choice.

We shall presently show the applicability of our doctrine to the various departments of poetical composition; first, however, it will be right to volunteer an explanation which may save it from much misconception and objection. Let not our notion be thought arbitrarily to limit the number of poets, generally considered such. It will be found to lower particular works, or parts of works, rather than the writers themselves; sometimes to condemn only the vehicle in which the poetry is conveyed. There is an ambiguity in the word poetry, which is taken to signify both the talent itself, and the written composition which is the result of it. Thus there is an apparent, but no real contradiction, in saying a poem may be but partially poetical; in some passages more so than in others; and sometimes not poetical at all. We only maintain—not that writers forfeit the name of poet who fail at times to answer to our requisitions, but—that they are poets only so far forth and inasmuch as they do answer to them. We may grant, for instance, that the vulgarities of old Phoenix in the ninth *Iliad*, or of the nurse of Orestes in the *Choephoroe*, or perhaps of the grave-diggers in *Hamlet*, are in themselves unworthy of their respective authors, and refer them to the wantonness of exuberant genius; and yet maintain that the scenes in question contain much *incidental* poetry. Now and then the lustre of the true metal catches the eye, redeeming whatever is unseemly and worthless in the rude ore; still the ore is not the metal. Nay sometimes, and not unfrequently in Shakespeare, the introduction of unpoetical matter may be necessary for the sake of relief, or as a vivid expression of recondite conceptions, and (as it were) to make friends with the reader's imagination. This necessity, however, cannot make the additions in themselves beautiful and pleasing. Sometimes, on the other hand, while we do not deny the incidental beauty of a poem, we are ashamed and indignant on witnessing the unworthy substance in which that beauty is imbedded. This remark applies strongly to the immoral compositions to which Lord Byron devoted his last years. Now to proceed with our proposed investigation.

We will notice *descriptive poetry* first. Empedocles wrote his physics in verse, and Oppian his history of animals. Neither were poets—the one was an historian of nature, the other a sort of biographer of brutes. Yet a poet may make natural history or philosophy the material of his composition. But under his hands they are no longer a bare collection of facts or principles, but are painted with a meaning, beauty, and harmonious order not their own. Thomson has sometimes been commended for the novelty and minuteness of his remarks upon nature. This is not the praise of a poet; whose office rather is to represent *known* phenomena in a new connexion or medium. In *L'Allegro* and *Il Penseroso* the poetical magician invests the commonest scenes of a country life with the hues, first of a mirthful, then of a pensive mind.[1] Pastoral poetry is a description of rustics, agriculture, and cattle, softened off and corrected from the rude health of nature. Virgil, and much more Pope and others, have run into the fault of colouring too highly;—instead of drawing generalized and ideal forms of *shepherds*, they have given us pictures of *gentlemen* and *beaux*. Their composition may be poetry, but it is not pastoral poetry.

The difference between poetical and historical *narrative* may be illustrated by the 'Tales Founded on Facts', generally of a religious character, so common in the present day, which we must not be thought to approve, because we use them for our purpose. The author finds in the circumstances of the case many particulars too trivial for public notice, or irrelevant to the main story, or partaking perhaps too much of the peculiarity of individual minds:—these he omits. He finds connected events separated from each other by time or place, or a course of action distributed

---

[1] It is the charm of the descriptive poetry of a religious mind, that nature is viewed in a moral connexion. Ordinary writers (e.g.) compare aged men to trees in autumn—a gifted poet will reverse the metaphor. Thus:—
'How quiet shows the woodland scene!
  Each flower and tree, its duty done,
  Reposing in decay serene,
  Like weary men when age is won,' &c.

among a multitude of agents; he limits the scene or duration of the tale, and dispenses with his host of characters by condensing the mass of incident and action in the history of a few. He compresses long controversies into a concise argument—and exhibits characters by dialogue—and (if such be his object) brings prominently forward the course of Divine Providence by a fit disposition of his materials. Thus he selects, combines, refines, colours—in fact, *poetizes*. His facts are no longer *actual* but *ideal*—a tale *founded on* facts is a tale *generalized from* facts. The authors of *Peveril of the Peak*, and of *Brambletye House*, have given us their respective descriptions of the profligate times of Charles II. Both accounts are interesting, but for different reasons. That of the latter writer has the fidelity of history; Walter Scott's picture is the hideous reality unintentionally softened and decorated by the poetry of his own mind. Miss Edgeworth sometimes apologizes for certain incidents in her tales, by stating they took place 'by one of those strange chances which occur in life, but seem incredible when found in writing'. Such an excuse evinces a misconception of the principle of fiction, which, being the *perfection* of the actual, prohibits the introduction of any such anomalies of experience. It is by a similar impropriety that painters sometimes introduce unusual sunsets, or other singular phenomena of lights and forms. Yet some of Miss Edgeworth's works contain much poetry of narrative. *Manœuvring* is perfect in its way—the plot and characters are natural, without being too real to be pleasing.

Character is made poetical by a like process. The writer draws indeed from experience; but unnatural peculiarities are laid aside, and harsh contrasts reconciled. If it be said, the fidelity of the imitation is often its greatest merit, we have only to reply, that in such cases the pleasure is not poetical, but consists in the mere recognition. All novels and tales which introduce real characters, are in the same degree unpoetical. Portrait-painting, to be poetical, should furnish an abstract representation of an individual; the abstraction being more rigid, inasmuch as the painting is confined to one point of time. The artist should draw independently of the accidents of attitude, dress, occasional feeling, and transient action. He should depict the general spirit of his subject—as if he were copying from memory, not from a few particular sittings. An ordinary painter will delineate with rigid fidelity, and will make a caricature. But the learned artist contrives so to temper his composition, as to sink all offensive peculiarities and hardnesses of individuality, without diminishing the striking effect of the likeness, or acquainting the casual spectator with the secret of his art. Miss Edgeworth's representations of the Irish character are actual, and not poetical—nor were they intended to be so. They are interesting, because they are faithful. If there is poetry about them, it exists in the personages themselves, not in her representation of them. She is only the accurate reporter in word of what was poetical in fact. Hence, moreover, when a deed or incident is striking in itself, a judicious writer is led to describe it in the most simple and colourless terms, his own being unnecessary; e.g. if the greatness of the action itself excites the imagination, or the depth of the suffering interests the feelings. In the usual phrase, the circumstances are left to 'speak for themselves'.

Let it not be said that our doctrine is adverse to that individuality in the delineation of character, which is a principal charm of fiction. It is not necessary for the ideality of a composition to avoid those minuter shades of difference between man and man, which give to poetry its plausibility and life; but merely such violation of general nature, such improbabilities, wanderings, or coarsenesses, as interfere with the refined and delicate enjoyment of the imagination; which would have the elements of beauty extracted out of the confused multitude of ordinary actions and habits, and combined with consistency and ease. Nor does it exclude the introduction of imperfect or odious characters. The original conception of a weak or guilty mind may have its intrinsic beauty. And much more so, when it is connected with a tale which finally adjusts whatever is reprehensible in the personages themselves. Richard and Iago are subservient to the plot. Moral excellence of character may sometimes be even a fault. The Clytemnestra of Euripides is so interesting, that the divine vengeance, which is the main subject of the drama, seems almost unjust. Lady Macbeth, on the contrary, is the conception of one deeply learned in the poetical art. She is polluted with the most heinous crimes, and meets the fate she deserves. Yet there is nothing in the picture to offend the taste, and much to feed the imagination. Romeo and Juliet are too good for the termination to which the plot leads—so are Ophelia and the bride of Lammermoor. In these cases there is something inconsistent with correct beauty, and therefore unpoetical. We do not say the fault could be avoided without sacrificing more than would be gained; still it is a fault. It is scarcely possible for a poet satisfactorily to connect innocence with ultimate unhappiness, when the notion of a future life is excluded. Honours paid to the memory of the dead are some alleviation of the harshness. In his use of the doctrine of a future life, Southey is admirable. Other writers are content to conduct their heroes to temporal happiness—Southey refuses present comfort to his Ladurlad, Thalaba, and Roderick, but carries them on through suffering to another world. The death of his hero is the termination of the action; yet so little in two of them, at least, does this catastrophe excite sorrowful feelings, that some readers may be startled to be reminded of the fact. If a melancholy is thrown over the conclusion of the *Roderick*, it is from the peculiarities of the hero's previous history.

Opinions, feelings, manners, and customs, are made poetical by the delicacy or splendour with which they are expressed. This is seen in the *ode, elegy, sonnet,* and *ballad*; in which a single idea perhaps, or familiar occurrence, is invested by the poet with pathos or dignity. The ballad of *Old Robin Gray* will serve, for an instance, out of a multitude; again, Lord Byron's *Hebrew Melody,* beginning 'Were my bosom as false', &c.; or Cowper's *Lines on his Mother's Picture*; or Milman's 'Funeral Hymn' in the *Martyr of Antioch*; or Milton's *Sonnet on his Blindness*; or Bernard Barton's *Dream.* As picturesque specimens, we may name Campbell's *Battle of the Baltic*; or Joanna Baillie's *Chough and Crow*; and for the more exalted and splendid style, Gray's *Bard*; or Milton's *Hymn on the Nativity*; in which facts, with which every one is familiar, are made new by the colouring of a poetical imagination. It must all along be observed, that we are not adducing instances for their own sake; but in order to illustrate our general doctrine, and to show its applicability to those compositions which are, by universal consent, acknowledged to be poetical.

The department of poetry we are now speaking of, is of much wider extent than might at first sight appear. It will include such moralizing and philosophical poems as Young's *Night Thoughts,* and Byron's *Childe Harold.*[1] There is much bad taste, at present, in the judgement passed on compositions of this kind. It is the fault of the day to mistake mere eloquence for poetry; whereas, in direct opposition to the conciseness and simplicity of the poet, the talent of the orator consists in making much of a single idea. '*Sic dicet ille ut verset saepe multis modis eandem et unam rem, ut haereat in eadem commoreturque sententia.*' This is the great art of Cicero himself, who, whether he is engaged in statement, argument, or raillery, never

[1] We would here mention Rogers's *Italy,* if such a cursory notice could convey our high opinion of its merit.

ceases till he has exhausted the subject; going round about it, and placing it in every different light, yet without repetition to offend or weary the reader. This faculty seems to consist in the power of throwing off harmonious sentences, which, while they have a respectable proportion of meaning, yet are especially intended to charm the ear. In popular poems, common ideas are unfolded with copiousness, and set off in polished verse—and this is called poetry. In the *Pleasures of Hope* we find this done with exquisite taste; but it is in his minor poems that the author's powerful and free poetical genius rises to its natural elevation. In *Childe Harold*, too, the writer is carried through his Spenserian stanza with the unweariness and equable fullness of accomplished eloquence; opening, illustrating, and heightening one idea, before he passes on to another. His composition is an extended funeral oration over buried joys and pleasures. His laments over Greece, Rome, and the fallen in various engagements, have quite the character of panegyrical orations; while by the very attempt to describe the celebrated buildings and sculptures of antiquity, he seems to confess that *they* are the poetical text, his the rhetorical comment. Still it is a work of splendid talent, though, as a whole, not of the highest poetical excellence. Juvenal is, perhaps, the only ancient author who habitually substitutes declamation for poetry.[1]

[1] The difference between oratory and poetry is well illustrated by a passage in a recent tragedy.

> *Col.* Joined! by what tie?
> *Rien.* By hatred—
> By danger—the two hands that tightest grasp
> Each other—the two cords that soonest knit
> A fast and stubborn tie; your true love knot
> Is nothing to it. Faugh! the supple touch
> Of pliant interest, or the dust of time,
> Or the pin-point of temper, loose or rot
> Or snap love's silken band. Fear and old hate,

The *philosophy of mind* may equally be made subservient to poetry, as the philosophy of nature. It is a common fault to mistake a mere knowledge of the heart for poetical talent. Our greatest masters have known better;—they have subjected metaphysics to their art. In *Hamlet, Macbeth, Richard,* and *Othello,* the philosophy of mind is but the material of the poet. These personages are ideal; they are effects of the contact of a given internal character with given outward circumstances, the results of combined conditions determining (so to say) a moral curve of original and inimitable properties. Philosophy is exhibited in the same subserviency to poetry in many parts of Crabbe's *Tales of the Hall.* In the writings of this author there is much to offend a refined taste; but at least in the work in question there is much of a highly poetical cast. It is a representation of the action and re-action of two minds upon each other and upon the world around them. Two brothers of different characters and fortunes, and strangers to each other, meet. Their habits of mind, the formation of those habits by external circumstances, their respective media of judgement, their points of mutual attraction and repulsion, the mental position of each in relation to a variety of trifling phenomena of every-day nature and life, are beautifully developed in a series of tales moulded into a connected narrative. We are tempted to single out the fourth book, which gives an account of the childhood and education of the younger brother, and which for variety of thought as well as fidelity of description is in our judgement beyond praise. The Waverley novels would afford us specimens of a similar excellence. One striking peculiarity

> They are sure weavers—they work for the storm,
> The whirlwind, and the rocking surge; their knot
> Endures till death.

The idea is good, and, if expressed in a line or two, might have been poetry—spread out into nine or ten lines, it yields but a languid and ostentatious declamation.

of these tales is the author's practice of describing a group of characters bearing the same general features of mind, and placed in the same general circumstances; yet so contrasted with each other in minute differences of mental constitution, that each diverges from the common starting-place into a path peculiar to himself. The brotherhood of villains in *Kenilworth*, of knights in *Ivanhoe*, and of enthusiasts in *Old Mortality* are instances of this. This bearing of character and plot on each other is not often found in Byron's poems. The Corsair is intended for a remarkable personage. We pass by the inconsistencies of his character, considered by itself. The grand fault is that, whether it be natural or not, we are obliged to accept the author's word for the fidelity of his portrait. We are told, not shown, what the hero was. There is nothing in the plot which results from his peculiar formation of mind. An every-day bravo might equally well have satisfied the requirements of the action. Childe Harold, again, if he is any thing, is a being professedly isolated from the world, and uninfluenced by it. One might as well draw Tityrus's stags grazing in the air, as a character of this kind; which yet, with more or less alteration passes through successive editions in his other poems. Byron had very little versatility or elasticity of genius; he did not know how to make poetry out of existing materials. He declaims in his own way, and has the upper hand as long as he is allowed to go on; but, if interrogated on principles of nature and good sense, he is at once put out and brought to a stand. Yet his conception of Sardanapalus and Myrrha is fine and ideal, and in the style of excellence which we have just been admiring in Shakespeare and Scott.

These illustrations of Aristotle's doctrine may suffice.

Now let us proceed to a fresh position; which, as before, shall first be broadly stated, then modified and explained. How does originality differ from the poetical talent? Without affecting the accuracy of a definition, we may call the latter the originality of right moral feeling.

Originality may perhaps be defined as the power of abstracting for oneself, and is in thought what strength of mind is in action. Our opinions are commonly derived from education and society. Common minds transmit as they receive, good and bad, true and false; minds of original talent feel a continual propensity to investigate subjects and strike out views for themselves;—so that even old and established truths do not escape modification and accidental change when subjected to this process of mental digestion. Even the style of original writers is stamped with the peculiarities of their minds. When originality is found apart from good sense, which more or less is frequently the case, it shows itself in paradox and rashness of sentiment, and eccentricity of outward conduct. Poetry, on the other hand, cannot be separated from its good sense, or taste, as it is called; which is one of its elements. It is originality energizing in the world of beauty; the originality of grace, purity, refinement, and feeling. We do not hesitate to say, that poetry is ultimately founded on correct moral perception;—that where there is no sound principle in exercise there will be no poetry, and that on the whole (originality being granted) in proportion to the standard of a writer's moral character, will his compositions vary in poetical excellence. This position, however, requires some explanation.[1]

---

[1] A living prelate, in his Academical Prelections, even suggests the converse of our position—'*Neque enim facile crediderim de eo qui semel hac imbutus fuerit disciplina, qui in id tota mentis acie assuefactus fuerit incumbere, ut quid sit in rebus decens, quid pulchrum, quid congruum, penitus intueretur, quin idem harum rerum perpetuum amorem foveat, et cum ab his studiis discesserit, etiam ad reliqua vitae officia earum imaginem quasi animo infixam transferat.*'

Of course, then, we do not mean to imply that a poet must necessarily *display* virtuous and religious feeling;—we are not speaking of the actual *material* of poetry, but of its *sources*. A right moral state of heart is the formal and scientific condition of a poetical mind. Nor does it follow from our position that every poet must in fact be a man of consistent and practical principle; except so far as good feeling commonly produces or results from good practice. Burns was a man of inconsistent practice—still, it is known, of much really sound principle at bottom. Thus his acknowledged poetical talent is in no wise inconsistent with the truth of our doctrine, which will refer the beauty which exists in his compositions to the remains of a virtuous and diviner nature within him. Nay, further than this, our theory holds good even though it be shown that a bad man may write a poem. As motives short of the purest lead to actions intrinsically good, so frames of mind short of virtuous will produce a partial and limited poetry. But even where it is exhibited, the poetry of a vicious mind will be inconsistent and debased; i.e. so far only such, as the traces and shadows of holy truth still remain upon it. On the other hand, a right moral feeling places the mind in the very centre of that circle from which all the rays have their origin and range; whereas minds otherwise placed command but a portion of the whole circuit of poetry. Allowing for human infirmity and the varieties of opinion, Milton, Spenser, Cowper, Wordsworth, and Southey, may be considered, as far as their writings go, to approximate to this moral centre. The following are added as further illustrations of our meaning. Walter Scott's centre is chivalrous honour; Shakespeare exhibits the ἦθος, the physiognomy of an unlearned and undisciplined piety; Homer the religion of nature and the heart, at times debased by polytheism. All these poets are religious:—the occasional irreligion of Virgil's poetry is painful to the admirers of his general taste and delicacy. Dryden's *Alexander's Feast* is a magnificent composition, and has high poetical beauties; but to a delicate judgement there is something intrinsically unpoetical in the end to which it is devoted, the praises of revel and sensuality. It corresponds to a process of clever reasoning erected on an untrue foundation—the one is a fallacy, the other is out of taste. Lord Byron's *Manfred* is in parts intensely poetical; yet the refined mind naturally shrinks from the spirit which here and there reveals itself, and the basis on which the fable is built. From a perusal of it we should infer, according to the above theory, that there was right and fine feeling in the poet's mind, but that the central and consistent character was wanting. From the history of his life we know this to be the fact. The connexion between want of the religious principle and want of poetical feeling, is seen in the instances of Hume and Gibbon; who had radically unpoetical minds. Rousseau is not an exception to our doctrine, for his heart was naturally religious. Lucretius too had much poetical talent; but his work evinces that his miserable philosophy was rather the result of a bewildered judgement than a corrupt heart.

According to the above theory, revealed religion should be especially poetical—and it is so in fact. While its disclosures have an originality in them to engage the intellect, they have a beauty to satisfy the moral nature. It presents us with those ideal forms of excellence in which a poetical mind delights, and with which all grace and harmony are associated. It brings us into a new world—a world of overpowering interest, of the sublimest views, and the tenderest and purest feelings. The peculiar grace of mind of the New Testament writers is as striking as the actual effect produced upon the hearts of those who have imbibed their spirit. At present we are not concerned with the practical, but the poetical nature of revealed truth. With Christians a poetical view of things is a

duty—we are bid to colour all things with hues of
faith, to see a divine meaning in every event, and a
superhuman tendency. Even our friends around
are invested with unearthly brightness—no longer
imperfect men, but beings taken into divine favour,
stamped with his seal, and in training for future
happiness. It may be added that the virtues peculiarly Christian are especially poetical;—meekness,
gentleness, compassion, contentment, modesty, not
to mention the devotional virtues: whereas the ruder
and more ordinary feelings are the instruments of
rhetoric more justly than of poetry—anger, indignation, emulation, martial spirit, and love of independence.

A few remarks on poetical composition, and we
have done.—The art of composition is merely accessory to the poetical talent. But where that talent
exists it necessarily gives its own character to the style,
and renders it perfectly different from all others. As
the poet's habits of mind lead to contemplation rather
than communication with others, he is more or less
obscure, according to the particular style of poetry
he has adopted; less so, in epic or narrative and
dramatic representation—more so, in odes and
choruses. He will be obscure, moreover, from the
depth of his feelings, which require a congenial reader
to enter into them—and from their acuteness, which
shrinks from any formal accuracy in the expression
of them. And he will be obscure, not only from the
carelessness of genius and from the originality of his
conceptions, but (it may be) from natural deficiency
in the power of clear and eloquent expression, which,
we must repeat, is a talent distinct from poetry,
though often mistaken for it.

Dexterity in composition, or *eloquence* as it may be
called in a contracted sense of the word, is however
manifestly more or less necessary in every branch of
literature, though its elements may be different in
each. *Poetical* eloquence consists, first in the power

of illustration—which the poet uses, not as the orator, voluntarily, for the sake of clearness or ornament; but almost by constraint, as the sole outlet and expression of intense inward feeling. The spontaneous power of comparison is in some poetical minds entirely wanting; these of course cannot show to advantage as poets.—Another talent necessary to composition is the power of unfolding the meaning in an orderly manner. A poetical mind is often too impatient to explain itself justly; it is overpowered by a rush of emotions, which sometimes want of power, sometimes the indolence of inward enjoyment, prevents it from describing. Nothing is more difficult than to analyse the feelings of our own minds; and the power of doing so, whether natural or acquired, is clearly distinct from experiencing them. Yet, though distinct from the poetical talent, it is obviously necessary to its exhibition. Hence it is a common praise bestowed upon writers, that they express what we have often felt but could never describe. The power of arrangement, which is necessary for an extended poem, is a modification of the same talent;—being to poetry what method is to logic. Besides these qualifications, poetical composition requires that command of language which is the mere effect of practice. The poet is a compositor; words are his types; he must have them within reach, and in unlimited abundance. Hence the need of careful labour to the accomplished poet—not in order that his diction may attract, but that language may be subjected to him. He studies the art of composition as we might learn dancing or elocution; not that we may move or speak according to rule, but that by the very exercise our voice and carriage may become so unembarrassed as to allow of our doing what we will with them.

A talent for composition then is no essential part of poetry, though indispensable to its exhibition. Hence it would seem that attention to the language *for its own sake* evidences not the true poet but the mere artist. Pope is said to have tuned our tongue. We certainly owe much to him—his diction is rich, musical, and expressive. Still he is not on this account a poet; he elaborated his composition for its own sake. If we give him poetical praise on this account, we may as appropriately bestow it on a tasteful cabinet-maker. This does not forbid us to ascribe the grace of his verse to an inward principle of poetry, which supplied him with archetypes of the beautiful and splendid to work by. But a similar internal gift must direct the skill of every fancy-artist who subserves the luxuries and elegancies of life. On the other hand, though Virgil is celebrated as a master of composition, yet his style is so identified with his conceptions, as their outward development, as to preclude the possibility of our viewing the one apart from the other. In Milton, again, the harmony of the verse is but the echo of the inward music which the thoughts of the poet breathe. In Moore's style the ornament continually outstrips the sense. Cowper and Walter Scott, on the other hand, are slovenly in their versification. Sophocles writes, on the whole, without studied attention to the style; but Euripides frequently affects a simplicity and prettiness which exposed him to the ridicule of the comic poets. Lastly, the style of Homer's poems is perfect in their particular department. It is free, manly, simple, perspicuous, energetic, and varied. It is the style of one who rhapsodized without deference to hearer or judge, in an age prior to the temptations which more or less prevailed over succeeding writers—before the theatre had degraded poetry into an exhibition, and criticism narrowed it into an art.

THOMAS CARLYLE
1795–1881

THE HERO AS POET. DANTE; SHAKESPEARE
[From *Heroes and Hero-worship*, 1840]

THE Hero as Divinity, the Hero as Prophet, are productions of old ages; not to be repeated in the new. They presuppose a certain rudeness of conception, which the progress of mere scientific knowledge puts an end to. There needs to be, as it were, a world vacant, or almost vacant of scientific forms, if men in their loving wonder are to fancy their fellow-man either a god or one speaking with the voice of a god. Divinity and Prophet are past. We are now to see our Hero in the less ambitious, but also less questionable, character of Poet; a character which does not pass. The Poet is a heroic figure belonging to all ages; whom all ages possess, when once he is produced, whom the newest age as the oldest may produce;—and will produce, always when Nature pleases. Let Nature send a Hero-soul; in no age is it other than possible that he may be shaped into a Poet.

Hero, Prophet, Poet,—many different names, in different times and places, do we give to Great Men; according to varieties we note in them, according to the sphere in which they have displayed themselves! We might give many more names, on this same principle. I will remark again, however, as a fact not unimportant to be understood, that the different *sphere* constitutes the grand origin of such distinction; that the Hero can be Poet, Prophet, King, Priest or what you will, according to the kind of world he finds himself born into. I confess, I have no notion of a truly great man that could not be *all* sorts of men. The Poet who could merely sit on a chair, and compose stanzas, would never make a stanza worth much.

He could not sing the Heroic warrior, unless he himself were at least a Heroic warrior too. I fancy there is in him the Politician, the Thinker, Legislator, Philosopher;—in one or the other degree, he could have been, he is all these. So too I cannot understand how a Mirabeau, with that great glowing heart, with the fire that was in it, with the bursting tears that were in it, could not have written verses, tragedies, poems, and touched all hearts in that way, had his course of life and education led him thitherward. The grand fundamental character is that of Great Man; that the man be great. Napoleon has words in him which are like Austerlitz Battles. Louis Fourteenth's Marshals are a kind of poetical men withal; the things Turenne says are full of sagacity and geniality, like sayings of Samuel Johnson. The great heart, the clear deep-seeing eye: there it lies; no man whatever, in what province soever, can prosper at all without these. Petrarch and Boccaccio did diplomatic messages, it seems, quite well: one can easily believe it; they had done things a little harder than these! Burns, a gifted song-writer, might have made a still better Mirabeau. Shakespeare,—one knows not what *he* could not have made, in the supreme degree.

True, there are aptitudes of Nature too. Nature does not make all great men, more than all other men, in the self-same mould. Varieties of aptitude doubtless; but infinitely more of circumstance; and far oftenest it is the *latter* only that are looked to. But it is as with common men in the learning of trades. You take any man, as yet a vague capability of a man, who could be any kind of craftsman; and make him into a smith, a carpenter, a mason: he is then and thenceforth that and nothing else. And if, as Addison complains, you sometimes see a street-porter staggering under his load on spindle-shanks, and near at hand a tailor with the frame of a Samson handling a bit of cloth and small Whitechapel needle, —it cannot be considered that aptitude of Nature alone has been consulted here either!—The Great Man also, to what shall he be bound apprentice? Given your Hero, is he to become Conqueror, King, Philosopher, Poet? It is an inexplicably complex controversial-calculation between the world and him! He will read the world and its laws; the world with its laws will be there to be read. What the world, on *this* matter, shall permit and bid is, as we said, the most important fact about the world.—

Poet and Prophet differ greatly in our loose modern notions of them. In some old languages, again, the titles are synonymous; *Vates* means both Prophet and Poet: and indeed at all times, Prophet and Poet, well understood, have much kindred of meaning. Fundamentally indeed they are still the same; in this most important respect especially, That they have penetrated both of them into the sacred mystery of the Universe; what Goethe calls 'the open secret'. 'Which is the great secret?' asks one.—'The *open* secret,'—open to all, seen by almost none! That divine mystery, which lies everywhere in all Beings, 'the Divine Idea of the World, that which lies at the bottom of Appearance,' as Fichte styles it; of which all Appearance, from the starry sky to the grass of the field, but especially the Appearance of Man and his work, is but the *vesture*, the embodiment that renders it visible. This divine mystery *is* in all times and in all places; veritably is. In most times and places it is greatly overlooked; and the Universe, definable always in one or the other dialect, as the realized Thought of God, is considered a trivial, inert, commonplace matter,—as if, says the Satirist, it were a dead thing, which some upholsterer had put together! It could do no good, at present, to *speak* much about this; but it is a pity for every one of us if we do not know it, live ever in the knowledge of it. Really a most mournful pity;—a failure to live at all, if we live otherwise!

But now, I say, whoever may forget this divine mystery, the *Vates*, whether Prophet or Poet, has penetrated into it; is a man sent hither to make it more impressively known to us. That always is his message; he is to reveal that to us,—that sacred mystery which he more than others lives ever present with. While others forget it, he knows it;—I might say, he has been driven to know it; without consent asked of *him*, he finds himself living in it, bound to live in it. Once more, here is no Hearsay, but a direct Insight and Belief; this man too could not help being a sincere man! Whosoever may live in the shows of things, it is for him a necessity of nature to live in the very fact of things. A man, once more, in earnest with the Universe, though all others were but toying with it. He is a *Vates*, first of all, in virtue of being sincere. So far Poet and Prophet, participators in the 'open secret,' are one.

With respect to their distinction again: The *Vates* Prophet, we might say, has seized that sacred mystery rather on the moral side, as Good and Evil, Duty and Prohibition; the *Vates* Poet on what the Germans call the æsthetic side, as Beautiful, and the like. The one we may call a revealer of what we are to do, the other of what we are to love. But indeed these two provinces run into one another, and cannot be disjoined. The Prophet too has his eye on what we are to love: how else shall he know what it is we are to do? The highest Voice ever heard on this Earth said withal, 'Consider the lilies of the field; they toil not, neither do they spin: yet Solomon in all his glory was not arrayed like one of these.' A glance, that, into the deepest deep of Beauty. 'The lilies of the field,'— dressed finer than earthly princes, springing up there in the humble furrow-field; a beautiful *eye* looking out on you, from the great inner Sea of Beauty! How could the rude Earth make these, if her Essence, rugged as she looks and is, were not inwardly Beauty? —In this point of view, too, a saying of Goethe's, which has staggered several, may have meaning: 'The Beautiful', he intimates, 'is higher than the Good; the Beautiful includes in it the Good.' The *true* Beautiful; which however, I have said somewhere, 'differs from the *false*, as Heaven does from Vauxhall!' So much for the distinction and identity of Poet and Prophet.—

In ancient and also in modern periods, we find a few Poets who are accounted perfect; whom it were a kind of treason to find fault with. This is noteworthy; this is right: yet in strictness it is only an illusion. At bottom, clearly enough, there is no perfect Poet! A vein of Poetry exists in the hearts of all men; no man is made altogether of Poetry. We are all poets when we *read* a poem well. The 'imagination that shudders at the Hell of Dante,' is not that the same faculty, weaker in degree, as Dante's own? No one but Shakespeare can embody, out of Saxo Grammaticus, the story of *Hamlet* as Shakespeare did: but every one models some kind of story out of it; every one embodies it better or worse. We need not spend time in defining. Where there is no specific difference, as between round and square, all definition must be more or less arbitrary. A man that has *so* much more of the poetic element developed in him as to have become noticeable, will be called Poet by his neighbours. World-Poets too, those whom we are to take for perfect Poets, are settled by critics in the same way. One who rises *so* far above the general level of Poets will, to such and such critics, seem a Universal Poet; as he ought to do. And yet it is, and must be, an arbitrary distinction. All Poets, all men, have some touches of the Universal; no man is wholly made of that. Most Poets are very soon forgotten: but not the noblest Shakespeare or Homer of them can be remembered *for ever*;—a day comes when he too is not!

Nevertheless, you will say, there must be a difference between true Poetry and true Speech not

Poetical: what is the difference? On this point many things have been written, especially by late German Critics, some of which are not very intelligible at first. They say, for example, that the Poet has an *infinitude* in him; communicates an *Unendlichkeit*, a certain character of 'infinitude', to whatsoever he delineates. This, though not very precise, yet on so vague a matter is worth remembering: if well meditated, some meaning will gradually be found in it. For my own part, I find considerable meaning in the old vulgar distinction of Poetry being *metrical*, having music in it, being a Song. Truly, if pressed to give a definition, one might say this as soon as anything else: If your delineation be authentically *musical*, musical not in word only, but in heart and substance, in all the thoughts and utterances of it, in the whole conception of it, then it will be poetical; if not, not.—Musical: how much lies in that! A *musical* thought is one spoken by a mind that has penetrated into the inmost heart of the thing; detected the inmost mystery of it, namely the *melody* that lies hidden in it; the inward harmony of coherence which is its soul, whereby it exists, and has a right to be, here in this world. All inmost things, we may say, are melodious; naturally utter themselves in Song. The meaning of Song goes deep. Who is there that, in logical words, can express the effect music has on us? A kind of inarticulate unfathomable speech, which leads us to the edge of the Infinite, and lets us for moments gaze into that!

Nay all speech, even the commonest speech, has something of song in it: not a parish in the world but has its parish-accent;—the rhythm or *tune* to which the people there *sing* what they have to say! Accent is a kind of chanting; all men have accent of their own,—though they only *notice* that of others. Observe too how all passionate language does of itself become musical,—with a finer music than the mere accent; the speech of a man even in zealous anger becomes a chant, a song. All deep things are Song. It seems somehow the very central essence of us, Song; as if all the rest were but wrappages and hulls! The primal element of us; of us, and of all things. The Greeks fabled of Sphere-Harmonies: it was the feeling they had of the inner structure of Nature; that the soul of all her voices and utterances was perfect music. Poetry, therefore, we will call *musical Thought*. The Poet is he who *thinks* in that manner. At bottom, it turns still on power of intellect; it is a man's sincerity and depth of vision that makes him a Poet. See deep enough, and you see musically; the heart of Nature *being* everywhere music, if you can only reach it.

The *Vates* Poet, with his melodious Apocalypse of Nature, seems to hold a poor rank among us, in comparison with the *Vates* Prophet; his function, and our esteem of him for his function, alike slight. The Hero taken as Divinity; the Hero taken as Prophet; then next the Hero taken only as Poet: does it not look as if our estimate of the Great Man, epoch after epoch, were continually diminishing? We take him first for a god, then for one god-inspired; and now in the next stage of it, his most miraculous word gains from us only the recognition that he is a Poet, beautiful verse-maker, man of genius, or such-like!— It looks so; but I persuade myself that intrinsically it is not so. If we consider well, it will perhaps appear that in man still there is the *same* altogether peculiar admiration for the Heroic Gift, by what name soever called, that there at any time was.

I should say, if we do not now reckon a Great Man literally divine, it is that our notions of God, of the supreme unattainable Fountain of Splendour, Wisdom and Heroism, are ever rising *higher*; not altogether that our reverence for these qualities, as manifested in our like, is getting lower. This is worth taking thought of. Sceptical Dilettantism, the curse of these ages, a curse which will not last for ever, does indeed in this the highest province of human things,

THE HERO AS POET

as in all provinces, make sad work; and our reverence for great men, all crippled, blinded, paralytic as it is, comes out in poor plight, hardly recognizable. Men worship the shows of great men; the most disbelieve that there is any reality of great men to worship. The dreariest, fatallest faith; believing which, one would literally despair of human things. Nevertheless look, for example, at Napoleon! A Corsican lieutenant of artillery; that is the show of *him*: yet is he not obeyed, *worshipped* after his sort, as all the Tiaraed and Diademed of the world put together could not be? High Duchesses, and ostlers of inns, gather round the Scottish rustic, Burns;—a strange feeling dwelling in each that they never heard a man like this; that, on the whole, this is the man! In the secret heart of these people it still dimly reveals itself, though there is no accredited way of uttering it at present, that this rustic, with his black brows and flashing sun-eyes, and strange words moving laughter and tears, is of a dignity far beyond all others, incommensurable with all others. Do not we feel it so? But now, were Dilettantism, Scepticism, Triviality, and all that sorrowful brood, cast-out of us,—as, by God's blessing, they shall one day be; were faith in the shows of things entirely swept out, replaced by clear faith in the *things*, so that a man acted on the impulse of that only, and counted the other non-extant; what a new livelier feeling towards this Burns were it!

Nay here in these ages, such as they are, have we not two mere Poets, if not deified, yet we may say beatified? Shakespeare and Dante are Saints of Poetry; really, if we will think of it, *canonized*, so that it is impiety to meddle with them. The unguided instinct of the world, working across all these perverse impediments, has arrived at such result. Dante and Shakespeare are a peculiar Two. They dwell apart, in a kind of royal solitude; none equal, none second to them: in the general feeling of the world, a certain transcendentalism, a glory as of complete perfection, invests these two. They *are* canonized, though no Pope or Cardinals took hand in doing it! Such, in spite of every perverting influence, in the most unheroic times, is still our indestructible reverence for heroism.—We will look a little at these Two, the Poet Dante and the Poet Shakespeare: what little it is permitted us to say here of the Hero as Poet will most fitly arrange itself in that fashion.

Many volumes have been written by way of commentary on Dante and his Book; yet, on the whole, with no great result. His Biography is, as it were, irrecoverably lost for us. An unimportant, wandering, sorrowstricken man, not much note was taken of him while he lived; and the most of that has vanished, in the long space that now intervenes. It is five centuries since he ceased writing and living here. After all commentaries, the Book itself is mainly what we know of him. The Book;—and one might add that Portrait commonly attributed to Giòtto, which, looking on it, you cannot help inclining to think genuine, whoever did it. To me it is a most touching face; perhaps of all faces that I know, the most so. Lonely there, painted as on vacancy, with the simple laurel wound round it; the deathless sorrow and pain, the known victory which is also deathless;—significant of the whole history of Dante! I think it is the mournfullest face that ever was painted from reality; an altogether tragic, heart-affecting face. There is in it, as foundation of it, the softness, tenderness, gentle affection as of a child; but all this is as if congealed into sharp contradiction, into abnegation, isolation, proud hopeless pain. A soft ethereal soul looking out so stern, implacable, grim-trenchant, as from imprisonment of thick-ribbed ice! Withal it is a silent pain too, a silent scornful one: the lip is curled in a kind of god-like disdain of the thing that is eating-out his heart,—as if it were withal a mean insignificant thing, as if

THE HERO AS POET

he whom it had power to torture and strangle were greater than it. The face of one wholly in protest, and lifelong unsurrendering battle, against the world. Affection all converted into indignation: an implacable indignation; slow, equable, silent, like that of a god! The eye too, it looks out as in a kind of *surprise*, a kind of inquiry, Why the world was of such a sort? This is Dante: so he looks, this 'voice of ten silent centuries', and sings us 'his mystic unfathomable song'.

The little that we know of Dante's Life corresponds well enough with this Portrait and this Book. He was born at Florence, in the upper class of society, in the year 1265. His education was the best then going; much school-divinity, Aristotelean logic, some Latin classics,—no inconsiderable insight into certain provinces of things: and Dante, with his earnest intelligent nature, we need not doubt, learned better than most all that was learnable. He has a clear cultivated understanding, and of great subtlety; this best fruit of education he had contrived to realize from these scholastics. He knows accurately and well what lies close to him; but, in such a time, without printed books or free intercourse, he could not know well what was distant: the small clear light, most luminous for what is near, breaks itself into singular *chiaroscuro* striking on what is far off. This was Dante's learning from the schools. In life, he had gone through the usual destinies; been twice out campaigning as a soldier for the Florentine State, been on embassy; had in his thirty-fifth year, by natural gradation of talent and service, become one of the Chief Magistrates of Florence. He had met in boyhood a certain Beatrice Portinari, a beautiful little girl of his own age and rank, and grown-up thenceforth in partial sight of her, in some distant intercourse with her. All readers know his graceful affecting account of this; and then of their being parted; of her being wedded to another, and of her death soon after. She makes a great figure in Dante's

Poem; seems to have made a great figure in his life. Of all beings it might seem as if she, held apart from him, far apart at last in the dim Eternity, were the only one he had ever with his whole strength of affection loved. She died: Dante himself was wedded; but it seems not happily, far from happily. I fancy, the rigorous earnest man, with his keen excitabilities, was not altogether easy to make happy.

We will not complain of Dante's miseries: had all gone right with him as he wished it, he might have been Prior, Podestà, or whatsoever they call it, of Florence, well accepted among neighbours,—and the world had wanted one of the most notable words ever spoken or sung. Florence would have had another prosperous Lord Mayor; and the ten dumb centuries continued voiceless, and the ten other listening centuries (for there will be ten of them and more) had no *Divina Commedia* to hear! We will complain of nothing. A nobler destiny was appointed for this Dante; and he, struggling like a man led towards death and crucifixion, could not help fulfilling it. Give *him* the choice of his happiness! He knew not, more than we do, what was really happy, what was really miserable.

In Dante's Priorship, the Guelf-Ghibelline, Bianchi-Neri, or some other confused disturbances rose to such a height, that Dante, whose party had seemed the stronger, was with his friends cast unexpectedly forth into banishment; doomed thenceforth to a life of woe and wandering. His property was all confiscated and more; he had the fiercest feeling that it was entirely unjust, nefarious in the sight of God and man. He tried what was in him to get reinstated; tried even by warlike surprisal, with arms in his hand: but it would not do; bad only had become worse. There is a record, I believe, still extant in the Florence Archives, dooming this Dante, wheresoever caught, to be burnt alive. Burnt alive; so it stands, they say: a very curious civic document. Another curious

THE HERO AS POET

document, some considerable number of years later, is a Letter of Dante's to the Florentine Magistrates, written in answer to a milder proposal of theirs, that he should return on condition of apologizing and paying a fine. He answers, with fixed stern pride: 'If I cannot return without calling myself guilty, I will never return, *nunquam revertar.*'

For Dante there was now no home in this world. He wandered from patron to patron, from place to place; proving, in his own bitter words, 'How hard is the path, *Come è duro calle.*' The wretched are not cheerful company. Dante, poor and banished, with his proud earnest nature, with his moody humours, was not a man to conciliate men. Petrarch reports of him that being at Can della Scala's court, and blamed one day for his gloom and taciturnity, he answered in no courtier-like way. Della Scala stood among his courtiers, with mimes and buffoons (*nebulones ac histriones*) making him heartily merry; when, turning to Dante, he said: 'Is it not strange, now, that this poor fool should make himself so entertaining; while you, a wise man, sit there day after day, and have nothing to amuse us with at all?' Dante answered bitterly: 'No, not strange; your Highness is to recollect the Proverb, *Like to Like*;'—given the amuser, the amusee must also be given! Such a man, with his proud silent ways, with his sarcasms and sorrows, was not made to succeed at court. By degrees, it came to be evident to him that he had no longer any resting-place, or hope of benefit, in this earth. The earthly world had cast him forth, to wander, wander; no living heart to love him now; for his sore miseries there was no solace here.

The deeper naturally would the Eternal World impress itself on him; that awful reality over which, after all, this Time-world, with its Florences and banishments, only flutters as an unreal shadow. Florence thou shalt never see: but Hell and Purgatory and Heaven thou shalt surely see! What is Florence,

Can della Scala, and the World and Life altogether?
ETERNITY: thither, of a truth, not elsewhither, art
thou and all things bound! The great soul of Dante,
homeless on earth, made its home more and more
in that awful other world. Naturally his thoughts
brooded on that, as on the one fact important for
him. Bodied or bodiless, it is the one fact important for all men:—but to Dante, in that age, it was
bodied in fixed certainty of scientific shape; he no
more doubted of that *Malebolge* Pool, that it all
lay there with its gloomy circles, with its *alti guai*, and
that he himself should see it, than we doubt that we
should see Constantinople if we went thither. Dante's
heart, long filled with this, brooding over it in
speechless thought and awe, bursts forth at length
into 'mystic unfathomable song'; and this his *Divine
Comedy*, the most remarkable of all modern Books,
is the result.

It must have been a great solacement to Dante,
and was, as we can see, a proud thought for him at
times, That he, here in exile, could do this work; that
no Florence, nor no man or men, could hinder him
from doing it, or even much help him in doing it.
He knew too, partly, that it was great; the greatest
a man could do. 'If thou follow thy star, *Se tu segui
tua stella*,'—so could the Hero, in his forsakenness, in
his extreme need, still say to himself: 'Follow thou
thy star, thou shalt not fail of a glorious heaven!'
The labour of writing, we find, and indeed could
know otherwise, was great and painful for him;
he says, This Book, 'which has made me lean for
many years.' Ah yes, it was won, all of it, with pain
and sore toil,—not in sport, but in grim earnest. His
Book, as indeed most good Books are, has been
written, in many senses, with his heart's blood. It is
his whole history, this Book. He died after finishing
it; not yet very old, at the age of fifty-six;—broken-
hearted rather, as is said. He lies buried in his death-
city Ravenna: *Hic claudor Dantes patriis extorris ab oris*.

THE HERO AS POET

The Florentines begged back his body, in a century after; the Ravenna people would not give it. 'Here am I Dante laid, shut out from my native shores.'

I said, Dante's Poem was a Song: it is Tieck who calls it 'a mystic unfathomable Song'; and such is literally the character of it. Coleridge remarks very pertinently somewhere, that wherever you find a sentence musically worded, of true rhythm and melody in the words, there is something deep and good in the meaning too. For body and soul, word and idea, go strangely together here as everywhere. Song: we said before, it was the Heroic of Speech! All *old* Poems, Homer's and the rest, are authentically Songs. I would say, in strictness, that all right Poems are; that whatsoever is not *sung* is properly no Poem, but a piece of Prose cramped into jingling lines,—to the great injury of the grammar, to the great grief of the reader, for most part! What we want to get at is the *thought* the man had, if he had any: why should he twist it into jingle, if he *could* speak it out plainly? It is only when the heart of him is rapt into true passion of melody, and the very tones of him, according to Coleridge's remark, become musical by the greatness, depth and music of his thoughts, that we can give him right to rhyme and sing; that we call him a Poet, and listen to him as the Heroic of Speakers,—whose speech *is* Song. Pretenders to this are many; and to an earnest reader, I doubt, it is for most part a very melancholy, not to say an insupportable business, that of reading rhyme! Rhyme that had no inward necessity to be rhymed;—it ought to have told us plainly, without any jingle, what it was aiming at. I would advise all men who *can* speak their thought, not to sing it; to understand that, in a serious time, among serious men, there is no vocation in them for singing it. Precisely as we love the true song, and are charmed by it as by something divine, so shall we hate the false song, and account it a mere wooden noise, a thing hollow, superfluous, altogether an insincere and offensive thing.

I give Dante my highest praise when I say of his *Divine Comedy* that it is, in all senses, genuinely a Song. In the very sound of it there is a *canto fermo*; it proceeds as by a chant. The language, his simple *terza rima*, doubtless helped him in this. One reads along naturally with a sort of *lilt*. But I add, that it could not be otherwise; for the essence and material of the work are themselves rhythmic. Its depth, and rapt passion and sincerity, makes it musical;—go *deep* enough, there is music everywhere. A true inward symmetry, what one calls an architectural harmony, reigns in it, proportionates it all: architectural; which also partakes of the character of music. The three kingdoms, *Inferno, Purgatorio, Paradiso*, look out on one another like compartments of a great edifice; a great supernatural world-cathedral, piled up there, stern, solemn, awful; Dante's World of Souls! It is, at bottom, the *sincerest* of all Poems; sincerity, here too, we find to be the measure of worth. It came deep out of the author's heart of hearts; and it goes deep, and through long generations, into ours. The people of Verona, when they saw him on the streets, used to say, '*Eccovi l' uom ch' è stato all' Inferno*, See, there is the man that was in Hell!' Ah, yes, he had been in Hell;—in Hell enough, in long severe sorrow and struggle; as the like of him is pretty sure to have been. Commedias that come-out *divine* are not accomplished otherwise. Thought, true labour of any kind, highest virtue itself, is it not the daughter of Pain? Born as out of the black whirlwind;—true *effort*, in fact, as of a captive struggling to free himself: that is Thought. In all ways we are 'to become perfect through *suffering*.'—But, as I say, no work known to me is so elaborated as this of Dante's. It has all been as if molten, in the hottest furnace of his soul. It had made him 'lean' for many years. Not the general whole only; every compartment of it is worked-out, with intense

earnestness, into truth, into clear visuality. Each
answers to the other; each fits in its place, like a
marble stone accurately hewn and polished. It is
the soul of Dante, and in this the soul of the Middle
Ages, rendered for ever rhythmically visible there.
No light task; a right intense one: but a task which is
done.

Perhaps one would say, *intensity*, with the much
that depends on it, is the prevailing character of
Dante's genius. Dante does not come before us as
a large catholic mind; rather as a narrow, and even
sectarian mind: it is partly the fruit of his age and
position, but partly too of his own nature. His greatness has, in all senses, concentered itself into fiery
emphasis and depth. He is world-great not because
he is world-wide, but because he is world-deep.
Through all objects he pierces as it were down into
the heart of Being. I know nothing so intense as
Dante. Consider, for example, to begin with the
outermost development of his intensity, consider how
he paints. He has a great power of vision; seizes the
very type of a thing; presents that and nothing more.
You remember that first view he gets of the Hall of
Dite: *red* pinnacle, red-hot cone of iron glowing
through the dim immensity of gloom;—so vivid, so
distinct, visible at once and for ever! It is as an
emblem of the whole genius of Dante. There is a
brevity, an abrupt precision in him: Tacitus is not
briefer, more condensed; and then in Dante it seems
a natural condensation, spontaneous to the man.
One smiting word; and then there is silence, nothing
more said. His silence is more eloquent than words.
It is strange with what a sharp decisive grace he
snatches the true likeness of a matter: cuts into the
matter as with a pen of fire. Plutus, the blustering
giant, collapses at Virgil's rebuke; it is 'as the sails
sink, the mast being suddenly broken'. Or that poor
Sordello, with the *cotto aspetto*, 'face *baked*', parched
brown and lean; and the 'fiery snow' that falls on

them there, a 'fiery snow without wind', slow, deliberate, never-ending! Or the lids of those Tombs; square sarcophaguses, in that silent dim-burning Hall, each with its Soul in torment; the lids laid open there; they are to be shut at the Day of Judgement, through Eternity. And how Farinata rises; and how Cavalcante falls—at hearing of his Son, and the past tense *'fue'!* The very movements in Dante have something brief; swift, decisive, almost military. It is of the inmost essence of his genius this sort of painting. The fiery, swift Italian nature of the man, so silent, passionate, with its quick abrupt movements, its silent 'pale rages', speaks itself in these things.

For though this of painting is one of the outermost developments of a man, it comes like all else from the essential faculty of him; it is physiognomical of the whole man. Find a man whose words paint you a likeness, you have found a man worth something; mark his manner of doing it, as very characteristic of him. In the first place, he could not have discerned the object at all, or seen the vital type of it, unless he had, what we may call, *sympathized* with it,— had sympathy in him to bestow on objects. He must have been *sincere* about it too; sincere and sympathetic: a man without worth cannot give you the likeness of any object; he dwells in vague outwardness, fallacy and trivial hearsay, about all objects. And indeed may we not say that intellect altogether expresses itself in this power of discerning what an object is? Whatsoever of faculty a man's mind may have will come out here. Is it even of business, a matter to be done? The gifted man is he who *sees* the essential point, and leaves all the rest aside as surplusage: it is his faculty too, the man of business's faculty, that he discern the true *likeness*, not the false superficial one, of the thing he has got to work in. And how much of *morality* is in the kind of insight we get of anything; 'the eye seeing in all things what it brought with it the faculty of seeing!' To the mean eye all things are trivial, as certainly as to the jaundiced they are yellow. Raphael, the Painters tell us, is the best of all Portrait-painters withal. No most gifted eye can exhaust the significance of any object. In the commonest human face there lies more than Raphael will take away with him.

Dante's painting is not graphic only, brief, true, and of a vividness as of fire in dark night; taken on the wider scale, it is everyway noble, and the outcome of a great soul. Francesca and her Lover, what qualities in that! A thing woven as out of rainbows, on a ground of eternal black. A small flute-voice of infinite wail speaks there, into our very heart of hearts. A touch of womanhood in it too: *della bella persona, che mi fu tolta*; and how, even in the Pit of woe, it is a solace that *he* will never part from her! Saddest tragedy in these *alti guai*. And the racking winds, in that *aer bruno*, whirl them away again, to wail for ever!—Strange to think: Dante was the friend of this poor Francesca's father; Francesca herself may have sat upon the Poet's knee, as a bright innocent little child. Infinite pity, yet also infinite rigour of law: it is so Nature is made; it is so Dante discerned that she was made. What a paltry notion is that of his *Divine Comedy*'s being a poor splenetic impotent terrestrial libel; putting those into Hell whom he could not be avenged upon on earth! I suppose if ever pity, tender as a mother's, was in the heart of any man, it was in Dante's. But a man who does not know rigour cannot pity either. His very pity will be cowardly, egoistic,—sentimentality, or little better. I know not in the world an affection equal to that of Dante. It is a tenderness, a trembling, longing, pitying love: like the wail of Aeolean harps, soft, soft; like a child's young heart;—and then that stern, sore-saddened heart! These longings of his towards his Beatrice; their meeting together in the *Paradiso*; his gazing in her pure transfigured eyes, her that had been purified by death so long, separated from him so far:—one likens it to the song of angels; it is among the purest utterances of affection, perhaps the very purest, that ever came out of a human soul.

For the *intense* Dante is intense in all things; he has got into the essence of all. His intellectual insight as painter, on occasion too as reasoner, is but the result of all other sorts of intensity. Morally great, above all, we must call him; it is the beginning of all. His scorn, his grief are as transcendent as his love;— as indeed, what are they but the *inverse* or *converse* of his love? '*A Dio spiacenti, ed a' nemici sui*, Hateful to God and to the enemies of God:' lofty scorn, unappeasable silent reprobation and aversion; '*Non ragionam di lor*, We will not speak of *them*, look only and pass.' Or think of this: 'They have not the *hope* to die, *Non han speranza di morte*.' One day, it had risen sternly benign on the scathed heart of Dante, that he, wretched, never-resting, worn as he was, would full surely *die*; 'that Destiny itself could not doom him not to die.' Such words are in this man. For rigour, earnestness and depth, he is not to be paralleled in the modern world; to seek his parallel we must go into the Hebrew Bible, and live with the antique Prophets there.

I do not agree with much modern criticism, in greatly preferring the *Inferno* to the two other parts of the Divine *Commedia*. Such preference belongs, I imagine, to our general Byronism of taste, and is like to be a transient feeling. The *Purgatorio* and *Paradiso*, especially the former, one would almost say, is even more excellent than it. It is a noble thing that *Purgatorio*, 'Mountain of Purification'; an emblem of the noblest conception of that age. If Sin is so fatal, and Hell is and must be so rigorous, awful, yet in Repentance too is man purified; Repentance is the grand Christian act. It is beautiful how Dante works it out. The *tremolar dell' onde*, that 'trembling' of the ocean-waves, under the first pure gleam of morning, dawning afar on the wandering Two, is as

THE HERO AS POET

the type of an altered mood. Hope has now dawned; never-dying Hope, if in company still with heavy sorrow. The obscure sojourn of daemons and reprobate is under foot; a soft breathing of penitence mounts higher and higher, to the Throne of Mercy itself. 'Pray for me,' the denizens of that Mount of Pain all say to him. 'Tell my Giovanna to pray for me,' my daughter Giovanna; 'I think her mother loves me no more!' They toil painfully up by that winding steep, 'bent-down like corbels of a building,' some of them,—crushed together so 'for the sin of pride'; yet nevertheless in years, in ages and aeons, they shall have reached the top, which is Heaven's gate, and by Mercy shall have been admitted in. The joy too of all, when one has prevailed; the whole Mountain shakes with joy, and a psalm of praise rises, when one soul has perfected repentance, and got its sin and misery left behind! I call all this a noble embodiment of a true noble thought.

But indeed the Three compartments mutually support one another, are indispensable to one another. The *Paradiso*, a kind of inarticulate music to me, is the redeeming side of the *Inferno*; the *Inferno* without it were untrue. All three make up the true Unseen World, as figured in the Christianity of the Middle Ages; a thing for ever memorable, for ever true in the essence of it, to all men. It was perhaps delineated in no human soul with such depth of veracity as in this of Dante's; a man *sent* to sing it, to keep it long memorable. Very notable with what brief simplicity he passes out of the every-day reality, into the Invisible one; and in the second or third stanza, we find ourselves in the World of Spirits; and dwell there, as among things palpable, indubitable! To Dante they *were* so; the real world, as it is called, and its facts, was but the threshold to an infinitely higher Fact of a World. At bottom, the one was as *preter*natural as the other. Has not each man a soul? He will not only be a spirit, but is one. To the earnest

Dante it is all one visible Fact; he believes it, sees it; is the Poet of it in virtue of that. Sincerity, I say again, is the saving merit, now as always.

Dante's Hell, Purgatory, Paradise, are a symbol withal, an emblematic representation of his Belief about this Universe:—some Critic in a future age, like those Scandinavian ones the other day, who has ceased altogether to think as Dante did, may find this too all an 'Allegory', perhaps an idle Allegory! It is a sublime embodiment, or sublimest, of the soul of Christianity. It expresses, as in huge world-wide architectural emblems, how the Christian Dante felt Good and Evil to be the two polar elements of this Creation, on which it all turns; that these two differ not by *preferability* of one to the other, but by incompatibility absolute and infinite; that the one is excellent and high as light and Heaven, the other hideous, black as Gehenna and the Pit of Hell! Everlasting Justice, yet with Penitence, with everlasting Pity,—all Christianism, as Dante and the Middle Ages had it, is emblemed there. Emblemed: and yet, as I urged the other day, with what entire truth of purpose; how unconscious of any embleming! Hell, Purgatory, Paradise: these things were not fashioned as emblems; was there, in our Modern European Mind, any thought at all of their being emblems! Were they not indubitable awful facts; the whole heart of man taking them for practically true, all Nature everywhere confirming them? So is it always in these things. Men do not believe an Allegory. The future Critic, whatever his new thought may be, who considers this of Dante to have been all got-up as an Allegory, will commit one sore mistake!—Paganism we recognized as a veracious expression of the earnest awe-struck feeling of man towards the Universe; veracious, true once, and still not without worth for us. But mark here the difference of Paganism and Christianism; one great difference. Paganism emblemed chiefly the Operations of Nature; the destinies, efforts, combinations, vicissitudes of things and men in this world; Christianism emblemed the Law of Human Duty, the Moral Law of Man. One was for the sensuous nature: a rude helpless utterance of the *first* Thought of men,—the chief recognized virtue, Courage, Superiority to Fear. The other was not for the sensuous nature, but for the moral. What a progress is here, if in that one respect only!—

And so in this Dante, as we said, had ten silent centuries, in a very strange way, found a voice. The *Divina Commedia* is of Dante's writing; yet in truth *it* belongs to ten Christian centuries, only the finishing of it is Dante's. So always. The craftsman there, the smith with that metal of his, with these tools, with these cunning methods,—how little of all he does is properly *his* work! All past inventive men work there with him;—as indeed with all of us, in all things. Dante is the spokesman of the Middle Ages; the Thought they lived by stands here, in everlasting music. These sublime ideas of his, terrible and beautiful, are the fruit of the Christian Meditation of all the good men who had gone before him. Precious they; but also is not he precious? Much, had not he spoken, would have been dumb; not dead, yet living voiceless.

On the whole, is it not an utterance, this mystic Song, at once of one of the greatest human souls, and of the highest thing that Europe had hitherto realized for itself? Christianism, as Dante sings it, is another than Paganism in the rude Norse mind; another than 'Bastard Christianism' half articulately spoken in the Arab desert, seven hundred years before!—The noblest *idea* made *real* hitherto among men, is sung, and emblemed forth abidingly, by one of the noblest men. In the one sense and in the other, are we not right glad to possess it? As I calculate, it may last yet for long thousands of years. For the thing that is uttered from the inmost parts of a man's soul, differs altogether from what is uttered by the outer part. The outer is of the day, under the empire of mode; the outer passes away, in swift endless changes; the inmost is the same yesterday, to-day, and for ever. True souls, in all generations of the world, who look on this Dante, will find a brotherhood in him; the deep sincerity of his thoughts, his woes and hopes, will speak likewise to their sincerity; they will feel that this Dante too was a brother. Napoleon in Saint-Helena is charmed with the genial veracity of old Homer. The oldest Hebrew Prophet, under a vesture the most diverse from ours, does yet, because he speaks from the heart of man, speak to all men's hearts. It is the one sole secret of continuing long memorable. Dante, for depth of sincerity, is like an antique Prophet too; his words, like theirs, come from his very heart. One need not wonder if it were predicted that his Poem might be the most enduring thing our Europe has yet made; for nothing so endures as a truly spoken word. All cathedrals, pontificalities, brass and stone, and outer arrangement never so lasting, are brief in comparison to an unfathomable heart-song like this: one feels as if it might survive, still of importance to men, when these had all sunk into new irrecognizable combinations, and had ceased individually to be. Europe has made much; great cities, great empires, encyclopaedias, creeds, bodies of opinion and practice: but it has made little of the class of Dante's Thought. Homer yet *is*, veritably present face to face with every open soul of us; and Greece, where is *it*? Desolate for thousands of years; away, vanished; a bewildered heap of stones and rubbish, the life and existence of it all gone. Like a dream; like the dust of King Agamemnon! Greece was; Greece, except in the *words* it spoke, is not.

The uses of this Dante? We will not say much about his 'uses'. A human soul who has once got into that primal element of *Song*, and sung forth fitly somewhat therefrom, has worked in the *depths* of our existence; feeding through long times the life-*roots* of all excellent human things whatsoever,—in a way that 'utilities' will not succeed well in calculating! We will not estimate the Sun by the quantity of gaslight it saves us; Dante shall be invaluable, or of no value. One remark I may make: the contrast in this respect between the Hero-Poet and the Hero-Prophet. In a hundred years, Mahomet, as we saw, had his Arabians at Grenada and at Delhi; Dante's Italians seem to be yet very much where they were. Shall we say, then, Dante's effect on the world was small in comparison? Not so: his arena is far more restricted; but also it is far nobler, clearer;—perhaps not less but more important. Mahomet speaks to great masses of men, in the coarse dialect adapted to such; a dialect filled with inconsistencies, crudities, follies: on the great masses alone can he act, and there with good and with evil strangely blended. Dante speaks to the noble, the pure and great, in all times and places. Neither does he grow obsolete, as the other does. Dante burns as a pure star, fixed there in the firmament, at which the great and the high of all ages kindle themselves: he is the possession of all the chosen of the world for uncounted time. Dante, one calculates, may long survive Mahomet. In this way the balance may be made straight again.

But, at any rate, it is not by what is called their effect on the world by what *we* can judge of their effect there, that a man and his work are measured. Effect? Influence? Utility? Let a man *do* his work; the fruit of it is the care of Another than he. It will grow its own fruit; and whether embodied in Caliph Thrones and Arabian Conquests, so that it 'fills all Morning and Evening Newspapers', and all Histories, which are a kind of distilled Newspapers; or not embodied so at all;—what matters that? That is not the real fruit of it! The Arabian Caliph, in so far only as he did something, was something. If the great Cause of Man, and Man's work in God's Earth, got no furtherance from the Arabian Caliph, then no matter how many scimitars he drew, how many gold piastres pocketed, and what uproar and blaring he made in this world,—*he* was but a loud-sounding inanity and futility; at bottom, he *was* not at all. Let us honour the great empire of *Silence*, once more! The boundless treasury which we do *not* jingle in our pockets, or count up and present before men! It is perhaps, of all things, the usefulest for each of us to do, in these loud times.——

As Dante, the Italian man, was sent into our world to embody musically the Religion of the Middle Ages, the Religion of our Modern Europe, its Inner Life; so Shakespeare, we may say, embodies for us the Outer Life of our Europe as developed then, its chivalries, courtesies, humours, ambitions, what practical way of thinking, acting, looking at the world, men then had. As in Homer we may still construe Old Greece; so in Shakespeare and Dante, after thousands of years, what our Modern Europe was, in Faith and in Practice, will still be legible. Dante has given us the Faith or soul; Shakespeare, in a not less noble way, has given us the Practice or body. This latter also we were to have; a man was sent for it, the man Shakespeare. Just when that chivalry way of life had reached its last finish, and was on the point of breaking down into slow or swift dissolution, as we now see it everywhere, this other sovereign Poet, with his seeing eye, with his perennial singing voice, was sent to take note of it, to give long-enduring record of it. Two fit men: Dante, deep, fierce as the central fire of the world; Shakespeare, wide, placid, far-seeing, as the Sun, the upper light of the world. Italy produced the one world-voice; we English had the honour of producing the other.

Curious enough how, as it were by mere accident, this man came to us. I think always, so great, quiet, complete and self-sufficing is this Shakespeare, had the Warwickshire Squire not prosecuted him for deer-stealing, we had perhaps never heard of him as a Poet! The woods and skies, the rustic Life of Man in Stratford there, had been enough for this man! But indeed that strange outbudding of our whole English Existence, which we call the Elizabethan Era, did not it too come as of its own accord? The 'Tree Igdrasil' buds and withers by its own laws,— too deep for our scanning. Yet it does bud and wither, and every bough and leaf of it is there, by fixed eternal laws; not a Sir Thomas Lucy but comes at the hour fit for him. Curious, I say, and not sufficiently considered: how everything does co-operate with all; not a leaf rotting on the highway but is indissoluble portion of solar and stellar systems; no thought, word or act of man but has sprung withal out of all men, and works sooner or later, recognizably or irrecognizably, on all men! It is all a Tree: circulation of sap and influences, mutual communication of every minutest leaf with the lowest talon of a root, with every other greatest and minutest portion of the whole. The Tree Igdrasil, that has its roots down in the Kingdoms of Hela and Death, and whose boughs overspread the highest Heaven!—

In some sense it may be said that this glorious Elizabethan Era with its Shakespeare, as the outcome and flowerage of all which had preceded it, is itself attributable to the Catholicism of the Middle Ages. The Christian Faith, which was the theme of Dante's Song, had produced this Practical Life which Shakespeare was to sing. For Religion then, as it now and always is, was the soul of Practice; the primary vital fact in men's life. And remark here, as rather curious, that Middle-Age Catholicism was abolished, so far as Acts of Parliament could abolish it, before Shakespeare, the noblest product of it, made his appearance. He did make his appearance nevertheless. Nature at her own time, with Catholicism or what else might be necessary, sent him forth; taking small thought of Acts of Parliament. King-Henrys, Queen-Elizabeths go their way; and Nature too goes hers. Acts of Parliament, on the whole, are small, notwithstanding the noise they make. What Act of Parliament, debate at St. Stephens, on the hustings or elsewhere, was it that brought this Shakespeare into being? No dining at Freemasons' Tavern, opening subscription-lists, selling of shares, and infinite other jangling and true or false endeavouring! This Elizabethan Era, and all its nobleness and blessedness, came without proclamation, preparation of ours. Priceless Shakespeare was the free gift of Nature; given altogether silently;—received altogether silently, as if it had been a thing of little account. And yet, very literally, it is a priceless thing. One should look at that side of matters too.

Of this Shakespeare of ours, perhaps the opinion one sometimes hears a little idolatrously expressed is, in fact, the right one; I think the best judgement not of this country only, but of Europe at large, is slowly pointing to the conclusion, That Shakespeare is the chief of all Poets hitherto; the greatest intellect who, in our recorded world, has left record of himself in the way of Literature. On the whole, I know not such a power of vision, such a faculty of thought, if we take all the characters of it, in any other man. Such a calmness of depth; placid joyous strength; all things imaged in that great soul of his so true and clear, as in a tranquil unfathomable sea! It has been said, that in the constructing of Shakespeare's Dramas there is, apart from all other 'faculties' as they are called, an understanding manifested, equal to that in Bacon's *Novum Organum*. That is true; and it is not a truth that strikes every one. It would become more apparent if we tried, any of us for himself, how, out of Shakespeare's dramatic materials, *we* could fashion such a result! The built house seems all so fit,—everyway as it should be. as if it came there

THE HERO AS POET

by its own law and the nature of things,—we forget the rude disorderly quarry it was shaped from. The very perfection of the house, as if Nature herself had made it, hides the builder's merit. Perfect, more perfect than any other man, we may call Shakespeare in this: he discerns, knows as by instinct, what condition he works under, what his materials are, what his own force and its relation to them is. It is not a transitory glance of insight that will suffice; it is deliberate illumination of the whole matter; it is a calmly *seeing* eye; a great intellect, in short. How a man, of some wide thing that he has witnessed, will construct a narrative, what kind of picture and delineation he will give of it,—is the best measure you could get of what intellect is in the man. Which circumstance is vital and shall stand prominent; which unessential, fit to be suppressed; where is the true *beginning*, the true sequence and ending? To find out this, you task the whole force of insight that is in the man. He must *understand* the thing; according to the depth of his understanding, will the fitness of his answer be. You will try him so. Does like join itself to like; does the spirit of method stir in that confusion, so that its embroilment becomes order? Can the man say, *Fiat lux*, Let there be light; and out of chaos make a world? Precisely as there is *light* in himself, will he accomplish this.

Or indeed we may say again, it is in what I called Portrait-painting, delineating of men and things, especially of men, that Shakespeare is great. All the greatness of the man comes out decisively here. It is unexampled, I think, that calm creative perspicacity of Shakespeare. The thing he looks at reveals not this or that face of it, but its inmost heart and generic secret: it dissolves itself as in light before him, so that he discerns the perfect structure of it. Creative, we said: poetic creation, what is this too but *seeing* the thing sufficiently? The *word* that will describe the thing, follows of itself from such clear intense sight of the thing. And is not Shakespeare's *morality*, his valour, candour, tolerance, truthfulness; his whole victorious strength and greatness, which can triumph over such obstructions, visible there too? Great as the world! No *twisted*, poor convex-concave mirror, reflecting all objects with its own convexities and concavities; a perfectly *level* mirror;—that is to say withal, if we will understand it, a man justly related to all things and men, a good man. It is truly a lordly spectacle how this great soul takes in all kinds of men and objects, a Falstaff, an Othello, a Juliet, a Coriolanus; sets them all forth to us in their round completeness; loving, just, the equal brother of all. *Novum Organum*, and all the intellect you will find in Bacon, is of a quite secondary order; earthy, material, poor in comparison with this. Among modern men, one finds, in strictness, almost nothing of the same rank. Goethe alone, since the days of Shakespeare, reminds me of it. Of him too you say that he *saw* the object; you may say what he himself says of Shakespeare: 'His characters are like watches with dial-plates of transparent crystal; they show you the hour like others, and the inward mechanism also is all visible.'

The seeing eye! It is this that discloses the inner harmony of things; what Nature meant, what musical idea Nature has wrapped up in these often rough embodiments. Something she did mean. To the seeing eye that something were discernible. Are they base, miserable things? You can laugh over them, you can weep over them; you can in some way or other genially relate yourself to them;—you can, at lowest, hold your peace about them, turn away your own and others' face from them, till the hour come for practically exterminating and extinguishing them! At bottom, it is the Poet's first gift, as it is all men's, that he have intellect enough. He will be a Poet if he have: a Poet in word; or failing that, perhaps still better, a Poet in act. Whether he write at all; and if so, whether in prose or in verse, will depend on accidents: who knows on what extremely trivial accidents,—perhaps on his having had a singing-master, on his being taught to sing in his boyhood! But the faculty which enables him to discern the inner heart of things, and the harmony that dwells there (for whatsoever exists has a harmony in the heart of it, or it would not hold together and exist), is not the result of habits or accidents, but the gift of Nature herself; the primary outfit for a Heroic Man in what sort soever. To the Poet, as to every other, we say first of all, *See*. If you cannot do that, it is of no use to keep stringing rhymes together, jingling sensibilities against each other, and *name* yourself a Poet; there is no hope for you. If you can, there is, in prose or verse, in action or speculation, all manner of hope. The crabbed old Schoolmaster used to ask, when they brought him a new pupil, 'But are ye sure he's *not a dunce*?' Why, really one might ask the same thing, in regard to every man proposed for whatsoever function; and consider it as the one inquiry needful: Are ye sure he's not a dunce? There is, in this world, no other entirely fatal person.

For, in fact, I say the degree of vision that dwells in a man is a correct measure of the man. If called to define Shakespeare's faculty, I should say superiority of Intellect, and think I had included all under that. What indeed are faculties? We talk of faculties as if they were distinct, things separable; as if a man had intellect, imagination, fancy, &c., as he has hands, feet and arms. That is a capital error. Then again, we hear of a man's 'intellectual nature', and of his 'moral nature', as if these again were divisible, and existed apart. Necessities of language do perhaps prescribe such forms of utterance; we must speak, I am aware, in that way, if we are to speak at all. But words ought not to harden into things for us. It seems to me, our apprehension of this matter is, for most part, radically falsified thereby. We ought to know withal, and to keep for ever in mind, that these divisions are at bottom but *names*; that man's spiritual nature, the vital Force which dwells in him, is essentially one and indivisible; that what we call imagination, fancy, understanding, and so forth, are but different figures of the same Power of Insight, all indissolubly connected with each other, physiognomically related; that if we knew one of them, we might know all of them. Morality itself, what we call the moral quality of a man, what is this but another *side* of the one vital Force whereby he is and works? All that a man does is physiognomical of him. You may see how a man would fight, by the way in which he sings; his courage, or want of courage, is visible in the word he utters, in the opinion he has formed, no less than in the stroke he strikes. He is *one*; and preaches the same Self abroad in all these ways.

Without hands a man might have feet, and could still walk: but, consider it,—without morality, intellect were impossible for him; a thoroughly immoral *man* could not know anything at all! To know a thing, what we can call knowing, a man must first *love* the thing, sympathize with it: that is, be *virtuously* related to it. If he have not the justice to put down his own selfishness at every turn, the courage to stand by the dangerous-true at every turn, how shall he know? His virtues, all of them, will lie recorded in his knowledge. Nature, with her truth, remains to the bad, to the selfish and the pusillanimous for ever a sealed book: what such can know of Nature is mean, superficial, small; for the uses of the day merely.—But does not the very Fox know something of Nature? Exactly so: it knows where the geese lodge! The human Reynard, very frequent everywhere in the world, what more does he know but this and the like of this? Nay, it should be considered too, that if the Fox had not a certain vulpine *morality*, he could not even know where the geese were, or get at the geese! If he spent his time in splenetic atrabiliar reflections on his own misery, his ill usage by Nature, Fortune and other Foxes, and so forth; and had not courage, promptitude, practicality, and other suitable vulpine gifts and graces, he would catch no geese. We may say of the Fox too, that his morality and insight are of the same dimensions; different faces of the same internal unity of vulpine life!—These things are worth stating; for the contrary of them acts with manifold very baleful perversion, in this time: what limitations, modifications they require, your own candour will supply.

If I say, therefore, that Shakespeare is the greatest of Intellects, I have said all concerning him. But there is more in Shakespeare's intellect than we have yet seen. It is what I call an unconscious intellect; there is more virtue in it than he himself is aware of. Novalis beautifully remarks of him, that those Dramas of his are Products of Nature too, deep as Nature herself. I find a great truth in this saying. Shakespeare's Art is not Artifice; the noblest worth of it is not there by plan or precontrivance. It grows up from the deeps of Nature, through this noble sincere soul, who is a voice of Nature. The latest generations of men will find new meanings in Shakespeare, new elucidations of their own human being; 'new harmonies with the infinite structure of the Universe; concurrences with later ideas, affinities with the higher powers and senses of man.' This well deserves meditating. It is Nature's highest award to a true simple great soul, that he get thus to be *a part of herself*. Such a man's works, whatsoever he with utmost conscious exertion and forethought shall accomplish, grow up withal *un*consciously, from the unknown deeps in him;—as the oak-tree grows from the Earth's bosom, as the mountains and waters shape themselves; with a symmetry grounded on Nature's own laws, conformable to all Truth whatsoever. How much in Shakespeare lies hid; his sorrows, his silent struggles known to himself; much that was not known at all, not speakable at all:

like *roots*, like sap and forces working underground! Speech is great; but Silence is greater.

Withal the joyful tranquillity of this man is notable. I will not blame Dante for his misery: it is as battle without victory; but true battle,—the first, indispensable thing. Yet I call Shakespeare greater than Dante, in that he fought truly, and did conquer. Doubt it not, he had his own sorrows: those *Sonnets* of his will even testify expressly in what deep waters he had waded, and swum struggling for his life;—as what man like him ever failed to have to do? It seems to me a heedless notion, our common one, that he sat like a bird on the bough; and sang forth, free and offhand, never knowing the troubles of other men. Not so; with no man is it so. How could a man travel forward from rustic deer-poaching to such tragedy-writing, and not fall in with sorrows by the way? Or, still better, how could a man delineate a Hamlet, a Coriolanus, a Macbeth, so many suffering heroic hearts, if his own heroic heart had never suffered?—And now, in contrast with all this, observe his mirthfulness, his genuine overflowing love of laughter! You would say, in no point does he *exaggerate* but only in laughter. Fiery objurgations, words that pierce and burn, are to be found in Shakespeare; yet he is always in measure here; never what Johnson would remark as a specially 'good hater'. But his laughter seems to pour from him in floods; he heaps all manner of ridiculous nicknames on the butt he is bantering, tumbles and tosses him in all sorts of horse-play; you would say, roars and laughs. And then, if not always the finest, it is always a genial laughter. Not at mere weakness, at misery or poverty; never. No man who *can* laugh, what we call laughing, will laugh at these things. It is some poor character only *desiring* to laugh, and have the credit of wit, that does so. Laughter means sympathy; good laughter is not 'the crackling of thorns under the pot'. Even at stupidity and pretension this Shakespeare does not laugh otherwise than genially. Dogberry and Verges

THE HERO AS POET

tickle our very hearts; and we dismiss them covered with explosions of laughter: but we like the poor fellows only the better for our laughing; and hope they will get on well there, and continue Presidents of the City-watch.—Such laughter, like sunshine on the deep sea, is very beautiful to me.

We have no room to speak of Shakespeare's individual works; though perhaps there is much still waiting to be said on that head. Had we, for instance, all his plays reviewed as *Hamlet*, in *Wilhelm Meister*, is! A thing which might, one day, be done. August Wilhelm Schlegel has a remark on his Historical Plays, *Henry Fifth* and the others, which is worth remembering. He calls them a kind of National Epic. Marlborough, you recollect, said, he knew no English History but what he had learned from Shakespeare. There are really, if we look to it, few as memorable Histories. The great salient points are admirably seized; all rounds itself off, into a kind of rhythmic coherence; it is, as Schlegel says, *epic*;—as indeed all delineation by a great thinker will be. There are right beautiful things in those Pieces, which indeed together form one beautiful thing. That battle of Agincourt strikes me as one of the most perfect things, in its sort, we anywhere have of Shakespeare's. The description of the two hosts: the worn-out, jaded English; the dread hour, big with destiny, when the battle shall begin; and then that deathless valour: 'Ye good yeomen, whose limbs were made in England!' There is a noble Patriotism in it,—far other than the 'indifference' you sometimes hear ascribed to Shakespeare. A true English heart breathes, calm and strong, through the whole business; not boisterous, protrusive; all the better for that. There is a sound in it like the ring of steel. This man too had a right stroke in him, had it come to that!

But I will say, of Shakespeare's works generally, that we have no full impress of him there; even as full as we have of many men. His works are so many windows, through which we see a glimpse of the world that was in him. All his works seem, comparatively speaking, cursory, imperfect, written under cramping circumstances; giving only here and there a note of the full utterance of the man. Passages there are that come upon you like splendour out of Heaven; bursts of radiance, illuminating the very heart of the thing: you say, 'That is *true*, spoken once and forever; wheresoever and whensoever there is an open human soul, that will be recognized as true!' Such bursts, however, make us feel that the surrounding matter is not radiant; that it is, in part, temporary, conventional. Alas, Shakespeare had to write for the Globe Playhouse: his great soul had to crush itself, as it could, into that and no other mould. It was with him, then, as it is with us all. No man works save under conditions. The sculptor cannot set his own free Thought before us; but his Thought as he could translate it into the stone that was given, with the tools that were given. *Disjecta membra* are all that we find of any Poet, or of any man.

Whoever looks intelligently at this Shakespeare may recognize that he too was a *Prophet*, in his way; of an insight analogous to the Prophetic, though he took it up in another strain. Nature seemed to this man also divine; *un*speakable, deep as Tophet, high as Heaven: 'We are such stuff as Dreams are made of!' That scroll in Westminster Abbey, which few read with understanding, is of the depth of any Seer. But the man sang; did not preach, except musically. We called Dante the melodious Priest of Middle-Age Catholicism. May we not call Shakespeare the still more melodious Priest of a *true* Catholicism, the 'Universal Church' of the Future and of all times? No narrow superstition, harsh asceticism, intolerance, fanatical fierceness or perversion: a Revelation, so far as it goes, that such a thousandfold hidden

THE HERO AS POET

beauty and divineness dwells in all Nature; which let all men worship as they can! We may say without offence, that there rises a kind of universal Psalm out of this Shakespeare too; not unfit to make itself heard among the still more sacred Psalms. Not in disharmony with these, if we understood them, but in unison!—I cannot call this Shakespeare a 'Sceptic', as some do; his indifference to the creeds and theological quarrels of his time misleading them. No: neither unpatriotic, though he says little about his Patriotism; no sceptic, though he says little about his Faith. Such 'indifference' was the fruit of his greatness withal: his whole heart was in his own grand sphere of worship (we may call it such); these other controversies, vitally important to other men, were not vital to him.

But call it worship, call it what you will, is it not a right glorious thing and set of things, this that Shakespeare has brought us? For myself, I feel that there is actually a kind of sacredness in the fact of such a man being sent into this Earth. Is he not an eye to us all; a blessed heaven-sent Bringer of Light?—And, at bottom, was it not perhaps far better that this Shakespeare, everyway an unconscious man, was *conscious* of no Heavenly message? He did not feel, like Mahomet, because he saw into those internal Splendours, that he specially was the 'Prophet of God': and was he not greater than Mahomet in that? Greater; and also, if we compute strictly, as we did in Dante's case, more successful. It was intrinsically an error that notion of Mahomet's, of his supreme Prophethood; and has come down to us inextricably involved in error to this day; dragging along with it such a coil of fables, impurities, intolerances, as makes it a questionable step for me here and now to say, as I have done, that Mahomet was a true Speaker at all, and not rather an ambitious charlatan, perversity, and simulacrum, no Speaker, but a Babbler! Even in Arabia, as I compute, Mahomet will have exhausted himself and become obsolete, while this Shakespeare, this Dante may still be young;—while this Shakespeare may still pretend to be a Priest of Mankind, of Arabia as of other places, for unlimited periods to come! Compared with any speaker or singer one knows, even with Aeschylus or Homer, why should he not, for veracity and universality, last like them? He is *sincere* as they; reaches deep down like them, to the universal and perennial. But as for Mahomet, I think it had been better for him *not* to be so conscious! Alas, poor Mahomet; all that he was *conscious* of was a mere error; a futility and triviality,—as indeed such ever is. The truly great in him too was the unconscious: that he was a wild Arab lion of the desert, and did speak out with that great thunder-voice of his, not by words which he *thought* to be great, but by actions, by feelings, by a history which *were* great! His Koran has become a stupid piece of prolix absurdity; we do not believe, like him, that God wrote that! The Great Man here too, as always, is a Force of Nature: whatsoever is truly great in him springs up from the *inarticulate deeps.*

Well: this is our poor Warwickshire Peasant, who rose to be Manager of a Playhouse, so that he could live without begging; whom the Earl of Southampton cast some kind glances on; whom Sir Thomas Lucy, many thanks to him, was for sending to the Treadmill! We did not account him a god, like Odin, while he dwelt with us;—on which point there were much to be said. But I will say rather, or repeat: In spite of the sad state Hero-worship now lies in, consider what this Shakespeare has actually become among us. Which Englishman we ever made, in this land of ours, which million of Englishmen, would we not give up rather than the Stratford Peasant? There is no regiment of highest Dignitaries that we would sell him for. He is the grandest thing we have yet done. For our honour among foreign nations, as an ornament to our

THE HERO AS POET 253

English Household, what item is there that we would not surrender rather than him? Consider now, if they asked us, Will you give up your Indian Empire or your Shakespeare, you English; never have had any Indian Empire, or never have had any Shakespeare? Really it were a grave question. Official persons would answer doubtless in official language; but we, for our part too, should not we be forced to answer: Indian Empire, or no Indian Empire; we cannot do without Shakespeare! Indian Empire will go, at any rate, some day; but this Shakespeare does not go, he lasts for ever with us; we cannot give up our Shakespeare!

Nay, apart from spiritualities; and considering him merely as a real, marketable, tangibly-useful possession. England, before long, this Island of ours, will hold but a small fraction of the English: in America, in New Holland, east and west to the very Antipodes, there will be a Saxondom covering great spaces of the Globe. And now, what is it that can keep all these together into virtually one Nation, so that they do not fall out and fight, but live at peace, in brotherlike intercourse, helping one another? This is justly regarded as the greatest practical problem, the thing all manner of sovereignties and governments are here to accomplish: what is it that will accomplish this? Acts of Parliament, administrative prime-ministers cannot. America is parted from us, so far as Parliament could part it. Call it not fantastic, for there is much reality in it: Here, I say, is an English King, whom no time or chance, Parliament or combination of Parliaments, can dethrone! This King Shakespeare, does not he shine, in crowned sovereignty, over us all, as the noblest, gentlest, yet strongest of rallying-signs; *in*destructible; really more valuable in that point of view, than any other means or appliance whatsoever? We can fancy him as radiant aloft over all the Nations of Englishmen, a thousand years hence. From Paramatta, from New York, wheresoever, under what sort of Parish-Constable soever, English men and women are, they will say to one another: 'Yes, this Shakespeare is ours: we produced him, we speak and think by him; we are of one blood and kind with him.' The most common-sense politician, too, if he pleases, may think of that.

Yes, truly, it is a great thing for a Nation that it get an articulate voice; that it produce a man who will speak forth melodiously what the heart of it means! Italy, for example, poor Italy lies dismembered, scattered asunder, not appearing in any protocol or treaty as a unity at all; yet the noble Italy is actually *one*: Italy produced its Dante: Italy can speak! The Czar of all the Russias, he is strong, with so many bayonets, Cossacks, and cannons: and does a great feat in keeping such a tract of Earth politically together; but he cannot yet speak. Something great in him, but it is a dumb greatness. He has had no voice of genius, to be heard of all men and times. He must learn to speak. He is a great dumb monster hitherto. His cannons and Cossacks will all have rusted into nonentity, while that Dante's voice is still audible. The Nation that has a Dante is bound together as no dumb Russia can be.—We must here end what we had to say of the *Hero-Poet*.

JAMES HENRY LEIGH HUNT
1784–1859
AN ANSWER TO THE QUESTION
WHAT IS POETRY? (1844)

POETRY, strictly and artistically so called, that is to say, considered not merely as poetic feeling, which is more or less shared by all the world, but as the operation of that feeling, such as we see it in the poet's book, is the utterance of a passion for truth, beauty, and power, embodying and illustrating its conceptions by imagination and fancy, and modulating its language on the principle of variety in uniformity. Its means are whatever the universe contains; and its ends, pleasure and exaltation. Poetry stands between nature and convention, keeping alive among us the enjoyment of the external and the spiritual world: it has constituted the most enduring fame of nations; and, next to Love and Beauty, which are its parents, is the greatest proof to man of the pleasure to be found in all things, and of the probable riches of infinitude.

Poetry is a passion,[1] because it seeks the deepest impressions; and because it must undergo, in order to convey, them.

It is a passion for truth, because without truth the impression would be false or defective.

It is a passion for beauty, because its office is to exalt and refine by means of pleasure, and because beauty is nothing but the loveliest form of pleasure.

It is a passion for power, because power is impression triumphant, whether over the poet, as desired by himself, or over the reader, as affected by the poet.

---

[1] *Passio*, suffering in a good sense,—ardent subjection of one's-self to emotion.

It embodies and illustrates its impressions by imagination, or images of the objects of which it treats, and other images brought in to throw light on those objects, in order that it may enjoy and impart the feeling of their truth in its utmost conviction and affluence.

It illustrates them by fancy, which is a lighter play of imagination, or the feeling of analogy coming short of seriousness, in order that it may laugh with what it loves, and show how it can decorate it with fairy ornament.

It modulates what it utters, because in running the whole round of beauty it must needs include beauty of sound; and because, in the height of its enjoyment, it must show the perfection of its triumph, and make difficulty itself become part of its facility and joy.

And lastly, Poetry shapes this modulation into uniformity for its outline, and variety for its parts, because it thus realizes the last idea of beauty itself, which includes the charm of diversity within the flowing round of habit and ease.

Poetry is imaginative passion. The quickest and subtlest test of the possession of its essence is in expression; the variety of things to be expressed shows the amount of its resources; and the continuity of the song completes the evidence of its strength and greatness. He who has thought, feeling, expression, imagination, action, character, and continuity, all in the largest amount and highest degree, is the greatest poet.

Poetry includes whatsoever of painting can be made visible to the mind's eye, and whatsoever of music can be conveyed by sound and proportion without singing or instrumentation. But it far surpasses those divine arts in suggestiveness, range, and intellectual wealth;—the first, in expression of thought, combination of images, and the triumph over space and time; the second, in all that can be done by speech, apart from the tones and modulations of pure sound. Painting and music, however,

WHAT IS POETRY?

include all those portions of the gift of poetry that can be expressed and heightened by the visible and melodious. Painting, in a certain apparent manner, is things themselves; music, in a certain audible manner, is their very emotion and grace. Music and painting are proud to be related to poetry, and poetry loves and is proud of them.

Poetry begins where matter of fact or of science ceases to be merely such, and to exhibit a further truth; that is to say, the connexion it has with the world of emotion, and its power to produce imaginative pleasure. Inquiring of a gardener, for instance, what flower it is we see yonder, he answers, 'a lily'. This is matter of fact. The botanist pronounces it to be of the order of 'Hexandria Monogynia'. This is matter of science. It is the 'lady' of the garden, says Spenser; and here we begin to have a poetical sense of its fairness and grace. It is

> The plant and flower of *light*,

says Ben Jonson; and poetry then shows us the beauty of the flower in all its mystery and splendour.

If it be asked, how we know perceptions like these to be true, the answer is, by the fact of their existence —by the consent and delight of poetic readers. And as feeling is the earliest teacher, and perception the only final proof, of things the most demonstrable by science, so the remotest imaginations of the poets may often be found to have the closest connexion with matter of fact; perhaps might always be so, if the subtlety of our perceptions were a match for the causes of them. Consider this image of Ben Jonson's— of a lily being the flower of light. Light, undecomposed, is white; and as the lily is white, and light is white, and whiteness itself is nothing *but* light, the two things, so far, are not merely similar, but identical. A poet might add, by an analogy drawn from the connexion of light and colour, that there is a 'golden dawn' issuing out of the white lily, in the rich yellow of the stamens. I have no desire to push this similarity farther than it may be worth. Enough has been stated to show that, in poetical as in other analogies, 'the same feet of Nature', as Bacon says, may be seen 'treading in different paths'; and that the most scornful, that is to say, dullest disciple of fact, should be cautious how he betrays the shallowness of his philosophy by discerning no poetry in its depths.

But the poet is far from dealing only with these subtle and analogical truths. Truth of every kind belongs to him, provided it can bud into any kind of beauty, or is capable of being illustrated and impressed by the poetic faculty. Nay, the simplest truth is often so beautiful and impressive of itself, that one of the greatest proofs of his genius consists in his leaving it to stand alone, illustrated by nothing but the light of its own tears or smiles, its own wonder, might, or playfulness. Hence the complete effect of many a simple passage in our old English ballads and romances, and of the passionate sincerity in general of the greatest early poets, such as Homer and Chaucer, who flourished before the existence of a 'literary world', and were not perplexed by a heap of notions and opinions, or by doubts how emotion ought to be expressed. The greatest of their successors never write equally to the purpose, except when they can dismiss everything from their minds but the like simple truth. In the beautiful poem of *Sir Eger, Sir Graham and Sir Gray-Steel* (see it in Ellis's *Specimens*, or Laing's *Early Metrical Tales*), a knight thinks himself disgraced in the eyes of his mistress:—

> Sir Eger said, 'If it be so,
> Then wot I well I must forgo
> Love-liking, and manhood, all clean!'
> *The water rush'd out of his een!*

Sir Gray-Steel is killed:

> Gray-Steel into his death thus thraws[1]
> He *walters*[2] *and the grass up draws;*
>
> . . . . .
>
> *A little while then lay he still*
> (*Friends that him saw, liked full ill*)
> *And bled into his armour bright.*

The abode of Chaucer's *Reeve,* or Steward, in the *Canterbury Tales,* is painted in two lines, which nobody ever wished longer:

> His wonning[3] was full fair upon an heath,
> With greeny trees yshadowed was his place.

Every one knows the words of Lear, 'most *matter-of-fact,* most melancholy.'

> Pray, do not mock me;
> I am a very foolish fond old man,
> Fourscore and upwards:
> Not an hour more, nor less; and, to deal plainly,
> I fear I am not in my perfect mind.

It is thus, by exquisite pertinence, melody, and the implied power of writing with exuberance, if need be, that beauty and truth become identical in poetry, and that pleasure, or at the very worst, a balm in our tears, is drawn out of pain.

It is a great and rare thing, and shows a lovely imagination, when the poet can write a commentary, as it were, of his own, on such sufficing passages of nature, and be thanked for the addition. There is an instance of this kind in Warner, an old Elizabethan poet, than which I know nothing sweeter in the world. He is speaking of Fair Rosamond, and of a blow given her by Queen Eleanor.

> With that she dash'd her on the lips,
>   *So dyèd double red:*
> *Hard was the heart that gave the blow,*
>   *Soft were those lips that bled.*

There are different kinds and degrees of imagina-

---

[1] throes?   [2] welters,—throws himself about.
[3] dwelling.

tion, some of them necessary to the formation of every true poet, and all of them possessed by the greatest. Perhaps they may be enumerated as follows:—First, that which presents to the mind any object or circumstance in every-day life; as when we imagine a man holding a sword, or looking out of a window;—Second, that which presents real, but not every-day circumstances; as King Alfred tending the loaves, or Sir Philip Sidney giving up the water to the dying soldier;—Third, that which combines character and events directly imitated from real life, with imitative realities of its own invention; as the probable parts of the histories of Priam and *Macbeth*, or what may be called natural fiction as distinguished from supernatural;—Fourth, that which conjures up things and events not to be found in nature; as Homer's gods, and Shakespeare's witches, enchanted horses and spears, Ariosto's hippogriff, &c.;—Fifth, that which, in order to illustrate or aggravate one image, introduces another; sometimes in simile, as when Homer compares Apollo descending in his wrath at noon-day to the coming of night-time: sometimes in metaphor, or simile comprised in a word, as in Milton's 'motes that *people* the sunbeams'; sometimes in concentrating into a word the main history of any person or thing, past or even future, as in the 'starry Galileo' of Byron, and that ghastly foregone conclusion of the epithet 'murdered' applied to the yet living victim in Keats's story from Boccaccio,—

> So the two brothers and their *murder'd* man
> Rode towards fair Florence;—

sometimes in the attribution of a certain representative quality which makes one circumstance stand for others; as in Milton's grey-fly winding its 'sultry horn', which epithet contains the heat of a summer's day;—Sixth, that which reverses this process, and makes a variety of circumstances take colour from one, like nature seen with jaundiced or glad eyes, or under the influence of storm or sunshine; as when in *Lycidas*, or the Greek pastoral poets, the flowers and the flocks are made to sympathize with a man's death; or, in the Italian poet, the river flowing by the sleeping Angelica seems talking of love—

> Parea che l'erba le fiorisse intorno,
> E d'amor ragionasse quella riva!
> *Orlando Innamorato*, Canto iii.

or in the voluptuous homage paid to the sleeping Imogen by the very light in the chamber, and the reaction of her own beauty upon itself; or in the 'witch element' of the tragedy of *Macbeth* and the May-day night of *Faust*;—Seventh, and last, that which by a single expression, apparently of the vaguest kind, not only meets but surpasses in its effect the extremest force of the most particular description; as in that exquisite passage of Coleridge's *Christabel*, where the unsuspecting object of the witch's malignity is bidden to go to bed:

> Quoth Christabel, So let it be!
> And as the lady bade, did she.
> Her gentle limbs did she undress,
> *And lay down in her loveliness*;—

a perfect verse surely, both for feeling and music. The very smoothness and gentleness of the limbs is in the series of the letter *l*'s.

I am aware of nothing of the kind surpassing that most lovely inclusion of physical beauty in moral, neither can I call to mind any instances of the imagination that turns accompaniments into accessories, superior to those I have alluded to. Of the class of comparison, one of the most touching (many a tear must it have drawn from parents and lovers) is in a stanza which has been copied into the *Friar of Orders Grey*, out of Beaumont and Fletcher:

> Weep no more, lady, weep no more,
>   Thy sorrow is in vain;
> *For violets pluck'd the sweetest showers*
>   *Will ne'er make grow again.*

And Shakespeare and Milton abound in the very grandest; such as Antony's likening his changing fortunes to the cloud-rack; Lear's appeal to the old age of the heavens; Satan's appearance in the horizon, like a fleet 'hanging in the clouds'; and the comparisons of him with the comet and the eclipse. Nor unworthy of this glorious company, for its extraordinary combination of delicacy and vastness, is that enchanting one of Shelley's in the *Adonais*:

> Life, like a dome of many-coloured glass,
> Stains the white radiance of eternity.

I multiply these particulars in order to impress upon the reader's mind the great importance of imagination in all its phases, as a constituent part of the highest poetic faculty.

The happiest instance I remember of imaginative metaphor, is Shakespeare's moonlight 'sleeping' on a bank; but half his poetry may be said to be made up of it, metaphor indeed being the common coin of discourse. Of imaginary creatures, none out of the pale of mythology and the East are equal, perhaps, in point of invention, to Shakespeare's Ariel and Caliban; though poetry may grudge to prose the discovery of a Winged Woman, especially such as she has been described by her inventor in the story of *Peter Wilkins*; and in point of treatment, the Mammon and Jealousy of Spenser, some of the monsters in Dante, particularly his Nimrod, his interchangements of creatures into one another, and (if I am not presumptuous in anticipating what I think will be the verdict of posterity) the Witch in Coleridge's *Christabel*, may rank even with the creations of Shakespeare. It may be doubted, indeed, whether Shakespeare had bile and nightmare enough in him to have thought of such detestable horrors as those of the interchanging adversaries (now serpent, now man), or even of the huge, half-blockish enormity of Nimrod,—in Scripture, the 'mighty hunter' and

WHAT IS POETRY?

builder of the tower of Babel,—in Dante, a tower of a man in his own person, standing with some of his brother giants up to the middle in a pit in hell, blowing a horn to which a thunderclap is a whisper, and hallooing after Dante and his guide in the jargon of a lost tongue! The transformations are too odious to quote: but of the towering giant we cannot refuse ourselves the 'fearful joy' of a specimen. It was twilight, Dante tells us, and he and his guide Virgil were silently pacing through one of the dreariest regions of hell, when the sound of a tremendous horn made him turn all his attention to the spot from which it came. He there discovered through the dusk, what seemed to be the towers of a city. Those are no towers, said his guide; they are giants, standing up to the middle in one of these circular pits.

> I look'd again; and as the eye makes out,
> By little and little, what the mist conceal'd
> In which, till clearing up, the sky was steep'd;
> So, looming through the gross and darksome air,
> As we drew nigh, those mighty bulks grew plain,
> And error quitted me, and terror join'd:
> For in like manner as all round its height
> Montereggione crowns itself with towers,
> So tower'd above the circuit of that pit,
> Though but half out of it, and half within,
> The horrible giants that fought Jove, and still
> Are threaten'd when he thunders. As we near'd
> The foremost, I discern'd his mighty face,
> His shoulders, breast, and more than half his trunk,
> With both the arms down hanging by the sides.
> His face appear'd to me, in length and breadth,
> Huge as St. Peter's pinnacle at Rome,
> And of a like proportion all his bones.
> He open'd, as we went, his dreadful mouth,
> Fit for no sweeter psalmody; and shouted
> After us, in the words of some strange tongue,
> Ràfel ma-èe amech zabèe almee!—
> 'Dull wretch!' my leader cried, 'keep to thine horn,
> And so vent better whatsoever rage
> Or other passion stuff thee. Feel thy throat

And find the chain upon thee, thou confusion!
Lo! what a hoop is clench'd about thy gorge.'
Then turning to myself, he said, 'His howl
Is its own mockery. This is Nimrod, he
Through whose ill thought it was that humankind
Were tongue-confounded. Pass him, and say nought:
For as he speaketh language known of none,
So none can speak save jargon to himself.'
Inferno, Canto xxxi, ver. 34.

Assuredly it could not have been easy to find a fiction so uncouthly terrible as this in the hypochondria of Hamlet. Even his father had evidently seen no such ghost in the other world. All his phantoms were in the world he had left. Timon, Lear, Richard, Brutus, Prospero, Macbeth himself, none of Shakespeare's men had, in fact, any thought but of the earth they lived on, whatever supernatural fancy crossed them. The thing fancied was still a thing of this world, 'in its habit as it lived,' or no remoter acquaintance than a witch or a fairy. Its lowest depths (unless Dante suggested them) were the cellars under the stage. Caliban himself is a crossbreed between a witch and a clown. No offence to Shakespeare; who was not bound to be the greatest of healthy poets, and to have every morbid inspiration besides. What he might have done, had he set his wits to compete with Dante, I know not: all I know is, that in the infernal line he did nothing like him; and it is not to be wished he had. It is far better that, as a higher, more universal, and more beneficent variety of the genus Poet, he should have been the happier man he was, and left us the plump cheeks on his monument, instead of the carking visage of the great, but over-serious, and comparatively one-sided Florentine. Even the imagination of Spenser, whom we take to have been a 'nervous gentleman' compared with Shakespeare, was visited with no such dreams as Dante. Or, if it was, he did not choose to make himself thinner (as Dante says *he* did) with

WHAT IS POETRY?

dwelling upon them. He had twenty visions of nymphs and bowers, to one of the mud of Tartarus. Chaucer, for all he was 'a man of this world' as well as the poets' world, and as great, perhaps a greater enemy of oppression than Dante, besides being one of the profoundest masters of pathos that ever lived, had not the heart to conclude the story of the famished father and his children, as finished by the inexorable anti-Pisan. But enough of Dante in this place. Hobbes, in order to daunt the reader from objecting to his friend Davenant's want of invention, says of these fabulous creations in general, in his letter prefixed to the poem of *Gondibert*, that 'impenetrable armours, enchanted castles, invulnerable bodies, iron men, flying horses, and a thousand other such things, are easily feigned by them that dare'. These are girds at Spenser and Ariosto. But, with leave of Hobbes (who translated Homer as if on purpose to show what execrable verses could be written by a philosopher), enchanted castles and flying horses are not easily feigned as Ariosto and Spenser feigned them; and that just makes all the difference. For proof, see the accounts of Spenser's enchanted castle in Book the Third, Canto Twelfth, of the *Faerie Queene*; and let the reader of Italian open the *Orlando Furioso* at its first introduction of the Hippogriff (Canto iii, st. 4), where Bradamante, coming to an inn, hears a great noise, and sees all the people looking up at something in the air; upon which, looking up herself, she sees a knight in shining armour riding towards the sunset upon a creature with variegated wings, and then dipping and disappearing among the hills. Chaucer's steed of brass, that was

> So horsly and so quick of eye,

is copied from the life. You might pat him and feel his brazen muscles. Hobbes, in objecting to what he thought childish, made a childish mistake. His criticism is just such as a boy might pique himself upon, who was educated on mechanical principles, and thought he had outgrown his Goody Two-shoes. With a wonderful dimness of discernment in poetic matters, considering his acuteness in others, he fancies he has settled the question by pronouncing such creations 'impossible'! To the brazier they are impossible, no doubt; but not to the poet. Their possibility, if the poet wills it, is to be conceded; the problem is, the creature being given, how to square its actions with probability, according to the nature assumed of it. Hobbes did not see, that the skill and beauty of these fictions lay in bringing them within those very regions of truth and likelihood in which he thought they could not exist. Hence the serpent Python of Chaucer,

Sleeping against the sun upon a day,

when Apollo slew him. Hence the chariot-drawing dolphins of Spenser, softly swimming along the shore lest they should hurt themselves against the stones and gravel. Hence Shakespeare's Ariel, living under blossoms, and riding at evening on the bat; and his domestic namesake in the *Rape of the Lock* (the imagination of the drawing-room) saving a lady's petticoat from the coffee with his plumes, and directing atoms of snuff into a coxcomb's nose. In the *Orlando Furioso* (Canto xv, st. 65) is a wild story of a cannibal necromancer, who laughs at being cut to pieces, coming together again like quicksilver, and picking up his head when it is cut off, sometimes by the hair, sometimes by the nose! This, which would be purely childish and ridiculous in the hands of an inferior poet, becomes interesting, nay grand, in Ariosto's, from the beauties of his style, and its conditional truth to nature. The monster has a fated hair on his head,— a single hair,—which must be taken from it before he can be killed. Decapitation itself is of no consequence, without that proviso. The Paladin Astolfo, who has fought this phenomenon on horseback, and succeeded in getting the head and galloping off with it, is therefore still at a loss what to be at. How is he to discover such a needle in such a bottle of hay? The trunk is spurring after him to recover it, and he seeks for some evidence of the hair in vain. At length he bethinks him of scalping the head. He does so; and the moment the operation arrives at the place of the hair, *the face of the head becomes pale, the eyes turn in their sockets*, and the lifeless pursuer tumbles from his horse.

> Then grew the visage pale, and deadly wet;
> The eyes turn'd in their sockets, drearily;
> And all things show'd the villain's sun was set.
> His trunk that was in chase, fell from its horse,
> And giving the last shudder, was a corse.

It is thus, and thus only, by making Nature his companion wherever he goes, even in the most supernatural region, that the poet, in the words of a very instructive phrase, takes the world along with him. It is true, he must not (as the Platonists would say) humanize weakly or mistakenly in that region; otherwise he runs the chance of forgetting to be true to the supernatural itself, and so betraying a want of imagination from that quarter. His nymphs will have no taste of their woods and waters; his gods and goddesses be only so many fair or frowning ladies and gentlemen, such as we see in ordinary paintings; he will be in no danger of having his angels likened to a sort of wild-fowl, as Rembrandt has made them in his Jacob's Dream. His Bacchuses will never remind us, like Titian's, of the force and fury, as well as of the graces, of wine. His Jupiter will reduce no females to ashes; his fairies be nothing fantastical; his gnomes not 'of the earth, earthy'. And this again will be wanting to Nature; for it will be wanting to the supernatural, as Nature would have made it, working in a supernatural direction. Nevertheless, the poet, even for imagination's sake, must not become a bigot to imaginative truth, dragging it down into the region of the mechanical and the limited, and losing sight of its paramount privilege, which is to make beauty, in a human sense, the lady and queen of the universe. He would gain nothing by making his ocean-nymphs mere fishy creatures, upon the plea that such only could live in the water; his wood-nymphs with faces of knotted oak; his angels without breath and song, because no lungs could exist between the earth's atmosphere and the empyrean. The Grecian tendency in this respect is safer than the Gothic; nay, more imaginative; for it enables us to imagine *beyond* imagination, and to bring all things healthily round to their only present final ground of sympathy, —the human. When we go to heaven, we may idealize in a superhuman mode, and have altogether different notions of the beautiful; but till then we must be content with the loveliest capabilities of earth. The sea-nymphs of Greece were still beautiful women, though they lived in the water. The gills and fins of the ocean's natural inhabitants were confined to their lowest semi-human attendants; or if Triton himself was not quite human, it was because he represented the fiercer part of the vitality of the seas, as they did the fairer.

To conclude this part of my subject, I will quote from the greatest of all narrative writers two passages; —one exemplifying the imagination which brings supernatural things to bear on earthly, without confounding them; the other, that which paints events and circumstances after real life. The first is where Achilles, who has long absented himself from the conflict between his countrymen and the Trojans, has had a message from heaven bidding him reappear in the enemy's sight, standing outside the camp-wall upon the trench, but doing nothing more; that is to say, taking no part in the fight. He is simply to be seen. The two armies down by the sea-side are contending which shall possess the body of Patroclus; and the mere sight of the dreadful Grecian chief—

WHAT IS POETRY?

supernaturally indeed impressed upon them, in order that nothing may be wanting to the full effect of his courage and conduct upon courageous men—is to determine the question. We are to imagine a slope of ground towards the sea, in order to elevate the trench; the camp is solitary; the battle ('a dreadful roar of men,' as Homer calls it) is raging on the sea-shore; and the goddess Iris has just delivered her message, and disappeared.

> But up Achilles rose, the lov'd of heaven;
> And Pallas on his mighty shoulders cast
> The shield of Jove; and round about his head
> She put the glory of a golden mist,
> From which there burnt a fiery-flaming light.
> And as, when smoke goes heavenward from a town,
> In some far island which its foes besiege,
> Who all day long with dreadful martialness
> Have pour'd from their own town; soon as the sun
> Has set, thick lifted fires are visible,
> Which, rushing upward, make a light in the sky,
> And let the neighbours know, who may perhaps
> Bring help across the sea; so from the head
> Of great Achilles went up an effulgence.
>
> Upon the trench he stood, without the wall,
> But mix'd not with the Greeks, for he rever'd
> His mother's word; and so, thus standing there,
> He shouted; and Minerva, to his shout,
> Added a dreadful cry; and there arose
> Among the Trojans an unspeakable tumult.
> And as the clear voice of a trumpet, blown
> Against a town by spirit-withering foes,
> So sprang the clear voice of Aeacides.
> And when they heard the brazen cry, their hearts
> All leap'd within them; and the proud-maned horses
> Ran with the chariots round, for they foresaw
> Calamity; and the charioteers were smitten,
> When they beheld the ever-active fire
> Upon the dreadful head of the great-minded one
> Burning; for bright-eyed Pallas made it burn.
> Thrice o'er the trench divine Achilles shouted;
> And thrice the Trojans and their great allies

Roll'd back; and twelve of all their noblest men
Then perish'd, crush'd by their own arms and chariots.
Iliad, xviii. 203.

Of course there is no further question about the body of Patroclus. It is drawn out of the press, and received by the awful hero with tears.

The other passage is where Priam, kneeling before Achilles, and imploring him to give up the dead body of Hector, reminds him of his own father; who, whatever (says the poor old king) may be his troubles with his enemies, has the blessing of knowing that his son is still alive, and may daily hope to see him return. Achilles, in accordance with the strength and noble honesty of the passions in those times, weeps aloud himself at this appeal, feeling, says Homer, 'desire' for his father in his very 'limbs'. He joins in grief with the venerable sufferer, and can no longer withstand the look of 'his grey head and his grey *chin*'. Observe the exquisite introduction of this last word. It paints the touching fact of the chin's being imploringly thrown upward by the kneeling old man, and the very motion of his beard as he speaks.

So saying, Mercury vanished up to heaven:
And Priam then alighted from his chariot,
Leaving Idaeus with it, who remain'd
Holding the mules and horses; and the old man
Went straight indoors, where the belov'd of Jove
Achilles sat, and found him. In the room
Were others, but apart; and two alone,
The hero Automedon, and Alcimus,
A branch of Mars, stood by him. They had been
At meals, and had not yet remov'd the board.
Great Priam came, without their seeing him,
And kneeling down, he clasp'd Achilles' knees,
And kiss'd those terrible, homicidal hands,
Which had deprived him of so many sons.
And as a man who is press'd heavily
For having slain another, flies away
To foreign lands, and comes into the house
Of some great man, and is beheld with wonder,

So did Achilles wonder to see Priam;
And the rest wonder'd, looking at each other.
But Priam, praying to him, spoke these words:—
'God-like Achilles, think of thine own father!
To the same age have we both come, the same
Weak pass; and though the neighbouring chiefs may vex
Him also, and his borders find no help,
Yet when he hears that thou art still alive,
He gladdens inwardly, and daily hopes
To see his dear son coming back from Troy.
But I, bereav'd old Priam! I had once
Brave sons in Troy, and now I cannot say
That one is left me. Fifty children had I,
When the Greeks came; nineteen were of one womb;
The rest my women bore me in my house.
The knees of many of these fierce Mars has loosen'd;
And he who had no peer, Troy's prop and theirs,
Him hast thou kill'd now, fighting for his country,
Hector; and for his sake am I come here
To ransom him, bringing a countless ransom.
But thou, Achilles, fear the gods, and think
Of thine own father, and have mercy on me:
For I am much more wretched, and have borne
What never mortal bore, I think on earth,
To lift unto my lips the hand of him
Who slew my boys.'
                  He ceased; and there arose
Sharp longing in Achilles for his father;
And taking Priam by the hand, he gently
Put him away; for both shed tears to think
Of other times; the one most bitter ones
For Hector, and with wilful wretchedness
Lay right before Achilles: and the other,
For his own father now, and now his friend;
And the whole house might hear them as they moan'd.
But when divine Achilles had refresh'd
His soul with tears, and sharp desire had left
His heart and limbs, he got up from his throne,
And rais'd the old man by the hand, and took
Pity on his grey head and his grey chin.
Iliad, xxiv. 468.

O lovely and immortal privilege of genius! that can stretch its hand out of the wastes of time, thousands of years back, and touch our eyelids with tears. In these passages there is not a word which a man of the most matter-of-fact understanding might not have written, *if he had thought of it*. But in poetry, feeling and imagination are necessary to the perception and presentation even of matters of fact. They, and they only, see what is proper to be told, and what to be kept back; what is pertinent, affecting, and essential. Without feeling, there is a want of delicacy and distinction; without imagination, there is no true embodiment. In poets, even good of their kind, but without a genius for narration, the action would have been encumbered or diverted with ingenious mistakes. The over-contemplative would have given us too many remarks; the over-lyrical, a style too much carried away; the over-fanciful, conceits and too many similes; the unimaginative, the facts without the feeling, and not even those. We should have been told nothing of the 'grey chin', of the house hearing them as they moaned, or of Achilles gently putting the old man aside; much less of that yearning for his father, which made the hero tremble in every limb. Writers without the greatest passion and power do not feel in this way, nor are capable of expressing the feeling; though there is enough sensibility and imagination all over the world to enable mankind to be moved by it, when the poet strikes his truth into their hearts.

The reverse of imagination is exhibited in pure absence of ideas, in commonplaces, and, above all, in conventional metaphor, or such images and their phraseology as have become the common property of discourse and writing. Addison's *Cato* is full of them.

> Passion unpitied and successless love
> *Plant daggers in my breast*.
>
> I've sounded my Numidians, man by man,
> And find them *ripe for a revolt*.
>
> The virtuous Marcia *towers above her sex*.

WHAT IS POETRY?

Of the same kind is his 'courting the yoke'—'distracting my very heart'—'calling up all' one's 'father' in one's soul—'working every nerve'—'copying a bright example'; in short, the whole play, relieved now and then with a smart sentence or turn of words. The following is a pregnant example of plagiarism and weak writing. It is from another tragedy of Addison's time—the *Mariamne* of Fenton:

> Mariamne, *with superior charms,*
> *Triumphs o'er reason;* in her looks she *bears*
> A paradise of ever-blooming sweets;
> Fair as the first idea beauty *prints*
> In the young lover's soul; a winning grace
> Guides every gesture, and obsequious love
> *Attends* on all her steps.

'Triumphing o'er reason' is an old acquaintance of everybody's. 'Paradise in her look' is from the Italian poets through Dryden. 'Fair as the first idea', &c., is from Milton, spoilt;—'winning grace' and 'steps' from Milton and Tibullus, both spoilt. Whenever beauties are stolen by such a writer, they are sure to be spoilt: just as when a great writer borrows, he improves.

To come now to Fancy,—she is a younger sister of Imagination, without the other's weight of thought and feeling. Imagination indeed, purely so called, is all feeling; the feeling of the subtlest and most affecting analogies; the perception of sympathies in the natures of things, or in their popular attributes. Fancy is a sporting with their resemblance, real or supposed, and with airy and fantastical creations.

> —Rouse yourself; and the weak wanton Cupid
> Shall from your neck unloose his amorous fold,
> *And, like a dew-drop from the lion's mane,*
> *Be shook to air.*   *Troilus and Cressida*, Act iii, sc. 3.

That is imagination;—the strong mind sympathizing with the strong beast, and the weak love identified with the weak dew-drop.

> Oh!—and I forsooth
> In love! I that have been love's whip!

> *A very beadle to a humorous sigh!—*
> *A domineering pedant o'er the boy,—*
> *This whimpled, whining, purblind, wayward boy,*
> *This senior-junior, giant-dwarf, Dan Cupid,*
> *Regent of love-rhymes, lord of folded arms,*
> *The anointed sovereign of sighs and groans,* &c.
> *Love's Labour's Lost*, Act iii, sc. 1.

That is fancy;—a combination of images not in their nature connected, or brought together by the feeling, but by the will and pleasure; and having just enough hold of analogy to betray it into the hands of its smiling subjector.

> Silent icicles
> *Quietly shining to the quiet moon.*
> Coleridge's *Frost at Midnight*.

That, again, is imagination;—analogical sympathy; and exquisite of its kind it is.

> 'You are now sailed *into the north of my lady's opinion;* where you will hang *like an icicle on a Dutchman's beard,* unless you do redeem it by some laudable attempt.'
> *Twelfth Night*, Act iii, sc. 2.

And that is fancy;—one image capriciously suggested by another, and but half connected with the subject of discourse; nay, half opposed to it; for in the gaiety of the speaker's animal spirits, the 'Dutchman's beard' is made to represent the lady!

Imagination belongs to Tragedy, or the serious muse; Fancy to the comic. *Macbeth, Lear, Paradise Lost*, the poem of Dante, are full of imagination: the *Midsummer Night's Dream* and the *Rape of the Lock*, of fancy: *Romeo and Juliet*, the *Tempest*, the *Faerie Queene*, and the *Orlando Furioso* of both. The terms were formerly identical, or used as such; and neither is the best that might be found. The term Imagination is too confined: often too material. It presents too invariably the idea of a solid body;—of 'images' in the sense of the plaster-cast cry about the streets. Fancy, on the other hand, while it means nothing but a spiritual image or apparition (Φάντασμα, appearance, *phantom*), has rarely that freedom from visibility which is one of the highest privileges of imagination. Viola, in *Twelfth Night*, speaking of some beautiful music, says:

> It gives a very echo to the seat
> Where Love is throned.

In this charming thought, fancy and imagination are combined; yet the fancy, the assumption of Love's sitting on a throne, is the image of a solid body; while the imagination, the sense of sympathy between the passion of love and impassioned music, presents us no image at all. Some new term is wanting to express the more spiritual sympathies of what is called Imagination.

One of the teachers of Imagination is Melancholy; and like Melancholy, as Albert Dürer has painted her, she looks out among the stars, and is busied with spiritual affinities and the mysteries of the universe. Fancy turns her sister's wizard instruments into toys. She takes a telescope in her hand, and puts a mimic star on her forehead, and sallies forth as an emblem of astronomy. Her tendency is to the child-like and sportive. She chases butterflies, while her sister takes flight with angels. She is the genius of fairies, of gallantries, of fashions; of whatever is quaint and light, showy and capricious; of the poetical part of wit. She adds wings and feelings to the images of wit; and delights as much to people nature with smiling ideal sympathies, as wit does to bring antipathies together, and make them strike light on absurdity. Fancy, however, is not incapable of sympathy with Imagination. She is often found in her company; always, in the case of the greatest poets; often in that of less, though with them she is the greater favourite. Spenser has great imagination and fancy too, but more of the latter; Milton both also, the very greatest, but with imagination predominant; Chaucer, the strongest imagination of real life, beyond any writers but Homer, Dante, and Shakespeare, and in comic painting inferior to none; Pope has hardly any imagination, but he has a great deal of fancy; Coleridge little fancy, but imagination exquisite. Shakespeare alone, of all poets that ever lived, enjoyed the regard of both in equal perfection. A whole fairy poem of his writing [the Oberon-Titania scenes from the *Midsummer-Night's Dream*] will be found in the present volume.[1] See also his famous description of Queen Mab and her equipage, in *Romeo and Juliet*:

> Her waggon-spokes made of long spinners' legs;
> The cover, of the wings of grasshoppers:
> Her traces of the smallest spider's web;
> Her collars of the moonshine's watery beams, &c.

That is Fancy, in its playful creativeness. As a small but pretty rival specimen, less known, take the description of a fairy palace from Drayton's *Nymphidia*:

> This palace standeth in the air,
> By necromancy placèd there,
> That it no tempest needs to fear,
>   which way so'er it blow it:
> And somewhat southward tow'rd the noon,
> Whence lies a way up to the moon,
> And thence the Fairy can as soon
>   Pass to the earth below it.
> The walls of spiders' legs are made,
> Well morticèd and finely laid:
> He was the master of his trade
>   It curiously that builded:
> *The windows of the eyes of cats:*

(because they see best at night)

> And for the roof instead of slats
> Is cover'd with the skins of bats
>   *With moonshine that are gilded.*

Here also is a fairy bed, very delicate, from the same poet's *Muse's Elysium*:

> Of leaves of roses, *white and red*,
> Shall be the covering of the bed;

[1] Leigh Hunt's *Imagination and Fancy, or Selections from the English Poets*, 1844.

WHAT IS POETRY?

> The curtains, vallens, tester all,
> Shall be the flower imperial;
> And for the fringe it all along
> *With azure hare-bells shall be hung.*
> *Of lilies shall the pillows be,*
> *With down stuft of the butterfly.*

Of fancy, so full of gusto as to border on imagination, Sir John Suckling, in his *Ballad on a Wedding*, has given some of the most playful and charming specimens in the language. They glance like twinkles of the eye, or cherries bedewed:

> *Her feet beneath her petticoat,*
> *Like little mice stole in and out.*
>   *As if they fear'd the light:*
> But oh! she dances such a way!
> *No sun upon an Easter day*
>   Is half so fine a sight.

It is very daring, and has a sort of playful grandeur, to compare a lady's dancing with the sun. But as the sun has it all to himself in the heavens, so she, in the blaze of her beauty, on earth. This is imagination fairly displacing fancy. The following has enchanted everybody:

> *Her lips were red, and one was thin*
> *Compared with that was next her chin,*
> *Some bee had stung it newly.*

Every reader has stolen a kiss at that lip, gay or grave.

With regard to the principle of Variety in Uniformity by which verse ought to be modulated, and oneness of impression diversely produced, it has been contended by some, that Poetry need not be written in verse at all; that prose is as good a medium, provided poetry be conveyed through it; and that to think otherwise is to confound letter with spirit, or form with essence. But the opinion is a prosaical mistake. Fitness and unfitness for *song*, or metrical excitement, just make all the difference between a poetical and prosaical subject; and the reason why verse is necessary to the form of poetry, is, that the perfection of poetical spirit demands it;—that the circle of its enthusiasm, beauty and power, is incomplete without it. I do not mean to say that a poet can never show himself a poet in prose; but that, being one, his desire and necessity will be to write in verse; and that, if he were unable to do so, he would not, and could not, deserve his title. Verse to the true poet is no clog. It is idly called a trammel and a difficulty. It is a help. It springs from the same enthusiasm as the rest of his impulses, and is necessary to their satisfaction and effect. Verse is no more a clog than the condition of rushing upward is a clog to fire, or than the roundness and order of the globe we live on is a clog to the freedom and variety that abound within its sphere. Verse is no dominator over the poet, except inasmuch as the bond is reciprocal, and the poet dominates over the verse. They are lovers, playfully challenging each other's rule, and delighted equally to rule and to obey. Verse is the final proof to the poet that his mastery over his art is complete. It is the shutting up of his powers in '*measureful* content'; the answer of form to his spirit; of strength and ease to his guidance. It is the willing action, the proud and fiery happiness, of the winged steed on whose back he has vaulted,

To witch the world with wondrous horsemanship.

Verse, in short, is that finishing, and rounding, and 'tuneful planetting' of the poet's creations, which is produced of necessity by the smooth tendencies of their energy or inward working, and the harmonious dance into which they are attracted round the orb of the beautiful. Poetry, in its complete sympathy with beauty, must, of necessity, leave no sense of the beautiful, and no power over its forms, unmanifested; and verse flows as inevitably from this condition of its integrity, as other laws of proportion do from any other kind of embodiment of beauty (say that of the human figure), however free and various the movements may be that play within their limits. What great poet ever wrote his poems in prose? or where is a good prose poem, of any length, to be found? The poetry of the Bible is understood to be in verse, in the original. Mr. Hazlitt has said a good word for those prose enlargements of some fine old song, which are known by the name of Ossian; and in passages they deserve what he said; but he judiciously abstained from saying anything about the form. Is Gesner's *Death of Abel* a poem? or Hervey's *Meditations*? The *Pilgrim's Progress* has been called one; and, undoubtedly, Bunyan had a genius which tended to make him a poet, and one of no mean order: and yet it was of as ungenerous and low a sort as was compatible with so lofty an affinity; and this is the reason why it stopped where it did. He had a craving after the beautiful, but not enough of it in himself to echo to its music. On the other hand, the possession of the beautiful will not be sufficient without force to utter it. The author of *Telemachus* had a soul full of beauty and tenderness. He was not a man who, if he had had a wife and children, would have run away from them, as Bunyan's hero did, to get a place by himself in heaven. He was 'a little lower than the angels', like our own Bishop Jewells and Berkeleys; and yet he was no poet. He was too delicately, not to say feebly, absorbed in his devotions, to join in the energies of the seraphic choir.

Every poet, then, is a versifier; every fine poet an excellent one; and he is the best whose verse exhibits the greatest amount of strength, sweetness, straightforwardness, unsuperfluousness, *variety*, and *oneness*;—oneness, that is to say, consistency, in the general impression, metrical and moral; and variety, or every pertinent diversity of tone and rhythm, in the process. *Strength* is the muscle of verse, and shows itself in the number and force of the marked syllables; as,

Sonòrous mètal blòwing màrtial sòunds.
Paradise Lost

> Behèmoth, bìggest born of eàrth, ùphèav'd
> His vàstness.   *Id.*

> Blòw wìnds and cràck your chèeks! ràge! blòw!
> You càtărăcts and hurricànoes, spòut,
> Till you have drènch'd our stèeples, dròwn'd the còcks!
> You sùlphurous and thoùght-èxecuting fìres,
> Vaùnt coùriers of òak-clèaving thùnderbòlts,
> Sìnge my whìte hèad! and thòu, àll-shàking thùnder,
> Strìke flàt the thìck rotùndity o' the wòrld!
>   *Lear.*

Unexpected locations of the accent double this force, and render it characteristic of passion and abruptness. And here comes into play the reader's corresponding fineness of ear, and his retardations and accelerations in accordance with those of the poet:

> Then in the keyhole turns
> The ĭntrĭcăte wards, and every bolt and bar
> Unfastens.—On ă sŭddĕn òpen fly
> With ĭmpètuous recoil and jarring sound
> The infernal doors, and on their hinges grate
> Harsh thunder.   *Paradise Lost,* Book II.

> Abòmĭnăblĕ—unùttĕrăblĕ—and worse
> Than fables yet have feigned.   *Id.*

> Wàllŏwĭng ŭnwĭĕldy—ĕnòrmous in their gait.   *Id.*

Of unusual passionate accent, there is an exquisite specimen in the *Faerie Queene,* where Una is lamenting her desertion by the Red-Cross Knight:

> But he, my lion, and my noble lord,
> How does he find in cruel heart to hate
> Her that him lov'd, and ever most ador'd
>   *As the gòd of my lìfe?*[1] Why hath he me abhorr'd?

---

[1] Pray let not the reader consent to read this first half of the line in any manner less marked and peremptory. It is a striking instance of the beauty of that 'acceleration and retardation of true verse' which Coleridge speaks of. There is to be a hurry on the words *as the,* and a passionate emphasis and passing stop on the word *god;* and so of the next three words.

WHAT IS POETRY?

The abuse of strength is harshness and heaviness; the reverse of it is weakness. There is a noble sentiment—it appears both in Daniel's and Sir John Beaumont's works, but is most probably the latter's,—which is a perfect outrage of strength in the sound of the words:

> Only the firmest and the *constant'st hearts*
> God sets to act the *stout'st* and hardest parts.

Stout'st and *constant'st* for 'stoutest' and 'most constant'! It is as bad as the intentional crabbedness of the line in *Hudibras*:

> He that hangs or *beats out 's* brains,
> The devil's in him if *he* feigns.

Beats out 's brains, for 'beats out his brains'. Of heaviness, Davenant's *Gondibert* is a formidable specimen, almost throughout:

> With sìlence (òrder's help, and màrk of càre)
>   They chìde thàt nòise which hèedless yòuth affèct;
> Still coùrse, for ùse, for heàlth thèy clèanness wèar,
>   And sàve in wèll-fìx'd àrms, all nìceness chèck'd.
> Thèy thoùght, thòse that, unàrm'd, expòs'd fràil lìfe,
>   But nàked nàture vàliantly betrày'd;
> Whò wàs, though nàked, sàfe, till prìde màde strìfe,
>   But màde defènce must ùse, nòw dànger's màde.

And so he goes digging and lumbering on, like a heavy preacher thumping the pulpit in italics, and spoiling many ingenious reflections.

Weakness in versification is want of accent and emphasis. It generally accompanies prosaicalness, and is the consequence of weak thoughts, and of the affectation of a certain well-bred enthusiasm. The writings of the late Mr. Hayley were remarkable for it; and it abounds among the lyrical imitators of Cowley, and the whole of what is called our French school of poetry, when it aspired above its wit and 'sense'. It sometimes breaks down in a horrible, hopeless manner, as if giving way at the first step.

The following ludicrous passage in Congreve, intended to be particularly fine, contains an instance:

> And lo! Silence himself is here;
> Methinks I see the midnight god appear.
> In all his downy pomp array'd,
> Behold the reverend shade.
> *An ancient sigh he sits upon!!!*
> Whose memory of sound is long since gone,
> *And purposely annihilated for his throne!!!*
> Ode on the singing of Mrs. Arabella Hunt.

See also the would-be enthusiasm of Addison about music:

> For ever consecrate the *day*
> To music and *Cecilia*;
> Music, the greatest good that mortals know,
> And all of heaven we have below,
> Music can noble HINTS *impart!!!*

It is observable that the unpoetic masters of ridicule are apt to make the most ridiculous mistakes, when they come to affect a strain higher than the one they are accustomed to. But no wonder. Their habits neutralize the enthusiasm it requires.

Sweetness, though not identical with smoothness, any more than feeling is with sound, always includes it; and smoothness is a thing so little to be regarded for its own sake, and indeed so worthless in poetry but for some taste of sweetness, that I have not thought necessary to mention it by itself; though such an all-in-all in versification was it regarded not a hundred years back, that Thomas Warton himself, an idolater of Spenser, ventured to wish the following line in the *Faerie Queene*,

And was admirèd much of fools, *wòmen*, and boys—

altered to

And was admirèd much of women, fools, and boys—

thus destroying the fine scornful emphasis on the first syllable of 'women'! (an ungallant intimation, by the way, against the fair sex, very startling in this

WHAT IS POETRY?

no less woman-loving than great poet). Any poetaster can be smooth. Smoothness abounds in all small poets, as sweetness does in the greater. Sweetness is the smoothness of grace and delicacy,—of the sympathy with the pleasing and lovely. Spenser is full of it,—Shakespeare—Beaumont and Fletcher—Coleridge. Of Spenser's and Coleridge's versification it is the prevailing characteristic. Its main secrets are a smooth progression between variety and sameness, and a voluptuous sense of the continuous,— 'linked sweetness long drawn out'. Observe the first and last lines of the stanza in the *Faerie Queene*, describing a shepherd brushing away the gnats;—the open and the close *e's* in the one,

> As gèntle shèphèrd in swēēt ēventide—

and the repetition of the word *oft*, and the fall from the vowel *a*, into the two *u's* in the other,—

> She brusheth *oft*, and *oft* doth màr their mŭrmŭrings.

So in his description of two substances in the handling, both equally smooth:

Each smoother seems than each, and each than each seems smoother.

An abundance of examples from his poetry will be found in the volume before us. His beauty revolves on itself with conscious loveliness. And Coleridge is worthy to be named with him, as the reader will see also, and has seen already. Let him take a sample meanwhile from the poem called the *Day Dream*! Observe both the variety and sameness of the vowels, and the repetition of the soft consonants:

> My eyes make pictures when they're shut:—
>   I see a fountain, large and fair,
> A willow and a ruin'd hut,
>   And *thee* and *me* and Mary there.
> O Mary! *make thy gentle lap our pillow;*
> *Bend o'er us, like a bower, my beautiful green willow.*

By *Straightforwardness* is meant the flow of words, in their natural order, free alike from mere prose, and from those inversions to which bad poets recur in order to escape the charge of prose, but chiefly to accommodate their rhymes. In Shadwell's play of *Psyche*, Venus gives the sisters of the heroine an answer, of which the following is the *entire* substance, literally, in so many words. The author had nothing better for her to say:

I receive your prayers with kindness, and will give success to your hopes. I have seen, with anger, mankind adore your sister's beauty and deplore her scorn: which they shall do no more. For I'll so resent their idolatry, as shall content your wishes to the full.

Now in default of all imagination, fancy, and expression, how was the writer to turn these words into poetry or rhyme? Simply by diverting them from their natural order, and twisting the halves of the sentences each before the other.

> With kindness I your prayers receive,
> And to your hopes success will give.
> I have, with anger, seen mankind adore
> Your sister's beauty and her scorn deplore;
> Which they shall do no more.
> For their idolatry I'll so resent,
> As shall your wishes to the full content!!

This is just as if a man were to allow that there was no poetry in the words, 'How do you find yourself?' 'Very well, I thank you'; but to hold them inspired, if altered into

> Yourself how do you find?
> Very well, you I thank.

It is true, the best writers in Shadwell's age were addicted to these inversions, partly for their own reasons, as far as rhyme was concerned, and partly because they held it to be writing in the classical and Virgilian manner. What has since been called Artificial Poetry was then flourishing, in contradistinction to Natural; or Poetry seen chiefly through art and books, and not in its first sources. But when the artificial poet partook of the natural, or, in other words, was a true poet after his kind, his best was always written in his most natural and straightforward manner. Hear Shadwell's antagonist Dryden. Not a particle of inversion, beyond what is used for the sake of emphasis in common discourse, and this only in one line (the last but three), is to be found in his immortal character of the Duke of Buckingham:

> A man so various, that he seemed to be
> Not one, but all mankind's epitome:
> Stiff in opinions, *always in the wrong,*
> *Was everything by starts, and nothing long;*
> But in the course of one revolving moon
> Was chemist, fiddler, statesman, and buffoon:
> Then all for women, rhyming, dancing, drinking,
> *Besides ten thousand freaks that died in thinking.*
> *Blest madman!* who could every hour employ
> *With something new to wish or to enjoy!*
> Railing and praising were his usual themes;
> And both, to show his judgement, in extremes:
> So over violent, or over civil,
> *That every man with him was god or devil.*
> In squandering wealth was his peculiar art;
> *Nothing went unrewarded but desert.*
> Beggar'd by fools, whom still he found too late,
> He had his *jest,* and *they* had his estate.

Inversion itself was often turned into a grace in these poets, and may be in others, by the power of being superior to it; using it only with a classical air, and as a help lying next to them, instead of a salvation which they are obliged to seek. In jesting passages also it sometimes gave the rhyme a turn agreeably wilful, or an appearance of choosing what lay in its way; as if a man should pick up a stone to throw at another's head, where a less confident foot would have stumbled over it. Such is Dryden's use of the word *might*—the mere sign of a tense—in his pretended ridicule of the monkish practice of rising to sing psalms in the night.

> And much they griev'd to see so nigh their hall
> The bird that warn'd St. Peter of his fall;

> That he should raise his mitred crest on high,
> And clap his wings and call his family
> To sacred rites; and vex th' ethereal powers
> With midnight matins at uncivil hours;
> Nay more, his quiet neighbours should molest
> *Just in the sweetness of their morning rest.*

(What a line full of 'another doze' is that!)

> *Beast of a bird!* supinely, when he *might*
> Lie snug and sleep, to rise before the light!
> What if his dull forefathers used that cry?
> Could he not let a bad example die?

I the more gladly quote instances like those of Dryden, to illustrate the points in question, because they are specimens of the very highest kind of writing in the heroic couplet upon subjects not heroical. As to prosaicalness in general, it is sometimes indulged in by young writers on the plea of its being natural; but this is a mere confusion of triviality with propriety, and is usually the result of indolence.

Unsuperfluousness is rather a matter of style in general, than of the sound and order of words: and yet versification is so much strengthened by it, and so much weakened by its opposite, that it could not but come within the category of its requisites. When superfluousness of words is not occasioned by overflowing animal spirits, as in Beaumont and Fletcher, or by the very genius of luxury, as in Spenser (in which cases it is enrichment as well as overflow), there is no worse sign for a poet altogether, except pure barrenness. Every word that could be taken away from a poem, unreferable to either of the above reasons for it, is a damage; and many such are death; for there is nothing that posterity seems so determined to resent as this want of respect for its time and trouble. The world is too rich in books to endure it. Even true poets have died of this Writer's Evil. Trifling ones have survived, with scarcely any pretensions but the terseness of their trifles. What hope can remain for wordy mediocrity? Let the discerning reader take up any poem, pen in hand, for the purpose of discovering how many words he can strike out of it that give him no requisite ideas, no relevant ones that he cares for, and no reasons for the rhyme beyond its necessity, and he will see what blot and havoc he will make in many an admired production of its day,—what marks of its inevitable fate. Bulky authors in particular, however safe they may think themselves, would do well to consider what parts of their cargo they might dispense with in their proposed voyage down the gulfs of time; for many a gallant vessel, thought indestructible in its age, has perished;—many a load of words, expected to be in eternal demand, gone to join the wrecks of self-love, or rotted in the warehouses of change and vicissitude. I have said the more on this point, because in an age when the true inspiration has undoubtedly been reawakened by Coleridge and his fellows, and we have so many new poets coming forward, it may be as well to give a general warning against that tendency to an accumulation and ostentation of *thoughts*, which is meant to be a refutation in full of the pretensions of all poetry less cogitabund, whatever may be the requirements of its class. Young writers should bear in mind, that even some of the very best materials for poetry are not poetry built; and that the smallest marble shrine, of exquisite workmanship, outvalues all that architect ever chipped away. Whatever can be so dispensed with is rubbish.

Variety in versification consists in whatsoever can be done for the prevention of monotony, by diversity of stops and cadences, distribution of emphasis, and retardation and acceleration of time; for the whole real secret of versification is a musical secret, and is not attainable to any vital effect, save by the ear of genius. All the mere knowledge of feet and numbers, of accent and quantity, will no more impart it, than a knowledge of the 'Guide to Music' will make a Beethoven or a Paisiello. It is a matter of sensibility and imagination; of the beautiful in poetical passion, accompanied by musical; of the imperative necessity for a pause here, and a cadence there, and a quicker or slower utterance in this or that place, created by analogies of sound with sense, by the fluctuations of feeling, by the demands of the gods and graces that visit the poet's harp, as the winds visit that of Aeolus. The same time and quantity which are occasioned by the spiritual part of this secret, thus become its formal ones,—not feet and syllables, long and short, iambics or trochees; which are the reduction of it to its *less* than dry bones. You might get, for instance, not only ten and eleven, but thirteen or fourteen syllables into a rhyming, as well as blank, heroical verse, if time and the feeling permitted; and in irregular measure this is often done; just as musicians put twenty notes in a bar instead of two, quavers instead of minims, according as the feeling they are expressing impels them to fill up the time with short and hurried notes, or with long; or as the choristers in a cathedral retard or precipitate the words of the chant, according as the quantity of its notes, and the colon which divides the verse of the psalm, conspire to demand it. Had the moderns borne this principle in mind when they settled the prevailing systems of verse, instead of learning them, as they appear to have done, from the first drawling and one-syllabled notation of the church hymns, we should have retained all the advantages of the more numerous versifications of the ancients, without being compelled to fancy that there was no alternative for us between our syllabical uniformity and the hexameters or other special forms unsuited to our tongues. But to leave this question alone, we will present the reader with a few sufficing specimens of the difference between monotony and variety in versification, first from Pope, Dryden, and Milton, and next from Gay and Coleridge. The following is the boasted melody of the nevertheless exquisite poet of the *Rape of the Lock*,—

WHAT IS POETRY?

exquisite in his wit and fancy, though not in his numbers. The reader will observe that it is literally *see-saw*, like the rising and falling of a plank, with a light person at one end who is jerked up in the briefer time, and a heavier one who is set down more leisurely at the other. It is in the otherwise charming description of the heroine of that poem:

> On her white breast—a sparkling cross she wore,
> Which Jews might kiss—and infidels adore;
> Her lively looks—a sprightly mind disclose,
> Quick as her eyes—and as unfix'd as those;
> Favours to none—to all she smiles extends,
> Oft she rejects—but never once offends;
> Bright as the sun—her eyes the gazers strike,
> And like the sun—they shine on all alike;
> Yet graceful ease—and sweetness void of pride,
> Might hide her faults—if belles had faults to hide;
> If to her share—some female errors fall,
> Look on her face—and you'll forget them all.

Compare with this the description of Iphigenia in one of Dryden's stories from Boccaccio:

It happen'd—on a summer's holiday,
That to the greenwood shade—he took his way,
For Cymon shunn'd the church—and used not much to pray.
His quarter-staff—which he could ne'er forsake,
Hung half before—and half behind his back:
He trudg'd along—not knowing what he sought,
And whistled as he went—for want of thought.

By chance conducted—or by thirst constrain'd,
The deep recesses of a grove he gain'd:—
Where—in a plain defended by a wood,
Crept through the matted grass—a crystal flood,
By which—an alabaster fountain stood;
And on the margent of the fount was laid—
Attended by her slaves—a sleeping maid;
Like Dian and her nymphs—when, tir'd with sport,
To rest by cool Eurotas they resort.—
The dame herself—the goddess well express'd,
Not more distinguished by her purple vest—

Than by the charming features of the face—
And e'en in slumber—a superior grace:
Her comely limbs—compos'd with decent care,
Her body shaded—by a light cymar,
Her bosom to the view—was only bare;
Where two beginning paps were scarcely spied—
For yet their places were but signified.—
The fanning wind upon her bosom blows—
To meet the fanning wind—the bosom rose;
The fanning wind—and purling stream—continue her
   repose.

For a further variety take, from the same author's *Theodore and Honoria*, a passage in which the couplets are run one into the other, and all of it modulated, like the former, according to the feeling demanded by the occasion:

> Whilst listening to the murmuring leaves he stood—
> More than a mile immers'd within the wood—
> At once the wind was laid.|—The whispering sound
> Was dumb.|—A rising earthquake rock'd the ground.
> With deeper brown the grove was overspread—
> A sudden horror seiz'd his giddy head—
> And his ears tinkled—and his colour fled.
>
> Nature was in alarm.—Some danger nigh
> Seem'd threaten'd—though unseen to mortal eye.
> Unus'd to fear—he summon'd all his soul,
> And stood collected in himself—and whole:
> Not long.—

But for a crowning specimen of variety of pause and accent, apart from emotion, nothing can surpass the account, in *Paradise Lost*, of the Devil's search for an accomplice:

>   There was a plàce,
> Nòw nòt—though Sìn—not Tìme—fìrst wroùght the chànge,
> Where Tìgris—at the foot of Pàradise,
> Into a gulf—shòt under ground—till pàrt
> Ròse up a foùntain by the Trèe of Lìfe.
> *In* with the river sunk—and *with* it *ròse*
> Sàtan—invòlv'd in rìsing mìst—then soùght
> Whère to lie hìd.—Sèa he had search'd—and lànd
> From Eden over Pòntus—and the pòol

Maeòtis—*ùp* beyond the river *Ob*;
Dòwnward as fàr antàrctic;—and in lèngth
Wèst from Oròntes—to the òcean bàrr'd
At Dàriën—thènce to the lànd whère flòws
Gànges and Indus.—Thùs the òrb he ròam'd
With nàrrow sèarch;—and with inspèction dèep
Consìder'd èvery crèature—whìch of àll
Mòst opportùne mìght sèrve his wìles—and foùnd
The sèrpent—sùbtlest bèast of all the fièld.

If the reader cast his eye again over this passage, he will not find a verse in it which is not varied and harmonized in the most remarkable manner. Let him notice in particular that curious balancing of the lines in the sixth and tenth verses:

> *In* with the river sunk, &c.

and

> *Up* beyond the river *Ob*.

It might, indeed, be objected to the versification of Milton, that it exhibits too constant a perfection of this kind. It sometimes forces upon us too great a sense of consciousness on the part of the composer. We miss the first sprightly runnings of verse,—the ease and sweetness of spontaneity. Milton, I think, also too often condenses weight into heaviness.

Thus much concerning the chief of our two most popular measures. The other, called octo-syllabic, or the measure of eight syllables, offered such facilities for *namby-pamby*, that it had become a jest as early as the time of Shakespeare, who makes Touchstone call it the 'butterwoman's rate to market', and the 'very false gallop of verses'. It has been advocated, in opposition to the heroic measure, upon the ground that ten syllables lead a man into epithets and other superfluities, while eight syllables compress him into a sensible and pithy gentleman. But the heroic measure laughs at it. So far from compressing, it converts one line into two, and sacrifices everything to the quick and importunate return of the rhyme.

With Dryden, compare Gay, even in the strength of Gay,—

> The wind was high, the window shakes;
> With sudden start the miser wakes;
> Along the silent room he stalks,

(A miser never 'stalks'; but a rhyme was desired for 'walks')

> Looks back, and trembles as he walks:
> Each lock and every bolt he tries.
> In every creek and corner pries;
> Then opes the chest with treasure stor'd,
> And stands in rapture o'er his hoard;

('Hoard' and 'treasure stor'd' are just made for one another)

> But now, with sudden qualms possess'd,
> He wrings his hands, he beats his breast;
> By conscience stung, he wildly stares,
> And thus his guilty soul declares.

And so he denounces his gold, as miser never denounced it; and sighs, because

> Virtue resides on earth no more!

Coleridge saw the mistake which had been made with regard to this measure, and restored it to the beautiful freedom of which it was capable, by calling to mind the liberties allowed its old musical professors the minstrels, and dividing it by *time* instead of *syllables*;—by the *beat of four* into which you might get as many syllables as you could, instead of allotting eight syllables to the poor time, whatever it might have to say. He varied it further with alternate rhymes and stanzas, with rests and omissions precisely analogous to those in music, and rendered it altogether worthy to utter the manifold thoughts and feelings of himself and his lady Christabel. He even ventures, with an exquisite sense of solemn strangeness and licence (for there is witchcraft going forward), to introduce a couplet of blank verse, itself as mystically

WHAT IS POETRY?

and beautifully modulated as anything in the music of Gluck or Weber.

> 'Tis the middle of night by the castle clock,
> And the owls have awaken'd the crowing cock;
> Tu-whit!—Tu-whoo!
> And hark, again! the crowing cock,
> *How drowsily he crew.*
> Sir Leoline, the baron rich,
> Hath a toothless mastiff bitch;
> From her kennel beneath the rock
> She maketh answer to the clock,
> *Fòur fŏr thĕ qùartĕrs ănd twèlve fŏr thĕ hoùr,*
> Ever and aye, by shine and shower,
> Sixteen short howls, not over loud:
> Some say, she sees my lady's shroud.
>
> *Is the nìght chìlly and dàrk?*
> *The nìght is chìlly, but nòt dàrk.*
> The thin grey cloud is spread on high,
> It covers, but not hides, the sky.
> The moon is behind, and at the full,
> And yet she looks both small and dull.
> The night is chilly, the cloud is grey;

(These are not superfluities, but mysterious returns of importunate feeling)

> *'Tis a month before the month of May,*
> *And the spring comes slowly up this way.*
> The lovely lady, Christabel,
> Whom her father loves so well,
> What makes her in the wood so late,
> A furlong from the castle-gate?
>
> She had dreams all yesternight
> Of her own betrothèd knight;
> And shè ĭn thĕ midnight wood will pray
> For the wèal ŏf hĕr lover that's far away.
>
> She stole along, she nothing spoke,
> The sighs she heav'd were soft and low,
> And nought was green upon the oak,
> But moss and rarest mistletoe;
> She kneels beneath the huge oak tree,
> And in silence prayeth she.

> The lady sprang up suddenly,
> The lovely lady, Christabel!
> It moan'd as near as near can be,
> But what it is, she cannot tell.
> On the other side it seems to be
> Of thĕ hùge, broàd-breàsted, òld oàk trèe.
>
> The night is chill, the forest bare;
> Is it the wind that moaneth bleak?

(This 'bleak moaning' is a witch's)

> There is not wind enough in the air
> To move away the ringlet curl
> From the lovely lady's cheek—
> There is not wind enough to twirl
> *The òne rèd lèaf, the làst ŏf ĭts clan,*
> *That dàncĕs ăs ŏftĕn ăs dànce it càn,*
> *Hàngĭng sŏ lìght and hàngĭng sŏ hìgh,*
> *On thĕ tòpmost twìg thăt loŏks ùp ăt thĕ sky.*
>
> Hush, beating heart of Christabel!
> Jesu Maria, shield her well!
> She folded her arms beneath her cloak,
> And stole to the other side of the oak.
>   What sees she there?
>
> There she sees a damsel bright,
> Drest in a robe of silken white,
> That shadowy in the moonlight shone:
> The neck that made that white robe wan,
> Her stately neck and arms were bare:
> Her blue-vein'd feet unsandall'd were;
> And wildly glitter'd, here and there,
> The gems entangled in her hair.
> I guess 'twas *frightful* there to see
> *A lady so richly clad as she—*
> *Beautiful exceedingly.*

The principle of Variety in Uniformity is here worked out in a style 'beyond the reach of art'. Everything is diversified according to the demand of the moment, of the sounds, the sights, the emotions; the very uniformity of the outline is gently varied; and yet we feel that *the whole is one and of the same*

WHAT IS POETRY?

character, the single and sweet unconsciousness of the heroine making all the rest seem more conscious, and ghastly, and expectant. It is thus that *versification itself becomes part of the sentiment of a poem*, and vindicates the pains that have been taken to show its importance. I know of no very fine versification unaccompanied with fine poetry; no poetry of a mean order accompanied with verse of the highest.

As to Rhyme, which might be thought too insignificant to mention, it is not at all so. The universal consent of modern Europe, and of the East in all ages, has made it one of the musical beauties of verse for all poetry but epic and dramatic, and even for the former with Southern Europe,—a sustainment for the enthusiasm, and a demand to enjoy. The mastery of it consists in never writing it for its own sake, or at least never appearing to do so; in knowing how to vary it, to give it novelty, to render it more or less strong, to divide it (when not in couplets) at the proper intervals, to repeat it many times where luxury or animal spirits demand it (see an instance in Titania's speech to the Fairies), to impress an affecting or startling remark with it, and to make it, in comic poetry, a new and surprising addition to the jest.

> Large was his bounty and his soul sincere,
>   Heav'n did a recompense as largely send;
> He gave to misery all he had, *a tear*;
>   He gain'd from heav'n ('twas all he wish'd) *a friend*.
> > Gray's *Elegy*.

> The fops are proud of scandal; for they cry
> At every lewd, low character, 'That's *I*'.
> > Dryden's *Prologue to the Pilgrim*.

> What makes all doctrines plain and clear?
> *About two hundred pounds a-year*.
> And that which was proved true before,
> Prove false again? *Two hundred more*.
> > Hudibras.

> Compound for sins they are *inclin'd to*,
> By damning those they have *no mind to*.   *Id*.

>   —Stor'd with deletery *med'cines*,
>   Which whosoever took is *dead since*.   *Hudibras.*

Sometimes it is a grace in a master like Butler to force his rhyme, thus showing a laughing wilful power over the most stubborn materials:

>   Win
>   The women, and make them draw in
>   The men, as Indians with a *fèmale*
>   Tame elephant inveigle *the* male.   *Id.*
>
>   He made an instrument to know
>   If the moon shines at full or no;
>   That would, as soon as e'er she *shone, straight*
>   Whether 'twere day or night *demonstrate*;
>   Tell what her diameter to an *inch is,*
>   And prove that she's not made of *green cheese.*   *Id.*

Pronounce it, by all means, *grinches*, to make the joke more wilful. The happiest triple rhyme, perhaps, that ever was written, is in *Don Juan*:

>   But oh! ye lords of ladies *intellectual,*
>   Inform us truly,—haven't they *hen-peck'd you all?*

The sweepingness of the assumption completes the flowing breadth of effect.

Dryden confessed that a rhyme often gave him a thought. Probably the happy word 'sprung' in the following passage from Ben Jonson was suggested by it; but then the poet must have had the feeling in him.

>   —Let our trumpets sound,
>   And cleave both air and ground
>   With beating of our drums.
>   Let every lyre be strung,
>   Harp, lute, theorbo, *sprung*
>   *With touch of dainty thumbs.*

Boileau's trick for appearing to rhyme naturally was to compose the second line of his couplet first! which gives one the crowning idea of the 'artificial school of poetry'. Perhaps the most perfect master

WHAT IS POETRY?

of rhyme, the easiest and most abundant, was the greatest writer of comedy that the world has seen,—Molière.

If a young reader should ask, after all, What is the quickest way of knowing bad poets from good, the best poets from the next best, and so on? the answer is, the only and twofold way: first, the perusal of the best poets with the greatest attention; and, second, the cultivation of that love of truth and beauty which made them what they are. Every true reader of poetry partakes a more than ordinary portion of the poetic nature; and no one can be completely such, who does not love, or take an interest in, everything that interests the poet, from the firmament to the daisy,—from the highest heart of man to the most pitiable of the low. It is a good practice to read with pen in hand, marking what is liked or doubted. It rivets the attention, realizes the greatest amount of enjoyment, and facilitates reference. It enables the reader also, from time to time, to see what progress he makes with his own mind, and how it grows up towards the stature of its exalter.

If the same person should ask, What class of poetry is the highest? I should say, undoubtedly, the Epic; for it includes the drama, with narration besides; or the speaking and action of the characters, with the speaking of the poet himself, whose utmost address is taxed to relate all well for so long a time, particularly in the passages least sustained by enthusiasm. Whether this class has included the greatest poet, is another question still under trial; for Shakespeare perplexes all such verdicts, even when the claimant is Homer; though, if a judgement may be drawn from his early narratives (*Venus and Adonis*, and the *Rape of Lucrece*), it is to be doubted whether even Shakespeare could have told a story like Homer, owing to that incessant activity and superfoetation of thought, a little less of which might be occasionally desired even in his plays;—if it were possible, once possessing anything of his, to wish it away. Next to Homer and Shakespeare come such narrators as the less universal, but still intenser Dante; Milton, with his dignified imagination; the universal, profoundly simple Chaucer; and luxuriant, remote Spenser—immortal child in poetry's most poetic solitudes: then the great second-rate dramatists; unless those who are better acquainted with Greek tragedy than I am, demand a place for them before Chaucer: then the airy yet robust universality of Ariosto; the hearty, out-of-door nature of Theocritus, also a universalist; the finest lyrical poets (who only take short flights, compared with the narrators); the purely contemplative poets who have more thought than feeling; the descriptive, satirical, didactic, epigrammatic. It is to be borne in mind, however, that the first poet of an inferior class may be superior to followers in the train of a higher one, though the superiority is by no means to be taken for granted; otherwise Pope would be superior to Fletcher, and Butler to Pope. Imagination, teeming with action and character, makes the greatest poets; feeling and thought the next; fancy (by itself) the next; wit the last. Thought by itself makes no poet at all; for the mere conclusions of the understanding can at best be only so many intellectual matters of fact. Feeling, even destitute of conscious thought, stands a far better poetical chance; feeling being a sort of thought without the process of thinking,—a grasper of the truth without seeing it. And what is very remarkable, feeling seldom makes the blunders that thought does. An idle distinction has been made between taste and judgement. Taste is the very maker of judgement. Put an artificial fruit in your mouth, or only handle it, and you will soon perceive the difference between judging from taste or tact, and judging from the abstract figment called judgement. The latter does but throw you into guesses and doubts. Hence the conceits that astonish us in the gravest, and even subtlest, thinkers, whose taste is not proportionate to their mental perceptions; men like Donne, for instance; who, apart from accidental personal impressions, seem to look at nothing as it really is, but only as to what may be thought of it. Hence, on the other hand, the delightfulness of those poets who never violate truth of feeling, whether in things real or imaginary; who are always consistent with their object and its requirements; and who run the great round of nature, not to perplex and be perplexed, but to make themselves and us happy. And luckily, delightfulness is not incompatible with greatness, willing soever as men may be in their present imperfect state to set the power to subjugate above the power to please. Truth, of any great kind whatsoever, makes great writing. This is the reason why such poets as Ariosto, though not writing with a constant detail of thought and feeling like Dante, are justly considered great as well as delightful. Their greatness proves itself by the same truth of nature, and sustained power, though in a different way. Their action is not so crowded and weighty; their sphere has more territories less fertile; but it has enchantments of its own, which excess of thought would spoil,—luxuries, laughing graces, animal spirits; and not to recognize the beauty and greatness of these, treated as they treat them, is simply to be defective in sympathy. Every planet is not Mars or Saturn. There is also Venus and Mercury. There is one genius of the south, and another of the north, and others uniting both. The reader who is too thoughtless or too sensitive to like intensity of any sort, and he who is too thoughtful or too dull to like anything but the greatest possible stimulus of reflection or passion, are equally wanting in complexional fitness for a thorough enjoyment of books. Ariosto occasionally says as fine things as Dante, and Spenser as Shakespeare; but the business of both is to enjoy; and in order to partake their enjoyment to its full extent, you must feel what poetry is in the general as well as the particular, must be aware that there are different songs of the spheres, some fuller of notes, and others of a sustained delight; and as the former keep you perpetually alive to thought or passion, so from the latter you receive a constant harmonious sense of truth and beauty, more agreeable perhaps on the whole, though less exciting. Ariosto, for instance, does not *tell a story* with the brevity and concentrated passion of Dante; every sentence is not so full of matter, nor the style so removed from the indifference of prose; yet you are charmed with a truth of another sort, equally characteristic of the writer, equally drawn from nature and substituting a healthy sense of enjoyment for intenser emotion. Exclusiveness of liking for this or that mode of truth, only shows, either that a reader's perceptions are limited, or that he would sacrifice truth itself to his favourite form of it. Sir Walter Raleigh, who was as trenchant with his pen as his sword, hailed the *Faerie Queene* of his friend Spenser in verses in which he said that 'Petrarch' was thenceforward to be no more heard of; and that in all English poetry, there was nothing he counted 'of any price' but the effusions of the new author. Yet Petrarch is still living; Chaucer was not abolished by Sir Walter; and Shakespeare is thought somewhat valuable. A botanist might as well have said, that myrtles and oaks were to disappear, because acacias had come up. It is with the poet's creations, as with nature's, great or small. Wherever truth and beauty, whatever their amount, can be worthily shaped into verse, and answer to some demand for it in our hearts, there poetry is to be found; whether in productions grand and beautiful as some great event, or some mighty, leafy solitude, or no bigger and more pretending than a sweet face or a bunch of violets; whether in Homer's epic or Gray's *Elegy*, in the enchanted gardens of Ariosto and Spenser, or the very pot-herbs of the

Schoolmistress of Shenstone, the balms of the simplicity of a cottage. Not to know and feel this, is to be deficient in the universality of Nature herself, who is a poetess on the smallest as well as the largest scale, and who calls upon us to admire all her productions; not indeed with the same degree of admiration, but with no refusal of it, except to defect.

I cannot draw this essay towards its conclusion better than with three memorable words of Milton; who has said, that poetry, in comparison with science, is 'simple, sensuous, and passionate'. By simple, he means unperplexed and self-evident; by sensuous, genial and full of imagery; by passionate, excited and enthusiastic. I am aware that different constructions have been put on some of these words; but the context seems to me to necessitate those before us. I quote, however, not from the original, but from an extract in the *Remarks on Paradise Lost* by Richardson.

What the poet has to cultivate above all things is love and truth;—what he has to avoid, like poison, is the fleeting and the false. He will get no good by proposing to be 'in earnest at the moment'. His earnestness must be innate and habitual; born with him, and felt to be his most precious inheritance. 'I expect neither profit nor general fame by my writings,' says Coleridge, in the Preface to his Poems; 'and I consider myself as having been amply repaid without either. Poetry has been to me its *"own exceeding great reward"*; it has soothed my afflictions; it has multiplied and refined my enjoyments; it has endeared solitude; and it has given me the habit of wishing to discover the good and the beautiful in all that meets and surrounds me.'

'Poetry', says Shelley, 'lifts the veil from the hidden beauty of the world, *and makes familiar objects be as if they were not familiar.* It reproduces all that it represents; and the impersonations clothed in its Elysian light stand thenceforward in the minds of those who have once contemplated them, as memorials of that gentle and exalted content which extends itself over all thoughts and actions with which it co-exists. The great secret of morals is love, or a going out of our own nature, and an identification of ourselves with the beautiful which exists in thought, action, or person, not our own. A man, to be greatly good, must imagine intensely and comprehensively; he must put himself in the place of another, and of many others: the pains and pleasures of his species must become his own. The great instrument of moral good is imagination; and poetry administers to the effect by acting upon the cause.'

I would not willingly say anything after perorations like these; but as treatises on poetry may chance to have auditors who think themselves called upon to vindicate the superiority of what is termed useful knowledge, it may be as well to add, that if the poet may be allowed to pique himself on any one thing more than another, compared with those who undervalue him, it is on that power of undervaluing nobody, and no attainments different from his own, which is given him by the very faculty of imagination they despise. The greater includes the less. They do not see that their inability to comprehend him argues the smaller capacity. No man recognizes the worth of utility more than the poet: he only desires that the meaning of the term may not come short of its greatness, and exclude the noblest necessities of his fellow-creatures. He is quite as much pleased, for instance, with the facilities for rapid conveyance afforded him by the railroad, as the dullest confiner of its advantages to that single idea, or as the greatest two-idea'd man who varies that single idea with hugging himself on his 'buttons' or his good dinner. But he sees also the beauty of the country through which he passes, of the towns, of the heavens, of the steam-engine itself, thundering and fuming along like a magic horse, of the affections that are carrying, perhaps, half the passengers on their journey, nay, of those of the great two-idea'd man; and, beyond all this, he discerns the incalculable amount of good, and knowledge, and refinement, and mutual consideration, which this wonderful invention is fitted to circulate over the globe, perhaps to the displacement of war itself, and certainly to the diffusion of millions of enjoyments.

'And a button-maker, after all, invented it!' cries our friend.

Pardon me—it was a nobleman. A button-maker may be a very excellent, and a very poetical man too, and yet not have been the first man visited by a sense of the gigantic powers of the combination of water and fire. It was a nobleman who first thought of this most poetical bit of science. It was a nobleman who first thought of it—a captain who first tried it—and a button-maker who perfected it. And he who put the nobleman on such thoughts was the great philosopher, Bacon, who said that poetry had 'something divine in it', and was necessary to the satisfaction of the human mind.

MATTHEW ARNOLD
1822–1888
THE CHOICE OF SUBJECTS IN POETRY
[Preface to 'Poems', 1853]

IN two small volumes of Poems, published anonymously, one in 1849, the other in 1852, many of the Poems which compose the present volume have already appeared. The rest are now published for the first time.

I have, in the present collection, omitted the Poem from which the volume published in 1852 took its title. I have done so, not because the subject of it was a Sicilian Greek born between two and three thousand years ago, although many persons would think this a sufficient reason. Neither have I done so because I had, in my own opinion, failed in the delineation which I intended to effect. I intended to delineate the feelings of one of the last of the Greek religious philosophers, one of the family of Orpheus and Musaeus, having survived his fellows, living on into a time when the habits of Greek thought and feeling had begun fast to change, character to dwindle, the influence of the Sophists to prevail. Into the feelings of a man so situated there entered much that we are accustomed to consider as exclusively modern; how much, the fragments of Empedocles himself which remain to us are sufficient at least to indicate. What those who are familiar only with the great monuments of early Greek genius suppose to be its exclusive characteristics, have disappeared; the calm, the cheerfulness, the disinterested objectivity have disappeared: the dialogue of the mind with itself has commenced; modern problems have presented themselves; we hear already the doubts, we witness the discouragement, of Hamlet and of Faust.

The representation of such a man's feelings must be interesting, if consistently drawn. We all naturally take pleasure, says Aristotle, in any imitation or representation whatever: this is the basis of our love of Poetry: and we take pleasure in them, he adds, because all knowledge is naturally agreeable to us; not to the philosopher only, but to mankind at large. Every representation therefore which is consistently drawn may be supposed to be interesting, inasmuch as it gratifies this natural interest in knowledge of all kinds. What is *not* interesting, is that which does not add to our knowledge of any kind; that which is vaguely conceived and loosely drawn; a representation which is general, indeterminate, and faint, instead of being particular, precise, and firm.

Any accurate representation may therefore be expected to be interesting; but, if the representation be a poetical one, more than this is demanded. It is demanded, not only that it shall interest, but also that it shall inspirit and rejoice the reader: that it shall convey a charm, and infuse delight. For the Muses, as Hesiod says, were born that they might be 'a forgetfulness of evils, and a truce from cares'; and it is not enough that the Poet should add to the knowledge of men, it is required of him also that he should add to their happiness. 'All Art', says Schiller, 'is dedicated to Joy, and there is no higher and no more serious problem, than how to make men happy. The right Art is that alone, which creates the highest enjoyment.'

A poetical work, therefore, is not yet justified when it has been shown to be an accurate, and therefore interesting, representation; it has to be shown also that it is a representation from which men can derive enjoyment. In presence of the most tragic circumstances, represented in a work of Art, the feeling of enjoyment, as is well known, may still subsist: the representation of the most utter calamity, of the liveliest anguish, is not sufficient to destroy it: the more tragic the situation, the deeper becomes the enjoyment; and the situation is more tragic in proportion as it becomes more terrible.

What then are the situations, from the representation of which, though accurate, no poetical enjoyment can be derived? They are those in which the suffering finds no vent in action; in which a continuous state of mental distress is prolonged, unrelieved by incident, hope, or resistance; in which there is everything to be endured, nothing to be done. In such situations there is inevitably something morbid, in the description of them something monotonous. When they occur in actual life, they are painful, not tragic; the representation of them in poetry is painful also.

To this class of situations, poetically faulty as it appears to me, that of Empedocles, as I have endeavoured to represent him, belongs; and I have therefore excluded the Poem from the present collection.

And why, it may be asked, have I entered into this explanation respecting a matter so unimportant as the admission or exclusion of the Poem in question? I have done so, because I was anxious to avow that the sole reason for its exclusion was that which has been stated above; and that it has not been excluded in deference to the opinion which many critics of the present day appear to entertain against subjects chosen from distant times and countries: against the choice, in short, of any subjects but modern ones.

'The Poet,' it is said, and by an intelligent critic, 'the Poet who would really fix the public attention must leave the exhausted past, and draw his subjects from matters of present import, and *therefore* both of interest and novelty.'

Now this view I believe to be completely false. It is worth examining, inasmuch as it is a fair sample of a class of critical dicta everywhere current at the present day, having a philosophical form and air,

THE CHOICE OF SUBJECTS IN POETRY

but no real basis in fact; and which are calculated to vitiate the judgement of readers of poetry, while they exert, so far as they are adopted, a misleading influence on the practice of those who write it.

What are the eternal objects of Poetry, among all nations and at all times? They are actions; human actions; possessing an inherent interest in themselves, and which are to be communicated in an interesting manner by the art of the Poet. Vainly will the latter imagine that he has everything in his own power; that he can make an intrinsically inferior action equally delightful with a more excellent one by his treatment of it: he may indeed compel us to admire his skill, but his work will possess, within itself, an incurable defect.

The Poet, then, has in the first place to select an excellent action; and what actions are the most excellent? Those, certainly, which most powerfully appeal to the great primary human affections: to those elementary feelings which subsist permanently in the race, and which are independent of time. These feelings are permanent and the same; that which interests them is permanent and the same also. The modernness or antiquity of an action, therefore, has nothing to do with its fitness for poetical representation; this depends upon its inherent qualities. To the elementary part of our nature, to our passions, that which is great and passionate is eternally interesting; and interesting solely in proportion to its greatness and to its passion. A great human action of a thousand years ago is more interesting to it than a smaller human action of to-day, even though upon the representation of this last the most consummate skill may have been expended, and though it has the advantage of appealing by its modern language, familiar manners, and contemporary allusions, to all our transient feelings and interests. These, however, have no right to demand of a poetical work that it shall satisfy them; their claims are to be directed elsewhere. Poetical works belong to the domain of our permanent passions: let them interest these, and the voice of all subordinate claims upon them is at once silenced.

Achilles, Prometheus, Clytemnestra, Dido—what modern poem presents personages as interesting, even to us moderns, as these personages of an 'exhausted past'? We have the domestic epic dealing with the details of modern life which pass daily under our eyes; we have poems representing modern personages in contact with the problems of modern life, moral, intellectual, and social; these works have been produced by poets the most distinguished of their nation and time; yet I fearlessly assert that *Hermann and Dorothea*, *Childe Harold*, *Jocelyn*, *The Excursion*, leave the reader cold in comparison with the effect produced upon him by the latter books of the Iliad, by the *Orestea*, or by the episode of Dido. And why is this? Simply because in the three latter cases the action is greater, the personages nobler, the situations more intense: and this is the true basis of the interest in a poetical work, and this alone.

It may be urged, however, that past actions may be interesting in themselves, but that they are not to be adopted by the modern Poet, because it is impossible for him to have them clearly present to his own mind, and he cannot therefore feel them deeply, nor represent them forcibly. But this is not necessarily the case. The externals of a past action, indeed, he cannot know with the precision of a contemporary; but his business is with its essentials. The outward man of Oedipus or of Macbeth, the houses in which they lived, the ceremonies of their courts, he cannot accurately figure to himself; but neither do they essentially concern him. His business is with their inward man; with their feelings and behaviour in certain tragic situations, which engage their passions as men; these have in them nothing local and casual; they are as accessible to the modern Poet as to a contemporary.

THE CHOICE OF SUBJECTS IN POETRY

The date of an action, then, signifies nothing: the action itself, its selection and construction, this is what is all-important. This the Greeks understood far more clearly than we do. The radical difference between their poetical theory and ours consists, as it appears to me, in this: that, with them, the poetical character of the action in itself, and the conduct of it, was the first consideration; with us, attention is fixed mainly on the value of the separate thoughts and images which occur in the treatment of an action. They regarded the whole; we regard the parts. With them, the action predominated over the expression of it; with us, the expression predominates over the action. Not that they failed in expression, or were inattentive to it; on the contrary, they are the highest models of expression, the unapproached masters of the *grand style*: but their expression is so excellent because it is so admirably kept in its right degree of prominence; because it is so simple and so well subordinated; because it draws its force directly from the pregnancy of the matter which it conveys. For what reason was the Greek tragic poet confined to so limited a range of subjects? Because there are so few actions which unite in themselves, in the highest degree, the conditions of excellence: and it was not thought that on any but an excellent subject could an excellent Poem be constructed. A few actions, therefore, eminently adapted for tragedy, maintained almost exclusive possession of the Greek tragic stage; their significance appeared inexhaustible; they were as permanent problems, perpetually offered to the genius of every fresh poet. This too is the reason of what appears to us moderns a certain baldness of expression in Greek tragedy; of the triviality with which we often reproach the remarks of the Chorus, where it takes part in the dialogue: that the action itself, the situation of Orestes, or Merope, or Alcmaeon, was to stand the central point of interest, unforgotten, absorbing, principal; that no accessories were for a moment to distract the spectator's attention from this; that the tone of the parts was to be perpetually kept down, in order not to impair the grandiose effect of the whole. The terrible old mythic story on which the drama was founded stood, before he entered the theatre, traced in its bare outlines upon the spectator's mind; it stood in his memory, as a group of statuary, faintly seen, at the end of a long and dark vista: then came the Poet, embodying outlines, developing situations, not a word wasted, not a sentiment capriciously thrown in; stroke upon stroke, the drama proceeded: the light deepened upon the group; more and more it revealed itself to the riveted gaze of the spectator: until at last, when the final words were spoken, it stood before him in broad sunlight, a model of immortal beauty.

This was what a Greek critic demanded; this was what a Greek poet endeavoured to effect. It signified nothing to what time an action belonged; we do not find that the *Persae* occupied a particularly high rank among the dramas of Aeschylus, because it represented a matter of contemporary interest: this was not what a cultivated Athenian required; he required that the permanent elements of his nature should be moved; and dramas of which the action, though taken from a long-distant mythic time, yet was calculated to accomplish this in a higher degree than that of the *Persae*, stood higher in his estimation accordingly. The Greeks felt, no doubt, with their exquisite sagacity of taste, that an action of present times was too near them, too much mixed up with what was accidental and passing, to form a sufficiently grand, detached, and self-subsistent object for a tragic poem: such objects belonged to the domain of the comic poet, and of the lighter kinds of poetry. For the more serious kinds, for *pragmatic* poetry, to use an excellent expression of Polybius, they were more difficult and severe in the range of subjects which they

THE CHOICE OF SUBJECTS IN POETRY

permitted. Their theory and practice alike, the admirable treatise of Aristotle, and the unrivalled works of their poets, exclaim with a thousand tongues—'All depends upon the subject; choose a fitting action, penetrate yourself with the feeling of its situations; this done, everything else will follow.'

But for all kinds of poetry alike there was one point on which they were rigidly exacting; the adaptability of the subject to the kind of poetry selected, and the careful construction of the poem.

How different a way of thinking from this is ours! We can hardly at the present day understand what Menander meant, when he told a man who inquired as to the progress of his comedy that he had finished it, not having yet written a single line, because he had constructed the action of it in his mind. A modern critic would have assured him that the merit of his piece depended on the brilliant things which arose under his pen as he went along. We have poems which seem to exist merely for the sake of single lines and passages; not for the sake of producing any total-impression. We have critics who seem to direct their attention merely to detached expressions, to the language about the action, not to the action itself. I verily think that the majority of them do not in their hearts believe that there is such a thing as a total-impression to be derived from a poem at all, or to be demanded from a poet; they think the term a commonplace of metaphysical criticism. They will permit the Poet to select any action he pleases, and to suffer that action to go as it will, provided he gratifies them with occasional bursts of fine writing, and with a shower of isolated thoughts and images. That is, they permit him to leave their poetical sense ungratified, provided that he gratifies their rhetorical sense and their curiosity. Of his neglecting to gratify these, there is little danger; he needs rather to be warned against the danger of attempting to gratify these alone; he needs rather to be perpetually reminded to prefer his action to everything else; so to treat this, as to permit its inherent excellences to develop themselves, without interruption from the intrusion of his personal peculiarities: most fortunate when he most entirely succeeds in effacing himself, and in enabling a noble action to subsist as it did in nature.

But the modern critic not only permits a false practice; he absolutely prescribes false aims.—'A true allegory of the state of one's own mind in a representative history,' the Poet is told, 'is perhaps the highest thing that one can attempt in the way of poetry.'—And accordingly he attempts it. An allegory of the state of one's own mind, the highest problem of an art which imitates actions! No assuredly, it is not, it never can be so: no great poetical work has ever been produced with such an aim. *Faust* itself, in which something of the kind is attempted, wonderful passages as it contains, and in spite of the unsurpassed beauty of the scenes which relate to Margaret, *Faust* itself, judged as a whole, and judged strictly as a poetical work, is defective: its illustrious author, the greatest poet of modern times, the greatest critic of all times, would have been the first to acknowledge it; he only defended his work, indeed, by asserting it to be 'something incommensurable'.

The confusion of the present times is great, the multitude of voices counselling different things bewildering, the number of existing works capable of attracting a young writer's attention and of becoming his models, immense: what he wants is a hand to guide him through the confusion, a voice to prescribe to him the aim which he should keep in view, and to explain to him that the value of the literary works which offer themselves to his attention is relative to their power of helping him forward on his road towards this aim. Such a guide the English writer at the present day will nowhere find. Failing this, all that can be looked for, all indeed that can be desired,

THE CHOICE OF SUBJECTS IN POETRY 313

is, that his attention should be fixed on excellent models; that he may reproduce, at any rate, something of their excellence, by penetrating himself with their works and by catching their spirit, if he cannot be taught to produce what is excellent independently.

Foremost among these models for the English writer stands Shakespeare: a name the greatest perhaps of all poetical names; a name never to be mentioned without reverence. I will venture, however, to express a doubt, whether the influence of his works, excellent and fruitful for the readers of poetry, for the great majority, has been of unmixed advantage to the writers of it. Shakespeare indeed chose excellent subjects; the world could afford no better than Macbeth, or Romeo and Juliet, or Othello: he had no theory respecting the necessity of choosing subjects of present import, or the paramount interest attaching to allegories of the state of one's own mind; like all great poets, he knew well what constituted a poetical action; like them, wherever he found such an action, he took it; like them, too, he found his best in past times. But to these general characteristics of all great poets, he added a special one of his own; a gift, namely, of happy, abundant, and ingenious expression, eminent and unrivalled: so eminent as irresistibly to strike the attention first in him, and even to throw into comparative shade his other excellences as a poet. Here has been the mischief. These other excellences were his fundamental excellences *as a poet*; what distinguishes the artist from the mere amateur, says Goethe, is *Architectonicè* in the highest sense; that power of execution, which creates, forms, and constitutes: not the profoundness of single thoughts, not the richness of imagery, not the abundance of illustration. But these attractive accessories of a poetical work being more easily seized than the spirit of the whole, and these accessories being possessed by Shakespeare in an unequalled degree, a young writer having recourse to Shakespeare as his model runs great risk of being vanquished and absorbed by them, and, in consequence, of reproducing, according to the measure of his power, these, and these alone. Of this preponderating quality of Shakespeare's genius, accordingly, almost the whole of modern English poetry has, it appears to me, felt the influence. To the exclusive attention on the part of his imitators to this it is in a great degree owing, that of the majority of modern poetical works the details alone are valuable, the composition worthless. In reading them one is perpetually reminded of that terrible sentence on a modern French poet—*il dit tout ce qu'il veut, mais malheureusement il n'a rien à dire*.

Let me give an instance of what I mean. I will take it from the works of the very chief among those who seem to have been formed in the school of Shakespeare: of one whose exquisite genius and pathetic death render him for ever interesting. I will take the poem of *Isabella, or the Pot of Basil*, by Keats. I choose this rather than the *Endymion*, because the latter work (which a modern critic has classed with the *Faerie Queene*!), although undoubtedly there blows through it the breath of genius, is yet as a whole so utterly incoherent, as not strictly to merit the name of a poem at all. The poem of *Isabella*, then, is a perfect treasure-house of graceful and felicitous words and images: almost in every stanza there occurs one of those vivid and picturesque turns of expression, by which the object is made to flash upon the eye of the mind, and which thrill the reader with a sudden delight. This one short poem contains, perhaps, a greater number of happy single expressions which one could quote than all the extant tragedies of Sophocles. But the action, the story? The action in itself is an excellent one; but so feebly is it conceived by the Poet, so loosely constructed, that the effect produced by it, in and for itself, is absolutely null. Let the reader, after he has finished the poem of Keats, turn to the same story in the *Decameron*: he will then feel how pregnant and interesting the same action has become in the hands of a great artist, who above all things delineates his object; who subordinates expression to that which it is designed to express.

I have said that the imitators of Shakespeare, fixing their attention on his wonderful gift of expression, have directed their imitation to this, neglecting his other excellences. These excellences, the fundamental excellences of poetical art, Shakespeare no doubt possessed them—possessed many of them in a splendid degree; but it may perhaps be doubted whether even he himself did not sometimes give scope to his faculty of expression to the prejudice of a higher poetical duty. For we must never forget that Shakespeare is the great poet he is from his skill in discerning and firmly conceiving an excellent action, from his power of intensely feeling a situation, of intimately associating himself with a character; not from his gift of expression, which rather even leads him astray, degenerating sometimes into a fondness for curiosity of expression, into an irritability of fancy, which seems to make it impossible for him to say a thing plainly, even when the press of the action demands the very directest language, or its level character the very simplest. Mr. Hallam, than whom it is impossible to find a saner and more judicious critic, has had the courage (for at the present day it needs courage) to remark, how extremely and faultily difficult Shakespeare's language often is. It is so: you may find main scenes in some of his greatest tragedies, *King Lear* for instance, where the language is so artificial, so curiously tortured, and so difficult, that every speech has to be read two or three times before its meaning can be comprehended. This overcuriousness of expression is indeed but the excessive employment of a wonderful gift—of the power of saying a thing in a happier way than any other man; nevertheless, it is carried so far that one understands what M. Guizot meant, when he said that Shakespeare appears in his language to have tried all styles except that of simplicity. He has not the severe and scrupulous self-restraint of the ancients, partly, no doubt, because he had a far less cultivated and exacting audience: he has indeed a far wider range than they had, a far richer fertility of thought; in this respect he rises above them: in his strong conception of his subject, in the genuine way in which he is penetrated with it, he resembles them, and is unlike the moderns: but in the accurate limitation of it, the conscientious rejection of superfluities, the simple and rigorous development of it from the first line of his work to the last, he falls below them, and comes nearer to the moderns. In his chief works, besides what he has of his own, he has the elementary soundness of the ancients; he has their important action and their large and broad manner: but he has not their purity of method. He is therefore a less safe model; for what he has of his own is personal, and inseparable from his own rich nature; it may be imitated and exaggerated, it canno be learned or applied as an art; he is above all suggestive; more valuable, therefore, to young writers as men than as artists. But clearness of arrangement, rigour of development, simplicity of style—these may to a certain extent be learned: and these may, I am convinced, be learned best from the ancients, who, although infinitely less suggestive than Shakespeare, are thus, to the artist, more instructive.

What then, it will be asked, are the ancients to be our sole models? the ancients with their comparatively narrow range of experience, and their widely different circumstances? Not, certainly, that which is narrow in the ancients, nor that in which we can no longer sympathize. An action like the action of the *Antigone* of Sophocles, which turns upon the conflict between the heroine's duty to her brother's corpse and that to the laws of her country, is no

THE CHOICE OF SUBJECTS IN POETRY 317

longer one in which it is possible that we should feel a deep interest. I am speaking too, it will be remembered, not of the best sources of intellectual stimulus for the general reader, but of the best models of instruction for the individual writer. This last may certainly learn of the ancients, better than anywhere else, three things which it is vitally important for him to know:—the all-importance of the choice of a subject; the necessity of accurate construction; and the subordinate character of expression. He will learn from them how unspeakably superior is the effect of the one moral impression left by a great action treated as a whole, to the effect produced by the most striking single thought or by the happiest image. As he penetrates into the spirit of the great classical works, as he becomes gradually aware of their intense significance, their noble simplicity, and their calm pathos, he will be convinced that it is this effect, unity and profoundness of moral impression, at which the ancient Poets aimed; that it is this which constitutes the grandeur of their works, and which makes them immortal. He will desire to direct his own efforts towards producing the same effect. Above all, he will deliver himself from the jargon of modern criticism, and escape the danger of producing poetical works conceived in the spirit of the passing time, and which partake of its transitoriness.

The present age makes great claims upon us: we owe it service, it will not be satisfied without our admiration. I know not how it is, but their commerce with the ancients appears to me to produce, in those who constantly practise it, a steadying and composing effect upon their judgement, not of literary works only, but of men and events in general. They are like persons who have had a very weighty and impressive experience; they are more truly than others under the empire of facts, and more independent of the language current among those with whom they live. They wish neither to applaud nor to revile their age: they wish to know what it is, what it can give them, and whether this is what they want. What they want, they know very well; they want to educe and cultivate what is best and noblest in themselves: they know, too, that this is no easy task —χαλεπὸν, as Pittacus said, χαλεπὸν ἐσθλὸν ἔμμεναι —and they ask themselves sincerely whether their age and its literature can assist them in the attempt. If they are endeavouring to practise any art, they remember the plain and simple proceedings of the old artists, who attained their grand results by penetrating themselves with some noble and significant action, not by inflating themselves with a belief in the pre-eminent importance and greatness of their own times. They do not talk of their mission, nor of interpreting their age, nor of the coming Poet; all this, they know, is the mere delirium of vanity; their business is not to praise their age, but to afford to the men who live in it the highest pleasure which they are capable of feeling. If asked to afford this by means of subjects drawn from the age itself, they ask what special fitness the present age has for supplying them: they are told that it is an era of progress, an age commissioned to carry out the great ideas of industrial development and social amelioration. They reply that with all this they can do nothing; that the elements they need for the exercise of their art are great actions, calculated powerfully and delightfully to affect what is permanent in the human soul; that so far as the present age can supply such actions, they will gladly make use of them; but that an age wanting in moral grandeur can with difficulty supply such, and an age of spiritual discomfort with difficulty be powerfully and delightfully affected by them.

A host of voices will indignantly rejoin that the present age is inferior to the past neither in moral grandeur nor in spiritual health. He who possesses the discipline I speak of will content himself with remembering the judgements passed upon the present age, in this respect, by the two men, the one of strongest head, the other of widest culture, whom it has produced; by Goethe and by Niebuhr. It will be sufficient for him that he knows the opinions held by these two great men respecting the present age and its literature; and that he feels assured in his own mind that their aims and demands upon life were such as he would wish, at any rate, his own to be; and their judgement as to what is impeding and disabling such as he may safely follow. He will not, however, maintain a hostile attitude towards the false pretensions of his age; he will content himself with not being overwhelmed by them. He will esteem himself fortunate if he can succeed in banishing from his mind all feelings of contradiction, and irritation, and impatience; in order to delight himself with the contemplation of some noble action of a heroic time, and to enable others, through his representation of it, to delight in it also.

I am far indeed from making any claim, for myself, that I possess this discipline; or for the following Poems, that they breathe its spirit. But I say, that in the sincere endeavour to learn and practise, amid the bewildering confusion of our times, what is sound and true in poetical art, I seemed to myself to find the only sure guidance, the only solid footing, among the ancients. They, at any rate, knew what they wanted in Art, and we do not. It is this uncertainty which is disheartening, and not hostile criticism. How often have I felt this when reading words of disparagement or of cavil: that it is the uncertainty as to what is really to be aimed at which makes our difficulty, not the dissatisfaction of the critic, who himself suffers from the same uncertainty. *Non me tua fervida terrent Dicta; Dii me terrent, et Jupiter hostis.*

Two kinds of *dilettanti*, says Goethe, there are in poetry: he who neglects the indispensable mechanical part, and thinks he has done enough if he shows spirituality and feeling; and he who seeks to arrive at poetry merely by mechanism, in which he can acquire an artisan's readiness, and is without soul and matter. And he adds, that the first does most harm to Art, and the last to himself. If we must be *dilettanti*: if it is impossible for us, under the circumstances amidst which we live, to think clearly, to feel nobly, and to delineate firmly: if we cannot attain to the mastery of the great artists—let us, at least, have so much respect for our Art as to prefer it to ourselves: let us not bewilder our successors: let us transmit to them the practice of Poetry, with its boundaries and wholesome regulative laws, under which excellent works may again, perhaps, at some future time, be produced, not yet fallen into oblivion through our neglect, not yet condemned and cancelled by the influence of their eternal enemy, Caprice.

ADVERTISEMENT TO THE SECOND EDITION
(1854)

I HAVE allowed the Preface to the former edition of these Poems to stand almost without change, because I still believe it to be, in the main, true. I must not, however, be supposed insensible to the force of much that has been alleged against portions of it, or unaware that it contains many things incompletely stated, many things which need limitation. It leaves, too, untouched the question, how far, and in what manner, the opinions there expressed respecting the choice of subjects apply to lyric poetry; that region of the poetical field which is chiefly cultivated at present. But neither have I time now to supply these deficiencies, nor is this the proper place for attempting it: on one or two points alone I wish to offer, in the briefest possible way, some explanation.

An objection has been ably urged to the classing

THE CHOICE OF SUBJECTS IN POETRY

together, as subjects equally belonging to a past time, Oedipus and Macbeth. And it is no doubt true that to Shakespeare, standing on the verge of the Middle Ages, the epoch of Macbeth was more familiar than that of Oedipus. But I was speaking of actions as they presented themselves to us moderns: and it will hardly be said that the European mind, since Voltaire, has much more affinity with the times of Macbeth than with those of Oedipus. As moderns, it seems to me, we have no longer any direct affinity with the circumstances and feelings of either; as individuals, we are attracted towards this or that personage, we have a capacity for imagining him, irrespective of his times, solely according to a law of personal sympathy; and those subjects for which we feel this personal attraction most strongly, we may hope to treat successfully. Alcestis or Joan of Arc, Charlemagne or Agamemnon—one of these is not really nearer to us now than another; each can be made present only by an act of poetic imagination: but this man's imagination has an affinity for one of them, and that man's for another.

It has been said that I wish to limit the Poet in his choice of subjects to the period of Greek and Roman antiquity: but it is not so: I only counsel him to choose for his subjects great actions, without regarding to what time they belong. Nor do I deny that the poetic faculty can and does manifest itself in treating the most trifling action, the most hopeless subject. But it is a pity that power should be wasted; and that the Poet should be compelled to impart interest and force to his subject, instead of receiving them from it, and thereby doubling his impressiveness. There is, it has been excellently said, an immortal strength in the stories of great actions: the most gifted poet, then, may well be glad to supplement with it that mortal weakness, which, in presence of the vast spectacle of life and the world, he must for ever feel to be his individual portion.

Again, with respect to the study of the classical writers of antiquity: it has been said that we should emulate rather than imitate them. I make no objection: all I say is, let us study them. They can help to cure us of what is, it seems to me, the great vice of our intellect, manifesting itself in our incredible vagaries in literature, in art, in religion, in morals; namely, that it is *fantastic*, and wants *sanity*. Sanity—that is the great virtue of the ancient literature: the want of that is the great defect of the modern, in spite of all its variety and power. It is impossible to read carefully the great ancients, without losing something of our caprice and eccentricity; and to emulate them we must at least read them.

JOHN RUSKIN
1819–1900
OF THE PATHETIC FALLACY
[*Modern Painters*, vol. iii, pt. 4, 1856]

§ 1. GERMAN dulness, and English affectation, have of late much multiplied among us the use of two of the most objectionable words that were ever coined by the troublesomeness of metaphysicians—namely, 'Objective' and 'Subjective'.

No words can be more exquisitely, and in all points, useless; and I merely speak of them that I may, at once and for ever, get them out of my way, and out of my reader's. But to get that done, they must be explained.

The word 'Blue', say certain philosophers, means the sensation of colour which the human eye receives in looking at the open sky, or at a bell gentian.

Now, say they farther, as this sensation can only be felt when the eye is turned to the object, and as, therefore, no such sensation is produced by the object when nobody looks at it, therefore the thing, when it is not looked at, is not blue; and thus (say they) there are many qualities of things which depend as much on something else as on themselves. To be sweet, a thing must have a taster; it is only sweet while it is being tasted, and if the tongue had not the capacity of taste, then the sugar would not have the quality of sweetness.

And then they agree that the qualities of things which thus depend upon our perception of them, and upon our human nature as affected by them, shall be called Subjective; and the qualities of things which they always have, irrespective of any other nature, as roundness or squareness, shall be called Objective.

From these ingenious views the step is very easy to a farther opinion, that it does not much matter what things are in themselves, but only what they are to us; and that the only real truth of them is their appearance to, or effect upon, us. From which position, with a hearty desire for mystification, and much egotism, selfishness, shallowness, and impertinence, a philosopher may easily go so far as to believe, and say, that everything in the world depends upon his seeing or thinking of it, and that nothing, therefore, exists, but what he sees or thinks of.

§ 2. Now, to get rid of all these ambiguities and troublesome words at once, be it observed that the word 'Blue' does *not* mean the *sensation* caused by a gentian on the human eye; but it means the *power* of producing that sensation; and this power is always there, in the thing, whether we are there to experience it or not, and would remain there though there were not left a man on the face of the earth. Precisely in the same way gunpowder has a power of exploding. It will not explode if you put no match to it. But it has always the power of so exploding, and is therefore called an explosive compound, which it very positively and assuredly is, whatever philosophy may say to the contrary.

In like manner, a gentian does not produce the sensation of blueness if you don't look at it. But it has always the power of doing so; its particles being everlastingly so arranged by its Maker. And, therefore, the gentian and the sky are always verily blue, whatever philosophy may say to the contrary; and if you do not see them blue when you look at them, it is not their fault but yours.

§ 3. Hence I would say to these philosophers: If, instead of using the sonorous phrase, 'It is objectively so,' you will use the plain old phrase, 'It *is* so;' and if instead of the sonorous phrase, 'It is subjectively so,' you will say, in plain old English, 'It does so,' or 'It seems so to me;' you will, on the whole, be more

OF THE PATHETIC FALLACY

intelligible to your fellow-creatures: and besides, if you find that a thing which generally 'does so' to other people (as a gentian looks blue to most men), does *not* so to you, on any particular occasion, you will not fall into the impertinence of saying, that the thing is not so, or did not so, but you will say simply (what you will be all the better for speedily finding out), that something is the matter with you. If you find that you cannot explode the gunpowder, you will not declare that all gunpowder is subjective, and all explosion imaginary, but you will simply suspect and declare yourself to be an ill-made match. Which, on the whole, though there may be a distant chance of a mistake about it, is, nevertheless, the wisest conclusion you can come to until farther experiment.

§ 4. Now, therefore, putting these tiresome and absurd words quite out of our way, we may go on at our ease to examine the point in question—namely, the difference between the ordinary, proper, and true appearances of things to us; and the extraordinary, or false appearances, when we are under the influence of emotion, or contemplative fancy; false appearances, I say, as being entirely unconnected with any real power or character in the object, and only imputed to it by us.

For instance—

> The spendthrift crocus, bursting through the mould
> Naked and shivering, with his cup of gold.

This is very beautiful, and yet very untrue. The crocus is not a spendthrift, but a hardy plant; its yellow is not gold, but saffron. How is it that we enjoy so much the having it put into our heads that it is anything else than a plain crocus?

It is an important question. For, throughout our past reasonings about art, we have always found that nothing could be good, or useful, or ultimately pleasurable, which was untrue. But here is something pleasurable in written poetry which is nevertheless *un*true. And what is more, if we think over our favourite poetry, we shall find it full of this kind of fallacy, and that we like it all the more for being so.

§ 5. It will appear also, on consideration of the matter, that this fallacy is of two principal kinds. Either, as in this case of the crocus, it is the fallacy of wilful fancy, which involves no real expectation that it will be believed; or else it is a fallacy caused by an excited state of the feelings, making us, for the time, more or less irrational. Of the cheating of the fancy we shall have to speak presently; but, in this chapter, I want to examine the nature of the other error, that which the mind admits when affected strongly by emotion. Thus, for instance, in *Alton Locke*—

> They rowed her in across the rolling foam—
> The cruel, crawling foam.

The foam is not cruel, neither does it crawl. The state of mind which attributes to it these characters of a living creature is one in which the reason is unhinged by grief. All violent feelings have the same effect. They produce in us a falseness in all our impressions of external things, which I would generally characterize as the 'Pathetic Fallacy'.

§ 6. Now we are in the habit of considering this fallacy as eminently a character of poetical description, and the temper of mind in which we allow it as one eminently poetical, because passionate. But, I believe, if we look well into the matter, that we shall find the greatest poets do not often admit this kind of falseness—that it is only the second order of poets who much delight in it.[1]

---

[1] I admit two orders of poets, but no third; and by these two orders I mean the Creative (Shakespeare, Homer, Dante), and Reflective or Perceptive (Wordsworth, Keats, Tennyson). But both of these must be *first*-rate in their range, though their range is different; and with poetry second-rate in *quality* no one ought to be allowed to trouble

Thus, when Dante describes the spirits falling from the bank of Acheron 'as dead leaves flutter from a bough', he gives the most perfect image possible of their utter lightness, feebleness, passiveness, and scattering agony of despair, without, however, for an instant losing his own clear perception that *these* are souls, and *those* are leaves; he makes no confusion of one with the other. But when Coleridge speaks of

> The one red leaf, the last of its clan,
> That dances as often as dance it can.

he has a morbid, that is to say, a so far false, idea about the leaf: he fancies a life in it, and will, which there are not; confuses its powerlessness with choice, its fading death with merriment, and the wind that

mankind. There is quite enough of the best,—much more than we can ever read or enjoy in the length of a life; and it is a literal wrong or sin in any person to encumber us with inferior work. I have no patience with apologies made by young pseudo-poets, 'that they believe there is *some* good in what they have written: that they hope to do better in time,' &c. *Some* good! If there is not *all* good, there is no good. If they ever hope to do better, why do they trouble us now? Let them rather courageously burn all they have done, and wait for the better days. There are few men, ordinarily educated, who in moments of strong feeling could not strike out a poetical thought, and afterwards polish it so as to be presentable. But men of sense know better than so to waste their time; and those who sincerely love poetry, know the touch of the master's hand on the chords too well to fumble among them after him. Nay, more than this; all inferior poetry is an injury to the good, inasmuch as it takes away the freshness of rhymes, blunders upon and gives a wretched commonalty to good thoughts; and, in general, adds to the weight of human weariness in a most woful and culpable manner. There are few thoughts likely to come across ordinary men, which have not already been expressed by greater men in the best possible way; and it is a wiser, more generous, more noble thing to remember and point out the perfect words, than to invent poorer ones, wherewith to encumber temporarily the world.

shakes it with music. Here, however, there is some beauty, even in the morbid passage; but take an instance in Homer and Pope. Without the knowledge of Ulysses, Elpenor, his youngest follower, has fallen from an upper chamber in the Circean palace, and has been left dead, unmissed by his leader, or companions, in the haste of their departure. They cross the sea to the Cimmerian land; and Ulysses summons the shades from Tartarus. The first which appears is that of the lost Elpenor. Ulysses, amazed, and in exactly the spirit of bitter and terrified lightness which is seen in Hamlet,[1] addresses the spirit with the simple, startled words:—

Elpenor! How camest thou under the shadowy darkness? Hast thou come faster on foot than I in my black ship?

Which Pope renders thus:—

O, say, what angry power Elpenor led
To glide in shades, and wander with the dead?
How could thy soul, by realms and seas disjoined,
Outfly the nimble sail, and leave the lagging wind?

I sincerely hope the reader finds no pleasure here, either in the nimbleness of the sail, or the laziness of the wind! And yet how is it that these conceits are so painful now, when they have been pleasant to us in the other instances?

§ 7. For a very simple reason. They are not a *pathetic* fallacy at all, for they are put into the mouth of the wrong passion—a passion which never could possibly have spoken them—agonized curiosity. Ulysses wants to know the facts of the matter; and the very last thing his mind could do at the moment would be to pause, or suggest in anywise what was *not* a fact. The delay in the first three lines, and conceit in the last, jar upon us instantly, like the most frightful discord in music. No poet of true

[1] 'Well said, old mole! can'st work i' the ground so fast?'

imaginative power could possibly have written the passage.[1]

Therefore, we see that the spirit of truth must guide us in some sort, even in our enjoyment of fallacy. Coleridge's fallacy has no discord in it, but Pope's has set our teeth on edge. Without farther questioning, I will endeavour to state the main bearings of this matter.

§ 8. The temperament which admits the pathetic fallacy, is, as I said above, that of a mind and body in some sort too weak to deal fully with what is before them or upon them; borne away, or overclouded, or over-dazzled by emotion; and it is a more or less noble state, according to the force of the emotion which has induced it. For it is no credit to a man that he is not morbid or inaccurate in his perceptions, when he has no strength of feeling to warp them; and it is in general a sign of higher capacity and stand in the ranks of being, that the emotions should be strong enough to vanquish, partly, the intellect, and make it believe what they choose. But it is still a grander condition when the intellect also rises, till it is strong enough to assert its rule against, or together with, the utmost efforts of the passions; and the whole man stands in an iron glow, white hot, perhaps, but still strong, and in no wise evaporating; even if he melts, losing none of his weight.

So, then, we have the three ranks: the man who

[1] It is worth while comparing the way a similar question is put by the exquisite sincerity of Keats:—

>   He wept, and his bright tears
>   Went trickling down the golden bow he held.
>   Thus, with half-shut, suffused eyes, he stood;
>   While from beneath some cumb'rous boughs hard by,
>   With solemn step, an awful goddess came.
>   And there was purport in her looks for him,
>   Which he with eager guess began to read:
>   Perplexed the while, melodiously he said,
>   '*How cam'st thou over the unfooted sea?*'

perceives rightly, because he does not feel, and to whom the primrose is very accurately the primrose, because he does not love it. Then, secondly, the man who perceives wrongly, because he feels, and to whom the primrose is anything else than a primrose: a star, or a sun, or a fairy's shield, or a forsaken maiden. And then, lastly, there is the man who perceives rightly in spite of his feelings, and to whom the primrose is for ever nothing else than itself—a little flower, apprehended in the very plain and leafy fact of it, whatever and how many soever the associations and passions may be, that crowd around it. And, in general, these three classes may be rated in comparative order, as the men who are not poets at all, and the poets of the second order, and the poets of the first; only however great a man may be, there are always some subjects which *ought* to throw him off his balance; some, by which his poor human capacity of thought should be conquered, and brought into the inaccurate and vague state of perception, so that the language of the highest inspiration becomes broken, obscure, and wild in metaphor, resembling that of the weaker man, overborne by weaker things.

§ 9. And thus, in full, there are four classes: the men who feel nothing, and therefore see truly; the men who feel strongly, think weakly, and see untruly (second order of poets); the men who feel strongly, think strongly, and see truly (first order of poets); and the men who, strong as human creatures can be, are yet submitted to influences stronger than they, and see in a sort untruly, because what they see is inconceivably above them. This last is the usual condition of prophetic inspiration.

§ 10. I separate these classes, in order that their character may be clearly understood; but of course they are united each to the other by imperceptible transitions, and the same mind, according to the influences to which it is subjected, passes at different times into the various states. Still, the difference

OF THE PATHETIC FALLACY

between the great and less man is, on the whole, chiefly in this point of *alterability*. That is to say, the one knows too much, and perceives and feels too much of the past and future, and of all things beside and around that which immediately affects him, to be in anywise shaken by it. His mind is made up; his thoughts have an accustomed current; his ways are steadfast; it is not this or that new sight which will at once unbalance him. He is tender to impression at the surface, like a rock with deep moss upon it; but there is too much mass of him to be moved. The smaller man, with the same degree of sensibility, is at once carried off his feet; he wants to do something he did not want to do before; he views all the universe in a new light through his tears; he is gay or enthusiastic, melancholy or passionate, as things come and go to him. Therefore the high creative poet might even be thought, to a great extent, impassive (as shallow people think Dante stern), receiving indeed all feelings to the full, but having a great centre of reflection and knowledge in which he stands serene, and watches the feeling, as it were, from far off.

Dante, in his most intense moods, has entire command of himself, and can look around calmly, at all moments, for the image or the word that will best tell what he sees to the upper or lower world. But Keats and Tennyson, and the poets of the second order, are generally themselves subdued by the feelings under which they write, or, at least, write as choosing to be so, and therefore admit certain expressions and modes of thought which are in some sort diseased or false.

§ 11. Now so long as we see that the *feeling* is true, we pardon, or are even pleased by, the confessed fallacy of sight which it induces: we are pleased, for instance, with those lines of Kingsley's, above quoted, not because they fallaciously describe foam, but because they faithfully describe sorrow. But the moment the mind of the speaker becomes cold, that moment every such expression becomes untrue, as being for ever untrue in the external facts. And there is no greater baseness in literature than the habit of using these metaphorical expressions in cold blood. An inspired writer, in full impetuosity of passion, may speak wisely and truly of 'raging waves of the sea, foaming out their own shame'; but it is only the basest writer who cannot speak of the sea without talking of 'raging waves', 'remorseless floods', 'ravenous billows', &c.; and it is one of the signs of the highest power in a writer to check all such habits of thought, and to keep his eyes fixed firmly on the *pure fact*, out of which if any feeling comes to him or his reader, he knows it must be a true one.

To keep to the waves, I forget who it is who represents a man in despair, desiring that his body may be cast into the sea,

> *Whose changing mound, and foam that passed away,*
> Might mock the eye that questioned where I lay.

Observe, there is not a single false, or even overcharged, expression. 'Mound' of the sea wave is perfectly simple and true; 'changing' is as familiar as may be; 'foam that passed away', strictly literal; and the whole line descriptive of the reality with a degree of accuracy which I know not any other verse, in the range of poetry, that altogether equals. For most people have not a distinct idea of the clumsiness and massiveness of a large wave. The word 'wave' is used too generally of ripples and breakers, and bendings in light drapery or grass: it does not by itself convey a perfect image. But the word 'mound' is heavy, large, dark, definite; there is no mistaking the kind of wave meant, nor missing the sight of it. Then the term 'changing' has a peculiar force also. Most people think of waves as rising and falling. But if they look at the sea carefully, they will perceive that the waves do not rise and fall. They change. Change both place and form, but they do not fall;

one wave goes on, and on, and still on; now lower, now higher, now tossing its mane like a horse, now building itself together like a wall, now shaking, now steady, but still the same wave, till at last it seems struck by something, and changes, one knows not how,—becomes another wave.

The close of the line insists on this image, and paints it still more perfectly,—'foam that passed away'. Not merely melting, disappearing, but passing on, out of sight, on the career of the wave. Then, having put the absolute ocean fact as far as he may before our eyes, the poet leaves us to feel about it as we may, and to trace for ourselves the opposite fact,—the image of the green mounds that do not change, and the white and written stones that do not pass away; and thence to follow out also the associated images of the calm life with the quiet grave, and the despairing life with the fading foam:

> Let no man move his bones.

As for Samaria, her king is cut off like the foam upon the water.

But nothing of this is actually told or pointed out, and the expressions, as they stand, are perfectly severe and accurate, utterly uninfluenced by the firmly governed emotion of the writer. Even the word 'mock' is hardly an exception, as it may stand merely for 'deceive' or 'defeat', without implying any impersonation of the waves.

§ 12. It may be well, perhaps, to give one or two more instances to show the peculiar dignity possessed by all passages which thus limit their expression to the pure fact, and leave the hearer to gather what he can from it. Here is a notable one from the Iliad. Helen, looking from the Scaean gate of Troy over the Grecian host, and telling Priam the names of its captains, says at last:

I see all the other dark-eyed Greeks; but two I cannot see,—Castor and Pollux,—whom one mother bore with me. Have they not followed from fair Lacedaemon, or have they indeed come in their sea-wandering ships, but now will not enter into the battle of men, fearing the shame and the scorn that is in Me?

Then Homer:

So she spoke. But them, already, the life-giving earth possessed, there in Lacedaemon, in the dear fatherland.

Note, here, the high poetical truth carried to the extreme. The poet has to speak of the earth in sadness, but he will not let that sadness affect or change his thoughts of it. No; though Castor and Pollux be dead, yet the earth is our mother still, fruitful, lifegiving. These are the facts of the thing. I see nothing else than these. Make what you will of them.

§ 13. Take another very notable instance from Casimir de la Vigne's terrible ballad, *La Toilette de Constance*. I must quote a few lines out of it here and there, to enable the reader who has not the book by him, to understand its close.

> Vite, Anna, vite; au miroir
> Plus vite, Anna. L'heure s'avance,
> Et je vais au bal ce soir
> Chez l'ambassadeur de France.

Y pensez-vous, ils sont fanés, ces nœuds,
Ils sont d'hier, mon Dieu, comme tout passe!
Que du réseau qui retient mes cheveux
Les glands d'azur retombent avec grâce.
Plus haut! Plus bas! Vous ne comprenez rien!
Que sur mon front ce saphir étincelle:
Vous me piquez, maladroite. Ah, c'est bien,
Bien,—chère Anna! Je t'aime, je suis belle.

Celui qu'en vain je voudrais oublier
(Anna, ma robe) il y sera, j'espère.
(Ah, fi! profane, est-ce là mon collier?
Quoi! ces grains d'or bénits par le Saint-Père!)
Il y sera; Dieu, s'il pressait ma main,
En y pensant, à peine je respire;
Père Anselmo doit m'entendre demain,
Comment ferai-je, Anna, pour tout lui dire?

> Vite un coup d'œil au miroir,
>   Le dernier. ——J'ai l'assurance
> Qu'on va m'adorer ce soir
>   Chez l'ambassadeur de France.
>
> Près du foyer, Constance s'admirait.
>   Dieu! sur sa robe il vole une étincelle!
> Au feu! Courez! Quand l'espoir l'enivrait,
>   Tout perdre ainsi! Quoi! Mourir,—et si belle!
> L'horrible feu ronge avec volupté
>   Ses bras, son sein, et l'entoure, et s'élève,
> Et sans pitié dévore sa beauté,
>   Ses dix-huit ans, hélas, et son doux rêve!
>
> Adieu, bal, plaisir, amour!
>   On disait, Pauvre Constance!
> Et on dansait, jusqu'au jour,
>   Chez l'ambassadeur de France.

Yes, that is the fact of it. Right or wrong, the poet does not say. What you may think about it, he does not know. He has nothing to do with that. There lie the ashes of the dead girl in her chamber. There they danced, till the morning, at the Ambassador's of France. Make what you will of it.

If the reader will look through the ballad, of which I have quoted only about the third part, he will find that there is not, from beginning to end of it, a single poetical (so called) expression, except in one stanza. The girl speaks as simple prose as may be; there is not a word she would not have actually used as she was dressing. The poet stands by, impassive as a statue, recording her words just as they come. At last the doom seizes her, and in the very presence of death, for an instant, his own emotions conquer him. He records no longer the facts only, but the facts as they seem to him. The fire gnaws with *voluptuousness—without pity*. It is soon past. The fate is fixed for ever; and he retires into his pale and crystalline atmosphere of truth. He closes all with the calm veracity,

> They said, 'Poor Constance!'

§ 14. Now in this there is the exact type of the

consummate poetical temperament. For, be it clearly and constantly remembered, that the greatness of a poet depends upon the two faculties, acuteness of feeling, and command of it. A poet is great, first in proportion to the strength of his passion, and then, that strength being granted, in proportion to his government of it; there being, however, always a point beyond which it would be inhuman and monstrous if he pushed this government, and, therefore, a point at which all feverish and wild fancy becomes just and true. Thus the destruction of the kingdom of Assyria cannot be contemplated firmly by a prophet of Israel. The fact is too great, too wonderful. It overthrows him, dashes him into a confused element of dreams. All the world is, to his stunned thought, full of strange voices. 'Yea, the fir-trees rejoice at thee, and the cedars of Lebanon, saying, "Since thou art gone down to the grave, no feller is come up against us."' So, still more, the thought of the presence of Deity cannot be borne without this great astonishment. 'The mountains and the hills shall break forth before you into singing, and all the trees of the field shall clap their hands.'

§ 15. But by how much this feeling is noble when it is justified by the strength of its cause, by so much it is ignoble when there is not cause enough for it; and beyond all other ignobleness is the mere affectation of it, in hardness of heart. Simply bad writing may almost always, as above noticed, be known by its adoption of these fanciful metaphorical expressions, as a sort of current coin; yet there is even a worse, at least a more harmful, condition of writing than this, in which such expressions are not ignorantly and feelinglessly caught up, but, by some master, skilful in handling, yet insincere, deliberately wrought out with chill and studied fancy; as if we should try to make an old lava stream look red-hot again, by covering it with dead leaves, or white-hot, with hoar-rost.

OF THE PATHETIC FALLACY

When Young is lost in veneration, as he dwells on the character of a truly good and holy man, he permits himself for a moment to be overborne by the feeling so far as to exclaim:

> Where shall I find him? angels, tell me where.
> You know him; he is near you; point him out.
> Shall I see glories beaming from his brow,
> Or trace his footsteps by the rising flowers?

This emotion has a worthy cause, and is thus true and right. But now hear the cold-hearted Pope say to a shepherd girl:

> Where'er you walk, cool gales shall fan the glade;
> Trees, where you sit, shall crowd into a shade;
> Your praise the birds shall chant in every grove,
> And winds shall waft it to the powers above.
> But would you sing, and rival Orpheus' strain,
> The wondering forests soon should dance again;
> The moving mountains hear the powerful call,
> And headlong streams hang, listening, in their fall.

This is not, nor could it for a moment be mistaken for, the language of passion. It is simple falsehood, uttered by hypocrisy; definite absurdity, rooted in affectation, and coldly asserted in the teeth of nature and fact. Passion will indeed go far in deceiving itself; but it must be a strong passion, not the simple wish of a lover to tempt his mistress to sing. Compare a very closely parallel passage in Wordsworth, in which the lover has lost his mistress:

> Three years had Barbara in her grave been laid,
> When thus his moan he made:—
>
> 'Oh move, thou cottage, from behind yon oak,
>   Or let the ancient tree uprooted lie,
> That in some other way yon smoke
>   May mount into the sky.
> If still behind yon pine-tree's ragged bough,
>   Headlong, the waterfall must come,
>   Oh, let it, then, be dumb—
> Be anything, sweet stream, but that which thou art now.'

Here is a cottage to be moved, if not a mountain, and a waterfall to be silent, if it is not to hang listening: but with what different relation to the mind that contemplates them! Here, in the extremity of its agony, the soul cries out wildly for relief, which at the same moment it partly knows to be impossible, but partly believes possible, in a vague impression that a miracle *might* be wrought to give relief even to a less sore distress,—that nature is kind, and God is kind, and that grief is strong: it knows not well what *is* possible to such grief. To silence a stream, to move a cottage wall,—one might think it could do as much as that!

§ 16. I believe these instances are enough to illustrate the main point I insist upon respecting the pathetic fallacy,—that so far as it *is* a fallacy, it is always the sign of a morbid state of mind, and comparatively of a weak one. Even in the most inspired prophet it is a sign of the incapacity of his human sight or thought to bear what has been revealed to it. In ordinary poetry, if it is found in the thoughts of the poet himself, it is at once a sign of his belonging to the inferior school; if in the thoughts of the characters imagined by him, it is right or wrong according to the genuineness of the emotion from which it springs; always, however, implying necessarily *some* degree of weakness in the character.

Take two most exquisite instances from master hands. The Jessy of Shenstone, and the Ellen of Wordsworth, have both been betrayed and deserted. Jessy, in the course of her most touching complaint, says:

> If through the garden's flowery tribes I stray,
>   Where bloom the jasmines that could once allure,
> 'Hope not to find delight in us,' they say.
>   'For we are spotless, Jessy; we are pure.'

Compare with this some of the words of Ellen:

> 'Ah, why,' said Ellen, sighing to herself,

'Why do not words, and kiss, and solemn pledge,
And nature, that is kind in woman's breast,
And reason, that in man is wise and good,
And fear of Him who is a righteous Judge,—
Why do not these prevail for human life,
To keep two hearts together, that began
Their springtime with one love, and that have need
Of mutual pity and forgiveness, sweet
To grant, or be received;—while that poor bird—
O, come and hear him! Thou who hast to me
Been faithless, hear him;—though a lowly creature,
One of God's simple children, that yet know not
The Universal Parent, *how* he sings!
As if he wished the firmament of heaven
Should listen, and give back to him the voice
Of his triumphant constancy and love.
The proclamation that he makes, how far
His darkness doth transcend our fickle light.'

The perfection of both these passages, as far as regards truth and tenderness of imagination in the two poets, is quite insuperable. But, of the two characters imagined, Jessy is weaker than Ellen, exactly in so far as something appears to her to be in nature which is not. The flowers do not really reproach her. God meant them to comfort her, not to taunt her; they would do so if she saw them rightly.

Ellen, on the other hand, is quite above the slightest erring emotion. There is not the barest film of fallacy in all her thoughts. She reasons as calmly as if she did not feel. And, although the singing of the bird suggests to her the idea of its desiring to be heard in heaven, she does not for an instant admit any veracity in the thought. 'As if,' she says,—'I know he means nothing of the kind; but it does verily seem as if.' The reader will find, by examining the rest of the poem, that Ellen's character is throughout consistent in this clear though passionate strength.[1]

---

[1] I cannot quit this subject without giving two more instances, both exquisite, of the pathetic fallacy, which I have just come upon, in *Maud*:

It is, I hope, now made clear to the reader in all respects that the pathetic fallacy is powerful only so far as it is pathetic, feeble so far as it is fallacious, and, therefore, that the dominion of Truth is entire, over this, as over every other natural and just state of the human mind.

[*Continuation of note.*]

       For a great speculation had fail'd;
And ever he mutter'd and madden'd, and ever wann'd
  with despair;
And out he walk'd, when the wind like a broken worldling
  wail'd,
And the *flying gold of the ruin'd woodlands drove thro' the air.*

   There has fallen a splendid tear
    From the passion-flower at the gate.
   The red rose cries, 'She is near, she is near!'
    And the white rose weeps, 'She is late.'
   The larkspur listens, 'I hear, I hear!'
    And the lily whispers, 'I wait.'

JOHN STUART MILL
1806–1873
THOUGHTS ON POETRY AND ITS VARIETIES (1859)

I

IT has often been asked, What is Poetry? And many and various are the answers which have been returned. The vulgarest of all—one with which no person possessed of the faculties to which Poetry addresses itself can ever have been satisfied—is that which confounds poetry with metrical composition: yet to this wretched mockery of a definition, many have been led back, by the failure of all their attempts to find any other that would distinguish what they have been accustomed to call poetry, from much which they have known only under other names.

That, however, the word 'poetry' imports something quite peculiar in its nature, something which may exist in what is called prose as well as in verse, something which does not even require the instrument of words, but can speak through the other audible symbols called musical sounds, and even through the visible ones which are the language of sculpture, painting, and architecture; all this, we believe, is and must be felt, though perhaps indistinctly, by all upon whom poetry in any of its shapes produces any impression beyond that of tickling the ear. The distinction between poetry and what is not poetry, whether explained or not, is felt to be fundamental: and where every one feels a difference, a difference there must be. All other appearances may be fallacious, but the appearance of a difference is a real difference. Appearances too, like other things, must have a cause, and that which can cause anything, even an illusion, must be a reality. And hence, while a half-philosophy disdains the classifications and distinctions indicated by popular language, philosophy carried to its highest point frames new ones, but rarely sets aside the old, content with correcting and regularizing them. It cuts fresh channels for thought, but does not fill up such as it finds ready-made; it traces, on the contrary, more deeply, broadly, and distinctly, those into which the current has spontaneously flowed.

Let us then attempt, in the way of modest inquiry, not to coerce and confine nature within the bounds of an arbitrary definition, but rather to find the boundaries which she herself has set, and erect a barrier round them; not calling mankind to account for having misapplied the word 'poetry', but attempting to clear up the conception which they already attach to it, and to bring forward as a distinct principle that which, as a vague feeling, has really guided them in their employment of the term.

The object of poetry is confessedly to act upon the emotions; and therein is poetry sufficiently distinguished from what Wordsworth affirms to be its logical opposite, namely, not prose, but matter of fact or science. The one addresses itself to the belief, the other to the feelings. The one does its work by convincing or persuading, the other by moving. The one acts by presenting a proposition to the understanding, the other by offering interesting objects of contemplation to the sensibilities.

This, however, leaves us very far from a definition of poetry. This distinguishes it from one thing, but we are bound to distinguish it from everything. To bring thoughts or images before the mind for the purpose of acting upon the emotions, does not belong to poetry alone. It is equally the province (for example) of the novelist: and yet the faculty of the poet and that of the novelist are as distinct as any other two faculties; as the faculties of the novelist and of the orator, or of the poet and the metaphysician. The two characters may be united, as characters the most disparate may; but they have no natural connexion.

Many of the greatest poems are in the form of fictitious narratives, and in almost all good serious fictions there is true poetry. But there is a radical distinction between the interest felt in a story as such, and the interest excited by poetry; for the one is derived from incident, the other from the representation of feeling. In one, the source of the emotion excited is the exhibition of a state or states of human sensibility; in the other, of a series of states of mere outward circumstances. Now, all minds are capable of being affected more or less by representations of the latter kind, and all, or almost all, by those of the former; yet the two sources of interest correspond to two distinct, and (as respects their greatest development) mutually exclusive, characters of mind.

At what age is the passion for a story, for almost any kind of story, merely as a story, the most intense? In childhood. But that also is the age at which poetry, even of the simplest description, is least relished and least understood; because the feelings with which it is especially conversant are yet undeveloped, and not having been even in the slightest degree experienced, cannot be sympathized with. In what stage of the progress of society, again, is storytelling most valued, and the story-teller in greatest request and honour?—In a rude state like that of the Tartars and Arabs at this day, and of almost all nations in the earliest ages. But in this state of society there is little poetry except ballads, which are mostly narrative, that is, essentially stories, and derive their principal interest from the incidents. Considered as poetry, they are of the lowest and most elementary kind: the feelings depicted, or rather indicated, are the simplest our nature has; such joys and griefs as the immediate pressure of some outward event excites in rude minds, which live wholly immersed in outward things, and have never, either from choice or a force they could not resist, turned themselves to the contemplation of the world within. Passing now from childhood, and from the childhood of society, to the grown-up men and women of this most grown-up and unchildlike age—the minds and hearts of greatest depth and elevation are commonly those which take greatest delight in poetry; the shallowest and emptiest, on the contrary, are, at all events, not those least addicted to novel-reading. This accords, too, with all analogous experience of human nature. The sort of persons whom not merely in books but in their lives, we find perpetually engaged in hunting for excitement from without, are invariably those who do not possess, either in the vigour of their intellectual powers or in the depth of their sensibilities, that which would enable them to find ample excitement nearer home. The most idle and frivolous persons take a natural delight in fictitious narrative; the excitement it affords is of the kind which comes from without. Such persons are rarely lovers of poetry, though they may fancy themselves so, because they relish novels in verse. But poetry, which is the delineation of the deeper and more secret workings of human emotion, is interesting only to those to whom it recalls what they have felt, or whose imagination it stirs up to conceive what they could feel, or what they might have been able to feel, had their outward circumstances been different.

Poetry, when it is really such, is truth; and fiction also, if it is good for anything, is truth: but they are different truths. The truth of poetry is to paint the human soul truly: the truth of fiction is to give a true picture of life. The two kinds of knowledge are different, and come by different ways, come mostly to different persons. Great poets are often proverbially ignorant of life. What they know has come by observation of themselves; they have found within them one highly delicate and sensitive specimen of human nature, on which the laws of emotion are written in large characters, such as can be read off without much study. Other knowledge of mankind, such as comes to men of the world by outward experience, is not indispensable to them as poets: but to the novelist such knowledge is all in all; he has to describe outward things, not the inward man; actions and events, not feelings; and it will not do for him to be numbered among those who, as Madame Roland said of Brissot, know man but not *men*.

All this is no bar to the possibility of combining both elements, poetry and narrative or incident, in the same work, and calling it either a novel or a poem; but so may red and white combine on the same human features, or on the same canvas. There is one order of composition which requires the union of poetry and incident, each in its highest kind—the dramatic. Even there the two elements are perfectly distinguishable, and may exist of unequal quality, and in the most various proportion. The incidents of a dramatic poem may be scanty and ineffective, though the delineation of passion and character may be of the highest order; as in Goethe's admirable *Torquato Tasso*; or again, the story as a mere story may be well got up for effect, as is the case with some of the most trashy productions of the Minerva press: it may even be, what those are not, a coherent and probable series of events, though there be scarcely a feeling exhibited which is not represented falsely, or in a manner absolutely commonplace. The combination of the two excellences is what renders Shakespeare so generally acceptable, each sort of readers finding in him what is suitable to their faculties. To the many he is great as a story-teller, to the few as a poet.

In limiting poetry to the delineation of states of feeling, and denying the name where nothing is delineated but outward objects, we may be thought to have done what we promised to avoid—to have not found, but made a definition, in opposition to the usage of language, since it is established by common consent that there is a poetry called descriptive. We deny the charge. Description is not poetry because there is descriptive poetry, no more than science is poetry because there is such a thing as a didactic poem. But an object which admits of being described, or a truth which may fill a place in a scientific treatise, may also furnish an occasion for the generation of poetry, which we thereupon choose to call descriptive or didactic. The poetry is not in the object itself, nor in the scientific truth itself, but in the state of mind in which the one and the other may be contemplated. The mere delineation of the dimensions and colours of external objects is not poetry, no more than a geometrical ground-plan of St. Peter's or Westminster Abbey is painting. Descriptive poetry consists, no doubt, in description, but in description of things as they appear, not as they are; and it paints them not in their bare and natural lineaments, but seen through the medium and arrayed in the colours of the imagination set in action by the feelings. If a poet describes a lion, he does not describe him as a naturalist would, nor even as a traveller would, who was intent upon stating the truth, the whole truth, and nothing but the truth. He describes him by imagery, that is, by suggesting the most striking likenesses and contrasts which might occur to a mind contemplating the lion, in the state of awe, wonder, or terror, which the spectacle naturally excites, or is, on the occasion, supposed to excite. Now this is describing the lion professedly, but the state of excitement of the spectator really. The lion may be described falsely or with exaggeration, and the poetry be all the better; but if the human emotion be not painted with scrupulous truth, the poetry is bad poetry, i.e. is not poetry at all, but a failure.

Thus far our progress towards a clear view of the essentials of poetry has brought us very close to the last two attempts at a definition of poetry which we happen to have seen in print, both of them by poets and men of genius. The one is by Ebenezer Elliott, the author of *Corn-Law Rhymes*, and other poems of still greater merit. 'Poetry', says he, 'is impassioned truth.' The other is by a writer in *Blackwood's Magazine*, and comes, we think, still nearer the mark. He defines poetry, 'man's thoughts tinged by his feelings'. There is in either definition a near approximation to what we are in search of. Every truth which a human being can enunciate, every thought, even every outward impression, which can enter into his consciousness, may become poetry when shown through any impassioned medium, when invested with the colouring of joy, or grief, or pity, or affection, or admiration, or reverence, or awe, or even hatred or terror: and, unless so coloured, nothing, be it as interesting as it may, is poetry. But both these definitions fail to discriminate between poetry and eloquence. Eloquence, as well as poetry, is impassioned truth; eloquence, as well as poetry, is thoughts coloured by the feelings. Yet common apprehension and philosophic criticism alike recognize a distinction between the two: there is much that every one would call eloquence, which no one would think of classing as poetry. A question will sometimes arise, whether some particular author is a poet; and those who maintain the negative commonly allow that, though not a poet, he is a highly eloquent writer. The distinction between poetry and eloquence appears to us to be equally fundamental with the distinction between poetry and narrative, or between poetry and description, while it is still farther from having been satisfactorily cleared up than either of the others.

Poetry and eloquence are both alike the expression or utterance of feeling. But if we may be excused the antithesis, we should say that eloquence is *heard*, poetry is *over*heard. Eloquence supposes an audience; the peculiarity of poetry appears to us to lie in the poet's utter unconsciousness of a listener. Poetry is feeling confessing itself to itself, in moments of solitude, and embodying itself in symbols which are the nearest possible representations of the feeling in the exact shape in which it exists in the poet's mind. Eloquence is feeling pouring itself out to other minds, courting their sympathy, or endeavouring to influence their belief or move them to passion or to action.

All poetry is of the nature of soliloquy. It may be said that poetry which is printed on hot-pressed paper and sold at a bookseller's shop, is a soliloquy in full dress, and on the stage. It is so; but there is nothing absurd in the idea of such a mode of soliloquizing. What we have said to ourselves, we may tell to others afterwards; what we have said or done in solitude, we may voluntarily reproduce when we know that other eyes are upon us. But no trace of consciousness that any eyes are upon us must be visible in the work itself. The actor knows that there is an audience present; but if he act as though he knew it, he acts ill. A poet may write poetry not only with the intention of printing it, but for the express purpose of being paid for it; that it should *be* poetry, being written under such influences, is less probable; not, however, impossible; but no otherwise possible than if he can succeed in excluding from his work every vestige of such lookings-forth into the outward and every-day world, and can express his emotions exactly as he has felt them in solitude, or as he is conscious that he should feel them though they were to remain for ever unuttered, or (at the lowest) as he knows that others feel them in similar circumstances of solitude. But when he turns round and addresses himself to another person; when the act of utterance is not itself the end, but a means to an end,—viz. by the feelings he himself expresses, to work upon the feelings, or upon the belief, or the will, of another,—when the expression of his emotions, or of his thoughts tinged by his emotions, is tinged also by that purpose, by that desire of making an impression upon another mind, then it ceases to be poetry, and becomes eloquence.

Poetry, accordingly, is the natural fruit of solitude and meditation; eloquence, of intercourse with the world. The persons who have most feeling of their own, if intellectual culture has given them a language in which to express it, have the highest faculty of poetry; those who best understand the feelings of others, are the most eloquent. The persons, and the nations, who commonly excel in poetry, are those whose character and tastes render them least dependent upon the applause, or sympathy, or concurrence of the world in general. Those to whom that applause, that sympathy, that concurrence are most necessary, generally excel most in eloquence. And hence, perhaps, the French, who are the least poetical of all great and intellectual nations, are among the most eloquent: the French, also, being the most sociable, the vainest, and the least self-dependent.

If the above be, as we believe, the true theory of the distinction commonly admitted between eloquence and poetry; or even though it be not so, yet if, as we cannot doubt, the distinction above stated be a real bona fide distinction, it will be found to hold, not merely in the language of words, but in all other language, and to intersect the whole domain of art.

Take, for example, music: we shall find in that art, so peculiarly the expression of passion, two perfectly distinct styles; one of which may be called the poetry, the other the oratory of music. This difference, being seized, would put an end to much musical sectarianism. There has been much contention whether the music of the modern Italian school, that of Rossini and his successors, be impassioned or not. Without doubt, the passion it expresses is not the musing, meditative tenderness, or pathos, or grief of Mozart or Beethoven. Yet it is passion, but garrulous passion —the passion which pours itself into other ears; and therein the better calculated for dramatic effect, having a natural adaptation for dialogue. Mozart also is great in musical oratory; but his most touching compositions are in the opposite style—that of soliloquy. Who can imagine 'Dove sono' *heard*? We imagine it *over*heard.

Purely pathetic music commonly partakes of soliloquy. The soul is absorbed in its distress, and though there may be bystanders, it is not thinking of them. When the mind is looking within, and not without, its state does not often or rapidly vary; and hence the even, uninterrupted flow, approaching almost to monotony, which a good reader, or a good singer, will give to words or music of a pensive or melancholy cast. But grief taking the form of a prayer, or of a complaint, becomes oratorical; no longer low, and even, and subdued, it assumes a more emphatic rhythm, a more rapidly returning accent; instead of a few slow equal notes, following one after another at regular intervals, it crowds note upon note, and often assumes a hurry and bustle like joy. Those who are familiar with some of the best of Rossini's serious compositions, such as the air 'Tu che i miseri conforti', in the opera of *Tancredi*, or the duet 'Ebben per mia memoria', in *La Gazza Ladra*, will at once understand and feel our meaning. Both are highly tragic and passionate; the passion of both is that of oratory, not poetry. The like may be said of that most moving invocation in Beethoven's *Fidelio*—

    Komm, Hoffnung, lass das letzte Stern
    Der Müde nicht erbleichen;

in which Madame Schröder Devrient exhibited such consummate powers of pathetic expression. How different from Winter's beautiful 'Paga fui', the very soul of melancholy exhaling itself in solitude; fuller of meaning, and, therefore, more profoundly poetical than the words for which it was composed—for it seems to express not simple melancholy, but the melancholy of remorse.

If, from vocal music, we now pass to instrumental, we may have a specimen of musical oratory in any fine military symphony or march: while the poetry of music seems to have attained its consummation in Beethoven's Overture to Egmont, so wonderful in its mixed expression of grandeur and melancholy.

In the arts which speak to the eye, the same distinctions will be found to hold, not only between poetry and oratory, but between poetry, oratory, narrative, and simple imitation or description.

Pure description is exemplified in a mere portrait or a mere landscape—productions of art, it is true, but of the mechanical rather than of the fine arts, being works of simple imitation, not creation. We say, a mere portrait, or a mere landscape, because it is possible for a portrait or a landscape, without ceasing to be such, to be also a picture; like Turner's landscapes, and the great portraits by Titian or Vandyke.

Whatever in painting or sculpture expresses human feeling—or character, which is only a certain state of feeling grown habitual—may be called, according to circumstances, the poetry, or the eloquence, of the painter's or the sculptor's art: the poetry, if the feeling declares itself by such signs as escape from us when we are unconscious of being seen; the oratory, if the signs are those we use for the purpose of voluntary communication.

The narrative style answers to what is called historical painting, which it is the fashion among connoisseurs to treat as the climax of the pictorial art. That it is the most difficult branch of the art we do not doubt, because, in its perfection, it includes the perfection of all the other branches: as in like manner an epic poem, though in so far as it is epic (i.e. narrative) it is not poetry at all, is yet esteemed the greatest effort of poetic genius, because there is no kind whatever of poetry which may not appropriately find a place in it. But an historical picture as such, that is, as the representation of an incident, must necessarily, as it seems to us, be poor and ineffective. The narrative powers of painting are extremely limited. Scarcely any picture, scarcely even any series of pictures, tells its own story without the aid of an interpreter. But it is the single figures which, to us, are the great charm even of an historical picture. It is in these that the power of the art is really seen. In the attempt to narrate, visible and permanent signs are too far behind the fugitive audible ones, which follow so fast one after another, while the faces and figures in a narrative picture, even though they be Titian's, stand still. Who would not prefer one Virgin and Child of Raphael, to all the pictures which Rubens, with his fat, frouzy Dutch Venuses, ever painted? Though Rubens, besides excelling almost every one in his mastery over the mechanical parts of his art, often shows real genius in *grouping* his figures, the peculiar problem of historical painting. But then, who, except a mere student of drawing and colouring, ever cared to look twice at any of the figures themselves? The power of painting lies in poetry, of which Rubens had not the slightest tincture—not in narrative, wherein he might have excelled.

The single figures, however, in an historical picture, are rather the eloquence of painting than the poetry: they mostly (unless they are quite out of place in the picture) express the feelings of one person as modified by the presence of others. Accordingly the minds whose bent leads them rather to eloquence than to poetry, rush to historical painting. The French painters, for instance, seldom attempt, because they could make nothing of, single heads, like those glorious ones of the Italian masters, with which they might feed themselves day after day in their own Louvre. They must all be historical; and they are, almost to a man, attitudinizers. If we wished to give any young artist the most impressive warning our imagination could devise against that kind of vice in the pictorial, which corresponds to rant in the histrionic art, we would advise him to walk once up and once down the gallery of the Luxembourg. Every figure in French painting or statuary seems to be showing itself off before spectators; they are not poetical, but in the worst style of corrupted eloquence.

II

Nascitur Poeta is a maxim of classical antiquity, which has passed to these latter days with less questioning than most of the doctrines of that early age. When it originated, the human faculties were occupied, fortunately for posterity, less in examining how the works of genius are created, than in creating them: and the adage, probably, had no higher source than the tendency common among mankind to consider all power which is not visibly the effect of practice, all skill which is not capable of being reduced to mechanical rules, as the result of a peculiar gift. Yet this aphorism, born in the infancy of psychology, will perhaps be found, now when that science is in its adolescence, to be as true as an epigram ever is, that is, to contain some truth: truth, however, which has been so compressed and bent out of shape, in order to tie it up into so small a knot of only two words that it requires an almost infinite amount of unrolling and laying straight, before it will resume its just proportions.

We are not now intending to remark upon the grosser misapplications of this ancient maxim, which have engendered so many races of poetasters. The days are gone by when every raw youth whose borrowed phantasies have set themselves to a borrowed tune, mistaking, as Coleridge says, an ardent desire of poetic reputation for poetic genius, while unable to disguise from himself that he had taken no means whereby he might *become* a poet, could fancy himself a born one. Those who would reap without sowing, and gain the victory without fighting the battle, are ambitious now of another sort of distinction, and are born novelists, or public speakers, not poets. And the wiser thinkers understand and acknowledge that poetic excellence is subject to the same necessary conditions with any other mental endowment; and that to no one of the spiritual benefactors of mankind is a higher or a more assiduous intellectual culture needful than to the poet. It is true, he possesses this advantage over others who use the 'instrument of words', that, of the truths which he utters, a larger proportion are derived from personal consciousness, and a smaller from philosophic investigation. But the power itself of discriminating between what really is consciousness, and what is only a process of inference completed in a single instant—and the capacity of distinguishing whether that of which the mind is conscious be an eternal truth, or but a dream—are among the last results of the most matured and perfect intellect. Not to mention that the poet, no more than any other person who writes, confines himself altogether to intuitive truths, nor has any means of communicating even these but by words, every one of which derives all its power of conveying a meaning, from a whole host of acquired notions, and facts learnt by study and experience.

Nevertheless, it seems undeniable in point of fact, and consistent with the principles of a sound metaphysics, that there are poetic *natures*. There is a mental and physical constitution or temperament, peculiarly fitted for poetry. This temperament will not of itself make a poet, no more than the soil will the fruit; and as good fruit may be raised by culture from indifferent soils, so may good poetry from naturally unpoetical minds. But the poetry of one who is a poet by nature, will be clearly and broadly distinguishable from the poetry of mere culture. It may not be truer; it may not be more useful; but it will be different: fewer will appreciate it, even though many should affect to do so; but in those few it will find a keener sympathy, and will yield them a deeper enjoyment.

One may write genuine poetry, and not be a poet; for whosoever writes out truly any human feeling, writes poetry. All persons, even the most unimaginative, in moments of strong emotion, speak poetry; and hence the drama is poetry, which else were always prose, except when a poet is one of the characters. What *is* poetry, but the thoughts and words in which emotion spontaneously embodies itself? As there are few who are not, at least for some moments and in some situations, capable of some strong feeling, poetry is natural to most persons at some period of their lives. And any one whose feelings are genuine, though but of the average strength,—if he be not diverted by uncongenial thoughts or occupations from the indulgence of them, and if he acquire by culture, as all persons may, the faculty of delineating them correctly,—has it in his power to be a poet, so far as a life passed in writing unquestionable poetry may be considered to confer that title. But *ought* it to do so? Yes, perhaps, in a collection of 'British Poets'. But 'poet' is the name also of a variety of man, not solely of the author of a particular variety of book: now, to have written whole volumes of real poetry is possible to almost all kinds of characters, and implies no greater peculiarity of mental construction, than to be the author of a history, or a novel.

Whom, then, shall we call poets? Those who are so constituted, that emotions are the links of association by which their ideas, both sensuous and spiritual, are connected together. This constitution belongs (within certain limits) to all in whom poetry is a pervading principle. In all others, poetry is something extraneous and superinduced: something out of themselves, foreign to the habitual course of their everyday lives and characters; a world to which they may make occasional visits, but where they are sojourners, not dwellers, and which, when out of it, or even when in it, they think of, peradventure, but as a phantom-world, a place of *ignes fatui* and spectral illusions. Those only who have the peculiarity of association which we have mentioned, and which is a natural though not a universal consequence of intense sensibility, instead of seeming not themselves when they are uttering poetry, scarcely seem themselves when uttering anything to which poetry is foreign. Whatever be the thing which they are contemplating, if it be capable of connecting itself with their emotions, the aspect under which it first and most naturally paints itself to them, is its poetic aspect. The poet of culture sees his object in prose, and describes it in poetry; the poet of nature actually sees it in poetry.

This point is perhaps worth some little illustration; the rather, as metaphysicians (the ultimate arbiters of all philosophical criticism), while they have busied themselves for two thousand years, more or less, about the few *universal* laws of human nature, have strangely neglected the analysis of its *diversities*. Of these, none lie deeper or reach further than the varieties which difference of nature and of education makes in what may be termed the habitual bond of association. In a mind entirely uncultivated, which is also without any strong feelings, objects whether of sense or of intellect arrange themselves in the mere casual order in which they have been seen, heard, or otherwise perceived. Persons of this sort may be said to think chronologically. If they remember a fact, it is by reason of a fortuitous coincidence with some trifling incident or circumstance which took place at the very time. If they have a story to tell, or testimony to deliver in a witness-box, their narrative must follow the exact order in which the events took place: *dodge* them, and the thread of association is broken; they cannot go on. Their associations, to use the language of philosophers, are chiefly of the successive, not the synchronous kind, and whether successive or synchronous, are mostly casual.

To the man of science, again, or of business, objects group themselves according to the artificial classifications which the understanding has voluntarily made for the convenience of thought or of practice. But where any of the impressions are vivid and intense, the associations into which these enter are the ruling ones: it being a well-known law of association, that the stronger a feeling is, the more quickly and strongly it associates itself with any other object or feeling. Where, therefore, nature has given strong feelings, and education has not created factitious tendencies stronger than the natural ones, the prevailing associations will be those which connect objects and ideas with emotions, and with each other through the intervention of emotions. Thoughts and images will be linked together, according to the similarity of the feelings which cling to them. A thought will introduce a thought by first introducing a feeling which is allied with it. At the centre of each group of thoughts or images will be found a feeling; and the thoughts or images will be there only because the feeling was there. The combinations which the mind puts together, the pictures which it paints, the wholes which Imagination constructs out of the materials supplied by Fancy, will be indebted to some dominant *feeling*, not as in other natures to a dominant *thought*, for their unity and consistency of character, for what distinguishes them from incoherencies.

The difference, then, between the poetry of a poet, and the poetry of a cultivated but not naturally poetic mind, is, that in the latter, with however bright a halo of feeling the thought may be surrounded and glorified, the thought itself is always the conspicuous object; while the poetry of a poet is Feeling itself, employing Thought only as the medium of its expression. In the one, feeling waits upon thought; in the other, thought upon feeling. The one writer has a distinct aim, common to him with any other didactic author; he desires to convey the thought, and he conveys it clothed in the feelings which it excites in himself, or which he deems most appropriate to it. The other merely pours forth the overflowing of his feelings; and all the thoughts which those feelings suggest are floated promiscuously along the stream.

It may assist in rendering our meaning intelligible, if we illustrate it by a parallel between the two English authors of our own day who have produced the greatest quantity of true and enduring poetry, Wordsworth and Shelley. Apter instances could not be wished for; the one might be cited as the type, the *exemplar*, of what the poetry of culture may accomplish: the other as perhaps the most striking example ever known of the poetic temperament. How different, accordingly, is the poetry of these two great writers! In Wordsworth, the poetry is almost always the mere setting of a thought. The thought may be more valuable than the setting, or it may be less valuable, but there can be no question as to which was first in his mind: what he is impressed with, and what he is anxious to impress, is some proposition, more or less distinctly conceived; some truth, or something which he deems such. He lets the thought dwell in his mind, till it excites, as is the nature of thought, other thoughts, and also such feelings as the measure of his sensibility is adequate to supply. Among these thoughts and feelings, had he chosen a different walk of authorship (and there are many in which he might equally have excelled), he would probably have made a different selection of media for enforcing the parent thought: his habits, however, being those of poetic composition, he selects in preference the strongest feelings, and the thoughts with which most of feeling is naturally or habitually connected. His poetry, therefore, may be defined to be, his thoughts, coloured by, and impressing themselves by means of, emotions. Such poetry, Wordsworth has occupied a long life in producing. And well and wisely has he so done. Criticisms, no doubt, may be made occasionally both upon the thoughts themselves, and upon the skill he has demonstrated in the choice of his media: for an affair of skill and study, in the most rigorous sense, it evidently was. But he has not laboured in vain; he has exercised, and continues to exercise, a powerful, and mostly a highly beneficial influence over the formation and growth of not a few of the most cultivated and vigorous of the youthful minds of our time, over whose heads poetry of the opposite description would have flown, for want of an original organization, physical or mental, in sympathy with it.

On the other hand, Wordsworth's poetry is never bounding, never ebullient; has little even of the appearance of spontaneousness: the well is never so full that it overflows. There is an air of calm deliberateness about all he writes, which is not characteristic of the poetic temperament: his poetry seems one thing, himself another; he seems to be poetical because he wills to be so, not because he cannot help it: did he will to dismiss poetry, he need never again, it might almost seem, have a poetical thought. He never seems *possessed* by any feeling; no emotion seems ever so strong as to have entire sway, for the time being, over the current of his thoughts. He never, even for the space of a few stanzas, appears entirely given up to exultation, or grief, or pity, or love, or admiration, or devotion, or even animal spirits. He now and then, though seldom, attempts to write as if he were: and never, we think, without leaving an impression of poverty: as the brook which on nearly level ground quite fills its banks, appears but a thread when running rapidly down a precipitous declivity. He has feeling enough to form a decent, graceful, even beautiful decoration to a thought which is in itself interesting and moving; but not so much as suffices to stir up the soul by mere sympathy with itself in its simplest manifestation, nor enough to summon up that array of 'thoughts of power' which in a richly stored mind always attends the call of really intense feeling. It is for this reason, doubtless, that the genius of Wordsworth is essentially unlyrical. Lyric poetry, as it was the earliest kind, is also, if the view we are now taking of poetry be correct, more eminently and peculiarly poetry than any other: it is the poetry most natural to a really poetic temperament, and least capable of being successfully imitated by one not so endowed by nature.

Shelley is the very reverse of all this. Where Wordsworth is strong, he is weak; where Wordsworth is weak, he is strong. Culture, that culture by which Wordsworth has reared from his own inward nature the richest harvest ever brought forth by a soil of so little depth, is precisely what was wanting to Shelley: or let us rather say, he had not, at the period of his deplorably early death, reached sufficiently far in that intellectual progression of which he was capable, and which, if it has done so much for greatly inferior natures, might have made of him the most perfect, as he was already the most gifted of our poets. For him, voluntary mental discipline had done little: the vividness of his emotions and of his sensations had done all. He seldom follows up an idea; it starts into life, summons from the fairy-land of his inexhaustible fancy some three or four bold images, then vanishes, and straight he is off on the wings of some casual association into quite another sphere. He had scarcely yet acquired the consecutiveness of thought necessary for a long poem; his more ambitious compositions too often resemble the scattered fragments of a mirror; colours brilliant as life, single images without end, but no picture. It is only when under the overruling influence of some one state of feeling, either actually experienced, or summoned up in the vividness of reality by a fervid imagination, that he writes as a great poet; unity of feeling being to him the harmonizing principle which a central idea is to minds of another class, and supplying the coherency and consistency which would else have been wanting. Thus it is in many of his smaller, and especially his lyrical poems. They are obviously written to exhale, perhaps to relieve, a state of feeling, or of conception of feeling, almost oppressive from its vividness. The thoughts and imagery are suggested by the feeling, and are such as it finds unsought. The state of feeling may be either of soul or of sense, or oftener (might we not say invariably?) of both: for the poetic temperament is usually, perhaps always, accompanied by exquisite senses. The exciting cause may be either an object or an idea. But whatever of sensation enters into the feeling, must not be local, or consciously organic; it is a condition of the whole frame, not of a part only. Like the state of sensation produced by a fine climate, or indeed like all strongly pleasurable or painful sensations in an impassioned nature, it pervades the entire nervous system. States of feeling, whether sensuous or spiritual, which thus possess the whole being, are the fountains of that which we have called the poetry of poets; and which is little else than a pouring forth of the thoughts and images that pass across the mind while some permanent state of feeling is occupying it.

To the same original fineness of organization, Shelley was doubtless indebted for another of his rarest gifts, that exuberance of imagery, which when unrepressed, as in many of his poems it is, amounts to a fault. The susceptibility of his nervous system, which made his emotions intense, made also the impressions of his external senses deep and clear; and agreeably to the law of association by which, as already remarked, the strongest impressions are those which associate themselves the most easily and strongly, these vivid sensations were readily recalled to mind by all objects or thoughts which had co-existed with them, and by all feelings which in any degree resembled them. Never did a fancy so teem with sensuous imagery as Shelley's. Wordsworth economizes an image, and detains it until he has distilled all the poetry out of it, and it will not yield a drop more: Shelley lavishes his with a profusion which is unconscious because it is inexhaustible.

If, then, the maxim *Nascitur poeta* mean, either that the power of producing poetical compositions is a peculiar faculty which the poet brings into the world with him, which grows with his growth like any of his bodily powers, and is as independent of culture as his height, and his complexion; or that any natural peculiarity whatever is implied in producing poetry, real poetry, and in any quantity—such poetry too, as, to the majority of educated and intelligent readers, shall appear quite as good as, or even better than, any other; in either sense the doctrine is false. And nevertheless, there *is* poetry which could not emanate but from a mental and physical constitution peculiar, not in the kind, but in the degree of its susceptibility: a constitution which makes its possessor capable of greater happiness than mankind in general, and also of greater unhappiness; and because greater, so also more various. And such poetry, to all who know enough of nature to own it as being in nature, is much more poetry, is poetry in a far higher sense, than any other; since the common element of all poetry, that which constitutes poetry, human feeling, enters far more largely into this than into the poetry of culture. Not only because the natures which we have called poetical, really feel more, and consequently have more feeling to express; but because, the capacity of feeling being so great, feeling, when excited and not voluntarily resisted, seizes the helm of their thoughts, and the succession of ideas and images becomes the mere utterance of an emotion; not, as in other natures, the emotion a mere ornamental colouring of the thought.

Ordinary education and the ordinary course of life are constantly at work counteracting this quality of mind, and substituting habits more suitable to their own ends: if instead of substituting they were content to superadd, there would be nothing to complain of. But when will education consist, not in repressing any mental faculty or power, from the uncontrolled action of which danger is apprehended, but in training up to its proper strength the corrective and antagonist power?

In whomsoever the quality which we have described exists, and is not stifled, that person is a poet. Doubtless he is a greater poet in proportion as the fineness of his perceptions, whether of sense or of internal consciousness, furnishes him with an ampler supply of lovely images—the vigour and richness of his intellect, with a greater abundance of moving thoughts. For it is through these thoughts and images that the feeling speaks, and through their impressiveness that it impresses itself, and finds response in other hearts; and from these media of transmitting it (contrary to the laws of physical nature) increase of intensity is reflected back upon the feeling itself. But all these it is possible to have, and not be a poet; they are mere materials, which the poet shares in common with other people. What constitutes the poet is not the imagery nor the thoughts, nor even the feelings, but the law according to which they are called up. He is a poet, not because he has ideas of any particular kind, but because the succession of his ideas is subordinate to the course of his emotions.

Many who have never acknowledged this in theory, bear testimony to it in their particular judgements. In listening to an oration, or reading a written discourse not professedly poetical, when do we begin to feel that the speaker or author is putting off the character of the orator or the prose writer, and is passing into the poet? Not when he begins to show strong feeling; *then* we merely say, he is in earnest, he feels what he says; still less when he expresses himself in imagery; then, unless illustration be manifestly his sole object, we are apt to say, this is affectation. It is when the feeling (instead of passing away, or, if it continue, letting the train of thoughts run on exactly as they would have done if there were no influence at work but the mere intellect) becomes itself the originator of another train of association, which expels or blends with the former; when (for example) either his words, or the mode of their arrangement, are such as we spontaneously use only when in a state of excitement, proving that the mind is at least as much occupied by a passive state of its own feelings, as by the desire of attaining the premeditated end which the discourse has in view.[1]

Our judgements of authors who lay actual claim to the title of poets, follow the same principle. Whenever, after a writer's meaning is fully understood, it is still matter of reasoning and discussion whether he is a poet or not, he will be found to be wanting in the characteristic peculiarity of association so often adverted to. When, on the contrary, after reading or hearing one or two passages, we instinctively and without hesitation cry out, 'This is a poet', the probability is, that the passages are strongly marked with this peculiar quality. And we may add that in such case, a critic who, not having sufficient feeling to

[1] And this, we may remark by the way, seems to point to the true theory of poetic diction; and to suggest the true answer to as much as is erroneous of Wordsworth's celebrated doctrine on that subject. For on the one hand, *all* language which is the natural expression of feeling, is really poetical, and will be felt as such, apart from conventional associations; but on the other, whenever intellectual culture has afforded a choice between several modes of expressing the same emotion, the stronger the feeling is, the more naturally and certainly will it prefer the language which is most peculiarly appropriated to itself, and kept sacred from the contact of more vulgar objects of contemplation.

respond to the poetry, is also without sufficient philosophy to understand it though he feel it not, will be apt to pronounce, not 'this is prose', but 'this is exaggeration', 'this is mysticism', or, 'this is nonsense'.

Although a philosopher cannot, by culture, make himself, in the peculiar sense in which we now use the term, a poet, unless at least he have that peculiarity of nature which would probably have made poetry his earliest pursuit; a poet may always, by culture, make himself a philosopher. The poetic laws of association are by no means incompatible with the more ordinary laws; are by no means such as *must* have their course, even though a deliberate purpose require their suspension. If the peculiarities of the poetic temperament were uncontrollable in any poet, they might be supposed so in Shelley; yet how powerfully, in the *Cenci*, does he coerce and restrain all the characteristic qualities of his genius; what severe simplicity, in place of his usual barbaric splendour; how rigidly does he keep the feelings and the imagery in subordination to the thought.

The investigation of nature requires no habits or qualities of mind, but such as may always be acquired by industry and mental activity. Because at one time the mind may be so given up to a state of feeling, that the succession of its ideas is determined by the present enjoyment or suffering which pervades it, this is no reason but that in the calm retirement of study, when under no peculiar excitement either of the outward or of the inward sense, it may form any combinations, or pursue any trains of ideas, which are most conducive to the purposes of philosophic inquiry; and may, while in that state, form deliberate convictions, from which no excitement will afterwards make it swerve. Might we not go even further than this? We shall not pause to ask whether it be not a misunderstanding of the nature of passionate feeling to imagine that it is inconsistent with calmness; whether they who so deem of it, do not mistake passion in the militant or antagonistic state, for the type of passion universally; do not confound passion struggling towards an outward object, with passion brooding over itself. But without entering into this deeper investigation; that capacity of strong feeling, which is supposed necessarily to disturb the judgement, is also the material out of which all *motives* are made; the motives, consequently, which lead human beings to the pursuit of truth. The greater the individual's capability of happiness and of misery, the stronger interest has that individual in arriving at truth; and when once that interest is felt, an impassioned nature is sure to pursue this, as to pursue any other object, with greater ardour; for energy of character is commonly the offspring of strong feeling. If, therefore, the most impassioned natures do not ripen into the most powerful intellects, it is always from defect of culture, or something wrong in the circumstances by which the being has originally or successively been surrounded. Undoubtedly strong feelings require a strong intellect to carry them, as more sail requires more ballast: and when, from neglect, or bad education, that strength is wanting, no wonder if the grandest and swiftest vessels make the most utter wreck.

Where, as in some of our older poets, a poetic nature has been united with logical and scientific culture, the peculiarity of association arising from the finer nature so perpetually alternates with the associations attainable by commoner natures trained to high perfection, that its own particular law is not so conspicuously characteristic of the result produced, as in a poet like Shelley, to whom systematic intellectual culture, in a measure proportioned to the intensity of his own nature, has been wanting. Whether the superiority will naturally be on the side of the philosopher-poet or of the mere poet—whether the writings of the one ought, as a whole, to be truer, and their influence more beneficent, than those of the other—is too obvious in principle to need statement: it would be absurd to doubt whether two endowments are better than one; whether truth is more certainly arrived at by two processes, verifying and correcting each other, than by one alone. Unfortunately, in practice the matter is not quite so simple; there the question often is, which is least prejudicial to the intellect, uncultivation or malcultivation. For, as long as education consists chiefly of the mere inculcation of traditional opinions, many of which, from the mere fact that the human intellect has not yet reached perfection, must necessarily be false; so long as even those who are best taught, are rather taught to know the thoughts of others than to think, it is not always clear that the poet of acquired ideas has the advantage over him whose feeling has been his sole teacher. For the depth and durability of wrong as well as of right impressions is proportional to the fineness of the material; and they who have the greatest capacity of natural feeling are generally those whose artificial feelings are the strongest. Hence, doubtless, among other reasons, it is, that in an age of revolutions in opinion, the cotemporary poets, those at least who deserve the name, those who have any individuality of character, if they are not before their age, are almost sure to be behind it. An observation curiously verified all over Europe in the present century. Nor let it be thought disparaging. However urgent may be the necessity for a breaking up of old modes of belief, the most strong-minded and discerning, next to those who head the movement, are generally those who bring up the rear of it.

WALTER BAGEHOT
1826–1877
WORDSWORTH, TENNYSON, AND BROWNING

OR

PURE, ORNATE, AND GROTESQUE ART IN ENGLISH POETRY (1864)

Enoch Arden, &c. By Alfred Tennyson, D.C.L., Poet Laureate
Dramatis Personae. By Robert Browning

WE couple these two books together, not because of their likeness, for they are as dissimilar as books can be, nor on account of the eminence of their authors, for in general two great authors are too much for one essay, but because they are the best possible illustration of something we have to say upon poetical art—because they may give to it life and freshness. The accident of contemporaneous publication has here brought together two books, very characteristic of modern art, and we want to show how they are characteristic.

Neither English poetry nor English criticism have ever recovered the *eruption* which they both made at the beginning of this century into the fashionable world. The poems of Lord Byron were received with an avidity that resembles our present avidity for sensation novels, and were read by a class which at present reads little but such novels. Old men who remember those days may be heard to say, 'We hear nothing of poetry nowadays; it seems quite down.' And 'down' it certainly is, if for poetry it be a descent to be no longer the favourite excitement of the more frivolous part of the 'upper' world. That stimulating poetry is now little read. A stray schoolboy may still be detected in a wild admiration for the *Giaour* or the *Corsair* (and it is suitable to his age, and he should not be reproached for it), but the *real* posterity—the quiet students of a past literature—never read them or think of them. A line or two linger in the memory; a few telling strokes of occasional and felicitous energy are quoted, but this is all. As wholes, these exaggerated stories were worthless; they taught nothing, and, therefore, they are forgotten. If nowadays a dismal poet were, like Byron, to lament the fact of his birth, and to hint that he was too good for the world, the *Saturday Review* would say that 'they doubted if he *was* too good; that a sulky poet was a questionable addition to a tolerable world; that he need not have been born, as far as they were concerned.' Doubtless, there is much in Byron besides his dismal exaggeration, but it was that exaggeration which made 'the sensation', which gave him a wild moment of dangerous fame. As so often happens, the cause of his momentary fashion is the cause also of his lasting oblivion. Moore's former reputation was less excessive, yet it has not been more permanent. The prettiness of a few songs preserves the memory of his name, but as a poet to *read* he is forgotten. There is nothing to read in him; no exquisite thought, no sublime feeling, no consummate description of true character. Almost the sole result of the poetry of that time is the harm which it has done. It degraded for a time the whole character of the art. It said by practice, by a most efficient and successful practice, that it was the aim, the *duty* of poets, to catch the attention of the passing, the fashionable, the busy world. If a poem 'fell dead', it was nothing; it was composed to please the 'London' of the year, and if that London did not like it, why, it had failed. It fixed upon the minds of a whole generation, it engraved in popular memory and tradition, a vague conviction that poetry is but one of the many *amusements* for the light classes, for the lighter hours of all classes. The mere notion, the bare idea, that poetry is a deep thing, a teaching thing, the most surely and wisely elevating of human things, is even now to the coarse public mind nearly unknown.

As was the fate of poetry, so inevitably was that of criticism. The science that expounds which poetry is good and which is bad is dependent for its popular reputation on the popular estimate of poetry itself. The critics of that day had *a* day, which is more than can be said for some since; they professed to tell the fashionable world in what books it would find new pleasure, and therefore they were read by the fashionable world. Byron counted the critic and poet equal. The *Edinburgh Review* penetrated among the young, and into places of female resort where it does not go now. As people ask, 'Have you read *Henry Dunbar*? and what do you think of it?' so they then asked, 'Have you read the *Giaour*? and what do you think of it?' Lord Jeffrey, a shrewd judge of the world, employed himself in telling it what to think; not so much what it ought to think, as what at bottom it did think, and so by dexterous sympathy with current society he gained contemporary fame and power. Such fame no critic must hope for now. His articles will not penetrate where the poems themselves do not penetrate. When poetry was noisy, criticism was loud; now poetry is a still small voice, and criticism must be smaller and stiller. As the function of such criticism was limited so was its subject. For the great and (as time now proves) the *permanent* part of the poetry of his time—for Shelley and for Wordsworth—Lord Jeffrey had but one word. He said[1] 'It won't do'. And it will not do to amuse a drawing-room.

The doctrine that poetry is a light amusement for idle hours, a metrical species of sensational novel, has not indeed been without gainsayers wildly popular. Thirty years ago, Mr. Carlyle most rudely contradicted it. But perhaps this is about all that he has done. He has denied, but he has not disproved. He

[1] The first words in Lord Jeffrey's celebrated review of the *Excursion* were, 'This will never do.'

has contradicted the floating paganism, but he has not founded the deep religion. All about and around us a *faith* in poetry struggles to be extricated, but it is not extricated. Some day, at the touch of the true word, the whole confusion will by magic cease; the broken and shapeless notions cohere and crystallize into a bright and true theory. But this cannot be yet.

But though no complete theory of the poetic art as yet be possible for us, though perhaps only our children's children will be able to speak on this subject with the assured confidence which belongs to accepted truth, yet something of some certainty may be stated on the easier elements, and something that will throw light on these two new books. But it will be necessary to assign reasons, and the assigning of reasons is a dry task. Years ago, when criticism only tried to show how poetry could be made a good amusement, it was not impossible that criticism itself should be amusing. But now it must at least be serious, for we believe that poetry is a serious and a deep thing.

There should be a word in the language of literary art to express what the word 'picturesque' expresses for the fine arts. *Picturesque* means fit to be put into a picture; we want a word *literatesque*, 'fit to be put into a book.' An artist goes through a hundred different country scenes, rich with beauties, charms, and merits, but he does not paint any of them. He leaves them alone; he idles on till he finds the hundred-and-first—a scene which many observers would not think much of, but which *he* knows by virtue of his art will look well on canvas, and this he paints and preserves. Susceptible observers, though not artists, feel this quality too; they say of a scene, 'How picturesque!' meaning by this a quality distinct from that of beauty, or sublimity, or grandeur—meaning to speak not only of the scene as it is in itself, but also of its fitness for imitation by art; meaning not only that it is good, but that its goodness is such as ought to be transferred to paper; meaning not simply that it fascinates, but also that its fascination is such as ought to be copied by man. A fine and insensible instinct has put language to this subtle use; it expresses an idea without which fine art criticism could not go on, and it is very natural that the language of pictorial should be better supplied with words than that of literary criticism, for the eye was used before the mind, and language embodies primitive sensuous ideas, long ere it expresses, or need express, abstract and literary ones.

The reason why a landscape is 'picturesque' is often said to be that such landscape represents an 'idea'. But this explanation, though in the minds of some who use it it is near akin to the truth, fails to explain that truth to those who did not know it before; the word 'idea' is so often used in these subjects when people do not know anything else to say; it represents so often a kind of intellectual insolvency, when philosophers are at their wits' end, that shrewd people will never readily on any occasion give it credit for meaning anything. A wise explainer must, therefore, look out for other words to convey what he has to say. *Landscapes*, like everything else in nature, divide themselves as we look at them into a sort of rude classification. We go down a river, for example, and we see a hundred landscapes on both sides of it, resembling one another in much, yet differing in something; with trees here, and a farmhouse there, and shadows on one side, and a deep pool far on; a collection of circumstances most familiar in themselves, but making a perpetual novelty by the magic of their various combinations. We travel so for miles and hours, and then we come to a scene which also has these various circumstances and adjuncts, but which combines them best, which makes the best whole of them, which shows them in their best proportion at a single glance before the eye. Then we say, 'This is the place to paint the river; this is the picturesque point!' Or, if not artists or critics of art, we feel without analysis or examination that somehow this bend or sweep of the river, shall, in future, *be the river to us*: that it is the image of it which we will retain in our mind's eye, by which we will remember it, which we will call up when we want to describe or think of it. Some fine countries, some beautiful rivers, have not this picturesque quality: they give us elements of beauty, but they do not combine them together; we go on for a time delighted, but *after* a time somehow we get wearied; we feel that we are taking in nothing and learning nothing; we get no collected image before our mind; we see the accidents and circumstances of that sort of scenery, but the summary scene we do not see; we find *disjecta membra*, but no form; various and many and faulty approximations are displayed in succession; but the absolute perfection in that country or river's scenery—its *type*—is withheld. We go away from such places in part delighted, but in part baffled; we have been puzzled by pretty things; we have beheld a hundred different inconsistent specimens of the same sort of beauty; but the rememberable idea, the full development, the characteristic individuality of it, we have not seen.

We find the same sort of quality in all parts of painting. We see a portrait of a person we know, and we say, 'It is like—yes, like, of course, but it is not *the man*;' we feel it could not be any one else, but still, somehow it fails to bring home to us the individual as we know him to be. *He* is not there. An accumulation of features like his are painted, but his essence is not painted; an approximation more or less excellent is given, but the characteristic expression, the *typical* form, of the man is withheld.

Literature—the painting of words—has the same quality but wants the analogous word. The word '*literatesque*' would mean, if we possessed it, that perfect combination in the *subject-matter* of literature, which suits the *art* of literature. We often meet people, and say of them, sometimes meaning well and sometimes ill, 'How well so-and-so would do in a book!'

Such people are by no means the best people; but they are the most effective people—the most rememberable people. Frequently when we first know them, we like them because they explain to us so much of our experience; we have known many people 'like that', in one way or another, but we did not seem to understand them; they were nothing to us, for their traits were indistinct; we forgot them, for they *hitched* on to nothing, and we could not classify them; but when we see the *type* of the genus, at once we seem to comprehend its character; the inferior specimens are explained by the perfect embodiment; the approximations are definable when we know the ideal to which they draw near. There are an infinite number of classes of human beings, but in each of these classes there is a distinctive type which, if we could expand it out in words, would define the class. We cannot expand it in formal terms any more than a landscape or a species of landscapes; but we have an art, an art of words, which can draw it. Travellers and others often bring home, in addition to their long journals—which though so living to them, are so dead, so inanimate, so undescriptive to all else—a pen-and-ink sketch, rudely done very likely, but which, perhaps, even the more for the blots and strokes, gives a distinct notion, an emphatic image, to all who see it. They say at once, '*Now* we know the sort of thing'. The sketch has *hit* the mind. True literature does the same. It describes sorts, varieties, and permutations, by delineating the type of each sort, the ideal of each variety, the central, the marking trait of each permutation.

On this account, the greatest artists of the world have ever shown an enthusiasm for reality. To care for notions and abstractions; to philosophize; to reason out conclusions; to care for schemes of thought, are signs in the artistic mind of secondary excellence. A Schiller, a Euripides, a Ben Jonson, cares for *ideas*— for the parings of the intellect, and the distillation of the mind; a Shakespeare, a Homer, a Goethe, finds his mental occupation, the true home of his natural thoughts, in the real world—'which is the world of all of us'—where the face of nature, the moving masses of men and women, are ever changing, ever multiplying, ever mixing one with the other. The reason is plain—the business of the poet, of the artist, is with *types*; and those types are mirrored in reality. As a painter must not only have a hand to execute, but an eye to distinguish—as he must go here and then there through the real world to catch the picturesque man, the picturesque scene, which is to live on his canvas—so the poet must find in that reality, the *literatesque* man, the *literatesque* scene which nature intends for him, and which will live in his page. Even in reality he will not find this type complete, or the characteristics perfect; but there, at least, he will find *something*, some hint, some intimation, some suggestion; whereas, in the stagnant home of his own thoughts he will find nothing pure, nothing *as it is*, nothing which does not bear his own mark, which is not somehow altered by a mixture with himself.

The first conversation of Goethe and Schiller illustrates this conception of the poet's art. Goethe was at that time prejudiced against Schiller, we must remember, partly from what he considered the *outrages* of the *Robbers*, partly because of the philosophy of Kant. Schiller's 'Essay on *Grace and Dignity*', he tells us, 'was yet less of a kind to reconcile me. The philosophy of Kant, which exalts the dignity of mind so highly, while appearing to restrict it, Schiller had joyfully embraced: it unfolded the extraordinary qualities which Nature had implanted in him; and in the lively feeling of freedom and self-direction, he showed himself unthankful to the Great Mother, who surely had not acted like a step-dame towards him. Instead of viewing her as self-subsisting, as producing with a living force, and according to appointed laws, alike the highest and the lowest of her works, he took her up under the aspect of some empirical native qualities of the human mind. Certain harsh passages I could even directly apply to myself: they exhibited my confession of faith in a false light; and I felt that if written without particular attention to me they were still worse; for in that case, the vast chasm which lay between us, gaped but so much the more distinctly.' After a casual meeting at a Society for Natural History, they walked home and Goethe proceeds:

'We reached his house; the talk induced me to go in. I then expounded to him, with as much vivacity as possible, the *Metamorphosis of Plants*, drawing out on paper, with many characteristic strokes, a symbolic Plant for him, as I proceeded. He heard and saw all this, with much interest and distinct comprehension; but when I had done, he shook his head and said: "This is no experiment, this is an idea." I stopped with some degree of irritation; for the point which separated us was most luminously marked by this expression. The opinions in *Dignity and Grace*, again occurred to me; the old grudge was just awakening; but I smothered it, and merely said: "I was happy to find that I had got ideas without knowing it, nay that I saw them before my eyes."

'Schiller had much more prudence and dexterity of management than I; he was also thinking of his periodical the *Horen*, about this time, and of course rather wished to attract than repel me. Accordingly he answered me like an accomplished Kantite; and as my stiff-necked Realism gave occasion to many contradictions, much battling took place between us, and at last a truce, in which neither party would consent to yield the victory, but each held himself invincible. Positions like the following grieved me to the very soul: *How can there ever be an experiment, that shall correspond with an idea? The specific quality of an idea is, that no experiment can reach it or agree with it.* Yet if he held as an idea, the same thing which I looked upon as an experiment; there must certainly, I thought, be some community between us, some ground whereon both of us might meet!'

With Goethe's natural history, or with Kant's philosophy, we have here no concern, but we can combine the expressions of the two great poets into a nearly complete description of poetry. The 'symbolic plant' is the *type* of which we speak, the ideal at which inferior specimens aim, the class-characteristic in which they all share, but which none shows forth fully: Goethe was right in searching for this in reality and nature; Schiller was right in saying that it was an 'idea', a transcending notion to which approximations could be found in experience, but only approximations—which could not be found there itself. Goethe, as a poet, rightly felt the primary necessity of outward suggestion and experience; Schiller as a philosopher, rightly felt its imperfection.

But in these delicate matters, it is easy to misapprehend. There is, undoubtedly, a sort of poetry which is produced as it were out of the author's mind. The description of the poet's own moods and feelings is a common sort of poetry—perhaps the commonest sort. But the peculiarity of such cases is, that the poet does not describe himself *as* himself: autobiography is not his object; he takes himself as a specimen of human nature; he describes, not himself, but a distillation of himself: he takes such of his moods as are most characteristic, as most typify certain moods of certain men, or certain moods of all men; he chooses preponderant feelings of special sorts of men, or occasional feelings of men of all sorts; but with whatever other difference and diversity, the essence is that such self-describing poets describe what is *in* them, but not *peculiar* to them,—what is generic, not what is special and individual. Gray's *Elegy* describes a mood which Gray felt more than other men, but which most others, perhaps all others, feel too. It is more popular, perhaps, than any other English poem, because that sort of feeling is the most diffused of high feelings, and because Gray added to a singular nicety of fancy an habitual proneness to a *contemplative*—a discerning but unbiassed—meditation on death and on life. Other poets cannot hope for such success: a subject, so popular, so grave, so wise, and yet so suitable to the writer's nature is hardly to be found. But the same ideal, the same unautobiographical character is to be found in the writings of meaner men. Take sonnets of Hartley Coleridge, for example:

I
TO A FRIEND

When we were idlers with the loitering rills,
The need of human love we little noted:
Our love was nature; and the peace that floated
On the white mist, and dwelt upon the hills,
To sweet accord subdued our wayward wills:
One soul was ours, one mind, one heart devoted,
That, wisely doating, ask'd not why it doated,
And ours the unknown joy, which knowing kills.
But now I find, how dear thou wert to me;
That man is more than half of nature's treasure,
Of that fair Beauty which no eye can see,
Of that sweet music which no ear can measure;
And now the streams may sing for others' pleasure,
The hills sleep on in their eternity.

II
TO THE SAME

In the great city we are met again,
Where many souls there are, that breathe and die,
Scarce knowing more of nature's potency,
Than what they learn from heat, or cold, or rain,
The sad vicissitude of weary pain;—
For busy man is lord of ear and eye,
And what hath nature, but the vast, void sky,
And the thronged river toiling to the main?
Oh! say not so, for she shall have her part
In every smile, in every tear that falls,
And she shall hide her in the secret heart,
Where love persuades, and sterner duty calls:
But worse it were than death, or sorrow's smart,
To live without a friend within these walls.

III
TO THE SAME

We parted on the mountains, as two streams
From one clear spring pursue their several ways;
And thy fleet course hath been through many a maze,
In foreign lands, where silvery Padus gleams
To that delicious sky, whose glowing beams
Brightened the tresses that old Poets praise;
Where Petrarch's patient love, and artful lays,
And Ariosto's song of many themes,
Moved the soft air. But I, a lazy brook,
As close pent up within my native dell,
Have crept along from nook to shady nook,
Where flowrets blow, and whispering Naiads dwell.
Yet now we meet, that parted were so wide,
O'er rough and smooth to travel side by side.

The contrast of instructive and enviable locomotion with refining but instructive meditation is not special and peculiar to these two, but general and universal. It was set down by Hartley Coleridge because he was the most meditative and refining of men.

What sort of literatesque types are fit to be described in the sort of literature called poetry, is a matter on which much might be written. Mr. Arnold, some years since, put forth a theory that the art of poetry could only delineate *great actions*. But though, rightly interpreted and understood—using the word action so as to include high and sound activity in contemplation—this definition may suit the highest poetry, it certainly cannot be stretched to include many inferior sorts and even many good sorts. Nobody in their senses would describe Gray's *Elegy* as the delineation of a 'great action'; some kinds of mental contemplation may be energetic enough to deserve this name, but Gray would have been frightened at the very word. He loved scholar-like calm and quiet inaction; his very greatness depended on his *not* acting, on his 'wise passiveness', on his indulging the grave idleness which so well appreciates so much of human life. But the best answer—the *reductio ad absurdum*—of Mr. Arnold's doctrine, is the mutilation which it has caused him to make of his own writings. It has forbidden him, he tells us, to reprint *Empedocles*—a poem undoubtedly containing defects and even excesses, but containing also these lines:

> And yet what days were those, Parmenides!
> When we were young, when we could number friends
> In all the Italian cities like ourselves,
> When with elated hearts we join'd your train,
> Ye Sun-born virgins! on the road of Truth.
> Then we could still enjoy, then neither thought
> Nor outward things were clos'd and dead to us,
> But we receiv'd the shock of mighty thoughts
> On simple minds with a pure natural joy;
> And if the sacred load oppress'd our brain,
> We had the power to feel the pressure eas'd,
> The brow unbound, the thoughts flow free again,
> In the delightful commerce of the world.
> We had not lost our balance then, nor grown
> Thought's slaves and dead to every natural joy.
> The smallest thing could give us pleasure then—
> The sports of the country people;
> A flute note from the woods;
> Sunset over the sea:
> Seed-time and harvest;
> The reapers in the corn;
> The vinedresser in his vineyard;
> The village-girl at her wheel.
> Fullness of life and power of feeling, ye
> Are for the happy, for the souls at ease,
> Who dwell on a firm basis of content.
> But he who has outliv'd his prosperous days,
> But he, whose youth fell on a different world
> From that on which his exil'd age is thrown;
> Whose mind was fed on other food, was train'd
> By other rules than are in vogue to-day;
> Whose habit of thought is fix'd, who will not change,
> But in a world he loves not must subsist
> In ceaseless opposition, be the guard
> Of his own breast, fetter'd to what he guards,
> That the world win no mastery over him;

Who has no friend, no fellow left, not one;
Who has no minute's breathing space allow'd
To nurse his dwindling faculty of joy:—
Joy and the outward world must die to him
As they are dead to me.

What freak of criticism can induce a man who has written such poetry as this, to discard it, and say it is not poetry? Mr. Arnold is privileged to speak of his own poems, but no other critic could speak so and not be laughed at.

We are disposed to believe that no very sharp definition can be given—at least in the present state of the critical art—of the boundary line between poetry and other sorts of imaginative delineation. Between the undoubted dominions of the two kinds there is a debateable land; everybody is agreed that the *Oedipus at Colonus is* poetry: every one is agreed that the wonderful appearance of Mrs. Veal is *not* poetry. But the exact line which separates grave novels in verse like *Aylmer's Field* or *Enoch Arden*, from grave novels not in verse like *Silas Marner* or *Adam Bede*, we own we cannot draw with any confidence. Nor, perhaps, is it very important; whether a narrative is thrown into verse or not certainly depends in part on the taste of the age, and in part on its mechanical helps. Verse is the only mechanical help to the memory in rude times, and there is little writing till a cheap something is found to write upon, and a cheap something to write with. Poetry—verse at least—is the literature of *all work* in early ages; it is only later ages which write in what *they* think a natural and simple prose. There are other casual influences in the matter too; but they are not material now. We need only say here that poetry, because it has a more marked rhythm than prose, must be more intense in meaning and more concise in style than prose. People expect a 'marked rhythm' to imply something worth marking; if it fails to do so they are disappointed. They are displeased at the visible waste of a powerful instrument; they call it 'doggerel,' and rightly call it, for the metrical expression of full thought and eager feeling—the burst of metre—incident to high imagination, should not be wasted on petty matters which prose does as well,—which it does better—which it suits by its very limpness and weakness, whose small changes it follows more easily, and to whose lowest details it can fully and without effort degrade itself. Verse, too, should be *more concise*, for long-continued rhythm tends to jade the mind, just as brief rhythm tends to attract the attention. Poetry should be memorable and emphatic, intense, and *soon over*.

The great divisions of poetry, and of all other literary art, arise from the different modes in which these *types*—these characteristic men, these characteristic feelings—may be variously described. There are three principal modes which we shall attempt to describe—the *pure*, which is sometimes, but not very wisely, called the classical; the *ornate*, which is also unwisely called romantic; and the *grotesque*, which might be called the mediaeval. We will describe the nature of these a little. Criticism we know must be brief—not, like poetry, because its charm is too intense to be sustained—but on the contrary, because its interest is too weak to be prolonged; but elementary criticism, if an evil, is a necessary evil; a little while spent among the simple principles of art is the first condition, the absolute pre-requisite, for surely apprehending and wisely judging the complete embodiments and miscellaneous forms of actual literature.

The definition of *pure* literature is that it describes the type in its simplicity, we mean, with the exact amount of accessory circumstance which is necessary to bring it before the mind in finished perfection, and *no more* than that amount. The *type* needs some accessories from its nature—a picturesque landscape does not consist wholly of picturesque features. There is a setting of surroundings—as the Americans would say, of *fixings*—without which the reality is not itself.

By a traditional mode of speech, as soon as we see a picture in which a complete effect is produced by detail so rare and so harmonized as to escape us, we say 'how classical'. The whole which is to be seen appears at once and through the detail, but the detail itself is not seen: we do not think of that which gives us the idea; we are absorbed in the idea itself. Just so in literature the pure art is that which works with the fewest strokes; the fewest, that is, for its purpose, for its aim is to call up and bring home to men an idea, a form, a character, and if that idea be twisted, that form be involved, that character perplexed, many strokes of literary art will be needful. Pure art does not mutilate its object: it represents it as fully as is possible with the slightest effort which is possible: it shrinks from no needful circumstances, as little as it inserts any which are needless. The precise peculiarity is not merely that no incidental circumstance is inserted which does not tell on the main design: no art is fit to be called *art* which permits a stroke to be put in without an object; but that only the minimum of such circumstance is inserted at all. The form is sometimes said to be bare, the accessories are sometimes said to be invisible, because the appendages are so choice that the shape only is perceived.

The English literature undoubtedly contains much impure literature; impure in its style if not in its meaning: but it also contains one great, one nearly perfect, model of the pure style in the literary expression of typical *sentiment*; and one not perfect, but gigantic and close approximation to perfection in the pure delineation of objective character. Wordsworth, perhaps, comes as near to choice purity of style in sentiment as is possible; Milton, with exceptions and conditions to be explained, approaches perfection by the strenuous purity with which he depicts character.

A wit once said, that '*pretty* women had more features than *beautiful* women', and though the expression may be criticized, the meaning is correct.

Pretty women seem to have a great number of attractive points, each of which attracts your attention, and each one of which you remember afterwards; yet these points have not *grown together*, their features have not linked themselves into a single inseparable whole. But a beautiful woman is a whole as she is; you no more take her to pieces than a Greek statue; she is not an aggregate of divisible charms, she is a charm in herself. Such ever is the dividing test of pure art; if you catch yourself admiring its details, it is defective; you ought to think of it as a single whole which you must remember, which you must admire, which somehow subdues you while you admire it, which is a 'possession' to you 'for ever'.

Of course no individual poem embodies this ideal perfectly; of course every human word and phrase has its imperfections, and if we choose an instance to illustrate that ideal, the instance has scarcely a fair chance. By contrasting it with the ideal we suggest its imperfections; by protruding it as an example, we turn on its defectiveness the microscope of criticism. Yet these two sonnets of Wordsworth may be fitly read in this place, not because they are quite without faults, or because they are the very best examples of their kind of style; but because they are *luminous* examples; the compactness of the sonnet and the gravity of the sentiment, hedging in the thoughts, restraining the fancy, and helping to maintain a singleness of expression:

THE TROSACHS

There's not a nook within this solemn Pass,
But were an apt Confessional for one
Taught by his summer spent, his autumn gone,
That Life is but a tale of morning grass
Withered at eve. From scenes of art which chase
That thought away, turn, and with watchful eyes
Feed it 'mid Nature's old felicities,
Rocks, rivers, and smooth lakes more clear than glass
Untouched, unbreathed upon. Thrice happy guest,

If from a golden perch of aspen spray
(October's workmanship to rival May)
The pensive warbler of the ruddy breast
That moral teaches by a heaven-taught lay,
Lulling the year, with all its cares, to rest!

COMPOSED UPON WESTMINSTER BRIDGE, SEPT. 3, 1802

Earth has not anything to show more fair:
Dull would he be of soul who could pass by
A sight so touching in its majesty:
This city now doth, like a garment, wear
The beauty of the morning; silent, bare,
Ships, towers, domes, theatres, and temples lie
Open unto the fields and to the sky;
All bright and open in the smokeless air.
Never did sun more beautifully steep
In his first splendour, valley, rock, or hill;
Ne'er saw I, never felt, a calm so deep!
The river glideth at his own sweet will:
Dear God! The very houses seem asleep;
And all that mighty heart is lying still!

Instances of barer style than this may easily be found, instances of colder style—few better instances of purer style. Not a single expression (the invocation in the concluding couplet of the second sonnet perhaps excepted) can be spared, yet not a single expression rivets the attention. If, indeed, we take out the phrase—

> The city now doth like a garment wear
> The beauty of the morning,

and the description of the brilliant yellow of autumn—

> October's workmanship to rival May,

they have independent value, but they are not noticed in the sonnet when we read it through; they fall into place there, and being in their place are not seen. The great subjects of the two sonnets, the religious aspect of the beautiful but grave nature—the religious aspect of a city about to awaken and be alive, are the only ideas left in our mind. To Wordsworth has been vouchsafed the last grace of the self-denying artist; you think neither of him nor his style, but you cannot help thinking of—you *must* recall—the exact phrase, the *very* sentiment he wished.

Milton's purity is more eager. In the most exciting parts of Wordsworth—and these sonnets are not very exciting—you always feel, you never forget, that what you have before you is the excitement of a recluse. There is nothing of the stir of life; nothing of the *brawl* of the world. But Milton though always a scholar by trade, though solitary in old age, was through life intent on great affairs, lived close to great scenes, watched a revolution, and if not an actor in it, was at least secretary to the actors. He was familiar—by daily experience and habitual sympathy—with the earnest debate of arduous questions, on which the life and death of the speakers certainly depended, on which the weal or woe of the country perhaps depended. He knew how profoundly the individual character of the speakers—their inner and real nature—modifies their opinion on such questions; he knew how surely that nature will appear in the expression of them. This great experience, fashioned by a fine imagination, gives to the debate of Satanic Council in Pandaemonium its reality and its life. It is a debate in the Long Parliament, and though the *theme* of *Paradise Lost* obliged Milton to side with the monarchical element in the universe, his old habits are often too much for him; and his real sympathy—the impetus and energy of his nature—side with the rebellious element. For the purposes of art this is much better—of a court, a poet can make but little; of a heaven he can make very little, but of a courtly heaven, such as Milton conceived, he can make nothing at all. The idea of a court and the idea of a heaven are so radically different, that a distinct combination of them is always grotesque and often ludicrous. *Paradise Lost*, as a whole, is radically tainted by a vicious principle. It professes to justify the ways of God to man, to account for sin and death, and it tells you that the whole originated in a political event; in a court squabble as to a particular act of patronage and the due or undue promotion of an eldest son. Satan may have been wrong, but on Milton's theory he had an *arguable* case at least. There was something arbitrary in the promotion; there were little symptoms of a job; in *Paradise Lost* it is always clear that the devils are the weaker, but it is never clear that the angels are the better. Milton's sympathy and his imagination slip back to the Puritan rebels whom he loved, and desert the courtly angels whom he could not love although he praised. There is no wonder that Milton's hell is better than his heaven, for he hated officials and he loved rebels, for he employs his genius below, and accumulates his pedantry above. On the great debate in Pandaemonium all his genius is concentrated. The question is very practical; it is, 'What are we devils to do, now we have lost heaven?' Satan who presides over and manipulates the assembly; Moloch

> the fiercest spirit
> That fought in Heaven, now fiercer by despair,

who wants to fight again; Belial, 'the man of the world', who does not want to fight any more; Mammon, who is for commencing an industrial career; Beelzebub, the official statesman,

> deep on his front engraven
> Deliberation sat and Public care,

who, at Satan's instance, proposes the invasion of earth—are as distinct as so many statues. Even Belial, 'the man of the world', the sort of man with whom Milton had least sympathy, is perfectly painted. An inferior artist would have made the actor who 'counselled ignoble ease and peaceful sloth', a degraded and ugly creature; but Milton knew better. He knew that low notions require a better garb than high notions. Human nature is not a high thing, but at least it has a high idea of itself; it will not accept mean maxims, unless they are gilded and made beautiful. A prophet in goatskin may cry, 'Repent, repent', but it takes 'purple and fine linen' to be able to say, 'Continue in your sins'. The world vanquishes with its speciousness and its show, and the orator who is to persuade men to worldliness must have a share in them. Milton well knew this; after the warlike speech of the fierce Moloch he introduces a brighter and a more graceful spirit:

> He ended frowning, and his look denounced
> Desp'rate revenge, and battle dangerous
> To less than Gods. On th' other side up rose
> Belial, in act more graceful and humane:
> A fairer person lost not Heaven; he seem'd
> For dignity composed and high exploit:
> But was all false and hollow, though his tongue
> Dropt manna, and could make the worse appear
> The better reason, to perplex and dash
> Maturest counsels; for his thoughts were low;
> To vice industrious, but to nobler deeds
> Tim'rous and slothful; yet he pleased the ear,
> And with persuasive accent thus began:

He does not begin like a man with a strong case, but like a man with a weak case; he knows that the pride of human nature is irritated by mean advice, and though he may probably persuade men to *take* it, he must carefully apologise for *giving* it. Here, as elsewhere, though the formal address is to devils, the real address is to men: to the human nature which we know, not to the fictitious demonic nature we do not know:

> I should be much for open war, O Peers!
> As not behind in hate, if what was urged
> Main reason to persuade immediate war,
> Did not dissuade me most, and seem to cast
> Ominous conjecture on the whole success:
> When he who most excels in fact of arms,
> In what he counsels and in what excels

> Mistrustful, grounds his courage on despair,
> And utter dissolution, as the scope
> Of all his aim, after some dire revenge.
> First, what revenge? The tow'rs of Heav'n are fill'd
> With armed watch, that render all access
> Impregnable; oft on the bord'ring deep
> Encamp their legions, or with obscure wing
> Scout far and wide into the realm of night,
> Scorning surprise. Or could we break our way
> By force, and at our heels all hell should rise
> With blackest insurrection, to confound
> Heav'n's purest light, yet our great Enemy,
> All incorruptible, would on his throne
> Sit unpolluted, and th' ethereal mould
> Incapable of stain would soon expel
> Her mischief, and purge off the baser fire
> Victorious. Thus repulsed, our final hope
> Is flat despair. We must exasperate
> Th' Almighty Victor to spend all his rage,
> And that must end us: that must be our cure,
> To be no more? Sad cure, for who would lose,
> Though full of pain, this intellectual being,
> Those thoughts that wander through eternity,
> To perish rather, swallow'd up and lost
> In the wide womb of uncreated night,
> Devoid of sense and motion? And who knows,
> Let this be good, whether our angry Foe
> Can give it, or will ever? How he can
> Is doubtful; that he never will is sure.
> Will he, so wise, let loose at once his ire
> Belike through impotence, or unaware,
> To give his enemies their wish, and end
> Them in his anger, whom his anger saves
> To punish endless? Wherefore cease we then?
> Say they who counsel war, we are decreed,
> Reserved, and destined, to eternal woe;
> Whatever doing, what can we suffer more,
> What can we suffer worse? Is this then worst,
> Thus sitting, thus consulting, thus in arms?
>   . . . .

And so on.

Mr. Pitt knew this speech by heart, and Lord Macaulay has called it incomparable; and these judges of the oratorical art have well decided. A mean foreign policy cannot be better defended. Its sensibleness is effectually explained, and its tameness as much as possible disguised.

But we have not here to do with the excellence of Belial's policy, but with the excellence of his speech; and with that speech in a peculiar manner. This speech, taken with the few lines of description with which Milton introduces them, embody, in as short a space as possible, with as much perfection as possible, the delineation of the type of character common at all times, dangerous in many times, sure to come to the surface in moments of difficulty, and never more dangerous than then. As Milton describes, it is one among several *typical* characters which will ever have their place in great councils, which will ever be heard at important decisions, which are part of the characteristic and inalienable whole of this statesmanlike world. The debate in Pandaemonium is a debate among these typical characters at the greatest conceivable crisis, and with adjuncts of solemnity which no other situation could rival. It is the greatest *classical* triumph, the highest achievement of the pure *style* in English literature; it is the greatest description of the highest and most typical characters with the most choice circumstances and in the fewest words.

It is not unremarkable that we should find in Milton and in *Paradise Lost* the best specimen of pure style. He was schoolmaster in a pedantic age, and there is nothing so unclassical—nothing so impure in style—as pedantry. The out-of-door conversational life of Athens was as opposed to bookish scholasticism as a life can be. The most perfect books have been written not by those who thought much of books, but by those who thought little, by those who were under the restraint of a sensitive talking world, to which books had contributed something, and a various eager life the rest. Milton is generally unclassical in spirit where he is learned, and naturally, because the purest poets do not overlay their conceptions with book knowledge, and the classical poets, having in comparison no books, were under little temptation to impair the purity of their style by the accumulation of their research. Over and above this, there is in Milton, and a little in Wordsworth also, one defect which is in the highest degree faulty and unclassical, which mars the effect and impairs the perfection of the pure style. There is a want of *spontaneity*, and a sense of effort. It has been happily said that Plato's words must have *grown* into their places. No one would say so of Milton or even of Wordsworth. About both of them there is a taint of duty; a vicious sense of the good man's task. Things seem right where they are, but they seem to be put where they are. *Flexibility* is essential to the consummate perfection of the pure style because the sensation of the poet's efforts carries away our thoughts from his achievements. We are admiring his labours when we should be enjoying his words. But this is a defect in those two writers, not a defect in pure art. Of course it *is* more difficult to write in few words than to write in many; to take the best adjuncts, and those only, for what you have to say, instead of using all which comes to hand; it *is* an additional labour if you write verses in the morning, to spend the rest of the day in *choosing*, or making those verses fewer. But a perfect artist in the pure style is as effortless and as natural as in any style, perhaps is more so. Take the well-known lines:

>   There was a little lawny islet
>   By anemone and violet,
>   Like mosaic, paven:
>   And its roof was flowers and leaves
>   Which the summer's breath enweaves,
>   Where nor sun, nor showers, nor breeze,
>   Pierce the pines and tallest trees,
>   Each a gem engraven;—

> Girt by many an azure wave
> With which the clouds and mountains pave
> A lake's blue chasm.

Shelley had many merits and many defects. This is not the place for a complete or indeed for *any* estimate of him. But one excellence is most evident. His words are as flexible as any words; the rhythm of some modulating air seems to move them into their place without a struggle by the poet and almost without his knowledge. This is the perfection of pure art, to embody typical conceptions in the choicest, the fewest accidents, to embody them so that each of these accidents may produce its full effect, and so to embody them without effort.

The extreme opposite to this pure art is what may be called ornate art. This species of art aims also at giving a delineation of the typical idea in its perfection and its fullness, but it aims at so doing in a manner most different. It wishes to surround the type with the greatest number of circumstances which it will *bear*. It works not by choice and selection, but by accumulation and aggregation. The idea is not, as in the pure style, presented with the least clothing which it will endure, but with the richest and most involved clothing that it will admit.

We are fortunate in not having to hunt out of past literature an illustrative specimen of the ornate style. Mr. Tennyson has just given one admirable in itself, and most characteristic of the defects and the merits of this style. The story of Enoch Arden, as he has enhanced and presented it, is a rich and splendid composite of imagery and illustration. Yet how simple that story is in itself. A sailor who sells fish, breaks his leg, gets dismal, gives up selling fish, goes to sea, is wrecked on a desert island, stays there some years, on his return finds his wife married to a miller, speaks to a landlady on the subject, and dies. Told in the pure and simple, the unadorned and classical style, this story would not have taken three pages, but

Mr. Tennyson has been able to make it the principal —the largest tale in his new volume. He has done so only by giving to every event and incident in the volume an accompanying commentary. He tells a great deal about the torrid zone which a rough sailor like Enoch Arden certainly would not have perceived; and he gives to the fishing village, to which all the characters belong, a softness and a fascination which such villages scarcely possess in reality.

The description of the tropical island on which the sailor is thrown, is an absolute model of adorned art:

> The mountain wooded to the peak, the lawns
> And winding glades high up like ways to Heaven,
> The slender coco's drooping crown of plumes,
> The lightning flash of insect and of bird,
> The lustre of the long convolvuluses
> That coil'd around the stately stems, and ran
> Ev'n to the limit of the land, the glows
> And glories of the broad belt of the world,
> All these he saw; but what he fain had seen
> He could not see, the kindly human face,
> Nor ever hear a kindly voice, but heard
> The myriad shriek of wheeling ocean-fowl,
> The league-long roller thundering on the reef,
> The moving whisper of huge trees that branch'd
> And blossom'd in the zenith, or the sweep
> Of some precipitous rivulet to the wave,
> As down the shore he ranged, or all day long
> Sat often in the seaward-gazing gorge,
> A shipwreck'd sailor, waiting for a sail:
> No sail from day to day, but every day
> The sunrise broken into scarlet shafts
> Among the palms and ferns and precipices;
> The blaze upon the waters to the east;
> The blaze upon his island overhead;
> The blaze upon the waters to the west;
> Then the great stars that globed themselves in Heaven,
> The hollower-bellowing ocean, and again
> The scarlet shafts of sunrise—but no sail.

No expressive circumstance can be added to this

description, no enhancing detail suggested. A much less happy instance is the description of Enoch's life before he sailed:

> While Enoch was abroad on wrathful seas,
> Or often journeying landward; for in truth
> Enoch's white horse, and Enoch's ocean spoil
> In ocean-smelling osier, and his face,
> Rough-redden'd with a thousand winter gales,
> Not only to the market-cross were known,
> But in the leafy lanes behind the down,
> Far as the portal-warding lion-whelp,
> And peacock yew-tree of the lonely Hall,
> Whose Friday fare was Enoch's ministering.

So much has not often been made of selling fish.

The essence of ornate art is in this manner to accumulate round the typical object, everything which can be said about it, every associated thought that can be connected with it without impairing the essence of the delineation.

The first defect which strikes a student of ornate art—the first which arrests the mere reader of it—is what is called a want of simplicity. Nothing is described as it is, everything has about it an atmosphere of *something else*. The combined and associated thoughts, though they set off and heighten particular ideas and aspects of the central conception, yet complicate it: a simple thing—'a daisy by the river's brim'—is never left by itself, something else is put with it; something not more connected with it than 'lion-whelp' and the 'peacock yew-tree' are with the 'fresh fish for sale' that Enoch carries past them. Even in the highest cases ornate art leaves upon a cultured and delicate taste, the conviction that it is not the highest art, that it is somehow excessive and over-rich, that it is not chaste in itself or chastening to the mind that sees it—that it is in an unexplained manner unsatisfactory, 'a thing in which we feel there is some hidden want!'

That want is a want of 'definition'. We must all

know landscapes, river landscapes especially, which are in the highest sense beautiful, which when we first see them give us a delicate pleasure; which in some—and these the best cases—give even a gentle sense of surprise that such things should be so beautiful, and yet when we come to live in them, to spend even a few hours in them, we seem stifled and oppressed. On the other hand there are people to whom the sea-shore is a companion, an exhilaration; and not so much for the brawl of the shore as for the *limited* vastness, the finite infinite of the ocean as they see it. Such people often come home braced and nerved, and if they spoke out the truth, would have only to say, 'We have seen the horizon line'; if they were let alone indeed, they would gaze on it hour after hour, so great to them is the fascination, so full the sustaining calm, which they gain from that union of form and greatness. To a very inferior extent, but still, perhaps, to an extent which most people understand better, a common arch will have the same effect. A bridge completes a river landscape; if of the old and many-arched sort it regulates by a long series of defined forms the vague outline of wood and river which before had nothing to measure it; if of the new scientific sort it introduces still more strictly a geometrical element; it stiffens the scenery which was before too soft, too delicate, too vegetable. Just such is the effect of pure style in literary art. It calms by conciseness; while the ornate style leaves on the mind a mist of beauty, an excess of fascination, a complication of charm, the pure style leaves behind it the simple, defined, measured idea, as it is, and by itself. That which is chaste chastens; there is a poised energy—a state half thrill, and half tranquillity—which pure art gives, which no other can give; a pleasure justified as well as felt; an ennobled satisfaction at what ought to satisfy us, and must ennoble us.

Ornate art is to pure art what a painted statue is to an unpainted. It is impossible to deny that a touch of colour *does* bring out certain parts, does convey certain expressions, does heighten certain features, but it leaves on the work as a whole, a want, as we say, 'of something'; a want of that inseparable chasteness which clings to simple sculpture, an impairing predominance of alluring details which impairs our satisfaction with our own satisfaction; which makes us doubt whether a higher being than ourselves will be satisfied even though we are so. In the very same manner, though the *rouge* of ornate literature excites our eye, it also impairs our confidence.

Mr. Arnold has justly observed that this self-justifying, self-*proving* purity of style, is commoner in ancient literature than in modern literature, and also that Shakespeare is not a great or an unmixed example of it. No one can say that he is. His works are full of undergrowth, are full of complexity, are not models of style; except by a miracle nothing in the Elizabethan age could be a model of style; the restraining taste of that age was feebler and more mistaken than that of any other equally great age. Shakespeare's mind so teemed with creation that he required the most just, most forcible, most constant restraint from without. He most needed to be guided of poets, and he was the least and worst guided. As a whole no one can call his works finished models of the pure style, or of any style. But he has many passages of the most pure style, passages which could be easily cited if space served. And we must remember that the task which Shakespeare undertook was the most difficult which any poet has ever attempted, and that it is a task in which after a million efforts every other poet has failed. The Elizabethan drama—as Shakespeare has immortalized it—undertakes to delineate in five acts, under stage restrictions, and in mere dialogue, a whole list of dramatis personae, a set of characters enough for a modern novel, and with the distinctness of a modern novel. Shakespeare is not content to give two or three great characters in solitude and in dignity, like the classical dramatists; he wishes to give a whole *party* of characters in the play of life, and according to the nature of each. He would 'hold the mirror up to nature', not to catch a monarch in a tragic posture, but a whole group of characters engaged in many actions, intent on many purposes, thinking many thoughts. There is life enough, there is action enough, in single plays of Shakespeare to set up an ancient dramatist for a long career. And Shakespeare succeeded. His characters, taken *en masse*, and as a whole, are as well-known as any novelist's characters; cultivated men know all about them, as young ladies know all about Mr. Trollope's novels. But no other dramatist has succeeded in such an aim. No one else's characters are staple people in English literature, hereditary people whom every one knows all about in every generation. The contemporary dramatists, Beaumont and Fletcher, Ben Jonson, Marlowe, &c., had many merits, some of them were great men. But a critic must say of them the worst thing he has to say; 'they were men who failed in their characteristic aim;' they attempted to describe numerous sets of complicated characters, and they failed. No one of such characters, or hardly one, lives in common memory; the Faustus of Marlowe, a really great idea, is not remembered. They undertook to write what they could not write, five acts full of real characters, and in consequence, the fine individual things they conceived are forgotten by the mixed multitude, and known only to a few of the few. Of the Spanish theatre we cannot speak; but there are no such characters in any French tragedy: the whole aim of that tragedy forbade it. Goethe has added to literature a few great characters; he may be said almost to have added to literature the idea of 'intellectual creation',—the idea of describing great characters through the intellect; but he has not added to the common stock what Shakespeare added, a new *multitude* of men and women;

and these not in simple attitudes, but amid the most complex parts of life, with all their various natures roused, mixed, and strained. The severest art must have allowed many details, much overflowing circumstance to a poet who undertook to describe what almost defies description. Pure art would have *commanded* him to use details lavishly, for only by a multiplicity of such could the required effect have been at all produced. Shakespeare could accomplish it, for his mind was a spring, an inexhaustible fountain of human nature, and it is no wonder that being compelled by the task of his time to let the fullness of his nature overflow, he sometimes let it overflow too much, and covered with erroneous conceits and superfluous images characters and conceptions which would have been far more justly, far more effectually, delineated with conciseness and simplicity. But there is an infinity of pure art *in* Shakespeare, although there is a great deal else also.

It will be said, if ornate art be as you say, an inferior species of art, why should it ever be used? If pure art be the best sort of art, why should it not always be used?

The reason is this: literary art, as we just now explained, is concerned with literatesque characters in literatesque situations; and the *best* art is concerned with the *most* literatesque characters in the *most* literatesque situations. Such are the subjects of pure art; it embodies with the fewest touches, and under the most select and choice circumstances, the highest conceptions; but it does not follow that only the best subjects are to be treated by art, and then only in the very best way. Human nature could not endure such a ritical commandment as that, and it would be an erroneous criticism which gave it. *Any* literatesque character may be described in literature under *any* circumstances which exhibit its literatesqueness.

The essence of pure art consists in its describing what is as it is, and this is very well for what can bear it, but there are many inferior things which will not bear it, and which nevertheless ought to be described in books. A certain kind of literature deals with illusions, and this kind of literature has given a colouring to the name romantic. A man of rare genius, and even of poetical genius, has gone so far as to make these illusions the true subject of poetry—almost the sole subject. 'Without,' says Father Newman, of one of his characters, 'being himself a poet, he was in the season of poetry, in the sweet spring-time, when the year is most beautiful because it is new. Novelty was beauty to a heart so open and cheerful as his; not only because it was novelty, and had its proper charm as such, but because when we first see things, we see them in a gay confusion, which is a principal element of the poetical. As time goes on, and we number and sort and measure things,—as we gain views,—we advance towards philosophy and truth, but we recede from poetry.

'When we ourselves were young, we once on a time walked on a hot summer-day from Oxford to Newington—a dull road, as any one who has gone it knows; yet it was new to us; and we protest to you, reader, believe it or not, laugh or not, as you will, to us it seemed on that occasion quite touchingly beautiful; and a soft melancholy came over us, of which the shadows fall even now, when we look back upon that dusty, weary journey. And why? because every object which met us was unknown and full of mystery. A tree or two in the distance seemed the beginning of a great wood, or park, stretching endlessly; a hill implied a vale beyond, with that vale's history; the bye-lanes, with their green hedges, wound on and vanished, yet were not lost to the imagination. Such was our first journey; but when we had gone it several times, the mind refused to act, the scene ceased to enchant, stern reality alone remained; and we thought it one of the most tiresome, odious roads we ever had occasion to traverse.'

That is to say, that the function of the poet is to introduce a 'gay confusion', a rich medley which does not exist in the actual world—which perhaps could not exist in any world—but which would seem pretty if it did exist. Everyone who reads *Enoch Arden* will perceive that this notion of all poetry is exactly applicable to this one poem. Whatever be made of Enoch's 'Ocean spoil in ocean-smelling osier', of the 'portal-warding lion-whelp, and peacock yew-tree', every one knows that in himself Enoch could not have been charming. People who sell fish about the country (and that is what he did, though Mr. Tennyson won't speak out, and wraps it up) never are beautiful. As Enoch was and must be coarse, in itself the poem must depend for its charm on a 'gay confusion'—on a splendid accumulation of impossible accessories.

Mr. Tennyson knows this better than many of us—he knows the country world; he has proved it that no one living knows it better; he has painted with pure art—with art which describes what is a race perhaps more refined, more delicate, more conscientious, than the sailor—the 'Northern Farmer', and we all know what a splendid, what a living thing, he has made of it. He could, if he only would, have given us the ideal sailor in like manner—the ideal of the natural sailor we mean—the characteristic present man as he lives and is. But this he has not chosen. He has endeavoured to describe an exceptional sailor, at an exceptionally refined port, performing a graceful act, an act of relinquishment. And with this task before him, his profound taste taught him that ornate art was a necessary medium—was the sole effectual instrument—for his purpose. It was necessary for him if possible to abstract the mind from reality, to induce us *not* to conceive or think of sailors as they are while we are reading of his sailors, but to think of what a person who did not know might fancy sailors to be. A casual traveller on the sea-shore, with the sensitive mood and the romantic imagination

Mr. Newman has described, might fancy, would fancy, a seafaring village to be like that. Accordingly, Mr. Tennyson has made it his aim to call off the stress of fancy from real life, to occupy it otherwise, to bury it with pretty accessories; to engage it on the 'peacock yew-tree', and the 'portal-warding lion-whelp'. Nothing, too, can be more splendid than the description of the tropics as Mr. Tennyson delineates them, but a sailor would not have felt the tropics in that manner. The beauties of nature would not have so much occupied him. He would have known little of the scarlet shafts of sunrise and nothing of the long convolvuluses. As in *Robinson Crusoe*, his own petty contrivances and his small ailments would have been the principal subject to him. 'For three years', he might have said, 'my back was bad, and then I put two pegs into a piece of drift wood and so made a chair, and after that it pleased God to send me a chill.' In real life his piety would scarcely have gone beyond that.

It will indeed be said, that though the sailor had no words for, and even no explicit consciousness of the splendid details of the torrid zone, yet that he had, notwithstanding, a dim latent inexpressible conception of them: though he could not speak of them or describe them, yet they were much to him. And doubtless such is the case. Rude people are impressed by what is beautiful—deeply impressed—though they could not describe what they see, or what they feel. But what is absurd in Mr. Tennyson's description— absurd when we abstract it from the gorgeous additions and ornaments with which Mr. Tennyson distracts us—is, that his hero feels nothing else but these great splendours. We hear nothing of the physical ailments, the rough devices, the low superstitions, which really would have been the *first* things, the favourite and principal occupations of his mind. Just so when he gets home he *may* have had such fine sentiments, though it is odd, and he *may* have spoken of them to his landlady, though that is odder still—but it is incredible that his whole mind should be made up of fine sentiments. Beside those sweet feelings, if he had them, there must have been many more obvious, more prosaic, and some perhaps more healthy. Mr. Tennyson has shown a profound judgement in distracting us as he does. He has given us a classic delineation of the 'Northern Farmer' with no ornament at all—as bare a thing as can be—because he then wanted to describe a true type of real men: he has given us a sailor crowded all over with ornament and illustration, because he then wanted to describe an unreal type of fancied men, not sailors as they are, but sailors as they might be wished.

Another prominent element in *Enoch Arden* is yet more suitable to, yet more requires the aid of, ornate art. Mr. Tennyson undertook to deal with *half belief*. The presentiments which Annie feels are exactly of that sort which everybody has felt, and which every one has half believed—which hardly any one has more than half believed. Almost every one, it has been said, would be angry if any one else reported that he believed in ghosts; yet hardly any one, when thinking by himself, wholly disbelieves them. Just so much presentiments as Mr. Tennyson depicts, impress the inner mind so much that the outer mind—the rational understanding—hardly likes to consider them nicely or to discuss them sceptically. For these dubious themes an ornate or complex style is needful. Classical art speaks out what it has to say plainly and simply. Pure style cannot hesitate; it describes in concisest outline what is, as it is. If a poet really believes in presentiments he can speak out in pure style. One who could have been a poet—one of the few in any age of whom one can say certainly that they could have been, and have not been—has spoken thus:

> When Heaven sends sorrow,
> Warnings go first,

> Lest it should burst
> With stunning might
> On souls too bright
>   To fear the morrow.
>
> Can science bear us
>   To the hid springs
>   Of human things?
> Why may not dream,
> Or thought's day-gleam,
>   Startle, yet cheer us?
>
> Are such thoughts fetters,
>   While faith disowns
>   Dread of earth's tones,
> Recks but Heaven's call,
> And on the wall,
>   Reads but Heaven's letters?

But if a poet is not sure whether presentiments are true or not true; if he wishes to leave his readers in doubt; if he wishes an atmosphere of indistinct illusion and of moving shadow, he must use the romantic style, the style of miscellaneous adjunct, the style 'which shirks, not meets' your intellect, the style which as you are scrutinizing disappears.

Nor is this all, or even the principal lesson, which *Enoch Arden* may suggest to us, of the use of ornate art. That art is the appropriate art for an *unpleasing type*. Many of the characters of real life, if brought distinctly, prominently, and plainly before the mind, as they really are, if shown in their inner nature, their actual essence, are doubtless very unpleasant. They would be horrid to meet and horrid to think of. We fear it must be owned that Enoch Arden is this kind of person. A dirty sailor who did *not* go home to his wife is not an agreeable thing: a varnish must be put on him to make him shine. It is true that he acts rightly; that he is very good. But such is human nature that it finds a little tameness in mere morality. Mere virtue belongs to a charity school-girl, and has a taint of the catechism. All of us feel this, though most of us are too timid, too scrupulous, too anxious about the virtue of others, to speak out. We are ashamed of our nature in this respect, but it is not the less our nature. And if we look deeper into the matter there are many reasons why we should not be ashamed of it. The soul of man, and as we necessarily believe of beings greater than man, has many parts beside its moral part. It has an intellectual part, an artistic part, even a religious part, in which mere morals have no share. In Shakespeare or Goethe, even in Newton or Archimedes, there is much which will not be cut down to the shape of the commandments. They have thoughts, feelings, hopes—immortal thoughts and hopes—which have influenced the life of men, and the souls of men, ever since their age, but which the 'whole duty of man', the ethical compendium, does not recognize. Nothing is more unpleasant than a virtuous person with a mean mind. A highly developed moral nature joined to an undeveloped intellectual nature, an undeveloped artistic nature, and a very limited religious nature, is of necessity repulsive. It represents a bit of human nature—a good bit, of course, but a bit only—in disproportionate, unnatural, and revolting prominence; and, therefore, unless an artist use delicate care, we are offended. The dismal act of a squalid man needed many condiments to make it pleasant, and therefore Mr. Tennyson was right to mix them subtly and to use them freely.

A mere act of self-denial can indeed scarcely be pleasant upon paper. An heroic struggle with an external adversary, even though it end in a defeat, may easily be made attractive. Human nature likes to see itself look grand, and it looks grand when it is making a brave struggle with foreign foes. But it does not look grand when it is divided against itself. An excellent person striving with temptation is a very admirable being in reality, but he is not a pleasant being in description. We hope he will win and overcome his temptation, but we feel that he would be a more interesting being, a higher being, if he had not felt that temptation so much. The poet must make the struggle great in order to make the self-denial virtuous, and if the struggle be too great, we are apt to feel some mixture of contempt. The internal metaphysics of a divided nature are but an inferior subject for art, and if they are to be made attractive, much else must be combined with them. If the excellence of *Hamlet* had depended on the ethical qualities of Hamlet, it would not have been the masterpiece of our literature. He acts virtuously of course, and kills the people he ought to kill, but Shakespeare knew that such goodness would not much interest the pit. He made him a handsome prince, and a puzzling meditative character; these secular qualities relieve his moral excellence, and so he becomes 'nice'. In proportion as an artist has to deal with types essentially imperfect, he must disguise their imperfections; he must accumulate around them as many first-rate accessories as may make his readers forget that they are themselves second-rate. The sudden *millionaires* of the present day hope to disguise their social defects by buying old places, and hiding among aristocratic furniture; just so a great artist who has to deal with characters artistically imperfect will use an ornate style, will fit them into a scene where there is much else to look at.

For these reasons ornate art is within the limits as legitimate as pure art. It does what pure art could not do. The very excellence of pure art confines its employment. Precisely because it gives the best things by themselves and exactly as they are, it fails when it is necessary to describe inferior things among other things, with a list of enhancements and a crowd of accompaniments that in reality do not belong to it. Illusion, half belief, unpleasant types, imperfect types, are as much the proper sphere of ornate art, as an inferior landscape is the proper sphere for the true efficacy of moonlight. A really great landscape needs sunlight and bears sunlight; but moonlight is an equalizer of beauties; it gives a romantic unreality to what will not stand the bare truth. And just so does romantic art.

There is, however, a third kind of art which differs from these on the point in which they most resemble one another. Ornate art and pure art have this in common, that they paint the types of literature in as good perfection as they can. Ornate art, indeed, uses undue disguises and unreal enhancements; it does not confine itself to the best types; on the contrary it is its office to make the best of imperfect types and lame approximations; but ornate art, as much as pure art, catches its subject in the best light it can, takes the most developed aspect of it which it can find, and throws upon it the most congruous colours it can use. But grotesque art does just the contrary. It takes the type, so to say, *in difficulties*. It gives a representation of it in its minimum development, amid the circumstances least favourable to it, just while it is struggling with obstacles, just where it is encumbered with incongruities. It deals, to use the language of science, not with normal types but with abnormal specimens; to use the language of old philosophy, not with what nature is striving to be, but with what by some lapse she has happened to become.

This art works by contrast. It enables you to see, it makes you see, the perfect type by painting the opposite deviation. It shows you what ought to be by what ought not to be, when complete it reminds you of the perfect image, by showing you the distorted and imperfect image. Of this art we possess in the present generation one prolific master. Mr. Browning is an artist working by incongruity. Possibly hardly one of his most considerable efforts can be found which is not great because of its odd mixture. He puts together things which no one else would have put together, and produces on our minds a result which no one else would have produced, or tried to produce. His admirers may not like all we may have to say of him. But in our way we too are among his admirers. No one ever read him without seeing not only his great ability but his great *mind*. He not only possesses superficial useable talents, but the strong something, the inner secret something which uses them and controls them; he is great, not in mere accomplishments, but in himself. He has applied a hard strong intellect to real life; he has applied the same intellect to the problems of his age. He has striven to know what *is*: he has endeavoured not to be cheated by counterfeits, not to be infatuated with illusions. His heart is in what he says. He has battered his brain against his creed till he believes it. He has accomplishments too, the more effective because they are mixed. He is at once a student of mysticism, and a citizen of the world. He brings to the club sofa distinct visions of old creeds, intense images of strange thoughts: he takes to the bookish student tidings of wild Bohemia, and little traces of the *demi-monde*. He puts down what is good for the naughty and what is naughty for the good. Over women his easier writings exercise that imperious power which belongs to the writings of a great man of the world upon such matters. He knows women, and therefore they wish to know him. If we blame many of Browning's efforts, it is in the interest of art, and not from a wish to hurt or degrade him.

If we wanted to illustrate the nature of grotesque art by an exaggerated instance we should have selected a poem which the chance of late publication brings us in this new volume. Mr. Browning has undertaken to describe what may be called *mind in difficulties*—mind set to make out the universe under the worst and hardest circumstances. He takes 'Caliban', not perhaps exactly Shakespeare's Caliban, but an analogous and worse creature; a strong thinking power, but a nasty creature—a gross animal, uncontrolled and unelevated by any feeling of religion or duty. The delineation of him will show that Mr. Browning does not wish to take undue advantage of his readers by a choice of nice subjects.

'Will sprawl, now that the heat of day is best,
Flat on his belly in the pit's much mire,
With elbows wide, fists clenched to prop his chin;
And, while he kicks both feet in the cool slush,
And feels about his spine small eft-things course,
Run in and out each arm, and make him laugh;
And while above his head a pompion-plant,
Coating the cave-top as a brow its eye,
Creeps down to touch and tickle hair and beard,
And now a flower drops with a bee inside,
And now a fruit to snap at, catch and crunch:

This pleasant creature proceeds to give his idea of the origin of the Universe, and it is as follows. Caliban speaks in the third person, and is of opinion that the maker of the Universe took to making it on account of his personal discomfort:

Setebos, Setebos, and Setebos!
'Thinketh, He dwelleth i' the cold o' the moon.

'Thinketh He made it, with the sun to match,
But not the stars: the stars came otherwise;
Only made clouds, winds, meteors, such as that:
Also this isle, what lives, and grows thereon,
And snaky sea which rounds and ends the same.

'Thinketh, it came of being ill at ease:
He hated that He cannot change His cold,
Nor cure its ache. 'Hath spied an icy fish
That longed to 'scape the rock-stream where she lived,
And thaw herself within the lukewarm brine
O' the lazy sea her stream thrusts far amid,
A crystal spike 'twixt two warm walls of wave;
Only she ever sickened, found repulse
At the other kind of water, not her life,
(Green-dense and dim-delicious, bred o' the sun)
Flounced back from bliss she was not born to breathe,
And in her old bounds buried her despair,
Hating and loving warmth alike: so He.

'Thinketh, He made thereat the sun, this isle,
Trees and the fowls here, beast and creeping thing.
Yon otter, sleek-wet, black, lithe as a leech;
Yon auk, one fire-eye, in a ball of foam,
That floats and feeds; a certain badger brown
He hath watched hunt with that slant white-wedge eye
By moonlight; and the pie with the long tongue
That pricks deep into oakwarts for a worm,
And says a plain word when she finds her prize,
But will not eat the ants; the ants themselves
That build a wall of seeds and settled stalks
About their hole—He made all these and more,
Made all we see, and us, in spite: how else?

It may seem perhaps to most readers that these lines are very difficult, and that they are unpleasant. And so they are. We quote them to illustrate, not the *success* of grotesque art, but the *nature* of grotesque art. It shows the end at which this species of art aims, and if it fails, it is from over-boldness in the choice of a subject by the artist, or from the defects of its execution. A thinking faculty more in difficulties —a great type,—an inquisitive, searching intellect under more disagreeable conditions, with worse helps, more likely to find falsehood, less likely to find truth, can scarcely be imagined. Nor is the mere description of the thought at all bad: on the contrary, if we closely examine it, it is very clever. Hardly any one could have amassed so many ideas at once nasty and suitable. But scarcely any readers—any casual readers—who are not of the sect of Mr. Browning's admirers will be able to examine it enough to appreciate it. From a defect, partly of subject, and partly of style, many of Mr. Browning's works make a demand upon the reader's zeal and sense of duty to which the nature of most readers is unequal. They have on the turf the convenient expression 'staying power': some horses can hold on and others cannot. But hardly any reader not of especial and peculiar nature can hold on through such composition. There is not enough of 'staying power' in human nature.

One of his greatest admirers once owned to us that he seldom or never began a new poem without looking on in advance, and foreseeing with caution what length of intellectual adventure he was about to commence. Whoever will work hard at such poems will find much mind in them: they are a sort of quarry of ideas, but whoever goes there will find these ideas in such a jagged, ugly, useless shape that he can hardly bear them.

We are not judging Mr. Browning simply from a hasty recent production. All poets are liable to misconceptions, and if such a piece as *Caliban upon Setebos* were an isolated error, a venial and particular exception, we should have given it no prominence. We have put it forward because it just elucidates both our subject and the characteristics of Mr. Browning. But many other of his best known pieces do so almost equally; what several of his devotees think his best piece is quite enough illustrative for anything we want. It appears that on Holy Cross day at Rome the Jews were obliged to listen to a Christian sermon in the hope of their conversion, though this is, according to Mr. Browning, what they really said when they came away:

Fee, faw, fum! bubble and squeak!
Blessedest Thursday's the fat of the week,
Rumble and tumble, sleek and rough,
Stinking and savoury, smug and gruff,
Take the church-road, for the bell's due chime
Gives us the summons—'t is sermon-time.

Boh, here's Barnabas! Job, that's you?
Up stumps Solomon—bustling too?
Shame, man! greedy beyond your years
To handsel the bishop's shaving-shears?
Fair play's a jewel! leave friends in the lurch?
Stand on a line ere you start for the church.

Higgledy, piggledy, packed we lie,
Rats in a hamper, swine in a stye,
Wasps in a bottle, frogs in a sieve,
Worms in a carcase, fleas in a sleeve.

> Hist! square shoulders, settle your thumbs
> And buzz for the bishop—here he comes.

And after similar nice remarks for a church, the edified congregation concludes:

> But now, while the scapegoats leave our flock,
> And the rest sit silent and count the clock,
> Since forced to muse the appointed time
> On these precious facts and truths sublime,—
> Let us fitly employ it, under our breath,
> In saying Ben Ezra's Song of Death.
>
> For Rabbi Ben Ezra, the night he died,
> Called sons and sons' sons to his side,
> And spoke, 'This world has been harsh and strange;
> Something is wrong: there needeth a change.
> But what, or where? at the last, or first?
> In one point only we sinned, at worst.
>
> 'The Lord will have mercy on Jacob yet,
> And again in his border see Israel set.
> When Judah beholds Jerusalem,
> The stranger-seed shall be joined to them:
> To Jacob's House shall the Gentiles cleave,
> So the Prophet saith and his sons believe.
>
> 'Ay, the children of the chosen race
> Shall carry and bring them to their place:
> In the land of the Lord shall lead the same,
> Bondsmen and handmaids. Who shall blame
> When the slaves enslave, the oppressed ones o'er
> The oppressor triumph for evermore?
>
> 'God spoke, and gave us the word to keep,
> Bade never fold the hands nor sleep
> 'Mid a faithless world,—at watch and ward,
> Till Christ at the end relieve our guard.
> By His servant Moses the watch was set:
> Though near upon cock-crow, we keep it yet.
>
> 'Thou! if Thou wast He, who at mid-watch came,
> By the starlight, naming a dubious Name!
> And if, too heavy with sleep—too rash
> With fear—O Thou, if that martyr-gash
> Fell on Thee coming to take Thine own,
> And we gave the Cross, when we owed the Throne—

'Thou art the Judge. We are bruised thus.
But, the judgement over, join sides with us!
Thine too is the cause! and not more Thine
Than ours, is the work of these dogs and swine,
Whose life laughs through and spits at their creed,
Who maintain Thee in word, and defy Thee in deed!

'We withstood Christ then? be mindful how
At least we withstand Barabbas now!
Was our outrage sore? But the worst we spared,
To have called these—Christians, had we dared!
Let defiance to them pay mistrust of Thee,
And Rome make amends for Calvary!

'By the torture, prolonged from age to age,
By the infamy, Israel's heritage,
By the Ghetto's plague, by the garb's disgrace,
By the badge of shame, by the felon's place,
By the branding-tool, the bloody whip,
And the summons to Christian fellowship,—

'We boast our proof that at least the Jew
Would wrest Christ's name from the Devil's crew.
Thy face took never so deep a shade
But we fought them in it, God our aid!
A trophy to bear, as we march, Thy band,
South, East, and on to the Pleasant Land!'

It is very natural that a poet whose wishes incline, or whose genius conducts him to a grotesque art, should be attracted towards mediaeval subjects. There is no age whose legends are so full of grotesque subjects, and no age where real life was so fit to suggest them. Then, more than at any other time, good principles have been under great hardships. The vestiges of ancient civilization, the germs of modern civilization, the little remains of what had been, the small beginnings of what is, were buried under a cumbrous mass of barbarism and cruelty. Good elements hidden in horrid accompaniments are the special theme of grotesque art, and these mediaeval life and legends afford more copiously than could have been furnished before Christianity gave its new elements of good, or since modern civilization has removed some few at least of the old elements of destruction. A *buried* life like the spiritual mediaeval was Mr. Browning's natural element, and he was right to be attracted by it. His mistake has been, that he has not made it pleasant; that he has forced his art to topics on which no one could charm, or on which he, at any rate, could not; that on these occasions and in these poems he has failed in fascinating men and women of sane taste.

We say 'sane' because there is a most formidable and estimable *insane* taste. The will has great though indirect power over the taste, just as it has over the belief. There are some horrid beliefs from which human nature revolts, from which at first it shrinks, to which, at first, no effort can force it. But if we fix the mind upon them they have a power over us just because of their natural offensiveness. They are like the sight of human blood: experienced soldiers tell us that at first men are sickened by the smell and newness of blood almost to death and fainting, but that as soon as they harden their hearts and stiffen their minds, as soon as they *will* bear it, then comes an appetite for slaughter, a tendency to gloat on carnage, to love blood, at least for the moment, with a deep eager love. It is a principle that if we put down a healthy instinctive aversion, nature avenges herself by creating an unhealthy insane attraction. For this reason the most earnest truth-seeking men fall into the worst delusions; they will not let their mind alone; they force it towards some ugly thing, which a crotchet of argument, a conceit of intellect recommends, and nature punishes their disregard of her warning by subjection to the ugly one, by belief in it. Just so the most industrious critics get the most admiration. They think it unjust to rest in their instinctive natural horror: they overcome it, and angry nature gives them over to ugly poems and marries them to detestable stanzas.

Mr. Browning possibly, and some of the worst of

Mr. Browning's admirers certainly, will say that these grotesque objects exist in real life, and therefore they ought to be, at least may be, described in art. But though pleasure is not the end of poetry, pleasing is a condition of poetry. An exceptional monstrosity of horrid ugliness cannot be made pleasing, except it be made to suggest—to recall—the perfection, the beauty, from which it is a deviation. Perhaps in extreme cases no art is equal to this; but then such self-imposed problems should not be worked by the artist; these out-of-the-way and detestable subjects should be let alone by him. It is rather characteristic of Mr. Browning to neglect this rule. He is the most of a realist, and the least of an idealist of any poet we know. He evidently sympathizes with some part at least of Bishop Blougram's apology. Anyhow this world exists. 'There *is* good wine—there *are* pretty women—there *are* comfortable benefices—there *is* money, and it *is* pleasant to spend it. Accept the creed of your age and you get these, reject that creed and you lose them. And for what do you lose them? For a fancy creed of your own, which no one else will accept, which hardly any one will call a "creed", which most people will consider a sort of unbelief.' Again, Mr. Browning evidently loves what we may call the realism, the grotesque realism, of orthodox Christianity. Many parts of it in which great divines have felt keen difficulties are quite pleasant to him. He must *see* his religion, he must have an 'object-lesson' in believing. He must have a creed that will *take*, which wins and holds the miscellaneous world, which stout men will heed, which nice women will adore. The spare moments of solitary religion—the 'obdurate questionings', the high 'instincts', the 'first affections', the 'shadowy recollections',

> Which, do they what they may,
> Are yet the fountain-light of all our day—
> Are yet a master-light of all our seeing;

the great but vague faith—the unutterable tenets

seem to him worthless, visionary; they are not enough immersed in matter; they move about 'in worlds not realized'. We wish he could be tried like the prophet once; he would have found God in the earthquake and the storm; he could have deciphered from them a bracing and a rough religion: he would have known that crude men and ignorant women felt them too, and he would accordingly have trusted them; but he would have distrusted and disregarded the 'still small voice'; he would have said it was 'fancy'—a thing you thought you heard to-day, but were not sure you had heard to-morrow: he would call it a nice illusion, an immaterial prettiness; he would ask triumphantly 'How are you to get the mass of men to heed this little thing?' he would have persevered and insisted '*My wife* does not hear it'.

But although a suspicion of beauty, and a taste for ugly reality, have led Mr. Browning to exaggerate the functions, and to caricature the nature of grotesque art, we own or rather we maintain that he has given many excellent specimens of that art within its proper boundaries and limits. Take an example, his picture of what we may call the *bourgeois* nature in *difficulties*; in the utmost difficulty, in contact with magic and the supernatural. He has made of it something homely, comic, true; reminding us of what *bourgeois* nature really is. By showing us the type under abnormal conditions, he reminds us of the type under its best and most satisfactory conditions—

>Hamelin Town's in Brunswick,
> By famous Hanover city;
>The river Weser, deep and wide,
>Washes its walls on the southern side;
>A pleasanter spot you never spied;
> But, when begins my ditty,
>Almost five hundred years ago,
>To see the townsfolk suffer so
> From vermin was a pity.

> Rats!
> They fought the dogs, and killed the cats,
> And bit the babies in the cradles,
> And ate the cheeses out of the vats,
>   And licked the soup from the cook's own ladles,
> Split open the kegs of salted sprats,
> Made nests inside men's Sunday hats,
> And even spoiled the women's chats
>   By drowning their speaking
>   With shrieking and squeaking
> In fifty different sharps and flats.
>
> At last the people in a body
>   To the Town Hall came flocking:
> ' 'Tis clear', cried they, 'our Mayor's a noddy;
>   And as for our Corporation—shocking
> To think we buy gowns lined with ermine
> For dolts that can't or won't determine
> What's best to rid us of our vermin!
> You hope, because you're old and obese,
> To find in the furry civic robe ease?
> Rouse up, Sirs! Give your brains a racking
> To find the remedy we're lacking,
> Or, sure as fate, we'll send you packing!'
> At this the Mayor and Corporation
> Quaked with a mighty consternation.

A person of musical abilities proposes to extricate the civic dignitaries from the difficulty, and they promise him a thousand guilders if he does.

> Into the street the Piper stept,
>   Smiling first a little smile,
> As if he knew what magic slept
>   In his quiet pipe the while;
> Then, like a musical adept,
> To blow the pipe his lips he wrinkled,
> And green and blue his sharp eye twinkled
> Like a candle-flame where salt is sprinkled;
> And ere three shrill notes the pipe uttered
> You heard as if an army muttered;
> And the muttering grew to a grumbling;
> And the grumbling grew to a mighty rumbling;
> And out of the houses the rats came tumbling.

Great rats, small rats, lean rats, brawny rats,
Brown rats, black rats, grey rats, tawny rats,
Grave old plodders, gay young friskers,
    Fathers, mothers, uncles, cousins,
Cocking tails and pricking whiskers,
    Families by tens and dozens,
Brothers, sisters, husbands, wives—
Followed the Piper for their lives.
From street to street he piped advancing,
And step for step they followed dancing,
Until they came to the river Weser,
Wherein all plunged and perished!
—Save one who, stout as Julius Cæsar,
Swam across and lived to carry
(As he, the manuscript he cherished)
To Rat-land home his commentary:
Which was, 'At the first shrill notes of the pipe,
I heard a sound as of scraping tripe,
And putting apples, wondrous ripe,
Into a cider-press's gripe:
And a moving away of pickle-tub boards,
And a leaving ajar of conserve-cupboards,
And a drawing the corks of train-oil flasks,
And a breaking the hoops of butter-casks:
And it seemed as if a voice
(Sweeter far than by harp or by psaltery
Is breathed) called out, "Oh rats, rejoice!
The world is grown to one vast drysaltery!
So, munch on, crunch on, take your nuncheon,
Breakfast, supper, dinner, luncheon!"
And just as a bulky sugar-puncheon,
All ready staved, like a great sun shone
Glorious scarce an inch before me,
Just as methought it said, "Come, bore me!"
—I found the Weser rolling o'er me.'
You should have heard the Hamelin people
Ringing the bells till they rocked the steeple.
'Go', cried the Mayor, 'and get long poles,
Poke out the nests and block up the holes!
Consult with carpenters and builders,
And leave in our town not even a trace
Of the rats!'—when suddenly, up the face
Of the Piper perked in the market-place,
With a 'First, if you please, my thousand guilders!'

A thousand guilders! The Mayor looked blue;
So did the Corporation too.
For council dinners made rare havoc
With Claret, Moselle, Vin-de-Grave, Hock;
And half the money would replenish
Their cellar's biggest butt with Rhenish.
To pay this sum to a wandering fellow
With a gipsy coat of red and yellow!
'Beside,' quoth the Mayor with a knowing wink,
'Our business was done at the river's brink;
We saw with our eyes the vermin sink,
And what's dead can't come to life, I think.
So, friend, we're not the folks to shrink
From the duty of giving you something for drink,
And a matter of money to put in your poke;
But as for the guilders, what we spoke
Of them, as you very well know, was in joke.
Besides, our losses have made us thrifty.
A thousand guilders! Come, take fifty!'

The piper's face fell, and he cried,
'No trifling! I can't wait, beside!
I've promised to visit by dinner time
Bagdat, and accept the prime
Of the Head-Cook's pottage, all he's rich in,
For having left, in the Caliph's kitchen,
Of a nest of scorpions no survivor—
With him I proved no bargain-driver,
With you, don't think I'll bate a stiver!
And folks who put me in a passion
May find me pipe to another fashion.'

'How?' cried the Mayor, 'd'ye think I'll brook
Being worse treated than a Cook?
Insulted by a lazy ribald
With idle pipe and vesture piebald?
You threaten us, fellow? Do your worst,
Blow your pipe there till you burst!'

Once more he stept into the street
   And to his lips again
Laid his long pipe of smooth straight cane;
   And ere he blew three notes (such sweet
Soft notes as yet musician's cunning
   Never gave the enraptured air)

There was a rustling, that seemed like a bustling
Of merry crowds justling at pitching and hustling,
Small feet were pattering, wooden shoes clattering,
Little hands clapping and little tongues chattering.
And, like fowls in a farm-yard when barley is scattering,
Out came the children running.

All the little boys and girls,
With rosy cheeks and flaxen curls,
And sparkling eyes and teeth like pearls,
Tripping and skipping ran merrily after
The wonderful music with shouting and laughter.

. . . .

And I must not omit to say
That in Transylvania there's a tribe
Of alien people that ascribe
The outlandish ways and dress
On which their neighbours lay such stress,
To their fathers and mothers having risen
Out of some subterraneous prison
Into which they were trepanned
Long time ago in a mighty band
Out of Hamelin town in Brunswick land,
But how or why, they don't understand.

Something more we had to say of Mr. Browning, but we must stop. It is singularly characteristic of this age that the poems which rise to the surface should be examples of ornate art, and grotesque art, not of pure art. We live in the realm of the *half* educated. The number of readers grows daily, but the quality of readers does not improve rapidly. The middle class is scattered, headless; it is well-meaning but aimless; wishing to be wise, but ignorant how to be wise. The aristocracy of England never was a literary aristocracy, never even in the days of its full power, of its unquestioned predominance, did it guide—did it even seriously try to guide—the taste of England. Without guidance young men and tired men are thrown amongst a mass of books; they have to choose which they like; many of them would much like to improve their culture, to chasten their taste, if they knew how. But left to themselves they take, not pure art, but showy art; not that which permanently relieves the eye and makes it happy whenever it looks, and as long as it looks, but *glaring* art which catches and arrests the eye for a moment, but which in the end fatigues it. But before the wholesome remedy of nature—the fatigue—arrives, the hasty reader has passed on to some new excitement, which in its turn stimulates for an instant, and then is passed by for ever. These conditions are not favourable to the due appreciation of pure art—of that art which must be known before it is admired—which must have fastened irrevocably on the brain before you appreciate it—which you must love ere it will seem worthy of your love. Women too, whose voice in literature counts as well as that of men—and in a light literature counts for more than that of men—women, such as we know them, such as they are likely to be, ever prefer a delicate unreality to a true or firm art. A dressy literature, an exaggerated literature seem to be fated to us. These are our curses, as other times had theirs.

            And yet
> Think not the living times forget,
> Ages of heroes fought and fell,
> That Homer in the end might tell;
> O'er grovelling generations past
> Upstood the Gothic fane at last;
> And countless hearts in countless years
> Had wasted thoughts, and hopes, and fears,
> Rude laughter and unmeaning tears;
> Ere England Shakespeare saw, or Rome
> The pure perfection of her dome.
> Others I doubt not, if not we,
> The issue of our toils shall see;
> And (they forgotten and unknown)
> Young children gather as their own
> The harvest that the dead had sown.

WALTER HORATIO PATER
1839–1894
COLERIDGE'S WRITINGS (1866)

[Reprinted with additions and revisions in
Appreciations, 1889]

Conversations, Letters, and Recollections of S. T. Coleridge.
Edited by THOMAS ALLSOP. London, 1864.

FORMS of intellectual and spiritual culture often exercise their subtlest and most artful charm when life is already passing from them. Searching and irresistible as are the changes of the human spirit on its way to perfection, there is yet so much elasticity of temper that what must pass away sooner or later is not disengaged all at once even from the highest order of minds. Nature, which by one law of development evolves ideas, moralities, modes of inward life, and represses them in turn, has in this way provided that the earlier growth should propel its fibres into the later, and so transmit the whole of its forces in an unbroken continuity of life. Then comes the spectacle of the reserve of the elder generation exquisitely refined by the antagonism of the new. That current of new life chastens them as they contend against it. Weaker minds do not perceive the change; clearer minds abandon themselves to it. To feel the change everywhere, yet not to abandon oneself to it, is a situation of difficulty and contention. Communicating in this way to the passing stage of culture the charm of what is chastened, high-strung, athletic, they yet detach the highest minds from the past by pressing home its difficulties and finally proving it impossible. Such is the charm of Julian, of St. Louis, perhaps of Luther; in the narrower compass of modern times, of Dr. Newman and Lacordaire; it is also the peculiar charm of Coleridge.

Modern thought is distinguished from ancient by its cultivation of the 'relative' spirit in place of the 'absolute'. Ancient philosophy sought to arrest every object in an eternal outline, to fix thought in a necessary formula, and types of life in a classification by 'kinds' or *genera*. To the modern spirit nothing is, or can be rightly known except relatively under conditions. An ancient philosopher indeed started a philosophy of the relative, but only as an enigma. So the germs of almost all philosophical ideas were enfolded in the mind of antiquity, and fecundated one by one in after ages by the external influences of art, religion, culture in the natural sciences, belonging to a particular generation, which suddenly becomes preoccupied by a formula or theory, not so much new as penetrated by a new meaning and expressiveness. So the idea of 'the relative' has been fecundated in modern times by the influence of the sciences of observation. These sciences reveal types of life evanescing into each other by inexpressible refinements of change. Things pass into their opposites by accumulation of undefinable quantities. The growth of those sciences consists in a continual analysis of facts of rough and general observation into groups of facts more precise and minute. A faculty for truth is a power of distinguishing and fixing delicate and fugitive details. The moral world is ever in contact with the physical; the relative spirit has invaded moral philosophy from the ground of the inductive science. There it has started a new analysis of the relations of body and mind, good and evil, freedom and necessity. Hard and abstract moralities are yielding to a more exact estimate of the subtlety and complexity of our life. Always, as an organism increases in perfection the conditions of its life become more complex. Man is the most complex of the products of nature. Character merges into temperament; the nervous system refines itself into intellect. His physical organism is played upon not only by the physical conditions about it, but by remote laws of inheritance, the vibrations of long past acts reaching him in the midst of the new order of things in which he lives. When we have estimated these conditions he is not yet simple and isolated; for the mind of the race, the character of the age, sway him this way or that through the medium of language and ideas. It seems as if the most opposite statements about him were alike true; he is so receptive, all the influences of the world and of society ceaselessly playing upon him, so that every hour in his life is unique, changed altogether by a stray word, or glance, or touch. The truth of these relations experience gives us; not the truth of eternal outlines effected once for all, but a world of fine gradations and subtly linked conditions, shifting intricately as we ourselves change; and bids us by constant clearing of the organs of observation and perfecting of analysis to make what we can of these. To the intellect, to the critical spirit, these subtleties of effect are more precious than anything else. What is lost in precision of form is gained in intricacy of expression. To suppose that what is called 'ontology' is what the speculative instinct seeks, is the misconception of a backward school of logicians. Who would change the colour or curve of a roseleaf for that οὐσία ἀχρώματος, ἀσχημάτιστος, ἀναφής. A transcendentalism that makes what is abstract more excellent than what is concrete has nothing akin to the leading philosophies of the world. The true illustration of the speculative temper is not the Hindoo, lost to sense, understanding, individuality; but such an one as Goethe, to whom every moment of life brought its share of experimental, individual knowledge, by whom no touch of the world of form, colour, and passion was disregarded.

The literary life of Coleridge was a disinterested struggle against the application of the relative spirit to moral and religious questions. Everywhere he is restlessly scheming to apprehend the absolute; to affirm it effectively; to get it acknowledged. Coleridge failed in that attempt, happily even for him, for it was a struggle against the increasing life of the mind itself. The real loss was, that this controversial interest betrayed him into a direction which was not for him the path of the highest intellectual success; a direction in which his artistic talent could never find the conditions of its perfection. Still, there is so much witchery about his poems, that it is as a poet that he will most probably be permanently remembered. How did his choice of a controversial interest, his determination to affirm the absolute, weaken or modify his poetical gift?

In 1798 he joined Wordsworth in the composition of a volume of poems—the *Lyrical Ballads*. What Wordsworth then wrote is already vibrant with that blithe *élan* which carried him to final happiness and self-possession. In Coleridge we feel already that faintness and obscure dejection which cling like some contagious damp to all his writings. Wordsworth was to be distinguished by a joyful and penetrative conviction of the existence of certain latent affinities between nature and the human mind, which reciprocally gild the mind and nature with a kind of 'heavenly alchemy':

> ... My voice proclaims
> How exquisitely the individual mind
> (And the progressive powers perhaps no less
> Of the whole species) to the external world
> Is fitted:—and how exquisitely, too,
> The external world is fitted to the mind:
> And the creation, by no lower name
> Can it be called, which they with blended might
> Accomplish.[1]

In Wordsworth this took the form of an unbroken dreaming over the aspects and transitions of nature, a reflective, but altogether unformulated, analysis of them.

[1] Preface to the *Excursion*.

There are in Coleridge's poems expressions of this conviction as deep as Wordsworth's. But Coleridge could never have abandoned himself to the dream as Wordsworth did, because the first condition of such abandonment is an unvexed quietness of heart. No one can read the *Lines composed above Tintern* without feeling how potent the physical element was among the conditions of Wordsworth's genius:—'felt in the blood and felt along the heart,'—'My whole life I have lived in quiet thought.' The stimulus which most artists require from nature he can renounce. He leaves the ready-made glory of the Swiss mountains to reflect a glory on a mouldering leaf. He loves best to watch the floating thistle-down, because of its hint at an unseen life in the air. Coleridge's temperament, ἀεὶ ἐν σφοδρᾷ ὀρέξει, with its faintness, its grieved dejection, could never have been like that.

> My genial spirits fail
> And what can these avail
> To lift the smothering weight from off my breast?
> It were a vain endeavour,
> Though I should gaze for ever
> On that green light that lingers in the west:
> I may not hope from outward forms to win
> The passion and the life whose fountains are within.

It is that flawless temperament in Wordsworth which keeps his conviction of a latent intelligence in nature within the limits of sentiment or instinct, and confines it to those delicate and subdued shades of expression which perfect art allows. In sadder dispositions, that is in the majority of cases, where such a conviction has existed, it has stiffened into a formula, it has frozen into a scientific or pseudo-scientific theory. For the perception of those affinities brings one so near the absorbing speculative problems of life—optimism, the proportion of man to his place in nature, his prospects in relation to it—that it ever tends to become theory through their contagion. Even in Goethe, who has brilliantly handled the subject in his lyrics entitled *Gott und Welt*, it becomes something stiffer than poetry; it is tempered by the 'pale cast' of his technical knowledge of the nature of colours, of anatomy, of the metamorphosis of plants.

That, however, which had only a limited power over Coleridge as sentiment, entirely possessed him as a philosophical idea. We shall see in what follows how deep its power was, how it pursued him everywhere, and seemed to him to interpret every question. Wordsworth's poetry is an optimism; it says man's relation to the world is, and may be seen by man to be, a perfect relation; but it is an optimism that begins and ends in an abiding instinct. Coleridge accepts the same optimism as a philosophical idea, but an idea is relative to an intellectual assent; sometimes it seems a better expression of facts, sometimes a worse, as the understanding weighs it in the logical balances. And so it is not a permanent consolation. It is only in the rarer moments of intellectual warmth and sunlight that it is entirely credible. In less exhilarating moments that perfect relation of man and nature seems to shift and fail; that is, the philosophical idea ceases to be realizable; and with Coleridge its place is not supplied, as with Wordsworth, by the corresponding sentiment or instinct.

What in Wordsworth is a sentiment or instinct, is in Coleridge a philosophical idea. In other words, Coleridge's talent is a more intellectual one than Wordsworth's, more dramatic, more self-conscious. Wordsworth's talent, deeply reflective as it is, because its base is an instinct, is deficient in self-knowledge. Possessed by the rumours and voices of the haunted country, the borders of which he has passed alone, he never thinks of withdrawing from it to look down upon it from one of the central heights of human life. His power absorbs him, not he it; he cannot turn it round or get without it; he does not estimate its general relation to life. But Coleridge, just because the essence of his talent is the intuition of an idea, commands his talent. He not only feels with Wordsworth the expression of mind in nature, but he can project that feeling outside him, reduce it to a psychological law, define its relation to other elements of culture, place it in a complete view of life.

And in some such activity as that, varied as his wide learning, in a many-sided dramatic kind of poetry, assigning its place and value to every mode of the inward life, seems to have been for Coleridge the original path of artistic success. But in order to follow that path one must hold ideas loosely in the relative spirit, not seek to stereotype any one of the many modes of that life; one must acknowledge that the mind is ever greater than its own products, devote ideas to the service of art rather than of γνῶσις, not disquiet oneself about the absolute. Perhaps Coleridge is more interesting because he did not follow this path. Repressing his artistic interest and voluntarily discolouring his own work, he turned to console and strengthen the human mind, vulgarized or dejected, as he believed, by the acquisition of new knowledge about itself in the *éclaircissement* of the eighteenth century.

What the reader of our own generation will least find in Coleridge's prose writings is the excitement of the literary sense. And yet in those grey volumes we have the production of one who made way ever by a charm, the charm of voice, of aspect, of language, above all, by the intellectual charm of new, moving, luminous ideas. Perhaps the chief offence in Coleridge is an excess of seriousness, a seriousness that arises not from any moral principle, but from a misconception of the perfect manner. There is a certain shade of levity and unconcern, the perfect manner of the eighteenth century, which marks complete culture in the handling of abstract questions. The humanist, he who possesses that complete culture, does not 'weep' over the failure of 'a theory of the quantification of the predicate', nor 'shriek' over the fall of a philosophical formula. A kind of humour is one of the conditions of the true mental attitude in the criticism of past stages of thought. Humanity cannot afford to be too serious about them, any more than a man of good sense can afford to be too serious in looking back upon his own childhood. Plato, whom Coleridge claims as the first of his spiritual ancestors, Plato, as we remember him, a true humanist, with Petrarch and Goethe and M. Renan, holds his theories lightly, glances with a blithe and naïve inconsequence from one view to another, not anticipating the burden of meaning 'views' will one day have for humanity. In reading him one feels how lately it was that Croesus thought it a paradox to say that external prosperity was not necessarily happiness. But on Coleridge lies the whole weight of the sad reflection that has since come into the world, with which for us the air is full, which the children in the market-place repeat to each other. Even his language is forced and broken, lest some saving formula should be lost—'distinctities', 'enucleation', 'pentad of operative Christianity'—he has a whole vocabulary of such phrases, and expects to turn the tide of human thought by fixing the sense of such expressions as 'reason', 'understanding', 'idea'.

Again, he has not the jealousy of the true artist in excluding all associations that have no charm or colour or gladness in them; everywhere he allows the impress of an inferior theological literature; he is often prolix and importunate about most indifferent heroes—Sir Alexander Ball, Dr. Bell, even Dr. Bowyer, the coarse pedant of the Blue-coat School. And the source of all this is closely connected with the source of his literary activity. For Coleridge had chosen as the mark of his literary egotism a kind of intellectual *tour de force*—to found a religious philosophy, to do something with the 'idea' in spite of the essential nature of the 'idea'. And therefore all is fictitious from the beginning. He had determined, that which is humdrum, insipid, which the human spirit has done with, shall yet stimulate and inspire. What he produced symbolizes this purpose—the mass of it *enn.uyant*, depressing: the *Aids to Reflection*, for instance, with Archbishop Leighton's vague pieties all twisted into the jargon of a spiritualistic philosophy. But sometimes 'the pulse of the God's blood' does transmute it, kindling here and there a spot that begins to live; as in that beautiful fragment at the end of the *Church and State*, or in the distilled and concentrated beauty of such a passage as this:

The first range of hills, that encircles the scanty vale of human life, is the horizon for the majority of its inhabitants. On its ridges the common sun is born and departs. From them the stars rise, and touching them they vanish. By the many, even this range, the natural limit and bulwark of the vale, is but imperfectly known. Its higher ascents are too often hidden by mists and clouds from uncultivated swamps, which few have courage or curiosity to penetrate. To the multitude below these vapours appear now as the dark haunts of terrific agents, on which none may intrude with impunity; and now all a-glow, with colours not their own, they are gazed at as the splendid palaces of happiness and power. But in all ages there have been a few who, measuring and sounding the rivers of the vale at the feet of their furthest inaccessible falls, have learned that the sources must be far higher and far inward; a few who, even in the level streams, have detected elements which neither the vale itself nor the surrounding mountains contained or could supply.
Biographia Literaria.

'I was driven from life in motion to life in thought and sensation.' So Coleridge sums up his childhood with its delicacy, its sensitiveness, and passion. From his tenth to his eighteenth year he was at a rough school in London. Speaking of this time, he says:

When I was first plucked up and transplanted from my birthplace and family, Providence, it has often occurred to me, gave me the first intimation that it was my lot, and

that it was best for me, to make or find my way of life a
detached individual, a *terrae filius*, who was to ask love or
service of no one on any more specific relation than that
of being a man, and as such to take my chance for the free
charities of humanity.[1]

Even his fine external nature was for years repressed, wronged, driven inward—'at fourteen I was in a continual state of low fever.' He becomes a dreamer, an eager student, but without ambition.

This depressed boy is nevertheless, on the spiritual side, the child of a noble house. At twenty-five he is exercising a wonderful charm, and has defined for himself a peculiar line of intellectual activity. He had left Cambridge without a degree, a Unitarian. Unable to take orders, he determined through Southey's influence to devote himself to literature. When he left Cambridge there was a prejudice against him which has given occasion to certain suspicions. Those who knew him best discredit these suspicions. What is certain is that he was subject to fits of violent, sometimes fantastic, despondency. He retired to Stowey, in Somersetshire, to study poetry and philosophy. In 1797 his poetical gift was in full flower; he wrote *Kubla Khan*, the first part of *Christabel*, and *The Ancient Mariner*. His literary success grew in spite of opposition. He had a strange attractive gift of conversation, or rather of monologue, as De Staël said, full of *bizarrerie*, with the rapid alternations of a dream, and here and there a sudden summons into a world strange to the hearer, abounding with images drawn from a sort of divided, imperfect life, as of one to whom the external world penetrated only in part, and, blended with all this, passages of the deepest obscurity, precious only for their musical cadence, the echo in Coleridge of the eloquence of the older English writers, of whom he

[1] Biographical Supplement to *Biographia Literaria*, chap. ii.

was so ardent a lover. All through this brilliant course we may discern the power of the Asiatic temperament, of that voluptuousness which is perhaps connected with his appreciation of the intimacy, the almost mystical *rapport*, between man and nature. 'I am much better', he writes, 'and my new and tender health is all over me like a voluptuous feeling.'

And whatever fame, or charm, or life-inspiring gift he has had is the vibration of the interest he excited then, the propulsion into years that clouded his early promise of that first buoyant, irresistible self-assertion: so great is even the indirect power of a sincere effort towards the ideal life, of even a temporary escape of the spirit from routine. Perhaps the surest sign of his election—that he was indeed, on the spiritual side, the child of a noble house—is that story of the Pantisocratic scheme, which at this distance looks so grotesque. In his enthusiasm for the French Revolution, the old communistic dream with its appeal to nature (perhaps a little theatrical), touched him, as it had touched Rousseau, Saint-Pierre, and Chateaubriand. He had married one, his affection for whom seems to have been only a passing feeling; with her and a few friends he was to found a communistic settlement on the banks of the Susquehannah—'the name was pretty and metrical.' It was one of Coleridge's lightest dreams; but also one which could only have passed through the liberal air of his earlier life. The later years of the French Revolution, which for us have discredited all such dreams, deprived him of that youthfulness which is the preservative element in a literary talent.

In 1798, he visited Germany. A beautiful fragment of this period remains, describing a spring excursion to the Brocken. His excitement still vibrates in it. Love, all joyful states of mind, are self-expressive; they loosen the tongue, they fill the thoughts with sensuous images, they harmonize one with the world of sight. We hear of the 'rich graciousness and courtesy' of Coleridge's manner, of the white and delicate skin, the abundant black hair, the full, almost animal lips, that whole physiognomy of the dreamer already touched with fanaticism. One says of the text of one of his Unitarian sermons, 'his voice rose like a stream of rich distilled perfumes'; another, 'he talks like an angel, and does—nothing.'

Meantime, he had designed an intellectual novelty in the shape of a religious philosophy. Socinian theology and the philosophy of Hartley had become distasteful. 'Whatever is against right reason, that no faith can oblige us to believe.' Coleridge quotes these words from Jeremy Taylor. And yet ever since the dawn of the Renaissance, had subsisted a conflict between reason and faith. From the first, indeed, the Christian religion had affirmed the existence of such a conflict, and had even based its plea upon its own weakness in it. In face of the classical culture, with its deep wide-struck roots in the world as it permanently exists, St. Paul asserted the claims of that which could not appeal with success to any genuinely human principle. Paradox as it was, that was the strength of the new spirit; for how much is there at all times in humanity which cannot appeal with success for encouragement or tolerance to any genuinely human principle. In the Middle Ages it might seem that faith had reconciled itself to philosophy; the Catholic church was the leader of the world's life as well as of the spirit's. Looking closer we see that the conflict is still latent there; the supremacy of faith is only a part of the worship of sorrow and weakness which marks the age. The weak are no longer merely a majority, they are all Europe. It is not that faith has become one with reason; but a strange winter, a strange suspension of life, has passed over the classical culture which is only the human reason in its most trenchant form. Glimpse after glimpse, as that pagan culture awoke to life, the conflict was felt once more. It is at the court of Frederick II that the

Renaissance first becomes discernible as an actual power in European society. How definite and unmistakable is the attitude of faith towards that! Ever since the Reformation all phases of theology had been imperfect philosophies—that is, in which there was a religious *arrière pensée*; philosophies which could never be in the ascendant in a sincerely scientific sphere. The two elements had never really mixed. Writers so different as Locke and Taylor have each his liberal philosophy, and each has his defence of the orthodox belief; but, also, each has a divided mind; we wonder how the two elements could have existed side by side; brought together in a single mind, but unable to fuse in it, they reveal their radical contrariety. The Catholic church and humanity are two powers that divide the intellect and spirit of man. On the Catholic side is faith, rigidly logical as Ultramontanism, with a proportion of the facts of life, that is, all that is despairing in life coming naturally under its formula. On the side of humanity is all that is desirable in the world, all that is sympathetic with its laws, and succeeds through that sympathy. Doubtless, for the individual, there are a thousand intermediate shades of opinion, a thousand resting-places for the religious spirit; still, τὸ διορίζειν οὐκ ἔστι τῶν πολλῶν, fine distinctions are not for the majority; and this makes time eventually a dogmatist, working out the opposition in its most trenchant form, and fixing the horns of the dilemma; until, in the present day, we have on one side Pius IX, the true descendant of the fisherman, issuing the Encyclical, pleading the old promise against the world with a special kind of justice; and on the other side, the irresistible modern culture, which, as religious men often remind us, is only Christian accidentally.

The peculiar temper of Coleridge's intellect made the idea of reconciling this conflict very seductive. With a true speculative talent he united a false kind of subtlety and the full share of vanity. A dexterous intellectual *tour de force* has always an independent charm; and therefore it is well for the cause of truth that the directness, sincerity, and naturalness of things are beyond a certain limit sacrificed in vain to a factitious interest. A method so forced as that of Coleridge's religious philosophy is from the first doomed to be insipid, so soon as the temporary interest or taste or curiosity it was designed to meet has passed away. Then, as to the manner of such books as the *Aids to Reflection,* or *The Friend*:—These books came from one whose vocation was in the world of art; and yet, perhaps, of all books that have been influential in modern times, they are farthest from the classical form—bundles of notes— the original matter inseparably mixed up with that borrowed from others—the whole, just that mere preparation for an artistic effect which the finished artist would be careful one day to destroy. Here, again, we have a trait profoundly characteristic of Coleridge. He often attempts to reduce a phase of thought, subtle and exquisite, to conditions too rough for it. He uses a purely speculative gift in direct moral edification. Scientific truth is something fugitive, relative, full of fine gradations; he tries to fix it in absolute formulas. The *Aids to Reflection,* or *The Friend,* is an effort to propagate the volatile spirit of conversation into the less ethereal fabric of a written book; and it is only here and there that the poorer matter becomes vibrant, is really lifted by the spirit.

At forty-two, we find Coleridge saying in a letter:

I feel with an intensity unfathomable by words my utter nothingness, impotence, and worthlessness in and for myself. I have learned what a sin is against an infinite, imperishable being such as is the soul of man. The consolations, at least the sensible sweetness of hope, I do not possess. On the contrary, the temptation which I have constantly to fight up against is a fear that, if annihilation and the possibility of heaven were offered to my choice, I should choose the former.

What was the cause of this change? That is precisely the point on which, after all the gossip there has been, we are still ignorant. At times Coleridge's opium excesses were great; but what led to those excesses must not be left out of account. From boyhood he had a tendency to low fever, betrayed by his constant appetite for bathing and swimming, which he indulged even when a physician had opposed it. In 1803, he went to Malta as secretary to the English Governor. His daughter suspects that the source of the evil was there, that for one of his constitution the climate of Malta was deadly. At all events, when he returned, the charm of those five wonderful years had failed at the source.

De Quincey said of him, 'he wanted better bread than can be made with wheat.' Lamb said of him that from boyhood he had 'hungered for eternity'. Henceforth those are the two notes of his life. From this time we must look for no more true literary talent in him. His style becomes greyer and greyer, his thoughts *outré*, exaggerated, a kind of credulity or superstition exercised upon abstract words. Like Clifford, in Hawthorne's beautiful romance—the born Epicurean, who by some strange wrong has passed the best of his days in a prison—he is the victim of a division of the will, often showing itself in trivial things: he could never choose on which side of the garden path he would walk. In 1803, he wrote a poem on 'The Pains of Sleep'. That unrest increased. Mr. Gillman tells us 'he had long been greatly afflicted with nightmare, and when residing with us was frequently aroused from this painful sleep by any one of the family who might hear him'.

That faintness and continual dissolution had its own consumptive refinements, and even brought, as to the 'Beautiful Soul' in *Wilhelm Meister*, a faint religious ecstasy—that 'singing in the sails' which is not of the breeze. Here, again, is a note of Coleridge's: 'In looking at objects of nature while I am thinking, as at yonder moon, dim-glimmering through the window-pane, I seem rather to be seeking, as it were asking, a symbolical language for something within me that already and for ever exists, than observing anything new. Even when that latter is the case, yet still I have always an obscure feeling, as if that new phenomenon were the dim awaking of a forgotten or hidden truth of my inner nature.' Then, 'while I was preparing the pen to write this remark, I lost the train of thought which had led me to it.'

What a distemper of the eye of the mind! What an almost bodily distemper there is in that!

Coleridge's intellectual sorrows were many; but he had one singular intellectual happiness. With an inborn taste for transcendental philosophy he lived just at the time when that philosophy took an immense spring in Germany, and connected itself with a brilliant literary movement. He had the luck to light upon it in its freshness, and introduce it to his countrymen. What an opportunity for one reared on the colourless English philosophies, but who feels an irresistible attraction towards metaphysical synthesis! How rare are such occasions of intellectual contentment! This transcendental philosophy, chiefly as systematized by Schelling, Coleridge applies, with an eager, unwearied subtlety, to the questions of theology and art-criticism. It is in his theory of art-criticism that he comes nearest to true and important principles; that is the least fugitive part of his work. Let us take this first; here we shall most clearly apprehend his main principle.

What, then, is the essence of this criticism? On the whole it may be described as an attempt to reclaim the world of art as a world of fixed laws—to show that the creative activity of genius and the simplest act of thought are but higher and lower products of the laws of a universal logic. Criticism, feeling its own unsuccess in dealing with the greater works of art, has sometimes made too much of those dark and capricious suggestions of genius which even the intellect possessed by them is unable to track or recall. It has seemed due to their half-sacred character to look for no link between the process by which they were produced and the slighter processes of the mind. Coleridge assumes that the highest phases of thought must be more, not less, than the lower, subjects of law.

With this interest, in the *Biographia Literaria*, he refines Schelling's 'Philosophy of Nature' into a theory of art. 'Es giebt kein Plagiat in der Philosophie' says Heine, alluding to the charge brought against Schelling of unacknowledged borrowing from Bruno, and certainly that which is common to Coleridge and Schelling is of far earlier origin than the Renaissance. Schellingism, the 'Philosophy of Nature', is indeed a constant tradition in the history of thought; it embodies a permanent type of the speculative temper. That mode of conceiving nature as a mirror or reflex of the intelligence of man may be traced up to the first beginnings of Greek speculation. There are two ways of envisaging those aspects of nature which appear to bear the impress of reason or intelligence. There is the deist's way, which regards them merely as marks of design, which separates the informing mind from nature, as the mechanist from the machine; and there is the pantheistic way, which identifies the two, which regards nature itself as the living energy of an intelligence of the same kind as, but vaster than, the human. Greek philosophy, finding indications of mind everywhere, dwelling exclusively in its observations on that which is general or formal, on that which modern criticism regards as the modification of things by the mind of the observer, adopts the latter, or pantheistic way, through the influence of the previous mythological period. Mythology begins in the early necessities of language, of which it is a kind of accident. But at a later period its essence changes; it becomes what it was not at its birth, the servant of a genuine poetic interest, a kind of *vivification* of nature. Played upon by those accidents of language, the Greek mind becomes possessed by the conception of nature as living, thinking, almost speaking to the mind of man. This unfixed poetical prepossession, reduced to an abstract form, petrified into an idea, is the conception which gives a unity of aim to Greek philosophy. Step by step it works out the substance of the Hegelian formula: 'Was ist, das ist vernünftig; was vernünftig ist, das ist'—'Whatever is, is according to reason; whatever is according to reason, that is.' A science of which that could be the formula is still but an intellectual aspiration; the formula of true science is different. Experience, which has gradually saddened the earth's colour, stiffened its motions, withdrawn from it some blithe and debonair presence, has moderated our demands upon science. The positive method makes very little account of marks of intelligence in nature; in its wider view of phenomena it sees that those incidents are a minority, and may rank as happy coincidences; it absorbs them in the simpler conception of law. But the suspicion of a mind latent in nature, struggling for release and intercourse with the intellect of man through true ideas, has never ceased to haunt a certain class of minds. Started again and again in successive periods by enthusiasts on the antique pattern, in each case the thought has seemed paler and more evanescent amidst the growing consistency and sharpness of outline of other and more positive forms of knowledge. Still, wherever a speculative instinct has been united with extreme inwardness of temperament, as in Jakob Böhme, there the old Greek conception, like some seed floating in the air, has taken root and sprung up anew. Coleridge, thrust inward upon himself, driven from 'life in thought and sensation' to life in thought only, feels in that dark London school a thread of the Greek mind vibrating strangely in him. At fifteen he is discoursing on Plotinus, and has translated the hymns of Synesius. So in later years he reflects from Schelling the flitting tradition. He conceives a subtle co-ordination between the ideas of the mind and the laws of the natural world. Science is to be attained, not by observation, analysis, generalization, but by the evolution or recovery of those ideas from within, by a sort of ἀνάμνησις, every group of observed facts remaining an enigma until the appropriate idea is struck upon them from the mind of Newton or Cuvier, the genius in whom sympathy with the universal reason is entire. Next he supposes that this reason or intelligence in nature gradually becomes reflective—self-conscious. He fancies he can track through all the simpler orders of life fragments of an eloquent prophecy about the human mind. He regards the whole of nature as a development of higher forms out of the lower, through shade after shade of systematic change. The dim stir of chemical atoms towards the axes of a crystal form, the trance-like life of plants, the animal troubled by strange irritabilities, are stages which anticipate consciousness. All through that increasing stir of life this was forming itself; each stage in its unsatisfied susceptibilities seeming to be drawn out of its own limits by the more pronounced current of life on its confines, the 'shadow of approaching humanity' gradually deepening, the latent intelligence working to the surface. At this point the law of development does not lose itself in caprice; rather it becomes more constraining and incisive. From the lowest to the highest acts of intelligence, there is another range of refining shades. Gradually the mind concentrates itself, frees itself from the limits of the particular, the individual, attains a strange power of modifying and centralizing what it receives from without according to an inward ideal. At last, in imaginative genius, ideas become effective; the intelligence of nature, with all its elements connected and justified, is clearly reflected; and the interpretation of its latent purposes is fixed in works of art.

In this fanciful and bizarre attempt to rationalize art, to range it under the dominion of law, there is still a gap to be filled up. What is that common law of the mind, of which a work of art and the slighter acts of thought are alike products? Here Coleridge weaves in Kant's fine-spun theory of the transformation of sense into perception. What every theory of perception has to explain is that associative power which gathers isolated sensible qualities into the objects of the world about us. Sense, without an associative power, would be only a threadlike stream of colours, sounds, odours—each struck upon one for a moment, and then withdrawn. The basis of this association may be represented as a material one, a kind of many-coloured 'etching' on the brain. Hartley has dexterously handled this hypothesis. The charm of his 'theory of vibrations' is the vivid image it presents to the fancy. How large an element in a speculative talent is the command of these happy images! Coleridge, by a finer effort of the same kind, a greater delicacy of fancy, detects all sorts of slips, transitions, breaks of continuity in Hartley's glancing cobweb. Coleridge, with Kant, regards all association as effected by a power within, to which he gives a fanciful Greek name.[1] In an act of perception there is the matter which sense presents, colour, tone, feeling; but also a form or mould, such as space, unity, causation, suggested from within. In these forms we arrest and frame the many attributes of sense. It is like that simple chemical phenomenon where two colourless fluids uniting reflect a full colour. Neither matter nor form can be perceived asunder; they unite into the many-coloured image of life. This theory has not been able to bear a loyal induction. Even if it were true, how little it would tell us; how it attenuates fact! There, again, the charm is all in the clear image;

[1] Esemplastic.

the image of the artist combining a few elementary colours, curves, sounds into a new whole. Well, this power of association, of concentrating many elements of sense in an object of perception, is refined and deepened into the creative acts of imagination.

We of the modern ages have become so familiarized with the greater works of art that we are little sensitive of the act of creation in them; they do not impress us as a new presence in the world. Only sometimes in productions which realize immediately a profound emotion and enforce a change in taste, such as *Werther* or *Emile*, we are actual witnesses of the moulding of an unforeseen type by some new principle of association. By imagination, the distinction between which and fancy is so thrust upon his readers, Coleridge means a vigorous act of association, which, by simplifying and restraining their natural expression to an artificial order, refines and perfects the types of human passion. It represents the excitements of the human kind, but reflected in a new manner, 'excitement itself imitating order.' 'Originally the offspring of passion,' he somewhere says, 'but now the adopted children of power.' So far there is nothing new or distinctive; every one who can receive from a poem or picture a total impression will admit so much. What makes the view distinctive in Coleridge are the Schellingistic associations with which he colours it, that faint glamour of the philosophy of nature which was ever influencing his thoughts. That suggested the idea of a subtly winding parallel, a 'rapport' in every detail, between the human mind and the world without it, laws of nature being so many transformed ideas. Conversely, the ideas of the human mind would be only transformed laws. Genius would be in a literal sense an exquisitely purged sympathy with nature. Those associative conceptions of the imagination, those unforeseen types of passion, would come, not so much of the artifice and invention of the understanding, as from self-surrender to the suggestions of nature;

they would be evolved by the stir of nature itself realizing the highest reach of its latent intelligence; they would have a kind of antecedent necessity to rise at some time to the surface of the human mind.

It is natural that Shakespeare should be the idol of all such criticism, whether in England or Germany. The first effect in Shakespeare is that of capricious detail, of the waywardness that plays with the parts careless of the impression of the whole. But beyond there is the constraining unity of effect, the uneffaceable impression, of *Hamlet* or *Macbeth*. His hand moving freely is curved round by some law of gravitation from within; that is, there is the most constraining unity in the most abundant variety. Coleridge exaggerates this unity into something like the unity of a natural organism, the associative act that effected it into something closely akin to the primitive power of nature itself. 'In the Shakespearian drama', he says, 'there is a vitality which grows and evolves itself from within.' Again:

He, too, worked in the spirit of nature, by evolving the germ from within by the imaginative power according to the idea. For as the power of seeing is to light, so is an idea in mind to a law in nature. They are correlatives which suppose each other.

Again:

The organic form is innate; it shapes, as it develops, itself from within, and the fulness of its development is one and the same with the perfection of its outward form. Such as the life is, such is the form. Nature, the prime genial artist, inexhaustible in diverse powers, is equally inexhaustible in forms; each exterior is the physiognomy of the being within, and even such is the appropriate excellence of Shakespeare, himself a nature humanized, a genial understanding, directing self-consciously a power and an implicit wisdom deeper even than our consciousness.

There 'the absolute' has been affirmed in the sphere of art; and thought begins to congeal. Coleridge has not only overstrained the elasticity of his hypothesis, but has also obscured the true interest of art. For, after all, the artist has become something almost mechanical; instead of being the most luminous and self-possessed phase of consciousness, the associative act itself looks like some organic process of assimilation. The work of art is sometimes likened to the living organism. That expresses the impression of a self-delighting, independent life which a finished work of art gives us; it does not express the process by which that work was produced. Here there is no blind ferment of lifeless elements to realize a type. By exquisite analysis the artist attains clearness of idea, then, by many stages of refining, clearness of expression. He moves slowly over his work, calculating the tenderest tone, and restraining the subtlest curve, never letting his hand or fancy move at large, gradually refining flaccid spaces to the higher degree of expressiveness. Culture, at least, values even in transcendent works of art the power of the understanding in them, their logical process of construction, the spectacle of supreme intellectual dexterity which they afford.

Coleridge's criticism may well be remembered as part of the long pleading of German culture for the things 'behind the veil'. It recalls us from the work of art to the mind of the artist; and, after all, this is what is infinitely precious, and the work of art only as the index of it. Still, that is only the narrower side of a complete criticism. Perhaps it is true, as some one says in Lessing's *Emilia Galotti*, that, if Michael Angelo had been born without hands, he would still have been the greatest of artists. But we must admit the truth also of an opposite view: 'In morals as in art', says M. Renan, 'the word is nothing—the fact is everything. The idea which lurks under a picture of Raphael is a slight matter; it is the picture itself only that counts.'

What constitutes an artistic gift is, first of all, a natural susceptibility to moments of strange excitement, in which the colours freshen upon our threadbare world, and the routine of things about us is broken by a novel and happier synthesis. These are moments into which other minds may be made to enter, but which they cannot originate. This susceptibility is the element of genius in an artistic gift. Secondly, there is what may be called the talent of projection, of throwing these happy moments into an external concrete form—a statue, or play, or picture. That projection is of all degrees of completeness; its facility and transparence are modified by the circumstances of the individual, his culture, and his age. When it is perfectly transparent, the work is classical. Compare the power of projection in Mr. Browning's *Sordello*, with that power in the *Sorrows of Werther*. These two elements determine the two chief aims of criticism. First, it has to classify those initiative moments according to the amount of interest excited in them, to estimate their comparative acceptability, their comparative power of giving joy to those who undergo them. Secondly, it has to test, by a study of the artistic product itself, in connexion with the intellectual and spiritual condition of its age, the completeness of the projection. These two aims form the positive, or concrete, side of criticism; their direction is not towards a metaphysical definition of the universal element in an artistic effort, but towards a subtle gradation of the shades of difference between one artistic gift and another. This side of criticism is infinitely varied; and it is what French culture more often achieves than the German.

Coleridge has not achieved this side in an equal degree with the other; and this want is not supplied by the *Literary Remains*, which contain his studies on Shakespeare. There we have a repetition, not an application, of the absolute formula. Coleridge is like one who sees in a picture only the rules of perspective, and is always trying to simplify even those. Thus: 'Where there is no humour, but only wit, or the like, there is no growth from within.' 'What is beauty'? he asks. 'It is the unity of the manifold, the coalescence of the diverse.' So of Dante: 'There is a total impression of infinity; the wholeness is not in vision or conception, but in an inner feeling of totality and absolute being.' Again, of the *Paradise Lost*: 'It has the totality of the poem as distinguished from the *ab ovo* birth and parentage or straight line of history.'

That exaggerated inwardness is barren. Here, too, Coleridge's thoughts require to be thawed, to be set in motion. He is admirable in the detection, the analysis, and statement of a few of the highest general laws of art-production. But he withdraws us too far from what we can see, hear, and feel. Doubtless, the idea, the intellectual element, is the spirit and life of art. Still, art is the triumph of the senses and the emotions; and the senses and the emotions must not be cheated of their triumph after all. That strange and beautiful psychology which he employs, with its evanescent delicacies, has not sufficient corporeity. Again, one feels that the discussion about Hartley, meeting us in the way, throws a tone of insecurity over the critical theory which it introduces. Its only effect is to win for the terms in which that criticism is expressed, the associations of one side in a metaphysical controversy.

The vagueness and fluidity of Coleridge's theological opinions have been exaggerated through an illusion, which has arisen from the occasional form in which they have reached us. Criticism, then, has to methodize and focus them. They may be arranged under three heads; the general principles of supernaturalism, orthodox dogmas, the interpretation of Scripture. With regard to the first and second, Coleridge ranks as a Conservative thinker; but his principles of Scriptural interpretation resemble Lessing's; they entitle him to be regarded as the founder of the modern liberal school of English theology. By supernaturalism is meant the theory of a divine person in immediate communication with the human mind, dealing with it out of that order of nature which includes man's body and his ordinary trains of thought, according to fixed laws, which the theologian sums up in the doctrines of 'grace' and 'sin'. Of this supernaturalism, the *Aids to Reflection* attempts to give a metaphysical proof. The first necessity of the argument is to prove that religion, with its supposed experiences of grace and sin, and the realities of a world above the world of sense, is the fulfilment of the constitution of every man, or, in the language of the 'philosophy of nature', is part of the 'idea' of man; so that, when those experiences are absent, all the rest of his nature is unexplained, like some enigmatical fragment, the construction and working of which we cannot surmise. According to Schelling's principle, the explanation of every phase of life is to be sought in that next above it. This axiom is applied to three supposed stages of man's reflective life: Prudence, Morality, Religion. Prudence, by which Coleridge means something like Bentham's 'enlightened principle of self-preservation', is, he says, an inexplicable instinct, a blind motion in the dark, until it is expanded into morality. Morality, again, is but a groundless prepossession until transformed into a religious recognition of a spiritual world, until, as Coleridge says in his rich figurative language, 'like the main feeder into some majestic lake, rich with hidden springs of its own, it flows into, and becomes one with, the spiritual life.' A spiritual life, then, being the fulfilment of human nature, implied, if we see clearly, in those instincts which enable one to live on from day to day, is part of the 'idea' of man.

The second necessity of the argument is to prove that 'the idea', according to the principle of the 'philosophy of nature', is an infallible index of the actual condition of the world without us. Here Coleridge introduces an analogy:

In the world, we see everywhere evidences of a unity,

which the component parts are so far from explaining, that they necessarily presuppose it as the cause and condition of their existing as those parts, or even of their existing at all. This antecedent unity, or cause and principle of each union, it has, since the time of Bacon and Kepler, been customary to call a law. This crocus for instance; or any other flower the reader may have before his sight, or choose to bring before his fancy; that the root, stem, leaves, petals, &c., cohere to one plant is owing to an antecedent power or principle in the seed which existed before a single particle of the matters that constitute the size and visibility of the crocus had been attracted from the surrounding soil, air, and moisture. Shall we turn to the seed? there, too, the same necessity meets us: an antecedent unity must here, too, be supposed. Analyse the seeds with the finest tools, and let the solar microscope come in aid of your senses, what do you find?—means and instruments; a wondrous fairy tale of nature, magazines of food, stores of various sorts, pipes, spiracles, defences; a house of many chambers, and the owner and inhabitant invisible.

Aids to Reflection.

Nature, that is, works by what we may call 'intact ideas'. It co-ordinates every part of the crocus to all the other parts; one stage of its growth to the whole process; and having framed its organism to assimilate certain external elements, it does not cheat it of those elements, soil, air, moisture. Well, if the 'idea' of man is to be intact, he must be enveloped in a supernatural world; and nature always works by intact ideas. The spiritual life is the highest development of the idea of man; there must be a supernatural world corresponding to it.

One finds, it is hard to say how many, difficulties in drawing Coleridge's conclusion. To mention only one of them—the argument looks too like the exploded doctrine of final causes. Of course the crocus would not live unless the conditions of its life were supplied. The flower is made for soil, air, moisture, and it has them; just as man's senses are made for a sensible world, and we have the sensible world. But give the flower the power of dreaming, nourish it on its own reveries, put man's wild hunger of heart and susceptibility to *ennui* in it, and what indication of the laws of the world without it, would be afforded by its longing to break its bonds?

In theology people are content with analogies, probabilities, with the empty schemes of arguments for which the data are still lacking; arguments, the rejection of which Coleridge tells us implies 'an evil heart of unbelief', but of which we might as truly say that they derive all their consistency from the peculiar atmosphere of the mind which receives them. Such arguments are received in theology because what chains men to a religion is not its claim on their reason, their hopes or fears, but the glow it affords to the world, its 'beau ideal'. Coleridge thinks that if we reject the supernatural, the spiritual element in life will evaporate also, that we shall have to accept a life with narrow horizons, without disinterestedness, harshly cut off from the springs of life in the past. But what is this spiritual element? It is the passion for inward perfection, with its sorrows, its aspirations, its joy. These mental states are the delicacies of the higher morality of the few, of Augustine, of the author of the 'Imitation', of Francis de Sales; in their essence they are only the permanent characteristics of the higher life. Augustine, or the author of the 'Imitation', agreeably to the culture of their age, had expressed them in the terms of a metaphysical theory, and expanded them into what theologians call the doctrines of grace and sin, the fluctuations of the union of the soul with its unseen friend. The life of those who are capable of a passion for perfection still produces the same mental states; but that religious expression of them is no longer congruous with the culture of the age. Still, all inward life works itself out in a few simple forms, and culture cannot go very far before the religious graces reappear in it in a subtilized intellectual shape. There are aspects of the religious character which have an artistic worth distinct from their religious import. Longing, a chastened temper, spiritual joy, are precious states of mind, not because they are part of man's duty or because God has commanded them, still less because they are means of obtaining a reward, but because like culture itself they are remote, refined, intense, existing only by the triumph of a few over a dead world of routine in which there is no lifting of the soul at all. If there is no other world, art in its own interest must cherish such characteristics as beautiful spectacles. Stephen's face, 'like the face of an angel', has a worth of its own, even if the opened heaven is but a dream.

Our culture, then, is not supreme, our intellectual life is incomplete, we fail of the intellectual throne, if we have no inward longing, inward chastening, inward joy. Religious belief, the craving for objects of belief, may be refined out of our hearts, but they must leave their sacred perfume, their spiritual sweetness behind. This law of the highest intellectual life has sometimes seemed hard to understand. Those who maintain the claims of the older and narrower forms of religious life against the claims of culture are often embarrassed at finding the intellectual life heated through with the very graces to which they would sacrifice it. How often in the higher class of theological writings—writings which really spring from an original religious genius, such as those of Dr. Newman —does the modern aspirant to perfect culture seem to find the expression of the inmost delicacies of his own life, the same yet different! The spiritualities of the Christian life have often drawn men on, little by little, into the broader spiritualities of systems opposed to it—pantheism, or positivism, or a philosophy of indifference. Many in our own generation, through religion, have become dead to religion. How often do we have to look for some feature of the ancient religious life, not in a modern saint, but in a modern artist or philosopher! For those who have passed out of Christianity, perhaps its most precious souvenir is the ideal of a transcendental disinterestedness. Where shall we look for this ideal? In Spinoza; or perhaps in Bentham or in Austin.

Some of those who have wished to save supernaturalism—as, for instance, Theodore Parker—have rejected more or less entirely the dogmas of the Church. Coleridge's instinct is truer than theirs; the two classes of principles are logically connected. It was in defence of the dogmas of the Church that Coleridge elaborated his unhappy crotchet of the diversity of the reason from the understanding. The weakness of these dogmas had ever been, not so much a failure of the authority of Scripture or tradition in their favour, as their conflict with the reason that they were words rather than conceptions. That analysis of words and conceptions which in modern philosophy has been a principle of continual rejuvenescence with Descartes and Berkeley, as well as with Bacon and Locke, had desolated the field of scholastic theology. It is the rationality of the dogmas of that theology that Coleridge had a taste for proving.

Of course they conflicted with the understanding, with the common daylight of the mind, but then might there not be some mental faculty higher than the understanding? The history of philosophy supplied many authorities for this opinion. Then, according to the 'philosophy of nature', science and art are both grounded upon the 'ideas' of genius, which are a kind of intuition, which are their own evidence. Again, this philosophy was always saying the ideas of the mind must be true, must correspond to reality; and what an aid to faith is that, if one is not too nice in distinguishing between ideas and mere convictions, or prejudices, or habitual views, or safe opinions! Kant also had made a distinction between the reason and the understanding. True, this harsh division of mental faculties is exactly what is most sterile in Kant, the essential tendency of the German school of thought being to show that the mind always acts *en masse.* Kant had defined two senses of reason as opposed to the understanding. First, there was the 'speculative reason', with its 'three categories of totality', God, the soul, and the universe—three mental forms which might give a sort of unity to science, but to which no actual intuition corresponded. The tendency of this part of Kant's critique is to destroy the rational groundwork of theism. Then there was the 'practical reason', on the relation of which to the 'speculative', we may listen to Heinrich Heine:

'After the tragedy comes the farce. [The tragedy is Kant's destructive criticism of the speculative reason.] So far Immanuel Kant has been playing the relentless philosopher; he has laid siege to heaven.' Heine goes on with some violence to describe the havoc Kant has made of the orthodox belief: 'Old Lampe,[1] with the umbrella under his arm, stands looking on much disturbed, perspiration and tears of sorrow running down his cheeks. Then Immanuel Kant grows pitiful, and shows that he is not only a great philosopher but also a good man. He considers a little; and then, half in good nature, half in irony, he says, "Old Lampe must have a god, otherwise the poor man will not be happy; but man ought to be happy in this life, the practical reason says that; let the practical reason stand surety for the existence of a god; it is all the same to me." Following this argument, Kant distinguishes between the theoretical and the practical reason, and, with the practical reason for a magic wand, he brings to life the dead body of deism, which the theoretical reason had slain.'

Coleridge first confused the speculative reason with the practical, and then exaggerated the variety and the sphere of their combined functions. Then he has given no consistent definition of the reason. It is 'the power of universal and necessary convictions'; it is 'the knowledge of the laws of the whole considered as one'; it is 'the science of all as a whole'. Again, the understanding is 'the faculty judging according to

[1] The servant who attended Kant in his walks.

sense', or 'the faculty of means to mediate ends'; and so on. The conception floating in his mind seems to have been a really valuable one; that, namely, of a distinction between an organ of adequate and an organ of inadequate ideas. But when we find him casting about for a definition, not precisely determining the functions of the reason, making long preparations for the 'deduction' of the faculty, as in the third volume of *The Friend*, but never actually starting, we suspect that the reason is a discovery in psychology which Coleridge has a good will to make, and that is all; that he has got no farther than the old vague desire to escape from the limitations of thought by some extraordinary mystical faculty. Some of the clergy eagerly welcomed the supposed discovery. In their difficulties they had often appealed in the old simple way to sentiment and emotion as of higher authority than the understanding, and on the whole had had to get on with very little philosophy. Like M. Jourdain, they were amazed to find that they had been all the time appealing to the reason; now they might actually go out to meet the enemy. Orthodoxy might be cured by a hair of the dog that had bitten it.

Theology is a great house, scored all over with hieroglyphics by perished hands. When we decipher one of these hieroglyphics, we find in it the statement of a mistaken opinion; but knowledge has crept onward since the hand dropped from the wall; we no longer entertain the opinion, and we can trace the origin of the mistake. Dogmas are precious as memorials of a class of sincere and beautiful spirits, who in a past age of humanity struggled with many tears, if not for true knowledge, yet for a noble and elevated happiness. That struggle is the substance, the dogma only its shadowy expression; received traditionally in an altered age, it is the shadow of a shadow, a mere τρίτον εἴδωλον, twice removed from substance and reality. The true method then in the treatment of dogmatic theology must be historical.

Englishmen are gradually finding out how much that method has done since the beginning of modern criticism by the hands of such writers as Baur. Coleridge had many of the elements of this method: learning, inwardness, a subtle psychology, a dramatic power of sympathy with modes of thought other than his own. Often in carrying out his own method he gives the true historical origin of a dogma, but, with a strange dullness of the historical sense, he regards this as a reason for the existence of the dogma now, not merely as reason for its having existed in the past. Those historical elements he could not envisage in the historical method, because this method is only one of the applications, the most fruitful of them all, of the relative spirit.

After Coleridge's death, seven letters of his on the inspiration of Scripture were published, under the title of *Confessions of an Inquiring Spirit*. This little book has done more than any other of Coleridge's writings to discredit his name with the orthodox. The frequent occurrence in it of the word 'bibliolatry', borrowed from Lessing, would sufficiently account for this pious hatred. From bibliolatry Coleridge was saved by the spiritualism, which, in questions less simple than that of the infallibility of Scripture, was so retarding to his culture. Bibliolators may remember that one who committed a kind of intellectual suicide by catching at any appearance of a fixed and absolute authority, never dreamed of resting on the authority of a book. His Schellingistic notion of the possibility of absolute knowledge, of knowing God, of a light within every man which might discover to him the doctrines of Christianity, tended to depreciate historical testimony, perhaps historical realism altogether. Scripture is a legitimate sphere for the understanding. He says, indeed, that there is more in the Bible that 'finds' him than he has experienced in all other books put together. But still, 'There is a Light higher than all, even the Word that was in the beginning. If between this Word and the written letter I shall anywhere seem to myself to find a discrepance, I will not conclude that such there actually is; nor on the other hand will I fall under the condemnation of them that would lie for God, but seek as I may, be thankful for what I have—and wait.' Coleridge is the inaugurator of that *via media* of Scriptural criticism which makes much of saving the word 'inspiration', while it attenuates its meaning; which supposes a sort of modified inspiration residing in the whole, not in the several parts. 'The Scriptures were not dictated by an infallible intelligence;' nor 'the writers each and all divinely informed as well as inspired'. 'They refer to other documents, and in all points express themselves as sober-minded and veracious writers under ordinary circumstances are known to do.' To make the Bible itself 'the subject of a special article of faith, is an unnecessary and useless abstraction'.

His judgement on the popular view of inspiration is severe. It is borrowed from the Cabbalists; it 'petrifies at once the whole body of Holy Writ, with all its harmonies and symmetrical gradations;—turns it at once into a colossal Memnon's head, a hollow passage for a voice, a voice that mocks the voices of many men, and speaks in their names, and yet is but one voice and the same;—and no man uttered it and never in a human heart was it conceived'. He presses very hard on the tricks of the 'routiniers of desk and pulpit'; forced and fantastic interpretations; 'the strange—in all other writings unexampled—practice of bringing together into logical dependency detached sentences from books composed at the distance of centuries, nay, sometimes a millennium, from each other, under different dispensations, and for different objects.'

Certainly he is much farther from bibliolatry than from the perfect freedom of the humanist interpreters. Still he has not freed himself from the notion of a sacred canon; he cannot regard the books of Scripture simply as fruits of the human spirit; his criticism is not entirely disinterested. The difficulties he finds are chiefly the supposed immoralities of Scripture; just those difficulties which fade away before the modern or relative spirit, which in the moral world, as in the physical, traces everywhere change, growth, development. Of historical difficulties, of those deeper moral difficulties which arise, for instance, from a consideration of the constitutional unveracity of the Oriental mind, he has no suspicion. He thinks that no book of the New Testament was composed so late as A.D. 120.

Coleridge's undeveloped opinions would be hardly worth stating except for the warning they afford against retarding compromises. In reading these letters one never doubts what Coleridge tells us of himself: 'that he loved truth with an indescribable awe,' or, as he beautifully says, 'that he would creep towards the light, even if the light had made its way through a rent in the wall of the temple.' And yet there is something sad in reading them by the light which twenty-five years have thrown back upon them. Taken as a whole, they contain a fallacy which a very ardent lover of truth might have detected.

The Bible is not to judge the spirit, but the spirit the Bible. The Bible is to be treated as a literary product. Well, but that is a conditional, not an absolute principle—that is not, if we regard it sincerely, a delivery of judgement, but only a suspension of it. If we are true to the spirit of that, we must wait patiently the complete result of modern criticism. Coleridge states that the authority of Scripture is on its trial—that at present it is not known to be an absolute resting-place; and then, instead of leaving that to aid in the formation of a fearless spirit, the spirit which, for instance, would accept the results of M. Renan's investigations, he turns it into a false security by anticipating the judgement of an undeveloped criticism. Twenty-five years of that criticism have gone by, and have hardly verified the anticipation.

The man of science asks, Are absolute principles attainable? What are the limits of knowledge? The answer he receives from science itself is not ambiguous. What the moralist asks is, Shall we gain or lose by surrendering human life to the relative spirit? Experience answers, that the dominant tendency of life is to turn ascertained truth into a dead letter—to make us all the phlegmatic servants of routine. The relative spirit, by dwelling constantly on the more fugitive conditions or circumstances of things, breaking through a thousand rough and brutal classifications, and giving elasticity to inflexible principles, begets an intellectual finesse, of which the ethical result is a delicate and tender justness in the criticism of human life. Who would gain more than Coleridge by criticism in such a spirit? We know how his life has appeared when judged by absolute standards. We see him trying to apprehend the absolute, to stereotype one form of faith, to attain, as he says, 'fixed principles' in politics, morals, and religion; to fix one mode of life as the essence of life, refusing to see the parts as parts only; and all the time his own pathetic history pleads for a more elastic moral philosophy than his, and cries out against every formula less living and flexible than life itself.

'From his childhood he hungered for eternity.' After all, that is the incontestable claim of Coleridge. The perfect flower of any elementary type of life must always be precious to humanity, and Coleridge is the perfect flower of the romantic type. More than Childe Harold, more than Werther, more than René, Coleridge, by what he did, what he was, and what he failed to do, represents that inexhaustible discontent, languor, and home-sickness, the chords of which ring all through our modern literature. Criticism may still discuss the claims of classical and romantic art, or literature, or sentiment; and perhaps one day we may come to forget the horizon, with full knowledge to be content with what is here and now;

and that is the essence of classical feeling. But by us of the present moment, by us for whom the Greek spirit, with its engaging naturalness, simple, chastened, debonair, τρυφῆς, ἀβρότητος, χλιδῆς, χαρίτων, ἱμέρου πόθου πατήρ, is itself the Sangraal of an endless pilgrimage, Coleridge, with his passion for the absolute, for something fixed where all is moving, his faintness, his broken memory, his intellectual disquiet, may still be ranked among the interpreters of one of the constituent elements of our life.

RALPH WALDO EMERSON
1803–1882
SHAKESPEARE; OR, THE POET
[From *Representative Men*, 1850]

GREAT men are more distinguished by range and extent than by originality. If we require the originality which consists in weaving, like a spider, their web from their own bowels; in finding clay, and making bricks, and building the house; no great men are original. Nor does valuable originality consist in unlikeness to other men. The hero is in the press of knights, and the thick of events; and, seeing what men want, and sharing their desire, he adds the needful length of sight and of arm, to come at the desired point. The greatest genius is the most indebted man. A poet is no rattlebrain, saying what comes uppermost, and, because he says everything, saying, at last, something good; but a heart in unison with his time and country. There is nothing whimsical and fantastic in his production, but sweet and sad earnest, freighted with the weightiest convictions, and pointed with the most determined aim which any man or class knows of in his times.

The Genius of our life is jealous of individuals, and will not have any individual great, except through the general. There is no choice to genius. A great man does not wake up on some fine morning, and say, 'I am full of life, I will go to sea, and find an Antarctic continent: to-day I will square the circle: I will ransack botany, and find a new food for man: I have a new architecture in my mind: I foresee a new mechanic power:' no, but he finds himself in the river of the thoughts and events, forced onward by the ideas and necessities of his contemporaries. He stands where all the eyes of men look one way, and their hands all point in the direction in which he should go. The church has reared him amidst rites and pomps, and he carries out the advice which her music gave him, and builds a cathedral needed by her chants and processions. He finds a war raging: it educates him, by trumpet, in barracks, and he betters the instruction. He finds two counties groping to bring coal, or flour, or fish, from the place of production to the place of consumption, and he hits on a railroad. Every master has found his material collected, and his power lay in his sympathy with his people, and in his love of the materials he wrought in. What an economy of power! and what a compensation for the shortness of life! All is done to his hand. The world has brought him thus far on his way. The human race has gone out before him, sunk the hills, filled the hollows, and bridged the rivers. Men, nations, poets, artisans, women, all have worked for him, and he enters into their labours. Choose any other thing, out of the line of tendency, out of the national feeling and history, and he would have all to do for himself; his powers would be expended in the first preparations. Great genial power, one would almost say, consists in not being original at all; in being altogether receptive; in letting the world do all, and suffering the spirit of the hour to pass unobstructed through the mind.

Shakespeare's youth fell in a time when the English people were importunate for dramatic entertainments. The court took offence easily at political allusions, and attempted to suppress them. The Puritans, a growing and energetic party, and the religious among the Anglican church, would suppress them. But the people wanted them. Inn-yards, houses without roofs, and extemporaneous enclosures at country fairs, were the ready theatres of strolling players. The people had tasted this new joy; and, as we could not hope to suppress newspapers now,—no, not by the strongest party,—neither then could king, prelate, or puritan, alone or united, suppress an organ, which was ballad, epic, newspaper, caucus, lecture, punch, and library, at the same time. Probably king, prelate, and puritan, all found their own account in it. It had become, by all causes, a national interest,—by no means conspicuous, so that some great scholar would have thought of treating it in an English history,—but not a whit less considerable, because it was cheap, and of no account, like a baker's shop. The best proof of its vitality is the crowd of writers which suddenly broke into this field: Kyd, Marlowe, Greene, Jonson, Chapman, Dekker, Webster, Heywood, Middleton, Peele, Ford, Massinger, Beaumont, and Fletcher.

The secure possession, by the stage, of the public mind, is of the first importance to the poet who works for it. He loses no time in idle experiments. Here is audience and expectation prepared. In the case of Shakespeare, there is much more. At the time when he left Stratford, and went up to London, a great body of stage-plays, of all dates and writers, existed in manuscript, and were in turn produced on the boards. Here is the Tale of Troy, which the audience will bear hearing some part of every week; the Death of Julius Cæsar, and other stories out of Plutarch, which they never tire of; a shelf full of English history, from the chronicles of Brut and Arthur, down to the royal Henries, which men hear eagerly; and a string of doleful tragedies, merry Italian tales, and Spanish voyages, which all the London prentices know. All the mass has been treated, with more or less skill, by every playwright, and the prompter has the soiled and tattered manuscripts. It is now no longer possible to say who wrote them first. They have been the property of the Theatre so long, and so many rising geniuses have enlarged or altered them, inserting a speech, or a whole scene, or adding a song, that no man can any longer claim copyright in this work of numbers. Happily, no man wishes to. They are not yet desired in that way. We have few readers, many spectators and hearers. They had best lie where they are.

Shakespeare, in common with his comrades, esteemed the mass of old plays, waste stock, in which any experiment could be freely tried. Had the *prestige* which hedges about a modern tragedy existed, nothing could have been done. The rude warm blood of the living England circulated in the play, as in street-ballads, and gave body which he wanted to his airy and majestic fancy. The poet needs a ground in popular tradition on which he may work, and which, again, may restrain his art within the due temperance. It holds him to the people, supplies a foundation for his edifice; and, in furnishing so much work done to his hand, leaves him at leisure, and in full strength for the audacities of his imagination. In short, the poet owes to his legend what sculpture owed to the temple. Sculpture in Egypt, and in Greece, grew up in subordination to architecture. It was the ornament of the temple wall: at first, a rude relief carved on pediments, then the relief became bolder, and a head or arm was projected from the wall, the groups being still arranged with reference to the building, which serves also as a frame to hold the figures; and when, at last, the greatest freedom of style and treatment was reached, the prevailing genius of architecture still enforced a certain calmness and continence in the statue. As soon as the statue was begun for itself, and with no reference to the temple or palace, the art began to decline; freak, extravagance, and exhibition, took the place of the old temperance. This balance-wheel, which the sculptor found in architecture, the perilous irritability of poetic talent found in the accumulated dramatic materials to which the people were already wonted, and which had a certain excellence which no single genius, however extraordinary, could hope to create.

In point of fact, it appears that Shakespeare did owe debts in all directions, and was able to use whatever he found; and the amount of indebtedness may be inferred from Malone's laborious computations in regard to the First, Second, and Third parts of *Henry VI*, in which, 'out of 6043 lines, 1771 were written by some author preceding Shakespeare; 2373 by him, on the foundation laid by his predecessors; and 1899 were entirely his own.' And the proceeding investigation hardly leaves a single drama of his absolute invention. Malone's sentence is an important piece of external history. In *Henry VIII*, I think I see plainly the cropping out of the original rock on which his own finer stratum was laid. The first play was written by a superior, thoughtful man, with a vicious ear. I can mark his lines, and know well their cadence. See Wolsey's soliloquy, and the following scene with Cromwell, where,—instead of the metre of Shakespeare, whose secret is, that the thought constructs the tune, so that reading for the sense will best bring out the rhythm,—here the lines are constructed on a given tune, and the verse has even a trace of pulpit eloquence. But the play contains, through all its length, unmistakable traits of Shakespeare's hand, and some passages, as the account of the coronation, are like autographs. What is odd, the compliment to Queen Elizabeth is in the bad rhythm.

Shakespeare knew that tradition supplies a better fable than any invention can. If he lost any credit of design, he augmented his resources; and, at that day, our petulant demand for originality was not so much pressed. There was no literature for the million. The universal reading, the cheap press, were unknown. A great poet, who appears in illiterate times, absorbs into his sphere all the light which is anywhere radiating. Every intellectual jewel, every flower of sentiment, it is his fine office to bring to his people; and he comes to value his memory equally with his invention. He is therefore little solicitous whence his thoughts have been derived; whether through translation, whether through tradition, whether by travel in distant countries, whether by inspiration; from whatever source, they are equally welcome to his uncritical audience. Nay, he borrows very near home. Other men say wise things as well as he; only they say a good many foolish things, and do not know when they have spoken wisely. He knows the sparkle of the true stone, and puts it in high place, wherever he finds it. Such is the happy position of Homer, perhaps; of Chaucer, of Saadi. They felt that all wit was their wit. And they are librarians and historiographers, as well as poets. Each romancer was heir and dispenser of all the hundred tales of the world,—

> Presenting Thebes' and Pelops' line,
> And the tale of Troy divine.

The influence of Chaucer is conspicuous in all our early literature; and, more recently, not only Pope and Dryden have been beholden to him, but, in the whole society of English writers, a large unacknowledged debt is easily traced. One is charmed with the opulence which feeds so many pensioners. But Chaucer is a huge borrower. Chaucer, it seems, drew continually, through Lydgate and Caxton, from Guido di Colonna, whose Latin romance of the Trojan war was in turn a compilation from Dares Phrygius, Ovid, and Statius. Then Petrarch, Boccaccio, and the Provençal poets are his benefactors: the *Romaunt of the Rose* is only judicious translation from William of Lorris and John of Meun: *Troilus and Creseide*, from Lollius of Urbino: *The Cock and the Fox*, from the *Lais* of Marie: *The House of Fame*, from the French or Italian: and poor Gower he uses as if he were only a brick-kiln or stone-quarry, out of which to build his house. He steals by this apology; that what he takes has no worth where he finds it, and the greatest where he leaves it. It has come to be practically a sort of rule in literature, that a man, having once shown himself capable of original writing, is entitled thenceforth to steal from the writings of others at discretion. Thought is the property of him who can entertain it; and of him who can adequately place it. A certain awkwardness marks the use of borrowed thoughts; but, as soon as we have learned what to do with them, they become our own.

Thus, all originality is relative. Every thinker is retrospective. The learned member of the legislature at Westminster or at Washington, speaks and votes for thousands. Show us the constituency, and the now invisible channels by which the senator is made aware of their wishes, the crowd of practical and knowing men, who, by correspondence or conversation, are feeding him with evidence, anecdotes, and estimates, and it will bereave his fine attitude and resistance of something of their impressiveness. As Sir Robert Peel and Mr. Webster vote, so Locke and Rousseau think for thousands; and so there were fountains all around Homer, Menu, Saadi, or Milton, from which they drew; friends, lovers, books, traditions, proverbs,— all perished,—which, if seen, would go to reduce the wonder. Did the bard speak with authority? Did he feel himself overmatched by any companion? The appeal is to the consciousness of the writer. Is there at last in his breast a Delphi whereof to ask concerning any thought or thing, whether it be verily so, yea or nay? and to have answer, and to rely on that? All the debts which such a man could contract to other wit, would never disturb his consciousness of originality: for the ministrations of books, and of other minds, are a whiff of smoke to that most private reality with which he has conversed.

It is easy to see that what is best written or done by genius, in the world, was no man's work, but came by wide social labour, when a thousand wrought like one, sharing the same impulse. Our English Bible is a wonderful specimen of the strength and music of the English language. But it was not made by one man, or at one time; but centuries and churches brought it to perfection. There never was a time when there was not some translation existing. The Liturgy, admired for its energy and pathos, is an anthology of the piety of ages and nations, a translation of the prayers and forms of the Catholic church,—these collected, too, in long periods, from the prayers and meditations of every saint and sacred writer, all over the world. Grotius makes the like remark in respect to the Lord's Prayer, that the single clauses of which it is composed, were already in use, in the time of Christ, in the rabbinical forms. He picked out the grains of gold. The nervous language of the Common Law, the impressive forms of our courts, and the precision and substantial truth of the legal distinctions, are the contribution of all the sharp-sighted, strong-minded men who have lived in the countries where these laws govern. The translation of Plutarch gets its excellence by being translation on translation. There never was a time when there was none. All the truly idiomatic and national phrases are kept, and all others successively picked out, and thrown away. Something like the same process had gone on, long before, with the originals of these books. The world takes liberties with world-books. Vedas, Æsop's Fables, Pilpay, Arabian Nights, Cid, Iliad, Robin Hood, Scottish Minstrelsy, are not the work of single men. In the composition of such works, the time thinks, the market thinks, the mason, the carpenter, the merchant, the farmer, the fop, all think for us. Every book supplies its time with one good word; every municipal law, every trade, every folly of the day, and the generic catholic genius who is not afraid or ashamed to owe his originality to the originality of all, stands with the next age as the recorder and embodiment of his own.

We have to thank the researches of antiquaries, and the Shakespeare Society, for ascertaining the steps of the English drama, from the Mysteries celebrated in churches and by churchmen, and the final detachment from the church, and the completion of secular plays, from *Ferrex and Porrex*, and *Gammer Gurton's Needle*, down to the possession of the stage by the very pieces which Shakespeare altered, remodelled, and finally made his own. Elated with success, and piqued by the growing interest of the problem, they have left no bookstall unsearched, no chest in a garret unopened, no file of old yellow accounts to decompose in damp and worms, so keen was the hope to discover whether the boy Shakespeare poached or not, whether he held horses at the theatre door, whether he kept school, and why he left in his will only his second-best bed to Ann Hathaway, his wife.

There is something touching in the madness with which the passing age mischooses the object on which all candles shine, and all eyes are turned; the care with which it registers every trifle touching Queen Elizabeth, and King James, and the Essexes, Leicesters, Burleighs, and Buckinghams; and lets pass without a single valuable note the founder of another dynasty, which alone will cause the Tudor dynasty to be remembered,—the man who carries the Saxon race in him by the inspiration which feeds him, and on whose thoughts the foremost people of the world are now for some ages to be nourished, and minds to receive this and· not another bias. A popular player,—nobody suspected he was the poet of the human race; and the secret was kept as faithfully from poets and intellectual men, as from courtiers and frivolous people. Bacon, who took the inventory of the human understanding for his times, never mentioned his name. Ben Jonson, though we have strained his few words of regard and panegyric, had no suspicion of the elastic fame whose first vibrations he was attempting. He no doubt thought the praise he has conceded to him generous, and esteemed himself, out of all question, the better poet of the two.

If it need wit to know wit, according to the proverb, Shakespeare's time should be capable of recognizing it. Sir Henry Wotton was born four years after Shakespeare, and died twenty-three years after him; and I find, among his correspondents and acquaintances, the following persons: Theodore Beza, Isaac Casaubon, Sir Philip Sidney, Earl of Essex, Lord Bacon, Sir Walter Raleigh, John Milton, Sir Henry Vane, Izaac Walton, Dr. Donne, Abraham Cowley, Bellarmine, Charles Cotton, John Pym, John Hales, Kepler, Vieta, Albericus Gentilis, Paul Sarpi, Arminius; with all of whom exists some token of his having communicated, without enumerating many others, whom doubtless he saw,—Shakespeare, Spenser, Jonson, Beaumont, Massinger, two Herberts, Marlowe, Chapman, and the rest. Since the constellation of great men who appeared in Greece in the time of Pericles, there was never any such society; yet their genius failed them to find out the best head in the universe. Our poet's mask was impenetrable. You cannot see the mountain near. It took a century to make it suspected; and not until two centuries had passed, after his death, did any criticism which we think adequate begin to appear. It was not possible to write the history of Shakespeare till now; for he is the father of German literature: it was on the introduction of Shakespeare into German, by Lessing, and the translation of his works by Wieland and Schlegel, that the rapid burst of German literature was most intimately connected. It was not until the nineteenth century, whose speculative genius is a sort of living Hamlet, that the tragedy of Hamlet could find such wondering readers. Now, literature, philosophy, and thought are Shakespearized. His mind is the horizon beyond which, at present, we do not see. Our ears are educated to music by his rhythm. Coleridge and Goethe are the only critics who have expressed our convictions with any adequate fidelity; but there is in all cultivated minds a silent appreciation of his superlative power and beauty, which, like Christianity, qualifies the period.

The Shakespeare Society have inquired in all directions, advertised the missing facts, offered money for any information that will lead to proof; and with what result? Beside some important illustration of the history of the English stage, to which I have adverted, they have gleaned a few facts touching the property, and dealings in regard to property, of the poet. It appears that, from year to year, he owned a larger share in the Blackfriars Theatre: its wardrobe and other appurtenances were his; that he bought an estate in his native village, with his earnings as writer and shareholder; that he lived in the best house in Stratford; was intrusted by his neighbours with their commissions in London, as of borrowing money, and the like; that he was a veritable farmer. About the time when he was writing *Macbeth*, he sues Philip Rogers, in the borough-court of Stratford, for thirty-five shillings, ten pence, for corn delivered to him at different times; and, in all respects, appears as a good husband, with no reputation for eccentricity or excess. He was a good-natured sort of man, an actor and shareholder in the theatre, not in any striking manner distinguished from other actors and managers. I admit the importance of this information. It was well worth the pains that have been taken to procure it.

But whatever scraps of information concerning his condition these researches may have rescued, they can shed no light upon that infinite invention which is the concealed magnet of his attraction for us. We are very clumsy writers of history. We tell the chronicle of parentage, birth, birth-place, schooling, schoolmates, earning of money, marriage, publication of books, celebrity, death; and when we have come to an end of this gossip, no ray of relation appears between it and the goddess-born; and it seems as if, had we dipped at random into the *Modern Plutarch* and read any other life there, it would have fitted the poems as well. It is the essence of poetry to spring, like the rainbow daughter of Wonder, from the invisible, to abolish the past, and refuse all history. Malone, Warburton, Dyce, and Collier have wasted their oil. The famed theatres, Covent Garden, Drury Lane, the Park, and Tremont, have vainly assisted. Betterton, Garrick, Kemble, Kean, and Macready dedicate their lives to this genius; him they crown, elucidate, obey, and express. The genius knows them not. The recitation begins; one golden word leaps out immortal from all this painted pedantry, and sweetly torments us with invitations to its own inaccessible homes. I remember, I went once to see the Hamlet of a famed performer, the pride of the English stage; and all I then heard, and all I now remember, of the tragedian, was that in which the tragedian had no part; simply, Hamlet's question to the ghost:

> What may this mean,
> That thou, dead corse, again in complete steel
> Revisit'st thus the glimpses of the moon?

That imagination which dilates the closet he writes in to the world's dimension, crowds it with agents in rank and order, as quickly reduces the big reality to be the glimpses of the moon. These tricks of his magic spoil for us the illusions of the green-room. Can any biography shed light on the localities into which the *Midsummer Night's Dream* admits me? Did Shakespeare confide to any notary or parish recorder, sacristan, or surrogate, in Stratford, the genesis of that delicate creation? The forest of Arden, the nimble air of Scone Castle, the moonlight of Portia's villa, 'the antres vast and desarts idle' of Othello's captivity,—where is the third cousin, or grand-nephew, the chancellor's file of accounts, or private letter, that has kept one word of those transcendent secrets? In fine, in this drama, as in all great works of art,—in the Cyclopean architecture of Egypt and India; in the Phidian sculpture; the Gothic minsters; the Italian painting; the Ballads of Spain and Scotland;—the Genius draws up the ladder after him, when the creative age goes up to heaven, and gives way to a new age, which sees the works, and asks in vain for a history.

Shakespeare is the only biographer of Shakespeare; and even he can tell nothing, except to the Shakespeare in us; that is, to our most apprehensive and sympathetic hour. He cannot step from off his tripod, and give us anecdotes of his inspirations. Read the antique documents extricated, analysed, and compared by the assiduous Dyce and Collier; and now read one of those skyey sentences,—aerolites,—which seem to have fallen out of heaven, and which, not your experience, but the man within the breast, has accepted as words of fate; and tell me if they match; if the former account in any manner for the latter; or which gives the most historical insight into the man.

Hence, though our external history is so meagre, yet with Shakespeare for biographer, instead of Aubrey and Rowe, we have really the information which is material, that which describes character and fortune, that which, if we were about to meet the man and deal with him, would most import us to know. We have his recorded convictions on those questions which knock for answer at every heart,— on life and death, on love, on wealth and poverty, on the prizes of life, and the ways whereby we come at them; on the characters of men, and the influences, occult and open, which affect their fortunes; and on those mysterious and demoniacal powers which defy our science, and which yet interweave their malice and their gift in our brightest hours. Who ever read the volume of the Sonnets, without finding that the poet had there revealed, under masks that are no masks to the intelligent, the lore of friendship and of love; the confusion of sentiments in the most susceptible, and, at the same time, the most intellectual of men? What trait of his private mind has he hidden in his dramas? One can discern, in his ample pictures of the gentleman and the king, what forms and humanities pleased him; his delight in troops of friends, in large hospitality, in cheerful giving. Let Timon, let Warwick, let Antonio the merchant, answer for his great heart. So far from Shakespeare's being the least known, he is the one person, in all modern history, known to us. What point of morals, of manners, of economy, of philosophy, of religion, of taste, of the conduct of life, has he not settled? What mystery has he not signified his knowledge of? What office, or function, or district of man's work, has he not remembered? What king has he not taught state, as Talma taught Napoleon? What maiden has not found him finer than her delicacy? What lover has he not outloved? What sage has he not outseen? What gentleman has he not instructed in the rudeness of his behaviour?

Some able and appreciating critics think no criticism on Shakespeare valuable, that does not rest purely on the dramatic merit; that he is falsely judged as poet and philosopher. I think as highly as these critics of his dramatic merit, but still think it secondary. He was a full man, who liked to talk; a brain exhaling thoughts and images, which, seeking vent, found the drama next at hand. Had he been less we should have had to consider how well he filled his place, how good a dramatist he was, and he is the best in the world. But it turns out, that what he has to say is of that weight as to withdraw some attention from the vehicle; and he is like some saint whose history is to be rendered into all languages, into verse and prose, into songs and pictures, and cut up into proverbs; so that the occasion which gave the saint's meaning the form of a conversation, or of a prayer, or of a code of laws, is immaterial, compared with the universality of its application. So it fares with the wise Shakespeare and his book of life. He wrote the airs for all our modern music: he wrote the text of modern life; the text of manners: he drew the man of England and Europe; the father of the man in

America: he drew the man, and described the day, and what is done in it; he read the hearts of men and women, their probity, and their second thought, and wiles; the wiles of innocence, and the transitions by which virtues and vices slide into their contraries: he could divide the mother's part from the father's part in the face of the child, or draw the fine demarcations of freedom and of fate: he knew the laws of repression which make the police of nature: and all the sweets and all the terrors of human lot lay in his mind as truly but as softly as the landscape lies on the eye. And the importance of this wisdom of life sinks the form, as of Drama or Epic, out of notice. 'Tis like making a question concerning the paper on which a king's message is written.

Shakespeare is as much out of the category of eminent authors, as he is out of the crowd. He is inconceivably wise; the others, conceivably. A good reader can, in a sort, nestle into Plato's brain, and think from thence; but not into Shakespeare's. We are still out of doors. For executive faculty, for creation, Shakespeare is unique. No man can imagine it better. He was the farthest reach of subtlety compatible with an individual self,—the subtilest of authors, and only just within the possibility of authorship. With this wisdom of life, is the equal endowment of imaginative and of lyric power. He clothed the creatures of his legend with form and sentiments, as if they were people who had lived under his roof; and few real men have left such distinct characters as these fictions. And they spoke in language as sweet as it was fit. Yet his talents never seduced him into an ostentation, nor did he harp on one string. An omnipresent humanity co-ordinates all his faculties. Give a man of talents a story to tell, and his partiality will presently appear. He has certain observations, opinions, topics, which have some accidental prominence, and which he disposes all to exhibit. He crams this part, and starves that other part, consulting not the fitness of the thing, but his fitness and strength. But Shakespeare has no peculiarity, no importunate topic; but all is duly given; no veins, no curiosities: no cow-painter, no bird-fancier, no mannerist is he: he has no discoverable egotism: the great he tells greatly; the small, subordinately. He is wise without emphasis or assertion; he is strong, as nature is strong, who lifts the land into mountain slopes without effort, and by the same rule as she floats a bubble in the air, and likes as well to do the one as the other. This makes that equality of power in farce, tragedy, narrative, and love-songs; a merit so incessant, that each reader is incredulous of the perception of other readers.

This power of expression, or of transferring the inmost truth of things into music and verse, makes him the type of the poet, and has added a new problem to metaphysics. This is that which throws him into natural history, as a main production of the globe, and as announcing new eras and ameliorations. Things were mirrored in his poetry without loss or blur; he could paint the fine with precision, the great with compass; the tragic and the comic indifferently, and without any distortion or favour. He carried his powerful execution into minute details, to a hair point; finishes an eyelash or a dimple as firmly as he draws a mountain; and yet these, like nature's, will bear the scrutiny of the solar microscope.

In short, he is the chief example to prove that more or less of production, more or fewer pictures, is a thing indifferent. He had the power to make one picture. Daguerre learned how to let one flower etch its image on his plate of iodine; and then proceeds at leisure to etch a million. There are always objects; but there was never representation. Here is perfect representation, at last; and now let the world of figures sit for their portraits. No recipe can be given for the making of a Shakespeare; but the possibility of the translation of things into song is demonstrated.

His lyric power lies in the genius of the piece. The sonnets, though their excellence is lost in the splendour of the dramas, are as inimitable as they; and it is not a merit of lines, but a total merit of the piece; like the tone of voice of some incomparable person, so is this a speech of poetic beings, and any clause as unproducible now as a whole poem.

Though the speeches in the plays, and single lines, have a beauty which tempts the ear to pause on them for their euphuism, yet the sentence is so loaded with meaning, and so linked with its foregoers and followers, that the logician is satisfied. His means are as admirable as his ends; every subordinate invention, by which he helps himself to connect some irreconcilable opposites, is a poem too. He is not reduced to dismount and walk, because his horses are running off with him in some distant direction: he always rides.

The finest poetry was first experience: but the thought has suffered a transformation since it was an experience. Cultivated men often attain a good degree of skill in writing verses; but it is easy to read, through their poems, their personal history: any one acquainted with parties can name every figure: this is Andrew, and that is Rachel. The sense thus remains prosaic. It is a caterpillar with wings, and not yet a butterfly. In the poet's mind, the fact has gone quite over into the new element of thought, and has lost all that is exuvial. This generosity abides with Shakespeare. We say, from the truth and closeness of his pictures, that he knows the lesson by heart. Yet there is not a trace of egotism.

One more royal trait properly belongs to the poet. I mean his cheerfulness, without which no man can be a poet,—for beauty is his aim. He loves virtue, not for its obligation, but for its grace: he delights in the world, in man, in woman, for the lovely light that sparkles from them. Beauty, the spirit of joy and hilarity, he sheds over the universe. Epicurus relates that poetry hath such charms that a lover might forsake his mistress to partake of them. And the true bards have been noted for their firm and cheerful temper. Homer lies in sunshine; Chaucer is glad and erect; and Saadi says, 'It was rumoured abroad that I was penitent; but what had I to do with repentance?' Not less sovereign and cheerful,— much more sovereign and cheerful, is the tone of Shakespeare. His name suggests joy and emancipation to the heart of men. If he should appear in any company of human souls, who would not march in his troop? He touches nothing that does not borrow health and longevity from his festal style.

And now, how stands the account of man with this bard and benefactor, when in solitude, shutting our ears to the reverberations of his fame, we seek to strike the balance? Solitude has austere lessons; it can teach us to spare both heroes and poets; and it weighs Shakespeare also, and finds him to share the halfness and imperfection of humanity.

Shakespeare, Homer, Dante, Chaucer, saw the splendour of meaning that plays over the visible world; knew that a tree had another use than for apples, and corn another than for meal, and the ball of the earth, than for tillage and roads: that these things bore a second and finer harvest to the mind, being emblems of its thoughts, and conveying in all their natural history a certain mute commentary on human life. Shakespeare employed them as colours to compose his picture. He rested in their beauty; and never took the step which seemed inevitable to such genius, namely, to explore the virtue which resides in these symbols, and imparts this power,—What is that which they themselves say? He converted the elements, which waited on his command, into entertainments. He was master of the revels to mankind. Is it not as if one should have, through majestic powers of science, the comets given into his hand, or the planets and their moons, and should draw them from their orbits to glare with the municipal fireworks on a holiday night, and advertise in all towns, 'very superior pyrotechny this evening!' Are the agents of nature, and the power to understand them, worth no more than a street serenade, or the breath of a cigar? One remembers again the trumpet-text in the Koran,—'The heavens and the earth, and all that is between them, think ye we have created them in jest?' As long as the question is of talent and mental power, the world of men has not his equal to show. But when the question is to life, and its materials, and its auxiliaries, how does he profit me? What does it signify? It is but a Twelfth Night, or Midsummer Night's Dream, or a Winter Evening's Tale: what signifies another picture more or less? The Egyptian verdict of the Shakespeare Societies comes to mind, that he was a jovial actor and manager. I cannot marry this fact to his verse. Other admirable men have led lives in some sort of keeping with their thought; but this man, in wide contrast. Had he been less, had he reached only the common measure of great authors, of Bacon, Milton, Tasso, Cervantes, we might leave the fact in the twilight of human fate: but, that this man of men, he who gave to the science of mind a new and larger subject than had ever existed, and planted the standard of humanity some furlongs forward into Chaos,—that he should not be wise for himself,—it must even go into the world's history, that the best poet led an obscure and profane life, using his genius for the public amusement.

Well, other men, priest and prophet, Israelite, German, and Swede, beheld the same objects: they also saw through them that which was contained. And to what purpose? The beauty straightway vanished; they read commandments, all-excluding mountainous duty; an obligation, a sadness, as of piled mountains, fell on them, and life became ghastly, joyless, a pilgrim's progress, a probation, beleaguered round with doleful histories of Adam's fall and curse, behind us; with doomsdays and purgatorial and penal fires before us; and the heart of the seer and the heart of the listener sank in them.

It must be conceded that these are half-views of half-men. The world still wants its poet-priest, a reconciler, who shall not trifle with Shakespeare the player, nor shall grope in graves with Swedenborg the mourner; but who shall see, speak, and act, with equal inspiration. For knowledge will brighten the sunshine; right is more beautiful than private affection; and love is compatible with universal wisdom.

JAMES RUSSELL LOWELL
1819–1891
WORDSWORTH

[From *Among my Books*, Series II, 1876]

A GENERATION has now passed away since Wordsworth was laid with the family in the churchyard at Grasmere. Perhaps it is hardly yet time to take a perfectly impartial measure of his value as a poet. To do this is especially hard for those who are old enough to remember the last shot which the foe was sullenly firing in that long war of critics which began when he published his manifesto as Pretender, and which came to a pause rather than end when they flung up their caps with the rest at his final coronation. Something of the intensity of the *odium theologicum* (if indeed the *aestheticum* be not in these days the more bitter of the two) entered into the conflict. The Wordsworthians were a sect, who, if they had the enthusiasm, had also not a little of the exclusiveness and partiality to which sects are liable. The verses of the master had for them the virtue of religious canticles stimulant of zeal and not amenable to the ordinary tests of cold-blooded criticism. Like the hymns of the Huguenots and Covenanters, they were songs of battle no less than of worship, and the combined ardours of conviction and conflict lent them a fire that was not naturally their own. As we read them now, that virtue of the moment is gone out of them, and whatever of Dr. Wattsiness there is gives us a slight shock of disenchantment. It is something like the difference between the *Marseillaise* sung by armed propagandists on the edge of battle, or by Brissotins in the tumbrel, and the words of it read coolly in the closet, or recited with the factitious frenzy of Thérèse. It was natural in the early days of Wordsworth's career to dwell most fondly on those profounder qualities to appreciate which settled in some sort the measure of a man's right to judge of poetry at all. But now we must admit the shortcomings, the failures, the defects, as no less essential elements in forming a sound judgement as to whether the seer and artist were so united in him as to justify the claim first put in by himself and afterwards maintained by his sect to a place beside the few great poets who exalt men's minds, and give a right direction and safe outlet to their passions through the imagination, while insensibly helping them toward balance of character and serenity of judgement by stimulating their sense of proportion, form, and the nice adjustment of means to ends. In none of our poets has the constant propulsion of an unbending will, and the concentration of exclusive, if I must not say somewhat narrow, sympathies done so much to make the original endowment of nature effective, and in none accordingly does the biography throw so much light on the works, or enter so largely into their composition as an element whether of power or of weakness. Wordsworth never saw, and I think never wished to see, beyond the limits of his own consciousness and experience. He early conceived himself to be, and through life was confirmed by circumstances in the faith that he was, a 'dedicated spirit',[1] a state of mind likely to further an intense but at the same time one-sided development of the intellectual powers. The solitude in which the greater part of his mature life was passed, while it doubtless ministered to the passionate

[1] In the *Prelude* he attributes this consecration to a sunrise seen (during a college vacation) as he walked homeward from some village festival where he had danced all night:

> My heart was full; I made no vows, but vows
> Were then made for me; bond unknown to me
> Was given that I should be, else sinning greatly,
> A dedicated Spirit.—Book IV.

intensity of his musings upon man and nature, was, it may be suspected, harmful to him as an artist, by depriving him of any standard of proportion outside himself by which to test the comparative value of his thoughts, and by rendering him more and more incapable of that urbanity of mind which could be gained only by commerce with men more nearly on his own level, and which gives tone without lessening individuality. Wordsworth never quite saw the distinction between the eccentric and the original. For what we call originality seems not so much anything peculiar, much less anything odd, but that quality in a man which touches human nature at most points of its circumference, which reinvigorates the consciousness of our own powers by recalling and confirming our own unvalued sensations and perceptions, gives classic shape to our own amorphous imaginings, and adequate utterance to our own stammering conceptions or emotions. The poet's office is to be a Voice, not of one crying in the wilderness to a knot of already magnetized acolytes, but singing amid the throng of men, and lifting their common aspirations and sympathies (so first clearly revealed to themselves) on the wings of his song to a purer ether and a wider reach of view. We cannot, if we would, read the poetry of Wordsworth as mere poetry; at every other page we find ourselves entangled in a problem of aesthetics. The world-old question of matter and form, of whether nectar *is* of precisely the same flavour when served to us from a Grecian chalice or from any jug of ruder pottery, comes up for decision anew. The Teutonic nature has always shown a sturdy preference of the solid bone with a marrow of nutritious moral to any shadow of the same on the flowing mirror of sense. Wordsworth never lets us long forget the deeply rooted stock from which he sprang,— *vien ben dà lui.*

William Wordsworth was born at Cockermouth

in Cumberland on the 7th of April, 1770, the second of five children. His father was John Wordsworth, an attorney-at-law, and agent of Sir James Lowther, afterwards first Earl of Lonsdale. His mother was Anne Cookson, the daughter of a mercer in Penrith. His paternal ancestors had been settled immemorially at Penistone in Yorkshire, whence his grandfather had emigrated to Westmorland. His mother, a woman of piety and wisdom, died in March 1778, being then in her thirty-second year. His father, who never entirely cast off the depression occasioned by her death, survived her but five years, dying in December 1783, when William was not quite fourteen years old.

The poet's early childhood was passed partly at Cockermouth, and partly with his maternal grandfather at Penrith. His first teacher appears to have been Mrs. Anne Birkett, a kind of Shenstone's Schoolmistress, who practised the memory of her pupils, teaching them chiefly by rote, and not endeavouring to cultivate their reasoning faculties, a process by which children are apt to be converted from natural logicians into impertinent sophists. Among his schoolmates here was Mary Hutchinson, who afterwards became his wife.

In 1778 he was sent to a school founded by Edwin Sandys, Archbishop of York, in the year 1585, at Hawkshead in Lancashire. Hawkshead is a small market-town in the vale of Esthwaite, about a third of a mile north-west of the lake. Here Wordsworth passed nine years, among a people of simple habits and scenery of a sweet and pastoral dignity. His earliest intimacies were with the mountains, lakes, and streams of his native district, and the associations with which his mind was stored during its most impressible period were noble and pure. The boys were boarded among the dames of the village, thus enjoying a freedom from scholastic restraints, which could be nothing but beneficial in a place where the temptations

were only to sports that hardened the body, while
they fostered a love of nature in the spirit and
habits of observation in the mind. Wordsworth's
ordinary amusements here were hunting and fishing,
rowing, skating, and long walks around the lake and
among the hills, with an occasional scamper on
horseback.[1] His life as a schoolboy was favourable
also to his poetic development, in being identified
with that of the people among whom he lived.
Among men of simple habits, and where there are
small diversities of condition, the feelings and passions are displayed with less restraint, and the young
poet grew acquainted with that primal human basis
of character where the Muse finds firm foothold,
and to which he ever afterward cleared his way
through all the overlying drift of conventionalism.
The dalesmen were a primitive and hardy race who
kept alive the traditions and often the habits of a
more picturesque time. A common level of interests
and social standing fostered unconventional ways of
thought and speech, and friendly human sympathies.
Solitude induced reflection, a reliance of the mind
on its own resources, and individuality of character.
Where everybody knew everybody, and everybody's
father had known everybody's father, the interest of
man in man was not likely to become a matter of cold
hearsay and distant report. When death knocked
at any door in the hamlet, there was an echo from
every fireside, and a wedding dropped its white
flowers at every threshold. There was not a grave
in the churchyard but had its story; not a crag or
glen or aged tree untouched with some ideal hue of
legend. It was here that Wordsworth learned that
homely humanity which gives such depth and sincerity to his poems. Travel, society, culture, nothing
could obliterate the deep trace of that early training
which enables him to speak directly to the primitive

---

[1] *Prelude*, Book II.

instincts of man. He was apprenticed early to the difficult art of being himself.

At school he wrote some task-verses on subjects imposed by the master, and also some voluntaries of his own, equally undistinguished by any peculiar merit. But he seems to have made up his mind as early as in his fourteenth year to become a poet.[1] 'It is recorded', says his biographer vaguely, 'that the poet's father set him very early to learn portions of the best English poets by heart, so that at an early age he could repeat large portions of Shakespeare, Milton, and Spenser.'

The great event of Wordsworth's schooldays was the death of his father, who left what may be called a hypothetical estate, consisting chiefly of claims upon the first Earl of Lonsdale, the payment of which, though their justice was acknowledged, that nobleman contrived in some unexplained way to elude so long as he lived. In October 1787 he left school for St. John's College, Cambridge. He was already, we are told, a fair Latin scholar, and had made some progress in mathematics. The earliest books we hear of his reading were *Don Quixote*, *Gil Blas*, *Gulliver's Travels*, and the *Tale of a Tub*; but at school he had also become familiar with the works of some English poets, particularly Goldsmith and Gray, of whose poems he had learned many by heart. What is more to the purpose, he had become, without knowing it, a lover of Nature in all her moods, and the same mental necessities of a solitary life which compel men to an interest in the transitory phenomena of scenery, had made him also studious of the movements of his own mind, and the mutual inter-action and dependence of the external and internal universe.

Doubtless his early orphanage was not without its effect in confirming a character naturally impatient

---

[1] I to the muses have been bound,
 These fourteen years, by strong indentures.
  Idiot Boy (1798).

of control, and his mind, left to itself, clothed itself with an indigenous growth, which grew fairly and freely, unstinted by the shadow of exotic plantations. It has become a truism, that remarkable persons have remarkable mothers; but perhaps this is chiefly true of such as have made themselves distinguished by their industry, and by the assiduous cultivation of faculties in themselves of only an average quality. It is rather to be noted how little is known of the parentage of men of the first magnitude, how often they seem in some sort foundlings, and how early an apparently adverse destiny begins the culture of those who are to encounter and master great intellectual or spiritual experiences.

Of his disposition as a child little is known, but that little is characteristic. He himself tells us that he was 'stiff, moody, and of violent temper'. His mother said of him that he was the only one of her children about whom she felt any anxiety,—for she was sure that he would be remarkable for good or evil. Once, in resentment at some fancied injury, he resolved to kill himself, but his heart failed him. I suspect that few boys of passionate temperament have escaped these momentary suggestions of despairing helplessness. 'On another occasion,' he says, 'while I was at my grandfather's house at Penrith, along with my eldest brother Richard, we were whipping tops together in the long drawing-room, on which the carpet was only laid down on particular occasions. The walls were hung round with family pictures, and I said to my brother, "Dare you strike your whip through that old lady's petticoat?" He replied, "No, I won't." "Then," said I, "here goes," and I struck my lash through her hooped petticoat, for which, no doubt, though I have forgotten it, I was properly punished. But, possibly from some want of judgement in punishments inflicted, I had become perverse and obstinate in defying chastisement, and rather proud of it than otherwise.' This last anecdote is as happily typical as a bit of Greek mythology which always prefigured the lives of heroes in the stories of their childhood. Just so do we find him afterward striking his defiant lash through the hooped petticoat of the artificial style of poetry, and proudly unsubdued by the punishment of the Reviewers.

Of his college life the chief record is to be found in *The Prelude*. He did not distinguish himself as a scholar, and if his life had any incidents, they were of that interior kind which rarely appear in biography, though they may be of controlling influence upon the life. He speaks of reading Chaucer, Spenser, and Milton while at Cambridge,[1] but no reflection from them is visible in his earliest published poems. The greater part of his vacations was spent in his native Lake-country, where his only sister, Dorothy, was the companion of his rambles. She was a woman of large natural endowments, chiefly of the receptive kind, and had much to do with the formation and tendency of the poet's mind. It was she who called forth the shyer sensibilities of his nature, and taught an originally harsh and austere imagination to surround itself with fancy and feeling, as the rock fringes itself with a sun-spray of ferns. She was his first public, and belonged to that class of prophetically appreciative temperaments whose apparent office it is to cheer the early solitude of original minds with messages from the future. Through the greater part of his life she continued to be a kind of poetical conscience to him.

Wordsworth's last college vacation was spent in a foot journey upon the Continent (1790). In January 1791 he took his degree of B.A., and left Cambridge. During the summer of this year he visited Wales, and, after declining to enter upon holy orders under the plea that he was not of age for ordination, went over to France in November, and remained during the winter at Orleans. Here he

[1] *Prelude*, Book III.

became intimate with the republican General Beaupuis, with whose hopes and aspirations he ardently sympathized. In the spring of 1792 he was at Blois, and returned thence to Orleans, which he finally quitted in October for Paris. He remained here as long as he could with safety, and at the close of the year went back to England, thus, perhaps, escaping the fate which soon after overtook his friends the Brissotins.

As hitherto the life of Wordsworth may be called a fortunate one, not less so in the training and expansion of his faculties was this period of his stay in France. Born and reared in a country where the homely and familiar nestles confidingly amid the most savage and sublime forms of nature, he had experienced whatever impulses the creative faculty can receive from mountain and cloud and the voices of winds and waters, but he had known man only as an actor in fireside histories and tragedies, for which the hamlet supplied an ample stage. In France he first felt the authentic beat of a nation's heart; he was a spectator at one of those dramas where the terrible footfall of the Eumenides is heard nearer and nearer in the pauses of the action; and he saw man such as he can only be when he is vibrated by the orgasm of a national emotion. He sympathized with the hopes of France and of mankind deeply, as was fitting in a young man and a poet; and if his faith in the gregarious advancement of men was afterward shaken, he only held the more firmly by his belief in the individual, and his reverence for the human as something quite apart from the popular and above it. Wordsworth has been unwisely blamed, as if he had been recreant to the liberal instincts of his youth. But it was inevitable that a genius so regulated and metrical as his, a mind which always compensated itself for its artistic radicalism by an involuntary leaning toward external respectability, should recoil from whatever was convulsionary and destructive in politics, and above all in religion. He reads the poems of Wordsworth without understanding, who does not find in them the noblest incentives to faith in man and the grandeur of his destiny, founded always upon that personal dignity and virtue, the capacity for whose attainment alone makes universal liberty possible and assures its permanence. He was to make men better by opening to them the sources of an inalterable well-being; to make them free, in a sense higher than political, by showing them that these sources are within them, and that no contrivance of man can permanently emancipate narrow natures and depraved minds. His politics were always those of a poet, circling in the larger orbit of causes and principles, careless of the transitory oscillation of events.

The change in his point of view (if change there was) certainly was complete soon after his return from France, and was perhaps due in part to the influence of Burke.

> While he [Burke] forewarns, denounces, launches forth,
> Against all systems built on abstract rights,
> Keen ridicule; the majesty proclaims
> Of institutes and laws hallowed by time;
> Declares the vital power of social ties
> Endeared by custom; and with high disdain,
> Exploding upstart theory, insists
> Upon the allegiance to which men are born.
> . . . . . Could a youth, and one
> In ancient story versed, whose breast had heaved
> Under the weight of classic eloquence,
> Sit, see, and hear, unthankful, uninspired?[1]

He had seen the French for a dozen years eagerly busy in tearing up whatever had roots in the past, replacing the venerable trunks of tradition and orderly growth with liberty-poles, then striving vainly to piece together the fibres they had broken, and to reproduce artificially that sense of permanence and

---

[1] *Prelude*, Book VII. Written before 1805, and referring to a still earlier date.

continuity which is the main safeguard of vigorous self-consciousness in a nation. He became a Tory through intellectual conviction, retaining, I suspect, to the last, a certain radicalism of temperament and instinct. Haydon tells us that in 1809 Sir George Beaumont said to him and Wilkie, 'Wordsworth may perhaps walk in; if he do, I caution you both against his terrific democratic notions'; and it must have been many years later that Wordsworth himself told Crabb Robinson, 'I have no respect whatever for Whigs, but I have a great deal of the Chartist in me'. In 1802, during his tour in Scotland, he travelled on Sundays as on the other days of the week. He afterwards became a theoretical churchgoer. 'Wordsworth defended earnestly the Church establishment. He even said he would shed his blood for it. Nor was he disconcerted by a laugh raised against him on account of his having confessed that he knew not when he had been in a church in his own country. "All our ministers are so vile," said he. The mischief of allowing the clergy to depend on the caprice of the multitude he thought more than outweighed all the evils of an establishment.'

In December 1792 Wordsworth had returned to England, and in the following year published *Descriptive Sketches* and the *Evening Walk*. He did this, as he says in one of his letters, to show that, although he had gained no honours at the University, he *could* do something. They met with no great success, and he afterward corrected them so much as to destroy all their interest as juvenile productions, without communicating to them any of the merits of maturity. In commenting, sixty years afterward, on a couplet in one of these poems,—

> And, fronting the bright west, the oak entwines
> Its darkening boughs and leaves in stronger lines,—

he says: 'This is feebly and imperfectly expressed, but I recollect distinctly the very spot where this first struck me.... The moment was important in my poetical history; for I date from it my consciousness of the infinite variety of natural appearances which had been unnoticed by the poets of any age or country, so far as I was acquainted with them, and I made a resolution to supply in some degree the deficiency.'

It is plain that Wordsworth's memory was playing him a trick here, misled by that instinct (it may almost be called) of consistency which leads men first to desire that their lives should have been without break or seam, and then to believe that they have been such. The more distant ranges of perspective are apt to run together in retrospection. How far could Wordsworth at fourteen have been acquainted with the poets of all ages and countries,—he who to his dying day could not endure to read Goethe and knew nothing of Calderon? It seems to me rather that the earliest influence traceable in him is that of Goldsmith, and later of Cowper, and it is, perhaps, some slight indication of its having already begun that his first volume of *Descriptive Sketches* (1793) was put forth by Johnson, who was Cowper's publisher. By and by the powerful impress of Burns is seen both in the topics of his verse and the form of his expression. But whatever their ultimate effect upon his style, certain it is that his juvenile poems were clothed in the conventional habit of the eighteenth century. 'The first verses from which he remembered to have received great pleasure were Miss Carter's *Poem on Spring*, a poem in the six-line stanza which he was particularly fond of and had composed much in,— for example, *Ruth*.' This is noteworthy, for Wordsworth's lyric range, especially so far as tune is concerned, was always narrow. His sense of melody was painfully dull, and some of his lighter effusions, as he would have called them, are almost ludicrously wanting in grace of movement. We cannot expect in a modern poet the thrush-like improvisation, the impulsively bewitching cadences, that charm us in our Elizabethan drama and whose last warble died with Herrick; but Shelley, Tennyson, and Browning have shown that the simple pathos of their music was not irrecoverable, even if the artless poignancy of their phrase be gone beyond recall. We feel this lack in Wordsworth all the more keenly if we compare such verses as

> Like an army defeated
> The snow hath retreated
> And now doth fare ill
> On the top of the bare hill,

with Goethe's exquisite *Ueber allen Gipfeln ist Ruh*, in which the lines (as if shaken down by a momentary breeze of emotion) drop lingeringly one after another like blossoms upon turf.

The Evening Walk and *Descriptive Sketches* show plainly the prevailing influence of Goldsmith, both in the turn of thought and the mechanism of the verse. They lack altogether the temperance of tone and judgement in selection which have made the *Traveller* and the *Deserted Village* perhaps the most truly classical poems in the language. They bear here and there, however, the unmistakable stamp of the maturer Wordsworth, not only in a certain blunt realism, but in the intensity and truth of picturesque epithet. Of this realism, from which Wordsworth never wholly freed himself, the following verses may suffice as a specimen. After describing the fate of a chamois-hunter killed by falling from a crag, his fancy goes back to the bereaved wife and son:

> Haply that child in fearful doubt may gaze,
> Passing his father's bones in future days,
> Start at the reliques of that very thigh
> On which so oft he prattled when a boy.

In these poems there is plenty of that 'poetic diction' against which Wordsworth was to lead the revolt nine years later.

> To wet the peak's impracticable sides
> He opens of his feet the sanguine tides,
> Weak and more weak the issuing current eyes
> Lapped by the panting tongue of thirsty skies.

Both of these passages have disappeared from the revised edition, as well as some curious outbursts of that motiveless despair which Byron made fashionable not long after. Nor are there wanting touches of fleshliness which strike us oddly as coming from Wordsworth.

> Farewell! those forms that in thy noontide shade
> Rest near their little plots of oaten glade,
> Those steadfast eyes that beating breasts inspire
> To throw the 'sultry ray' of young Desire;
> Those lips whose tides of fragrance come and go
> Accordant to the cheek's unquiet glow;
> Those shadowy breasts in love's soft light arrayed,
> And rising by the moon of passion swayed.

The political tone is also mildened in the revision; as where he changes 'despot courts' into 'tyranny'. One of the alterations is interesting. In the *Evening Walk* he had originally written

> And bids her soldier come her wars to share
> Asleep on Minden's charnel hill afar.

An erratum at the end directs us to correct the second verse, thus:

> Asleep on Bunker's charnel hill afar.

Wordsworth somewhere rebukes the poets for making the owl a bodeful bird. He had himself done so in the *Evening Walk*, and corrects his epithets to suit his later judgement, putting 'gladsome' for 'boding', and replacing

> The tremulous sob of the complaining owl

by

> The sportive outcry of the mocking owl.

Indeed, the character of the two poems is so much changed in the revision as to make the dates appended to them a misleading anachronism. But there is one truly Wordsworthian passage which already gives us a glimpse of that passion with which he was the first to irradiate descriptive poetry and which sets him on a level with Turner.

> 'Tis storm; and hid in mist from hour to hour
> All day the floods a deepening murmur pour:
> The sky is veiled and every cheerful sight;
> Dark is the region as with coming night;
> But what a sudden burst of overpowering light!
> Triumphant on the bosom of the storm,
> Glances the fire-clad eagle's wheeling form;
> Eastward, in long prospective glittering shine
> The wood-crowned cliffs that o'er the lake recline;
> Those eastern cliffs a hundred streams unfold,
> At once to pillars turned that flame with gold;
> Behind his sail the peasant tries to shun
> The West that burns like one dilated sun,
> Where in a mighty crucible expire
> The mountains, glowing hot like coals of fire.

Wordsworth has made only one change in these verses, and that for the worse, by substituting 'glorious' (which was already implied in 'glances' and 'fire-clad') for 'wheeling'. In later life he would have found it hard to forgive the man who should have made cliffs recline over a lake. On the whole, what strikes us as most prophetic in these poems is their want of continuity, and the purple patches of true poetry on a texture of unmistakable prose; perhaps we might add the incongruous clothing of prose thoughts in the ceremonial robes of poesy.

During the same year (1793) he wrote, but did not publish, a political tract, in which he avowed himself opposed to monarchy and to the hereditary principle, and desirous of a republic, if it could be had without a revolution. He probably continued to be all his life in favour of that ideal republic 'which never was on land or sea', but fortunately he gave up politics that he might devote himself to his own nobler calling, to which politics are subordinate, and for which he found freedom enough in England as it was. Dr. Wordsworth admits that his uncle's opinions were democratical so late as 1802. I suspect that they remained so in an esoteric way to the end of his days. He had himself suffered by the arbitrary selfishness of a great landholder, and he was born and bred in a part of England where there is a greater social equality than elsewhere. The look and manner of the Cumberland people especially are such as recall very vividly to a New-Englander the associations of fifty years ago, ere the change from New England to New Ireland had begun. But meanwhile, Want, which makes no distinctions of Monarchist or Republican, was pressing upon him. The debt due to his father's estate had not been paid, and Wordsworth was one of those rare idealists who esteem it the first duty of a friend of humanity to live for, and not on, his neighbour. He at first proposed establishing a periodical journal to be called *The Philanthropist*, but luckily went no further with it, for the receipts from an organ of opinion which professed republicanism, and at the same time discountenanced the plans of all existing or defunct republicans, would have been necessarily scanty. There being no appearance of any demand, present or prospective, for philanthropists, he tried to get employment as correspondent of a newspaper. Here also it was impossible that he should succeed; he was too great to be merged in the editorial We, and had too well defined a private opinion on all subjects to be able to express that average of public opinion which constitutes able editorials. But so it is that to the prophet in the wilderness the birds of ill omen are already on the wing with food from heaven; and while Wordsworth's relatives were getting impatient at what they considered his waste of time, while one thought he had gifts enough to make a good parson, and another lamented the rare attorney that was lost in him, the prescient muse guided the hand of Raisley Calvert while he wrote the poet's name in his will for a legacy of £900. By the death of Calvert, in 1795, this timely help came to Wordsworth at the turning-point of his life, and made it honest for him to write poems that will never die, instead of theatrical critiques as ephemeral as play-bills, or leaders that led only to oblivion.

In the autumn of 1795 Wordsworth and his sister took up their abode at Racedown Lodge, near Crewkerne, in Dorsetshire. Here nearly two years were passed, chiefly in the study of poetry, and Wordsworth to some extent recovered from the fierce disappointment of his political dreams, and regained that equable tenor of mind which alone is consistent with a healthy productiveness. Here Coleridge, who had contrived to see something more in the *Descriptive Sketches* than the public had discovered there, first made his acquaintance. The sympathy and appreciation of an intellect like Coleridge's supplied him with that external motive to activity which is the chief use of popularity, and justified to him his opinion of his own powers. It was now that the tragedy of *The Borderers* was for the most part written, and that plan of the *Lyrical Ballads* suggested which gave Wordsworth a clue to lead him out of the metaphysical labyrinth in which he was entangled. It was agreed between the two young friends, that Wordsworth was to be a philosophic poet, and, by a good fortune uncommon to such conspiracies, Nature had already consented to the arrangement. In July 1797, the two Wordsworths removed to Allfoxden in Somersetshire, that they might be near Coleridge, who in the meanwhile had married and settled himself at Nether Stowey. In November *The Borderers* was finished, and Wordsworth went up to London with his sister to offer it for the stage. The good Genius of the poet again interposing, the play was decisively rejected, and Wordsworth went back to Allfoxden, himself the hero of that first tragicomedy so common to young authors.

The play has fine passages, but is as unreal as *Jane Eyre*. It shares with many of Wordsworth's narrative poems the defect of being written to illustrate an abstract moral theory, so that the overbearing thesis is continually thrusting the poetry to the wall. Applied to the drama, such predestination makes all the personages puppets and disenables them for being characters. Wordsworth seems to have felt this when he published *The Borderers* in 1842, and says in a note that it was 'at first written . . . without any view to its exhibition upon the stage'. But he was mistaken. The contemporaneous letters of Coleridge to Cottle show that he was long in giving up the hope of getting it accepted by some theatrical manager.

He now applied himself to the preparation of the first volume of the *Lyrical Ballads* for the press, and it was published toward the close of 1798. The book, which contained also *The Ancient Mariner* of Coleridge, attracted little notice, and that in great part contemptuous. When Mr. Cottle, the publisher, shortly after sold his copyrights to Mr. Longman, that of the *Lyrical Ballads* was reckoned at *zero*, and it was at last given up to the authors. A few persons were not wanting, however, who discovered the dawn-streaks of a new day in that light which the critical fire-brigade thought to extinguish with a few contemptuous spurts of cold water.

Lord Byron describes himself as waking one morning and finding himself famous, and it is quite an ordinary fact, that a blaze may be made with a little saltpetre that will be stared at by thousands who would have thought the sunrise tedious. If we may believe his biographer, Wordsworth might have said that he awoke and found himself infamous, for the publication of the *Lyrical Ballads* undoubtedly raised him to the distinction of being the least popular poet in England. Parnassus has two peaks; the one where improvising poets cluster; the other where the singer of deep secrets sits alone,—a peak veiled sometimes from the whole morning of a generation by earth-born mists and smoke of kitchen fires, only to glow the more consciously at sunset, and after nightfall to crown itself with imperishable stars. Wordsworth had that self-trust which in the man of genius is sublime, and in the man of talent insufferable. It mattered not to him though all the reviewers had been in a chorus of laughter or conspiracy of silence behind him. He went quietly over to Germany to write more Lyrical Ballads, and to begin a poem on the growth of his own mind, at a time when there were only two men in the world (himself and Coleridge) who were aware that he had one, or at least one anywise differing from those mechanically uniform ones which are stuck drearily, side by side, in the great pin-paper of society.

In Germany Wordsworth dined in company with Klopstock, and after dinner they had a conversation, of which Wordsworth took notes. The respectable old poet, who was passing the evening of his days by the chimney-corner, Darby and Joan like, with his respectable Muse, seems to have been rather bewildered by the apparition of a living genius. The record is of value now chiefly for the insight it gives us into Wordsworth's mind. Among other things he said, 'that it was the province of a great poet to raise people up to his own level, not to descend to theirs',—memorable words, the more memorable that a literary life of sixty years was in keeping with them.

It would be instructive to know what were Wordsworth's studies during his winter in Goslar. De Quincey's statement is mere conjecture. It may be guessed fairly enough that he would seek an entrance to the German language by the easy path of the ballad, a course likely to confirm him in his theories as to the language of poetry. The Spinozism with which he has been not unjustly charged was certainly not due to any German influence, for it appears unmistakably in the *Lines composed at Tintern Abbey* in July 1798. It is more likely to have been derived from his talks with Coleridge in 1797. When Emerson visited him in 1833, he spoke with loathing of *Wilhelm Meister*, a part of which he had read in Carlyle's translation apparently. There was some affectation in this, it should seem, for he had read Smollett. On the whole, it may be fairly concluded that the help of Germany in the development of his genius may be reckoned as very small, though there is certainly a marked resemblance both in form and sentiment between some of his earlier lyrics and those of Goethe. His poem of the *Thorn*, though vastly more imaginative, may have been suggested by Bürger's *Pfarrers Tochter von Taubenhain*. The little grave *drei Spannen lang*, in its conscientious measurement, certainly recalls a famous couplet in the English poem.

After spending the winter at Goslar, Wordsworth and his sister returned to England in the spring of 1799, and settled at Grasmere in Westmorland. In 1800, the first edition of the *Lyrical Ballads* being exhausted, it was republished with the addition of another volume, Mr. Longman paying £100 for the copyright of two editions. The book passed to a second edition in 1802, and to a third in 1805. Wordsworth sent a copy of it, with a manly letter, to Mr. Fox, particularly recommending to his attention the poems *Michael* and *The Brothers*, as displaying the strength and permanence among a simple and rural population of those domestic affections which were certain to decay gradually under the influence of manufactories and poor-houses. Mr. Fox wrote a civil acknowledgement, saying that his favourites among the poems were *Harry Gill*, *We are Seven*, *The Mad Mother*, and *The Idiot*, but that he was prepossessed against the use of blank verse for simple subjects. Any political significance in the poems he was apparently unable to see. To this second edition

Wordsworth prefixed an argumentative Preface, in which he nailed to the door of the cathedral of English song the critical theses which he was to maintain against all comers in his poetry and his life. It was a new thing for an author to undertake to show the goodness of his verses by the logic and learning of his prose; but Wordsworth carried to the reform of poetry all that fervour and faith which had lost their political object, and it is another proof of the sincerity and greatness of his mind, and of that heroic simplicity which is their concomitant, that he could do so calmly what was sure to seem ludicrous to the greater number of his readers. Fifty years have since demonstrated that the true judgement of one man outweighs any counterpoise of false judgement, and that the faith of mankind is guided to a man only by a well-founded faith in himself. To this *Defensio* Wordsworth afterward added a supplement, and the two form a treatise of permanent value for philosophic statement and decorous English. Their only ill effect has been, that they have encouraged many otherwise deserving young men to set a Sibylline value on their verses in proportion as they were unsaleable. The strength of an argument for self-reliance drawn from the example of a great man depends wholly on the greatness of him who uses it; such arguments being like coats of mail, which, though they serve the strong against arrow-flights and lance-thrusts, may only suffocate the weak or sink him the sooner in the waters of oblivion.

An advertisement prefixed to the *Lyrical Ballads*, as originally published in one volume, warned the reader that 'they were written chiefly with a view to ascertain how far *the language of conversation in the middle and lower classes* of society is adapted to the purposes of poetic pleasure'. In his preface to the second edition, in two volumes, Wordsworth already found himself forced to shift his ground a little (perhaps in deference to the wider view and finer sense of Coleridge), and now says of the former volume that 'it was published as an experiment which, I hoped, might be of some use to ascertain how far, by fitting to metrical arrangement, *a selection of the real language of men in a state of vivid sensation*, that sort of pleasure and that quantity of pleasure may be imparted which a poet may *rationally endeavour* to impart'. Here is evidence of a retreat towards a safer position, though Wordsworth seems to have remained unconvinced at heart, and for many years longer clung obstinately to the passages of bald prose into which his original theory had betrayed him. In 1815 his opinions had undergone a still further change, and an assiduous study of the qualities of his own mind and of his own poetic method (the two subjects in which alone he was ever a thorough scholar) had convinced him that poetry was in no sense that appeal to the understanding which is implied by the words 'rationally endeavour to impart'. In the preface of that year he says, 'The observations prefixed to that portion of these volumes which was published many years ago under the title of *Lyrical Ballads* have so little of special application to the greater part of the present enlarged and diversified collection, that they could not with propriety stand as an introduction to it.' It is a pity that he could not have become an earlier convert to Coleridge's pithy definition, that 'prose was words in their best order, and poetry the *best* words in the best order'. But idealization was something that Wordsworth was obliged to learn painfully. It did not come to him naturally as to Spenser and Shelley and to Coleridge in his higher moods. Moreover, it was in the too frequent choice of subjects incapable of being idealized without a manifest jar between theme and treatment that Wordsworth's great mistake lay. For example, in the *The Blind Highland Boy* he had originally the following stanzas:

> Strong is the current, but be mild,
> Ye waves, and spare the helpless child!

> If ye in anger fret or chafe,
> A bee-hive would be ship as safe
>   As that in which he sails.
>
> But say, what was it? Thought of fear!
> Well may ye tremble when ye hear!
> —A household tub like one of those
> Which women use to wash their clothes,
>   This carried the blind boy.

In endeavouring to get rid of the downright vulgarity of phrase in the last stanza, Wordsworth invents an impossible tortoise-shell, and thus robs his story of the reality which alone gave it a living interest. Any extemporized raft would have floated the boy down to immortality. But Wordsworth never quite learned the distinction between Fact, which suffocates the Muse, and Truth, which is the very breath of her nostrils. Study and self-culture did much for him, but they never quite satisfied him that he was capable of making a mistake. He yielded silently to friendly remonstrance on certain points, and gave up, for example, the ludicrous exactness of

> I've measured it from side to side,
> 'Tis three feet long and two feet wide.

But I doubt if he was ever really convinced, and to his dying day he could never quite shake off that habit of over-minute detail which renders the narratives of uncultivated people so tedious, and sometimes so distasteful. *Simon Lee*, after his latest revision, still contains verses like these:

> And he is lean and he is sick;
> His body, dwindled and awry,
> Rests upon ankles swollen and thick;
> His legs are thin and dry;
>   . . . . .
> Few months of life he has in store,
> As he to you will tell,
> For still, the more he works, the more
> Do his weak ankles swell,—

which are not only prose, but *bad* prose, and moreover guilty of the same fault for which Wordsworth condemned Dr. Johnson's famous parody on the ballad-style,—that their *matter* is contemptible'. The sonorousness of conviction with which Wordsworth sometimes gives utterance to commonplaces of thought and trivialities of sentiment has a ludicrous effect on the profane and even on the faithful in unguarded moments. We are reminded of a passage in *The Excursion*:

> List! I heard
> From yon huge breast of rock *a solemn bleat*,
> Sent forth as if it were the mountain's voice.

In 1800 the friendship of Wordsworth with Lamb began, and was thenceforward never interrupted. He continued to live at Grasmere, conscientiously diligent in the composition of poems, secure of finding the materials of glory within and around him; for his genius taught him that inspiration is no product of a foreign shore, and that no adventurer ever found it, though he wandered as long as Ulysses. Meanwhile the appreciation of the best minds and the gratitude of the purest hearts gradually centred more and more towards him. In 1802 he made a short visit to France, in company with Miss Wordsworth, and soon after his return to England was married to Mary Hutchinson, on the 4th of October of the same year. Of the good fortune of this marriage no other proof is needed than the purity and serenity of his poems, and its record is to be sought nowhere else.

On the 18th of June, 1803, his first child, John, was born, and on the 14th of August of the same year he set out with his sister on a foot journey into Scotland. Coleridge was their companion during a part of this excursion, of which Miss Wordsworth kept a full diary. In Scotland he made the acquaintance of Scott, who recited to him a part of the *Lay of the Last Minstrel*, then in manuscript. The travellers returned to Grasmere on the 25th of

September. It was during this year that Wordsworth's intimacy with the excellent Sir George Beaumont began. Sir George was an amateur painter of considerable merit, and his friendship was undoubtedly of service to Wordsworth in making him familiar with the laws of a sister art and thus contributing to enlarge the sympathies of his criticism, the tendency of which was toward too great exclusiveness. Sir George Beaumont, dying in 1827, did not forgo his regard for the poet, but contrived to hold his affection in mortmain by the legacy of an annuity of £100, to defray the charges of a yearly journey.

In March 1805, the poet's brother, John, lost his life by the shipwreck of the *Abergavenny* East-Indiaman, of which he was captain. He was a man of great purity and integrity, and sacrificed himself to his sense of duty by refusing to leave the ship till it was impossible to save him. Wordsworth was deeply attached to him, and felt such grief at his death as only solitary natures like his are capable of, though mitigated by a sense of the heroism which was the cause of it. The need of mental activity as affording an outlet to intense emotion may account for the great productiveness of this and the following year. He now completed *The Prelude*, wrote *The Waggoner*, and increased the number of his smaller poems enough to fill two volumes, which were published in 1807.

This collection, which contained some of the most beautiful of his shorter pieces, and among others the incomparable *Odes* to Duty and on Immortality, did not reach a second edition till 1815. The reviewers had another laugh, and rival poets pillaged while they scoffed, particularly Byron, among whose verses a bit of Wordsworth showed as incongruously as a sacred vestment on the back of some buccaneering plunderer of an abbey. There was a general combination to put him down, but on the other hand there was a powerful party in his favour, consisting of William Wordsworth. He not only continued in good heart himself, but, reversing the order usual on such occasions, kept up the spirits of his friends.

Wordsworth passed the winter of 1806-7 in a house of Sir George Beaumont's, at Coleorton in Leicestershire, the cottage at Grasmere having become too small for his increased family. On his return to the Vale of Grasmere he rented the house at Allan Bank, where he lived three years. During this period he appears to have written very little poetry, for which his biographer assigns as a primary reason the smokiness of the Allan Bank chimneys. This will hardly account for the failure of the summer crop, especially as Wordsworth composed chiefly in the open air. It did not prevent him from writing a pamphlet upon the Convention of Cintra, which was published too late to attract much attention, though Lamb says that its effect upon him was like that which one of Milton's tracts might have had upon a contemporary. It was at Allan Bank that Coleridge dictated *The Friend*, and Wordsworth contributed to it two essays, one in answer to a letter of Mathetes (Professor Wilson), and the other on Epitaphs, republished in the Notes to *The Excursion*. Here also he wrote his *Description of the Scenery of the Lakes*. Perhaps a truer explanation of the comparative silence of Wordsworth's Muse during these years is to be found in the intense interest which he took in current events, whose variety, picturesqueness, and historical significance were enough to absorb all the energies of his imagination.

In the spring of 1811 Wordsworth removed to the Parsonage at Grasmere. Here he remained two years, and here he had his second intimate experience of sorrow in the loss of two of his children, Catharine and Thomas, one of whom died 4th June, and the other 1st December, 1812. Early in 1813 he bought Rydal Mount, and, having removed thither, changed his abode no more during the rest of his life. In

March of this year he was appointed Distributor of Stamps for the county of Westmorland, an office whose receipts rendered him independent, and whose business he was able to do by deputy, thus leaving him ample leisure for nobler duties. De Quincey speaks of this appointment as an instance of the remarkable good luck which waited upon Wordsworth through his whole life. In our view it is only another illustration of that scripture which describes the righteous as never forsaken. Good luck is the willing handmaid of upright, energetic character, and conscientious observance of duty. Wordsworth owed his nomination to the friendly exertions of the Earl of Lonsdale, who desired to atone as far as might be for the injustice of the first Earl, and who respected the honesty of the man more than he appreciated the originality of the poet. The Collectorship at Whitehaven (a more lucrative office) was afterwards offered to Wordsworth, and declined. He had enough for independence, and wished nothing more. Still later, on the death of the Stamp-Distributor for Cumberland, a part of that district was annexed to Westmorland, and Wordsworth's income was raised to something more than £1,000 a year.

In 1814 he made his second tour in Scotland, visiting Yarrow in company with the Ettrick Shepherd. During this year *The Excursion* was published, in an edition of five hundred copies, which supplied the demand for six years. Another edition of the same number of copies was published in 1827, and not exhausted till 1834. In 1815 *The White Doe of Rylstone* appeared, and in 1816 *A Letter to a Friend of Burns,* in which Wordsworth gives his opinion upon the limits to be observed by the biographers of literary men. It contains many valuable suggestions, but allows hardly scope enough for personal details, to which he was constitutionally indifferent. Nearly the same date may be ascribed to a rhymed translation of the first three books of the *Aeneid,* a specimen of which was printed in the Cambridge *Philological Museum* (1832). In 1819 *Peter Bell*, written twenty years before, was published, and, perhaps in consequence of the ridicule of the reviewers, found a more rapid sale than any of his previous volumes. *The Waggoner*, printed in the same year, was less successful. His next publication was the volume of *Sonnets on the river Duddon*, with some miscellaneous poems, 1820. A tour on the Continent in 1820 furnished the subjects for another collection, published in 1822. This was followed in the same year by the volume of *Ecclesiastical Sketches*. His subsequent publications were *Yarrow Revisited*, 1835, and the tragedy of *The Borderers*, 1842.

During all these years his fame was increasing slowly but steadily, and his age gathered to itself the reverence and the troops of friends which his poems and the nobly simple life reflected in them deserved. Public honours followed private appreciation. In 1838 the University of Dublin conferred upon him the degree of D.C.L. In 1839 Oxford did the same, and the reception of the poet (now in his seventieth year) at the University was enthusiastic. In 1842 he resigned his office of Stamp-Distributor, and Sir Robert Peel had the honour of putting him upon the civil list for a pension of £300. In 1843 he was appointed Laureate, with the express understanding that it was a tribute of respect, involving no duties except such as might be self-imposed. His only official production was an Ode for the installation of Prince Albert as Chancellor of the University of Cambridge. His life was prolonged yet seven years, almost, it should seem, that he might receive that honour which he had truly conquered for himself by the unflinching bravery of a literary life of half a century, unparalleled for the scorn with which its labours were received, and the victorious acknowledgement which at last crowned them. Surviving nearly all his contemporaries, he had, if ever any man had, a foretaste of immortality, enjoying in a sort his own posthumous renown, for the hardy slowness of its growth gave a safe pledge of its durability. He died on the 23rd of April, 1850, the anniversary of the death of Shakespeare.

We have thus briefly sketched the life of Wordsworth,—a life uneventful even for a man of letters; a life like that of an oak, of quiet self-development, throwing out stronger roots toward the side whence the prevailing storm-blasts blow, and of tougher fibre in proportion to the rocky nature of the soil in which it grows. The life and growth of his mind, and the influences which shaped it, are to be looked for, even more than is the case with most poets, in his works, for he deliberately recorded them there.

Of his personal characteristics little is related. He was somewhat above the middle height, but, according to De Quincey, of indifferent figure, the shoulders being narrow and drooping. His finest feature was the eye, which was grey and full of spiritual light. Leigh Hunt says: 'I never beheld eyes that looked so inspired, so supernatural. They were like fires, half burning, half smouldering, with a sort of acrid fixture of regard. One might imagine Ezekiel or Isaiah to have had such eyes.' Southey tells us that he had no sense of smell, and Haydon that he had none of form. The best likeness of him, in De Quincey's judgement, is the portrait of Milton prefixed to Richardson's notes on *Paradise Lost*. He was active in his habits, composing in the open air, and generally dictating his poems. His daily life was regular, simple, and frugal; his manners were dignified and kindly; and in his letters and recorded conversations it is remarkable how little that was personal entered into his judgement of contemporaries.

The true rank of Wordsworth among poets is, perhaps, not even yet to be fairly estimated, so hard is it to escape into the quiet hall of judgement uninflamed by the tumult of partisanship which besets the doors.

Coming to manhood, predetermined to be a great poet, at a time when the artificial school of poetry was enthroned with all the authority of long succession and undisputed legitimacy, it was almost inevitable that Wordsworth, who, both by nature and judgement was a rebel against the existing order, should become a partisan. Unfortunately, he became not only the partisan of a system, but of William Wordsworth as its representative. Right in general principle, he thus necessarily became wrong in particulars. Justly convinced that greatness only achieves its ends by implicitly obeying its own instincts, he perhaps reduced the following his instincts too much to a system, mistook his own resentments for the promptings of his natural genius, and, compelling principle to the measure of his own temperament or even of the controversial exigency of the moment, fell sometimes into the error of making naturalness itself artificial. If a poet resolve to be original, it will end commonly in his being merely peculiar.

Wordsworth himself departed more and more in practice, as he grew older, from the theories which he had laid down in his prefaces;[1] but those theories undoubtedly had a great effect in retarding the

---

[1] How far he swung backward toward the school under whose influence he grew up, and toward the style against which he had protested so vigorously, a few examples will show. The advocate of the language of common life has a verse in his *Thanksgiving Ode* which, if one met with it by itself, he would think the achievement of some later copyist of Pope:

While the *tubed engine* [the organ] feels the inspiring blast.

And in *The Italian Itinerant* and *The Swiss Goatherd* we find a thermometer or barometer called

> The well-wrought scale
> Whose sentient tube instructs to time
> A purpose to a fickle clime.

growth of his fame. He had carefully constructed a pair of spectacles through which his earlier poems were to be studied, and the public insisted on looking through them at his mature works, and were consequently unable to see fairly what required a different focus. He forced his readers to come to his poetry with a certain amount of conscious preparation, and thus gave them beforehand the impression of something like mechanical artifice, and deprived them of the contented repose of implicit faith. To the child a watch seems to be a living creature; but Wordsworth would not let his readers be children, and did injustice to himself by giving them an uneasy doubt whether creations which really throbbed with the very heart's-blood of genius, and were alive with nature's life of life, were not contrivances of wheels and springs. A naturalness which we are told to expect has lost the crowning grace of nature. The men who walked in Cornelius Agrippa's visionary gardens had probably no more pleasurable emotion than that of a shallow wonder, or an equally shallow self-satisfaction in thinking they had hit upon the secret of the thaumaturgy; but to a tree that has grown as God willed we come without a theory and with no botanical predilections, enjoying it simply and thankfully; or the Imagination recreates for us its past summers and winters, the birds that have nested and sung in it, the sheep that have clustered in its shade, the winds that have visited it, the cloud-bergs that have drifted over it, and the snows that have ermined

Still worse in the *Eclipse of the Sun*, 1821:

> High on her speculative tower
> Stood Science, waiting for the hour
> When Sol was destined to endure
>   That darkening.

So in *The Excursion*,

> The cold March wind raised in her tender throat
> Viewless obstructions.

it in winter. The Imagination is a faculty that flouts at foreordination, and Wordsworth seemed to do all he could to cheat his readers of her company by laying out paths with a peremptory *Do not step off the gravel!* at the opening of each, and preparing pitfalls for every conceivable emotion, with guideboards to tell each when and where it must be caught.

But if these things stood in the way of immediate appreciation, he had another theory which interferes more seriously with the total and permanent effect of his poems. He was theoretically determined not only to be a philosophic poet, but to be a *great* philosophic poet, and to this end he must produce an epic. Leaving aside the question whether the epic be obsolete or not, it may be doubted whether the history of a single man's mind is universal enough in its interest to furnish all the requirements of the epic machinery, and it may be more than doubted whether a poet's philosophy be ordinary metaphysics, divisible into chapter and section. It is rather something which is more energetic in a word than in a whole treatise, and our hearts unclose themselves instinctively at its simple *Open sesame!* while they would stand firm against the reading of the whole body of philosophy. In point of fact, the one element of greatness which *The Excursion* possesses indisputably is heaviness. It is only the episodes that are universally read, and the effect of these is diluted by the connecting and accompanying lectures on metaphysics. Wordsworth had his epic mould to fill, and, like Benvenuto Cellini in casting his Perseus, was forced to throw in everything, debasing the metal, lest it should run short. Separated from the rest, the episodes are perfect poems in their kind, and without example in the language.

Wordsworth, like most solitary men of strong minds, was a good critic of the substance of poetry, but somewhat niggardly in the allowance he made for those subsidiary qualities which make it the charmer of leisure and the employment of minds without definite object. It may be doubted, indeed, whether he set much store by any contemporary writing but his own, and whether he did not look upon poetry too exclusively as an exercise rather of the intellect than as a nepenthe of the imagination. He says of himself, speaking of his youth:

> In fine,
> I was a better judge of thoughts than words,
> Misled in estimating words, not only
> By common inexperience of youth,
> But by the trade in classic niceties,
> The dangerous craft of culling term and phrase
> From languages that want the living voice
> To carry meaning to the natural heart;
> To tell us what is passion, what is truth,
> What reason, what simplicity and sense.[1]

Though he here speaks in the preterite tense, this was always true of him, and his thought seems often to lean upon a word too weak to bear its weight. No reader of adequate insight can help regretting that he did not earlier give himself to 'the trade of classic niceties'. It was precisely this which gives to the blank-verse of Landor the severe dignity and reserved force which alone among later poets recall the tune of Milton, and to which Wordsworth never attained. Indeed, Wordsworth's blank-verse (though the passion be profounder) is always essentially that of Cowper. They were alike also in their love of outward nature and of simple things. The main difference between them is one of scenery rather than of sentiment, between the lifelong familiar of the mountains and the dweller on the plain.

It cannot be denied that in Wordsworth the very highest powers of the poetic mind were associated with a certain tendency to the diffuse and commonplace. It is in the understanding (always prosaic) that the great golden veins of his imagination are

[1] *Prelude*, Book VI.

imbedded. He wrote too much to write always well; for it is not a great Xerxes-army of words, but a compact Greek ten thousand, that march safely down to posterity. He set tasks to his divine faculty, which is much the same as trying to make Jove's eagle do the service of a clucking hen. Throughout *The Prelude* and *The Excursion* he seems striving to bind the wizard Imagination with the sand-ropes of dry disquisition, and to have forgotten the potent spell-word which would make the particles cohere. There is an arenaceous quality in the style which makes progress wearisome. Yet with what splendours as of mountain-sunsets are we rewarded! what golden rounds of verse do we not see stretching heavenward with angels ascending and descending! what haunting harmonies hover around us deep and eternal like the undying baritone of the sea! and if we are compelled to fare through sands and desert wildernesses, how often do we not hear airy shapes that syllable our names with a startling personal appeal to our highest consciousness and our noblest aspiration, such as we wait for in vain in any other poet!

Take from Wordsworth all which an honest criticism cannot but allow, and what is left will show how truly great he was. He had no humour, no dramatic power, and his temperament was of that dry and juiceless quality, that in all his published correspondence you shall not find a letter, but only essays. If we consider carefully where he was most successful, we shall find that it was not so much in description of natural scenery, or delineation of character, as in vivid expression of the effect produced by external objects and events upon his own mind, and of the shape and hue (perhaps momentary) which they in turn took from his mood or temperament. His finest passages are always monologues. He had a fondness for particulars, and there are parts of his poems which remind us of local histories in the undue relative importance given to trivial matters. He was the historian of Wordsworthshire. This power of particularization (for it is as truly a power as generalization) is what gives such vigour and greatness to single lines and sentiments of Wordsworth, and to poems developing a single thought or sentiment. It was this that made him so fond of the sonnet. That sequestered nook forced upon him the limits which his fecundity (if I may not say his garrulity) was never self-denying enough to impose on itself. It suits his solitary and meditative temper, and it was there that Lamb (an admirable judge of what was permanent in literature) liked him best. Its narrow bounds, but fourteen paces from end to end, turn into a virtue his too common fault of giving undue prominence to every passing emotion. He excels in monologue, and the law of the sonnet tempers monologue with mercy. In *The Excursion* we are driven to the subterfuge of a French verdict of extenuating circumstances. His mind had not that reach and elemental movement of Milton's, which, like the trade-wind, gathered to itself thoughts and images like stately fleets from every quarter; some deep with silks and spicery, some brooding over the silent thunders of their battailous armaments, but all swept forward in their destined track, over the long billows of his verse, every inch of canvas strained by the unifying breath of their common epic impulse. It was an organ that Milton mastered, mighty in compass, capable equally of the trumpet's ardours or the slim delicacy of the flute, and sometimes it bursts forth in great crashes through his prose, as if he touched it for solace in the intervals of his toil. If Wordsworth sometimes puts the trumpet to his lips, yet he lays it aside soon and willingly for his appropriate instrument, the pastoral reed. And it is not one that grew by any vulgar stream, but that which Apollo breathed through, tending the flocks of Admetus,—that which Pan endowed with every melody of the visible universe,—the same in which the soul of the despairing nymph took refuge and gifted with her dual nature,—so that ever and anon, amid the notes of human joy or sorrow, there comes suddenly a deeper and almost awful tone, thrilling us into dim consciousness of a forgotten divinity.

Wordsworth's absolute want of humour, while it no doubt confirmed his self-confidence by making him insensible both to the comical incongruity into which he was often led by his earlier theory concerning the language of poetry and to the not unnatural ridicule called forth by it, seems to have been indicative of a certain dullness of perception in other directions.[1] We cannot help feeling that the material

---

[1] Nowhere is this displayed with more comic self-complacency than when he thought it needful to rewrite the ballad of Helen of Kirconnel,—a poem hardly to be matched in any language for swiftness of movement and savage sincerity of feeling. Its shuddering compression is masterly. Compare:

> Curst be the heart that thought the thought,
> And curst the hand that fired the shot,
> When in my arms burd Helen dropt,
>   That died to succour me!
> O, think ye not my heart was sair
> When my love dropt down and spake na mair?

Compare this with,—

> Proud Gordon cannot bear the thoughts
>   That through his brain are travelling,
> And, starting up, to Bruce's heart
>   He launched a deadly javelin:
> Fair Ellen saw it when it came,
> And, *stepping forth to meet the same,*
> Did with her body cover
> The Youth, her chosen lover.
>
> . . . . .
>
> And Bruce (*as soon as he had slain
> The Gordon*) sailed away to Spain,
> And fought with rage incessant
> Against the Moorish Crescent.

of his nature was essentially prose, which, in his inspired moments, he had the power of transmuting, but which, whenever the inspiration failed or was factitious, remained obstinately leaden. The normal condition of many poets would seem to approach that temperature to which Wordsworth's mind could be raised only by the white heat of profoundly inward passion. And in proportion to the intensity needful to make his nature thoroughly aglow is the very high quality of his best verses. They seem rather the productions of nature than of man, and have the lastingness of such, delighting our age with the same startle of newness and beauty that pleased our youth. Is it his thought? It has the shifting inward lustre of diamond. Is it his feeling? It is as

These are surely the verses of an attorney's clerk 'penning a stanza when he should engross'. It will be noticed that Wordsworth here also departs from his earlier theory of the language of poetry by substituting a javelin for a bullet as less modern and familiar. Had he written

> And Gordon never gave a hint,
> But, having somewhat picked his flint,
> Let fly the fatal bullet
> That killed that lovely pullet,

it would hardly have seemed more like a parody than the rest. He shows the same insensibility in a note upon the *Ancient Mariner* in the second edition of the *Lyrical Ballads*: 'The poem of my friend has indeed great defects; first, that the principal person has no distinct character, either in his profession of mariner, or as a human being who, having been long under the control of supernatural impressions, might be supposed himself to partake of something supernatural; secondly, that he does not act, but is continually acted upon; thirdly, that the events, having no necessary connexion, do not produce each other; and lastly, that the imagery is somewhat laboriously accumulated.' Here is an indictment, to be sure, and drawn, plainly enough, by the attorney's clerk aforenamed. One would think that the strange charm of Coleridge's most truly original poems lay in this very emancipation from the laws of cause and effect.

delicate as the impressions of fossil ferns. He seems
to have caught and fixed for ever in immutable grace
the most evanescent and intangible of our intuitions,
the very ripple-marks on the remotest shores of being.
But this intensity of mood which insures high quality
is by its very nature incapable of prolongation, and
Wordsworth, in endeavouring it, falls more below
himself, and is, more even than many poets his inferiors in imaginative quality, a poet of passages.
Indeed, one cannot help having the feeling sometimes that the poem is there for the sake of these
passages, rather than that these are the natural jets
and elations of a mind energized by the rapidity of
its own motion. In other words, the happy couplet
or gracious image seems not to spring from the
inspiration of the poem conceived as a whole, but
rather to have dropped of itself into the mind of the
poet in one of his rambles, who then, in a less rapt
mood, has patiently built up around it a setting of
verse too often ungraceful in form and of a material
whose cheapness may cast a doubt on the priceless
quality of the gem it encumbers.[1] During the most
happily productive period of his life, Wordsworth
was impatient of what may be called the mechanical
portion of his art. His wife and sister seem from the
first to have been his scribes. In later years, he had
learned and often insisted on the truth that poetry
was an art no less than a gift, and corrected his
poems in cold blood, sometimes to their detriment.
But he certainly had more of the vision than of the
faculty divine, and was always a little numb on
the side of form and proportion. Perhaps his best
poem in these respects is the *Laodamia*, and it is not

[1] A hundred times when, roving high and low,
I have been harassed with the toil of verse,
Much pains and little progress, and at once
Some lovely Image in the song rose up,
Full-formed, like Venus rising from the sea.
Prelude, Book IV.

uninstructive to learn from his own lips that 'it cost him more trouble than almost anything of equal length he had ever written'. His longer poems (miscalled epical) have no more intimate bond of union than their more or less immediate relation to his own personality. Of character other than his own he had but a faint conception, and all the personages of *The Excursion* that are not Wordsworth are the merest shadows of himself upon mist, for his self-concentrated nature was incapable of projecting itself into the consciousness of other men and seeing the springs of action at their source in the recesses of individual character. The best parts of these longer poems are bursts of impassioned soliloquy, and his fingers were always clumsy at the *callida junctura*. The stream of narration is sluggish, if varied by times with pleasing reflections (*viridesque placido aequore sylvas*); we are forced to do our own rowing, and only when the current is hemmed in by some narrow gorge of the poet's personal consciousness do we feel ourselves snatched along on the smooth but impetuous rush of unmistakable inspiration. The fact that what is precious in Wordsworth's poetry was (more truly even than with some greater poets than he) a gift rather than an achievement should always be borne in mind in taking the measure of his power. I know not whether to call it height or depth, this peculiarity of his, but it certainly endows those parts of his work which we should distinguish as Wordsworthian with an unexpectedness and impressiveness of originality such as we feel in the presence of Nature herself. He seems to have been half conscious of this, and recited his own poems to all comers with an enthusiasm of wondering admiration that would have been profoundly comic but for its simple sincerity and for the fact that William Wordsworth, Esquire, of Rydal Mount, was one person, and the William Wordsworth whom he so heartily reverenced quite another. We recognize two voices in him, as Stephano did in Caliban. There are Jeremiah and his scribe Baruch. If the prophet cease from dictating, the amanuensis, rather than be idle, employs his pen in jotting down some anecdotes of his master, how he one day went out and saw an old woman, and the next day did *not*, and so came home and dictated some verses on this ominous phenomenon, and how another day he saw a cow. These marginal annotations have been carelessly taken up into the text, have been religiously held by the pious to be orthodox scripture, and by dexterous exegesis have been made to yield deeply oracular meanings. Presently the real prophet takes up the word again and speaks as one divinely inspired, the Voice of a higher and invisible power. Wordsworth's better utterances have the bare sincerity, the absolute abstraction from time and place, the immunity from decay, that belong to the grand simplicities of the Bible. They seem not more his own than ours and every man's, the word of the inalterable Mind. This gift of his was naturally very much a matter of temperament, and accordingly by far the greater part of his finer product belongs to the period of his prime, ere Time had set his lumpish foot on the pedal that deadens the nerves of animal sensibility.[1] He did not grow as those poets do in

[1] His best poetry was written when he was under the immediate influence of Coleridge. Coleridge seems to have felt this, for it is evidently to Wordsworth that he alludes when he speaks of 'those who have been so well pleased that I should, year after year, flow with a hundred nameless rills into *their* main stream' (*Letters, Conversations, and Recollections of S.T.C.*, vol. i, pp. 5–6). 'Wordsworth found fault with the repetition of the concluding sound of the participles in Shakespeare's line about bees:

The singing masons building roofs of gold.

This, he said, was a line that Milton never would have written. Keats thought, on the other hand, that the repetition was in harmony with the continued note of the singers' (Leigh Hunt's *Autobiography*). Wordsworth

whom the artistic sense is predominant. One of the most delightful fancies of the Genevese humorist, Toepffer, is the poet Albert, who, having had his portrait drawn by a highly idealizing hand, does his best afterwards to look like it. Many of Wordsworth's later poems seem like rather unsuccessful efforts to resemble his former self. They would never, as Sir John Harington says of poetry, 'keep a child from play and an old man from the chimney corner'.[1]

Chief Justice Marshall once blandly interrupted a junior counsel who was arguing certain obvious points of law at needless length, by saying, 'Brother Jones, there are *some* things which a Supreme Court of the United States sitting in equity may be presumed to know.' Wordsworth has this fault of enforcing and restating obvious points till the reader feels as if his own intelligence were somewhat underrated. He is over-conscientious in giving us full measure, and once profoundly absorbed in the sound of his own voice, he knows not when to stop. If he feel himself flagging, he has a droll way of keeping the floor, as it were, by asking himself a series of questions sometimes not needing, and often incapable of answer. There are three stanzas of such near the close of the First Part of *Peter Bell*, where Peter first catches a glimpse of the dead body in the water, all happily incongruous, and ending with one which reaches the height of comicality:

> Is it a fiend that to a stake
> Of fire his desperate self is tethering?
> Or stubborn spirit doomed to yell,
> In solitary ward or cell,
> Ten thousand miles from all his brethren?

The same want of humour which made him insen-
writes to Crabb Robinson in 1837, 'My ear is susceptible to the clashing of sounds almost to disease.' One cannot help thinking that his training in these niceties was begun by Coleridge.

[1] In the Preface to his translation of the *Orlando Furioso*.

sible to incongruity may perhaps account also for the singular unconsciousness of disproportion which so often strikes us in his poetry. For example, a little farther on in *Peter Bell* we find:

> *Now*—like a tempest-shattered bark
> That overwhelmed and prostrate lies,
> And in a moment to the verge
> Is lifted of a foaming surge—
> Full suddenly the Ass doth rise!

And one cannot help thinking that the similes of the huge stone, the sea-beast, and the cloud, noble as they are in themselves, are somewhat too lofty for the service to which they are put.[1]

The movement of Wordsworth's mind was too slow and his mood too meditative for narrative poetry. He values his own thoughts and reflections too much to sacrifice the least of them to the interests of his story. Moreover, it is never action that interests him, but the subtle motives that lead to or hinder it. *The Waggoner* involuntarily suggests a comparison with *Tam O'Shanter*, infinitely to its own disadvantage. *Peter Bell*, full though it be of profound touches and subtle analysis, is lumbering and disjointed. Even Lamb was forced to confess that he did not like it. *The White Doe*, the most Wordsworthian of them all in the best meaning of the epithet, is also only the more truly so for being diffuse and reluctant. What charms in Wordsworth and will charm for ever is the

> Happy tone
> Of meditation slipping in between
> The beauty coming and the beauty gone.

A few poets, in the exquisite adaptation of their words to the tune of our own feelings and fancies, in the charm of their manner, indefinable as the sympathetic grace of woman, *are* everything to us without our being able to say that they are much

---

[1] In *Resolution and Independence*.

in themselves. They rather narcotize than fortify.
Wordsworth must subject our mood to his own before
he admits us to his intimacy; but, once admitted, it
is for life, and we find ourselves in his debt, not for
what he has been to us in our hours of relaxation,
but for what he has done for us as a reinforcement
of faltering purpose and personal independence of
character. His system of a Nature-cure, first professed by Dr. Jean Jacques and continued by Cowper,
certainly breaks down as a whole. The Solitary of
The Excursion, who has not been cured of his scepticism by living among the medicinal mountains, is,
so far as we can see, equally proof against the lectures
of Pedlar and Parson. Wordsworth apparently felt
that this would be so, and accordingly never saw
his way clear to finishing the poem. But the treatment, whether a panacea or not, is certainly wholesome inasmuch as it inculcates abstinence, exercise,
and uncontaminate air. I am not sure, indeed, that
the Nature-cure theory does not tend to foster in
constitutions less vigorous than Wordsworth's what
Milton would call a fugitive and cloistered virtue
at a dear expense of manlier qualities. The ancients
and our own Elizabethans, ere spiritual megrims had
become fashionable, perhaps made more out of life
by taking a frank delight in its action and passion and
by grappling with the facts of this world, rather than
muddling themselves over the insoluble problems of
another. If they had not discovered the picturesque,
as we understand it, they found surprisingly fine
scenery in man and his destiny, and would have seen
something ludicrous, it may be suspected, in the
spectacle of a grown man running to hide his head
in the apron of the Mighty Mother whenever he had
an ache in his finger or got a bruise in the tussle for
existence.

But when, as I have said, our impartiality has
made all those qualifications and deductions against
which even the greatest poet may not plead his

privilege, what is left to Wordsworth is enough to justify his fame. Even where his genius is wrapped in clouds, the unconquerable lightning of imagination struggles through, flashing out unexpected vistas, and illuminating the humdrum pathway of our daily thought with a radiance of momentary consciousness that seems like a revelation. If it be the most delightful function of the poet to set our lives to music, yet perhaps he will be even more sure of our maturer gratitude if he do his part also as moralist and philosopher to purify and enlighten; if he define and encourage our vacillating perceptions of duty; if he piece together our fragmentary apprehensions of our own life and that larger life whose unconscious instruments we are, making of the jumbled bits of our dissected map of experience a coherent chart. In the great poets there is an exquisite sensibility both of soul and sense that sympathizes like gossamer sea-moss with every movement of the element in which it floats, but which is rooted on the solid rock of our common sympathies. Wordsworth shows less of this finer feminine fibre of organization than one or two of his contemporaries, notably than Coleridge or Shelley; but he was a masculine thinker, and in his more characteristic poems there is always a kernel of firm conclusion from far-reaching principles that stimulates thought and challenges meditation. Groping in the dark passages of life, we come upon some axiom of his, as it were a wall that gives us our bearings and enables us to find an outlet. Compared with Goethe we feel that he lacks that serene impartiality of mind which results from breadth of culture; nay, he seems narrow, insular, almost provincial. He reminds us of those saints of Dante who gather brightness by revolving on their own axis. But through this very limitation of range he gains perhaps in intensity and the impressiveness which results from eagerness of personal conviction. If we read Wordsworth through, as I have just done, we find ourselves changing our mind about him at every other page, so uneven is he. If we read our favourite poems or passages only, he will seem uniformly great. And even as regards *The Excursion* we should remember how few long poems will bear consecutive reading. For my part I know of but one,—the *Odyssey*.

None of our great poets can be called popular in any exact sense of the word, for the highest poetry deals with thoughts and emotions which inhabit, like rarest sea-mosses, the doubtful limits of that shore between our abiding divine and our fluctuating human nature, rooted in the one, but living in the other, seldom laid bare, and otherwise visible only at exceptional moments of entire calm and clearness. Of no other poet except Shakespeare have so many phrases become household words as of Wordsworth. If Pope has made current more epigrams of worldly wisdom, to Wordsworth belongs the nobler praise of having defined for us, and given us for a daily possession, those faint and vague suggestions of other-worldliness of whose gentle ministry with our baser nature the hurry and bustle of life scarcely ever allowed us to be conscious. He has won for himself a secure immortality by a depth of intuition which makes only the best minds at their best hours worthy, or indeed capable, of his companionship, and by a homely sincerity of human sympathy which reaches the humblest heart. Our language owes him gratitude for the habitual purity and abstinence of his style, and we who speak it, for having emboldened us to take delight in simple things, and to trust ourselves to our own instincts. And he hath his reward. It needs not to bid

> Renowned Chaucer lie a thought more nigh
> To rare Beaumont, and learned Beaumont lie
> A little nearer Spenser;

for there is no fear of crowding in that little society with whom he is now enrolled as fifth in the succession of the great English Poets.